2005 – 2006 EDITION

ILLUSTRATED AND PRICED OBJECTS

by

Dorothy Hammond

First published 2005

ISBN 1 85149 485 5

British Library Cataloguing-in-Publication Data
A catalogue record for this book is available from the British Library

Printed in China
Published in England by the Antique Collectors' Club Limited

Contents

Introduction

Now in its twenty-fourth edition, this 2005/06 full-color *Pictorial Price Guide To American Antiques And Objects Made For the American Market,* includes approximately 4,000 individual objects in full color. Entries are keyed to the auction gallery where an item was sold and the state abbreviation, to allow for regional price variations across the country. The year and month the item sold is also included. Anyone who has tried to translate the terminology of a standard price guide into something meaningful without an image will recognize the value of this approach. An introductory essay provides background information to each chapter with the exception of Miscellaneous.

Although the demographics for the antiques and collectibles market has lacked stability during the past few years, dealers and auction houses have recently reported accelerated market activity, and many predict a very strong outlook for 2005.

The serious collectors continue to look to auctions as the ultimate price determinant because they reflect market trends. As always, when comparing similar prices within this edition, the reader must take into consideration that fluctuations in the market, in addition to quality and popularity, and the region in which an item is sold, determine the hammer price. I have emphasized entries that are actively being sold in the market place, including harder-to-find objects which demonstrate the market spread.

Although the average collector is not a historian, but a person with a fascination with the American past, collecting has become one of our most popular American pastimes. We are seeing record attendance and fierce bidding at auction, in addition to record attendance at antiques shows throughout the country. Antiques and collectibles produced during the late nineteenth century, and well into the twentieth, continue to dominate a large segment of the market. Among the current trends is to blend historic and contemporary furnishing, either in period or modern interiors…and the combinations are endless.

Enthusiasm for fifties objects continues because of availability, and the field is extensive. However, many of the younger set are opting for more practical objects such as furniture because of its quality and craftsmanship.

The author has designed this pictorial price guide for use by antiques dealers and collectors, concentrating on antiques and collectibles that are relatively easy to obtain but including a number of upper end items that do come up for sale at shows and auctions.

Knowledge and perseverance are the keys to discovering great finds in this exciting field when forming a meaningful collection. Good hunting!

A-MA Nov. 2004 Skinner, Inc.

115 Portrait of the Barque Lizzie Boggs, sgn. R. Faxon Bordeaux, oil on canvas. The *Lizzie Boggs* was built in Warren, ME in 1854, and owned by P. Boggs and Company. Canvas size 19¾ x 28½in., framed. Relined w/minor inpainting in sky. $9,400

Acknowledgments

I am deeply grateful to my Publisher, Diana Steel, Managing Director of Antique Collectors' Club Ltd., Woodbridge, Suffolk, England, for her assistance in the preparation of this book. To those on her staff, my warmest thank you goes to Tom Conway, Primrose Elliott, Sandra Pond, and Pam Henderson, for their role in contributing to the final project. And as always, I am indebted to Dan Farrell, Managing Director of Antique Collectors' Club, North America, for his continued commitment and dedication to the book. His guidance has been invaluable.

This book has had its share of behind the scenes players, each of whom has played a very important part in the final production. I wish to express my sincere gratitude to the following individuals and auction houses who have so generously provided pictorial and textual material for this 2005/2006 edition. Without their support, this project would not have been possible

Front Cover Image:
Garth's Auctions Inc., Delaware, OH. Photo by: Thompson Creative Imaging, Columbus, OH

Back Cover Image:
Skinner, Inc., Boston, MA

Alderfer's Fine Art & Antiques
501 Fairgrounds Road
Hatfield, PA 19440
215-393-3000
www.alderferauction.com

Noel Barrett Antiques & Auction Ltd.
6183 Carversville Road
Carversville, PA 18913
215-297-5109

Brunk Auction Services, Inc.
P.O. Box 2135
Asheville, NC 28802
828-254-6846
www.brunkauctions.com

Charlton Hall Galleries, Inc.
912 Gervais Street
Columbia, SC 29201
803-779-5678
www.charltonhallauctions.com

Conestoga Auction Company, Inc.
768 Graystone Road
Manheim, PA 17545
717-898-7284
www.conestogaauction.com

Crocker Farm
P.O. Box 725
Riderwood, MD 21139
410-337-5090
stoneware @crockerfarm.com

David Rago Auctions
333 North Main Street
Lambertville, NJ 08530
609-397-9374
www.ragoarts.com

Early Auction Company
123 Main Street
Milford, OH 45150
513-831-4833
www.earlyauctionco.com

Robert C. Eldred Company, Inc.
1483 Route 6A
P.O. Box 796
East Dennis, MA 02641
508-385-3116
www.eldreds.com

Fontaines Auction Gallery
1485 West Housatonic Street
Pittsfield, MA 01201
413-448-8922
www.fontaineauction.com

Garth's Arts & Antiques
2690 Stratford Road
P.O. Box 369
Delaware, OH 43015
740-362-4771
www.garths.com

Glass Works Auctions
P.O. Box 180
East Greenville, PA 18041
215-679-5849
www.glswrk-auction.com

Guyette & Schmidt. Inc.
P.O. Box 522
West Farmington, ME 04992
207-778-6256
www.guyetteandschmidt.com

Tom Harris Auction Center, Inc.
203 South 18th Avenue
Marshalltown, IA 50158
641-754-4890
www.tomharrisauctions.com

Horst Auction Center
50 Durlach Road
Ephrata, PA 17522
717-738-3080
www.horstauction.com

Jackson's International Auctioneers, Inc.
2229 Lincoln Street
Cedar Falls, IA 50613
319-277-2256
www.jacksonsauction.com

James D. Julia, Inc.
P.O. Box 830
Fairfield, ME 04937
207-453-7125
www.juliaauctions.com

Northeast Auctions
93 Pleasant Street
Portsmouth, NH 03801
603-433-8400
www.northeastauctions.com

Pook & Pook, Inc.
P.O. Box 268
Downingtown, PA 19335
610-269-0695
www.pookandpook.com

R.O. Schmitt Fine Arts
P.O. Box 1941
Salem, NH 03079
603-893-5915

Skinner, Inc.
63 Park Plaza
Boston, MA 02116
617-350-5400
www.skinnerinc.com

Treadway Gallery, Inc.
2029 Madison Road
Cincinnati, OH 45208
513-321-6742
www.treadwaygallery.com

Willis Henry Auctions, Inc.
22 Main Street
Marshfield, MA 02050
781-834-7774
www.willishenry.com

The above auction houses charge a buyer's premium (a surcharge on the hammer or final bid price at auction) which will vary. For readers' convenience, I have included a complete address and website.

Although most auction houses give detailed catalog descriptions of items sold, others do not. Therefore, when interested in a particular illustrated item, it is always wise to ask for a condition report. In conclusion, every effort has been made to include accurate descriptions which have been carefully edited. However, neither the Publisher nor the author accepts any liability for any financial or other loss, or for errors that might have incurred as a result of typographical or other errors.

– Dorothy Hammond

Abbreviations

adv.	advertising
Am.	American
approx.	approximately
attrib.	attributed
C.	century
ca.	circa
comp.	composition
cond.	condition
const.	construction
decor.	decorated/decoration
dia.	diameter
dov.	dovetail/dovetailed
dp.	depth
D.Q.	diamond quilted
ea.	each
emb.	embossed/embossing
Eng.	England/English
est.	established
ex.	excellent
exc.	excluding
Fr.	France
gal.	gallon
Ger.	Germany
hdw.	hardware
ht.	height
illus.	illustrated
imp.	impressed
imper.	imperfect/imperfections
in.	inches
incl.	including
incor.	incorporating
int.	interior
L.	left
lb.	pound
lg.	length
litho.	lithograph
mah.	mahogany
mini	miniature
mkd.	marked
MOP	mother-of-pearl
mts.	mounts
OF	open face
N. Eng.	New England
n/s	no sale
orig.	original
oz.	ounce
pat.	patent
patt.	pattern
pc.	piece
pr.	pair
prof. restor.	professional restoration
Q.A.	Queen Anne
qt.	quart
qtr.	quarter
ref.	refinish
repl.	replaced/replacement
repr.	repair, repaired
rest.	restored/restoration
sgn.	signed
sm.	small
sq.	square
unmkd.	unmarked
w/	with
wd.	width
wt.	wrought
yrs.	years

The common and accepted abbreviations are used for states.

A-PA Oct. 2004 **Pook & Pook Inc.**

Still Life Oil Painting on canvas by Severin Roesen, German/American, 1815-1872 & sign. lower right. S. Roesen, 29in. x 36in. **$115,000**

The word advertising comes from the French word "avertir" meaning to notify. Advertising is actually as old as trade, probably beginning with what present day businessmen call personal selling. In essence, it informs people of the various advantages of a product, an idea, or a service. When manufacturing developed, few persons could read, as universal free education did not exist until the 1800s. Therefore, businessmen used symbols such as a shoemaker used a sign shaped like a shoe over his shop door, or a jeweler displayed a dummy clock. Later, when words were added, the symbols became trade signs.

Today, with new collectors appearing on the scene daily, the serious collecting of early advertising mementos has become widespread throughout the country. Searching out these collectibles is an endless adventure... and values have escalated which forces the serious collector to be more discriminating and build a more meaningful collection.

Nostalgia has created the current craze to acquire early advertising memorabilia because, in our hectic, parlous, plastic world today, the older generation, as well as the young, are fascinated by advertising collectibles in every media.

A-ME Jun. 2004 James D. Julia, Inc.
2536 **Yankee Girl Cigar Tin Sign,** late 1800s, embossed, lithographed by Standard Adv. Co., Coshocton, OH, ht. 27½, wd. 19½in. **$1,610**

A-MD Jun. 2004 James D. Julia, Inc.
550 **Cigar Store Indian,** attributed to Samuel A. Robb, 1851-1928. Provenance: part of the Schulte Cigar Store Collection, operating in New York City until early 1940s, some chips on surface & one repr. feather, overall ht. 73in. **$161,000**

A-ME Jun. 2004 James D. Julia, Inc.
2771 **Movie Lobby Poster of Seabiscuit,** 1949 w/some discoloration, ht. 36, wd. 14in. **$120**

A-ME Jun. 2004 James D. Julia, Inc.
2764 **Buster Brown Shoe Sign** showing a winking Buster Brown & Tige in relief, w/corner hairline & small chips, ht. 118, wd. 17¾in. **$172**

A-ME Jun. 2004 James D. Julia, Inc.
2563 **Red Goose Shoes Counter Display,** ht. 12, lg. 10in. **$258**

A-ME Jun. 2004 James D. Julia, Inc.
2525 **Lithograph,** Anheuser Busch Brewing Co., Custer's Last Fight, earlier 1876 edition, memorial to the Seventh Regiment U.S. Cavalry in orig. frame, ht. 38, wd. 48½in. **$1,035**

307

308

309

142

A-IA Oct. 2003
Jackson's International Auctioneers, Inc.
307 Miner's & Puddler Long Cut Smoking Tobacco, ht. 6¼in. $230

308 Dixie Queen Plug Cut Humidor, rust & scratches, ht. 6¼in. $143
309 Possum Cigar Tin, ht. 5¼in. $402

142 Standard Oil Gasoline Pump Globe, ca. 1940, ht. 16in. $374

294

295

296

297

298

299

304

301

A-PA Jun. 2004
Conestoga Auction Co., Inc.
200 Castle Hall Cigar Sidewalk Sign w/distressed paint, ht. 24¼, wd. 20½ in. $400

A-IA Oct. 2003
Jackson's International Auctioneers, Inc.
Chewing Tobacco Countertop Tins
294 Sweet Cuba, ht. 12, lg. 18in. $431
295 Polar Bear, ht. 12, lg. 14in. $316
296 Sure Shot Indian tin w/some rust & bent lid, ht. 7, lg.15½in. $259
297 Game Fine Cut w/bright colors, lg. 11¼, wd. 7in. $575
298 Winner Lunch Box Tin, lg. 8, wd. 4in. $375
299 Pastime Tobacco, 18lb. box, some missing paint, lg. 12, wd. 9in. $259
304 Green Turtle Cigar Lunch Box, lg. 7¼, ht. 5¼in. $402
301 Dan Patch Cut Plug Box w/hinged lid, 1g. 6¼in. $230

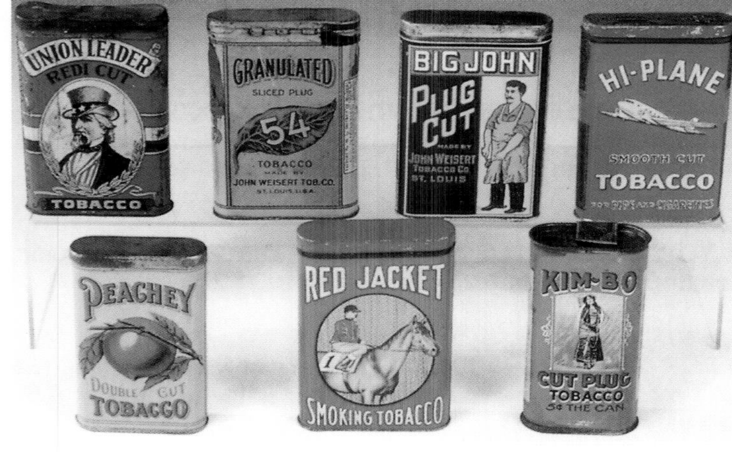

A-IA Oct. 2003 Jackson's International Auctioneers, Inc.
139 **Poll Parrot Neon Sign,** neon lighted, ca. 1950, small chip at base, ht. 24in. **$2,875**
140 **Poll Parrot Animated Store Display,** one of 25 made in Chicago by Sylvetri Display Co. for International Shoe Co., ht. 41in. **$1,380**

A-IA Oct. 2003 Jackson's International Auctioneers, Inc.
317 **Pocket Tins,** 7 including Union Leader, Granulated 54, Big John, Hi-Plane, Peachey, Red Jacket & Kim-Bo. **$402**

A-ME Jan. 2004
James D. Julia, Inc.
1164 **Columbus Buggy Sign,** Columbus, OH, image size ht. 23½, wd. 36in. **$2,500**

A-ME Jan. 2004
James D. Julia, Inc.
2688 **Diamond Dyes Cabinet,** small litho cabinet in mahogany of Washer Woman w/ drawers & some paper loss, ht. 14, wd. 13, dp. 8in. **$900**

1165

1166

1167

A-ME Jan. 2004 James D. Julia, Inc.
1165 **Ceresota Flower Tin Sign** for Consolidated Milling Co., Minneapolis, MN, image size ht. 26, wd. 21in. **$960**
1166 **Brasserie De Brive,** French litho. framed advertisement w/lower inset promoting their beers, lemonades & sodas, image ht. 25in. **$287**
1167 **Savannah Line Steamship Litho.** for Ocean Steamship Co. w/some water damage along bottom, ht. 22¼, wd. 15½in. **$920**

A-PA Jun. 2004
Conestoga Auction Co., Inc.
203 **Tin Trade Sign** for Ballantine's Brew, Newark, NJ w/pressed tin frame molding, printed in 1909 by Meek Company, dents & minor oxid., ht. 30⅝, wd. 22¾in. **$247**

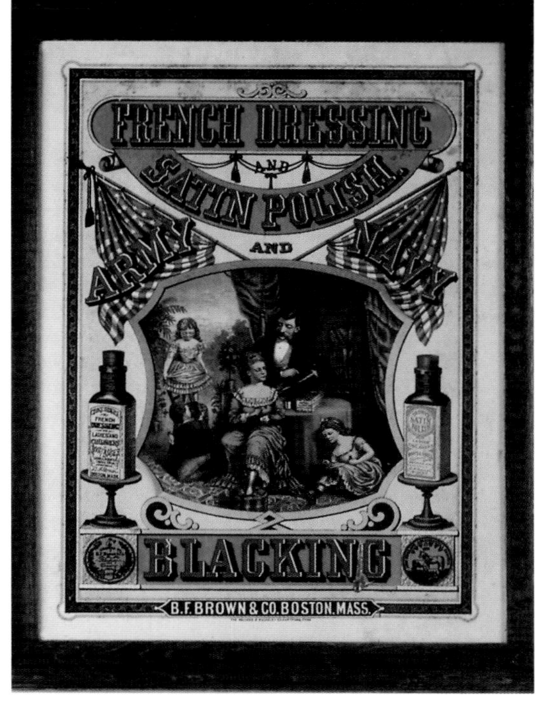

A-ME Jan. 2004 James D. Julia, Inc.
1163 **French Dressing Shoe Blacking Tin Sign,** litho by Kellogg & Bulkeley, Hartford, CT, for B.F. Brown & Co., Boston, ca. late 1870s. Some rust & blemishies, sight ht. 23½, wd. 17¾in. **$10,062**

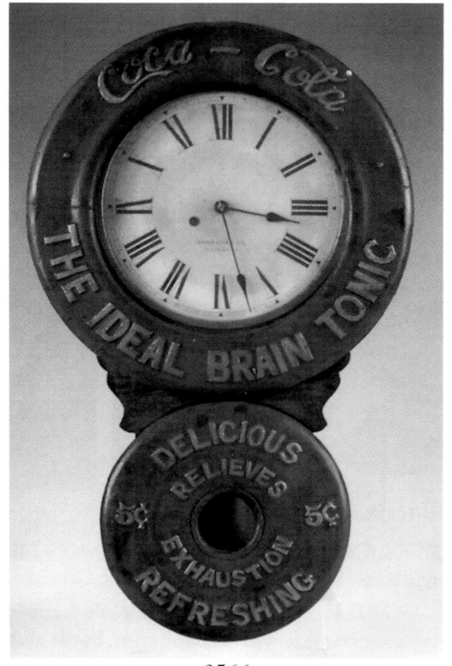

2566

2567

A-ME Jun. 2004 James D. Julia, Inc.
2566 **Coca-Cola Baird Clock,** mfg. between 1893-1896. Both papier-mache adv. bezels have been restored. Face shows some discoloration, orig. pendulum & key incl., ht. 30½in. **$2,160**
2567 **Gilbert Clock,** 31-day, w/Coca-Cola reverse painted glass panel & oak case, ht. 38in. **$373**

2720

2721

A-ME Jun. 2004 James D. Julia, Inc.
2720 **Coca-Cola Tip Tray,** ca. 1910 w/crazing to varnish & few chips, ht. 6, wd. 4¼in. **$900**

A-ME Jun. 2004 James D. Julia, Inc.
2721 **Coca-Cola Tip Tray,** ca. 1913 w/light surface crazing & rim chips, ht. 6, wd. 4¼in. **$780**

A-ME Jun. 2004 James D. Julia, Inc.
2554 **Case Threshing Machine Catalog** from 1905 w/72 pages filled w/images of various farming apparatuses incl. tractors, 9½ x 12in. **$270**

A-ME Jun. 2004 James D. Julia, Inc.
2539 **Hires Root Beer Store Display,** easel back missing & edge loss, ht. 18, wd. 32in. **$345**

A-ME Jun. 2004 James D. Julia, Inc.
2569 Crawford's Cherry-Fizz ceramic syrup dispenser, dated 1918, ht. 11in. $4,600

A-ME Jun. 2004 James D. Julia, Inc.
2571 Oak Barrel Dispenser for Liberty Root Beer, incl. orig. spigot, lid & insert w/orig. finish, ht. 25in. $920

A-IA Oct. 2003
Jackson's International Auctioneers
143 Lemp Brewery, St. Louis, MO, litho. tray, dia. 24in. $414

2730

2731

2732

2694

2733

2734

2735

2691

2736

2737

2738

2692

2704

2706

2715

2726

2729

A-ME Jun. 2004 James D. Julia, Inc.
2704 **Schneider Brewing Co. Trays,** one reglazed. **$74**
2706 **Whiskey Tip Trays,** Mellwood Distillery Co., and Old Boone Whiskey, Thixton Millett & Co., Louisville, KY. **$210**
2715 **Baker's Cocoa Tray Le Chocolatier,** for Walter Baker Co., Dorchester, MA, w/slight surface wear, dia. 6in. **$96**
2726 **Highland Evaporated Cream Tray,** early litho., w/crazing, dia. 3½in. **$120**
2729 **Beers, Ales & Porter Tray,** In Kegs & Bottles, together w/Potosi Special Brew tray & a Lily Beer Tray, not illus. **$345**

A-IA Oct. 2003
Jackson's International Auctioneers
327 **George Washington Cut Plug Lunch Box** w/paint loss & bent. **$23**

A-IA Oct. 2003
Jackson's International Auctioneers
354 **Japanese Tea Box,** tin lined w/minor paint losses, ht. 10¼in. **$69**

A-IA Oct. 2003
Jackson's International Auctioneers
346 **Counter Top Containers** for Beech Nut Tobacco. **$172**

Opposite
A-ME Jun. 2004 James D. Julia, Inc.
Tip Trays, Dia. 4¼in. unless noted
2730 **Stegmaier Brewing Co.,** Wilkes-Barre, PA, w/matt finish. **$60**
2731 **Seattle Brewing & Malting Co.** w/illus. of Mount Ranier for Ranier Beer, w/matt surface. **$270**
2732 **Buffalo Brewing Co.,** San Francisco, ca. 1915, ex. cond. **$316**
2733 **DeLaval Cream Separators** w/light scuff marks. **$180**
2734 **Ruhstaller's Gilt Edge Lager,** 1915 San Francisco Expo from Sacramento, CA brewer. **$180**
2735 **Old Reliable Coffee Tray** w/moderate crazing to paint. **$180**
2736 **Resinol Soap & Ointment tray** w/light crazing. **$96**
2737 **Coca-Cola Tray,** 1916 w/minor pitting & chips to perimeter, ht. 6in. **$201**
2738 **Coca-Cola Tray,** 1914 w/slight dimple & edge wear, ht. 6in. **$172**
2694 **Moxie Tray** w/few paint chips to perimeter edge, dia. 6in. **$316**
2691 **Coca-Cola 1906 Tray,** w/wear to outer edge, dia. 4in. **$840**
2692 **Coca-Cola 1909 Tray,** w/few chips to outer rim, ht. 6, wd. 4½in. **$510**

A-IA Oct. 2003
Jackson's International Auctioneers

328 **Poultry Medication,** IA Roup Remedy. **$23**
329 **Standard Oil Co. Tin,** Boston Coach & Axle Oil. **$46**
330 **Paragon Refining Co. Tin.** n/s

328

329

330

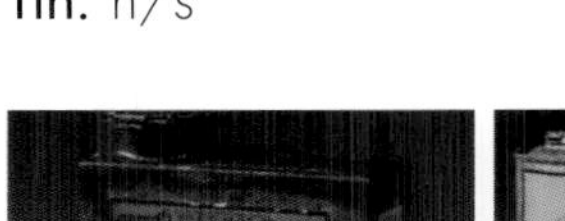
331

332

333

334

335

336

343

337

338

339

340

341

342

A-IA Oct. 2003 Jackson's International Auctioneers

331 **Wonder Mist Cleanser & Polisher Tin. $46**
332 **Tobacco Tins,** Sweet Burley w/denting & paint loss. **$143**
333 **Tiger Bright Sweet Chewing Tobacco Tins** w/paint loss, three. **$92**
334 **Tobacco Tins,** two flat Sweet Cuba & two Sweet Burley, paint loss. **$80**
335 **Tobacco Tins,** small incl. several flat 50's. **$80**
336 **Collection of five tins** & one lunch box. **$431**
337 **Tobacco Tins** incl. Bank Note, Eight Brothers, Dixie Queen, Hand Made, Plow Boy & Edgeworth. **$115**
338 **Tobacco Tins,** six incl. Topic, Sweet Cuba, Kre-ole,DeSoto, Country Club & Camel. **$373**
339 **Tobacco Tins,** eight incl. Parker-Gordons Class, Old Glory, Hand Made, Robert Emmet & Laughlins w/some paint loss. **$143**
340 **Tobacco Tins,** twelve in varying condition. **$143**
341 **Collection of Ten Tins** w/rust & paint loss. **$115**
342 **Tobacco Tins,** seven incl. Cinco, H-O, Piper Heidsieck, Ben Bey & P & G, **$92**
343 **Box Lot of Tobacco Tins,** 17 incl. a tin tankard Havana Blend cigars & Summertime. **$172**

344

345

347

348

349

350

351

352

353

A-IA Oct. 2003 Jackson's International Auctioneers

344 **Collection of 19 Tobacco Tins** incl. Baby's Bottom & Dutch Masters. **$86**

345 **Liner Coffee Tin** & five tobacco tins incl. Cuban Star, Stag, George Washington & Lincoln Hwy. **$161**

347 **Pocket Tobacco Tins,** 35 incl. Lucky Strike roll cut, Richmond & Maryland Club Mixture tins, Pat Hand, Phillip Morris & Dills Best. **$287**

348 **Collection of 22 Tins** incl. Granger, Catcher, Lucky Strike, Sir Walter Rawleigh & Boot Jack. **$86**

349 **Varied Collection** of 28 Tobacco Tins. **$373**

350 **Collection of 32 Tins** incl. Kipps, Gail Ax Navy, Emerson, Royal Gold, Star, American Beauty & others. **$345**

351 **Tobacco Tins,** 16 incl. Cubist, Amphora, Briggs & a Halligans Coffee tin. **$115**

352 **Collection of 25 tins,** mostly tobacco incl. Lucky Strike, Golden Twins & Best. **$115**

353 **Collection of 37 tins,** mostly tobacco incl. Between Acts, Little Cigars, Charm of the West & others. **$402**

A-ME June 2004
James D. Julia, Inc.

2451 **Brussell's Santa Lithograph** promoting Bissell's Cyco—Bearing Carpet Sweeper, by Michigan Litho. Company, Grand Rapids, w/several closed tears at bottom & upper left corners, ht. 50, wd. 31in. **$13,800**

BANKS, Still & Mechanical

Small banks for depositing coins became popular in the United States when hard currency was introduced in the 18th century. The adage "a penny saved is a penny earned" has represented an important part of Americana from the time of Benjamin Franklin. It was a time when parents taught their children the art of saving at a very early age, by giving them "penny" banks. Almost every substance has been used to make a still bank, all of which are very collectible. And hundreds of different types have been produced.

Still banks, so called to differentiate them from banks with mechanical parts, have been produced in quantities since the 19th century. They depict a range of buildings, animal and human figures. The most elaborate were made by leading manufacturing companies including Arcade, A.C. Williams, J. & E. Stevens and Kenton.

The most complex banks were mechanical cast-iron models produced from the 1870s. These banks operate on two principles: the weight of the deposited coin will cause the action to begin, or a person, after inserting a coin, presses a lever that activates a spring, setting the bank in motion. There were hundreds of different types of mechanical banks made until the 1930s by J. & E. Stevens and W.J. Shepard Hardware Company.

A-OH Jun. 2004 Garth's Arts & Antiques
Cast Iron Mechanical Banks, Working
424 **Novelty Bank** w/orig. paint & minor wear. Teller's wire replaced, ht. 6⅝in. **$891**
425 **I Always did `Spise A Mule,** Pat'd Apr 22d 1879 & Pending, orig. w/yellow base, remaining paint shows wear, lg. 10in. **$373**
426 **Eagle & Eaglets** w/worn orig. paint, eagle's eyes missing, lg. 8in. **$460**
427 **Hall's Excelsior Bank,** cashier has his orig. label, but repl. arms, minor wear, ht. 5¼in. **$345**
428 **Frog Bank** w/orig. worn paint, ht. 4¼in. **$517**

A-IA Oct. 2003

Jackson's International Auctioneers

01 **Rooster Mechanical Bank,** ca. 1880 by Kyser & Rex, cast iron, ht. 6¼in. **$62**

02 **General Pershing Still Bank,** ca. 1916, cast iron, ht. 8in. **$80**

03 **Eagle & Eaglets,** ca. 1883, by J&E Stevens Co., w/orig. paint. lg. 8in. **$747**

04 **Humpty Dumpty Still Bank,** ca. 1900 by Shepard Hdw., iron w/orig. paint, ht. 5¼in. **$546**

05 **Young N Still Bank,** ca. 1900, iron w/orig. paint, ht. 5¼in. **$172**

06 **Junior Safe Deposit Still Bank,** ca. 1900, iron & sheet metal. **$69**

07 **Wise Pig Still Bank,** early 20th C., by Hubley, iron w/orig. dec. **$80**

08 **Share Cropper Bank,** ca. 1900, Give Me A Penny, in iron. **$149**

09 **Middy Still Bank,** late 19th C., iron, missing clapper. **$69**

10 **Standing Rabbit Mechanical Bank,** ca. 1900 by Lockwood MEg., iron w/ remnants of bronze paint, ht. 6in. **$402**

11 **Donkey Still Bank,** ca. 1900, by A.C. Williams, cast iron w/orig. poly. dec., ht. 6¼in. **$184**

12 **Red Goose Shoes Still Bank,** early 20th C., by Arcade, cast iron w/orig. dec., ht. 4in. **$172**

13 **Small Pig Still Bank,** early 20th C., cast iron w/orig. paint,ht. 4in. **$46**

14 **Seated Rabbit Still Bank,** early 20th C., by Hubley, cast iron w/orig. brown paint, ht. 4¾in. **$103**

15 **Top Hat Still Bank,** ca. 1900, cast iron, ht. 2¼in. **$201**

16 **Colonial Home W/Porch Still Bank,** ca. 1900 by A.C. Williams, cast iron, ht. 4¼in. **$201**

17 **Toad On Stump Mechanical Bank,** late 19th C., by A&E Stevens Co., cast iron w/orig. paint, missing trap, lg. 4in. **$575**

18 **Pig Still Bank,** cast iron w/embossed words I Made Chicago Famous, lg. 4in. **$184**

Opposite

A-PA Mar. 2004 Pook & Pook, Inc.

Mechanical Banks, First Row

53 **Chief Big Moon** by J.E.Stevens Co., Pat. 1875, ht. 10in. **$2,300**

54 **Jonah and the Whale** by Shepard Hdw. Co., Pat. 1890 w/orig. dec. **$1,840**

55 **I Always Did `Spise A Mule Bank,** ca. 1900, jockey version. **$920**

56 **Magic Mechanical Bank** by J.E. Stevens Co., Pat. 1876, ht. 5½in. **$1,380**

Second Row

57 **Stump Speaker** by Shepard Hardware Co., w/orig. painted surface, ht. 6¾in. **$805**

58 **William Tell New Creedmore Bank,** ca. 1900 by J.E. Stevens Co. **$633**

59 **Tammany Bank** by J.E. Stevens Co., Pat. 1875, ht. 5¾in. **$316**

60 **Lion & Two Monkeys,** ca. 1900 by Kyser & Rex Co., ht. 9¼in. **$1,495**

61 **Leap-Frog Bank,** ca. 1900 by Shepard Hdw. Co., ht. 5, wd. 7¼in. **$805**

A-ME June 2004
James D. Julia, Inc.
2414 **Stump Speaker Mechanical Bank,** depicts a black carpet bagger traveling the south after the Civil War, ht. 10in. **$3,162**

A-ME June 2004
James D. Julia, Inc.
2412 **Ives Palace Still Bank** w/orig. spiral coin trap. **$1,380**

A-IA Mar. 2004
Jackson's International Auctioneers
Cast Iron Banks
456 **Bull Dog Mechanical Bank** Pat. by J.E. Stevens 4/27/1880, ht. 7¼in., missing trap. **$3,000**
457 **Punch & Judy Mechanical Bank,** Pat. 7/15/1884, repainted, ht. 7¾in. **$920**
458 **Jolly, Cast Iron Bank,** Pat. March 14, 1882, w/paint loss, missing tongue & eyes, ht. 7in. **$172**
459 **Magic Cast Iron Bank** by J&E Stevens, Pat. 3/7/76, ht. 5in. **$1,725**
460 **Cabin Mechanical Bank** by J&E Stevens, Pat. 6/2/85, w/minor paint loss. **$575**
461 **Zoo Mechanical Bank,** ca. 1960s, w/paint loss. **$316**
462 **Mutt & Jeff Still Bank** by A.C. Williams, w/minor paint loss. **$115**
463 **Rumplestiltskin Still Bank,** ca. 1910 w/paint loss, ht. 6in. **$86**
464 **Pair of Still Banks,** Boxer Dog & Elephant, both by A.C. Williams. **$115**
465 **Pair of Still Banks,** Coin Deposit, bank combination safe & Easy Chair, missing trap. **$69**

A-IA Sept 2003
Jackson's International Auctioneers
Iron, Metal & Ceramic Banks

19 **Standing Pig Still Bank,** 2nd half of 20th C., w/embossed words Bank On Repubic Pig, ht. 7in. **$69**
20 **Globe Mechanical Bank,** late 19th C., by Enterprise Mfg. w/orig. paint, ht. 5¼in. **$460**
21 **Two Faced Black Boy Still Bank,** ca. 1900, by A.C. Williams, ht. 3¼in. **$218**
22 **Thrift Registering Bank,** early 20th C., by American Can Co., ht. 5½in. **$115**
23 **Bugs Bunny At Tree Trunk Still Bank,** mid-20th C., by Metal Moss Mfg. Co. in white metal, missing trap, ht. 5¼in. **$126**
24 **European Ceramic Bank,** early 20th C., ht. 5½in. **$46**
25 **Lion On Wheels Still Bank,** ca. 1900, cast iron, lg. 4¼in. **$86**
26 **Crystal Bank,** ca. 1900 in cast iron & glass, ht. 4in. **$144**
27 **Basket Registering Bank,** ca. 1900, iron w/bronze finish, ht. 3in. **$46**
28 **Standing Bear Still Bank,** ca. 1900, iron w/orig. paint, ht. 5½in. **$144**
29 **Foxy Grandpa Still Bank,** early 20th C., by Hubley, iron, ht. 6in. **$195**
30 **Aunt Jemima Still Bank,** early 20th C., by A.C. Williams, iron w/orig. dec., ht. 6in. **$218**
31 **Boy Scout Still Bank,** early 20th C., by A.C. Williams, cast iron w/orig. finish, ht. 6in. **$149**
32 **Standing Rabbit Still Bank,** ca. 1900, iron w/orig. finish, ht. 5½in. **$92**
33 **Elephant W/Howdah Still Bank,** ca.1900, by A.C. Williams, iron, lg. 4¼in. **$69**
34 **Deckers Iowana Pig Bank,** ca. l900,iron w/lettering, ht. 4¼in. **$103**
35 **Cow Still Bank,** ca. 1900 by A.C. Williams, iron, lg. 5¼in. **$172**
36 **Campbell Kids Still Bank,** early 19th C., by A.C. Williams, iron, lg. 4in. **$149**
37 **Sitting Pig Still Banks,** pair, early 20th C., one cast iron, one silvered white metal w/locking trap, lg. 5½in. **$138**
38 **Turkey Still Bank,** ca. 1900, by A.C. Williams, cast iron w/orig. finish, ht. 3¼in. **$149**

A-ME June 2004
James D. Julia, Inc.
2411 **Speaking Dog Mechanical Bank** in untouched condition. **$2,875**

A-ME June 2004
James D. Julia, Inc.
2413 **Artillery Mechanical Bank,** the Union version w/orig. paint & old repair welding to base. **$3,105**

BASKETS

The art of basketry was one of our earliest crafts and is recognized today as yet another interesting form of folk art. Because basketry was common on the Continent, many of the first settlers were experienced basketmakers and quickly adopted new techniques from the Indians, who were excellent basketmakers.

During the decades following the first colonization, the need for containers and storage facilities was immense. Materials were abundant, so the art of basketmaking literally flourished until around the late 1800s when basket factories became established.

Among the most desirable baskets of interest to collectors these days are the Shaker, American Indian, the so-called Nantucket Lightship baskets, and the coiled rye straw baskets that are characteristically Pennsylvania Dutch.

Baskets continue enjoying much popularity among collectors, regardless of vintage. After all, everything collected these days was "new" once. An interesting collection can still be assembled inexpensively, unless one's taste preference includes one of the above types.

A-PA April 2004
Conestoga Auction Co., Inc.

26 **Rye Straw Sewing Basket** w/attached section for pin-cushion, attr. to Hanover, York Co., PA, ht. 7¾in. **$10,725**

27 **Miniature Rye Straw Covered Basket** w/open-work, woven hinges & latch, ht. 3, dia. 4½in. **$1,705**

28 **Round Rye Straw Basket** w/open-work & color banding, attr. to Andrew Sheely, Hanover, PA, died 1907, ht. 4, dia. 9¼in. **$990**

29 **Oval Rye Straw Basket** by unknown maker, York Co., PA. ht. 4, lg. 12½in. **$1,155**

30 **Ovoid Rye Straw Bee Skep** w/wood base & bee hole entrance, ht. 15, dp. 15in. **$3,960**

31 **Round Rye Straw Basket** w/tapered sides & two attached bent wood handles, ht. 8, dp. 14½in. **$1,760**

A-PA April 2004 Conestoga Auction Co., Inc.

34 **Oval Wooden Basket** w/wood slat & banded const. w/metal support to bentwood handle, ht. 15, lg. 15in. **$1,320**

37 **Oval Splint Market Basket** w/bent wood handle & pine base, Dauphin Co., PA maker, ht. 13½in. **$1,210**

24

A-PA April 2004

Conestoga Auction Co., Inc.

24 **Covered Rye Straw Oval Basket** w/carved bent wood handles, attr. to an Ephrata, PA maker, ht. 14¼, lg. 32½in. **$3,850**

25 **Bulbous Rye Straw Hamper Basket** w/cover, ht. 20, dp. 22in. **$2,750**

25

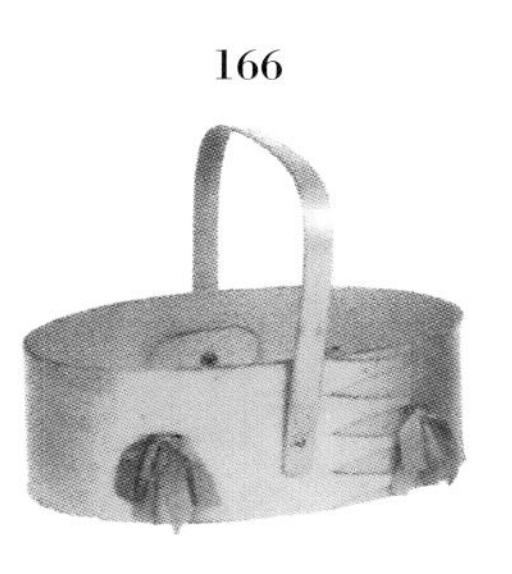
166

167

168

171

172

169

170

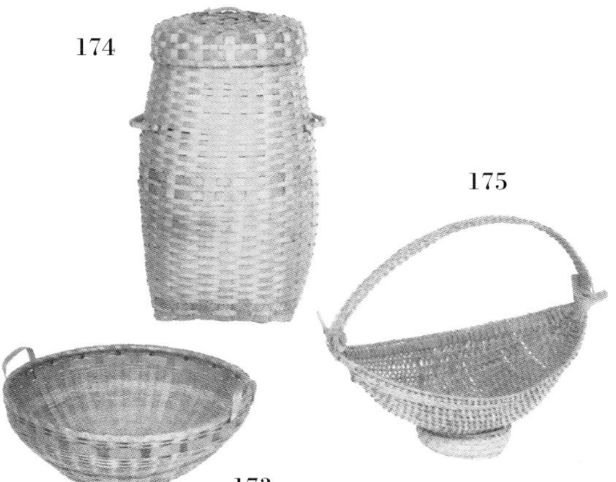
174 175 173

A-PA April 2004

Conestoga Auction Co., Inc.

166 **Shaker Bent Wood Sewing Box** w/straw woven needle holder, pin sharpener & cushion, mkd. Shaker Sabbath Day Lake Maine on base, ht. 3⅜in. **$231**

167 **Nantucket Light Ship Basket** w/hinged bent wood handle, ash splint & wood base w/label, ht. 5¼, dp. 8½in. **$632**

168 **Nantucket Ash Splint Basket** w/hinged bent wood handle & wooden base, sgn. & dated 1889, ht. 4½, dp. 6in. **$550**

169 **Round Potato Basket** w/bent oak wood handle & usage patina, ht. 13½, dp. 15in. **$385**

170 **Field Basket,** oak splint w/bent wood handle & red paint, ht. 17, dp. 19in. **$495**

171 **Square Splint Basket** w/two bent wood handles & stain color, ht. 7in. **$88**

172 **Straw Coil Basket** w/applied bent wood handles & base, ht. 7½in. **$605**

173 **Splint Basket** w/handles & color dec. banding, ht. 4½in. **$44**

174 **Bottle Basket,** splint w/lid, handle on lid & two sides, ht. 19in. **$77**

175 **Boat Form Splint Basket** w/woven handle & base, ht. 13½in. **$275**

164

165

A-PA Apr. 2004

Conestoga Auction Co., Inc.

164 **Field Basket,** oak splint & straw coiled w/willow bent handles, ht. 12, wd. 24in. **$687**

165 **Oak Splint & Coiled Straw Basket** w/horizontal woven side handles, ht. 14½, dp. 28in. **$2,420**

A-PA Apr. 2004 Conestoga Auction Co., Inc.
36 **Painted Rye Straw Basket,** unknown maker, York Co., PA, ht. 12in. **$2,970**

158 **Oval Splint Market Basket** w/bent wood handle attached w/God's eye & over sized ribs, ht. 10, lg. 12in. **$5,225**

160 **Oak Splint & Straw Coil Covered Basket** w/old reprs.to lid, ht. 9½, lg. 23, dia. 16in. **$1,870**

Top: 226, 227, 230, 230 Middle: 226, 227, 230, 227
Bottom: 228, 228, 229, 229, 228, 228, 227, 227, 229, 230

A-PA Mar. 2004 Pook & Pook, Inc.
First & Second Rows
226 **Oval Nantucket Basket,** 19th C., lg. 10½in., together with a small basket w/swing handles, dia. 5½in. **$1,725**
227 Miniature Buttocks Basket, 19th C., together w/2 splint baskets, 2 berry baskets & a small rye straw basket. **$345**
Third Row
228 **Lidded Shaker Basket,** together w/small bark snuff box w/relief dec., & 2 small berry baskets. **$575**
229 Cheese Baskets, 2, w/2 splint handled baskets & a rectangular basket. **$431**
230 **Miniature Splint Baskets,** 3, together w/ a larger rectangular splint basket. **$518**

A-OH July 2004 Cowan's Auctions, Inc.

82 **Buttocks Baskets,** split hickory, one w/ X wraps at terminals, ht. 9in; and one w/half Eye of God wraps at terminals, 19th C., ht. 15in. **$156**

83 **Buttocks Baskets,** probably Midwestern splint, both w/half of Eye of God wrap at handle ends, ht. 8in. w/splint breaks, the larger basket ht. 11in. **$161**

84 **Large Split Hickory & Maple Storage Basket,** Am., 19th C., w/orig. tinted splints, ht. 24in. **$218**

A-OH July 2004 Cowan's Auctions, Inc.

88 **Nantucket Gathering Basket** w/handles, ht. 4, dia. 6in. **$287**

A-OH July 2004 Cowan's Auctions, Inc.

86 **Split Hickory Gathering Basket,** Midwestern, 19th C., w/half Eye of God wraps where central spine meets rim, some breaks, ht. 11, ovoid 21 x 22in. **$172**

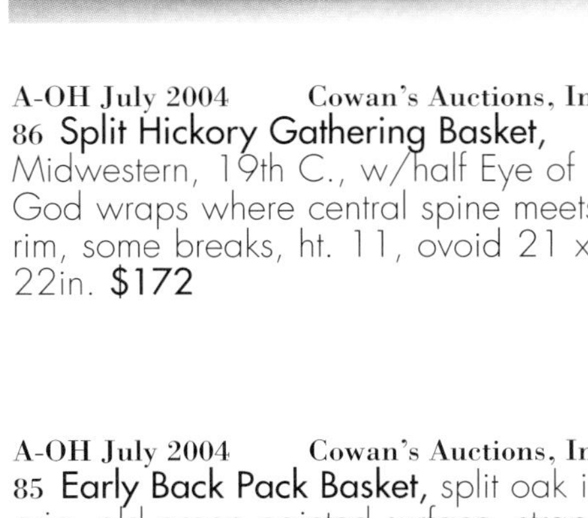

A-OH July 2004 Cowan's Auctions, Inc.

85 **Early Back Pack Basket,** split oak in orig. old green painted surface, straps missing, 19th C. ht. 21in. **$270**

A-OH July 2004 Cowan's Auctions, Inc.

89 **Early Basket Tree,** poplar & pine w/chamfered post, cross-form base & carved legs. Four pegs are period repl., 19th C., ht. 84in. **$2,990**

A-NH Aug. 2004 Northeast Auctions
793 **Two Large Gathering Baskets,** probably for drying herbs w/side handles, 13x17in. The second circular on square base w/side handles, ht. 14in., dia. 23in. **$200**
794 **Three Splint Baskets** incl. a New England Indian-made paint stamped example, w/side handles, red & black X & star motif overall, ht. over handles 8½in. The second basket has a stationary center handle, ht. 10in. & the third is a deep container w/square base & stationary wrapped center handle, ht. 17in. **$350**

A-NH Aug. 2004 Northeast Auctions
722 **Woodlands Indian Basket,** wide woven splint w/twin compartmented carrying case for pigeons, mid-19th C., ht. 19, wd. 10½, dp. 5¼in. **$1,200**

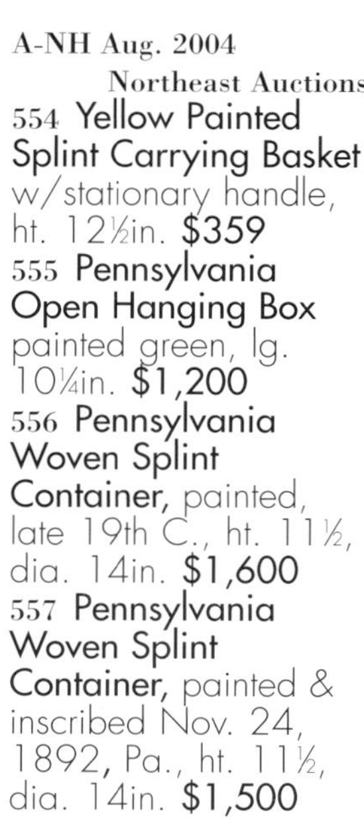

A-NH Aug. 2004
Northeast Auctions
554 **Yellow Painted Splint Carrying Basket** w/stationary handle, ht. 12½in. **$359**
555 **Pennsylvania Open Hanging Box** painted green, lg. 10¼in. **$1,200**
556 **Pennsylvania Woven Splint Container,** painted, late 19th C., ht. 11½, dia. 14in. **$1,600**
557 **Pennsylvania Woven Splint Container,** painted & inscribed Nov. 24, 1892, Pa., ht. 11½, dia. 14in. **$1,500**

200

203

201

202

204

A-PA April 2004
Conestoga Auction Co., Inc.
Rye Straw Baskets
200 **Oval Basket** w/straight sides & lid, ht. 7, dia. 10½, wd. 12in. **$1,320**
201 **Round Field Basket** w/tapered sides & woven handles, ht. 8½, dia. 18in. **$880**
202 **Bulbous Basket** w/flared rim, ht. 11½, dia. 11½in. **$990**
203 **Round Basket** w/open work, ht. 4¼, dia. 11in. **$770**
204 **Bulbous Hamper Basket** w/lid, ht. 22, dia. 16in. **$1,760**

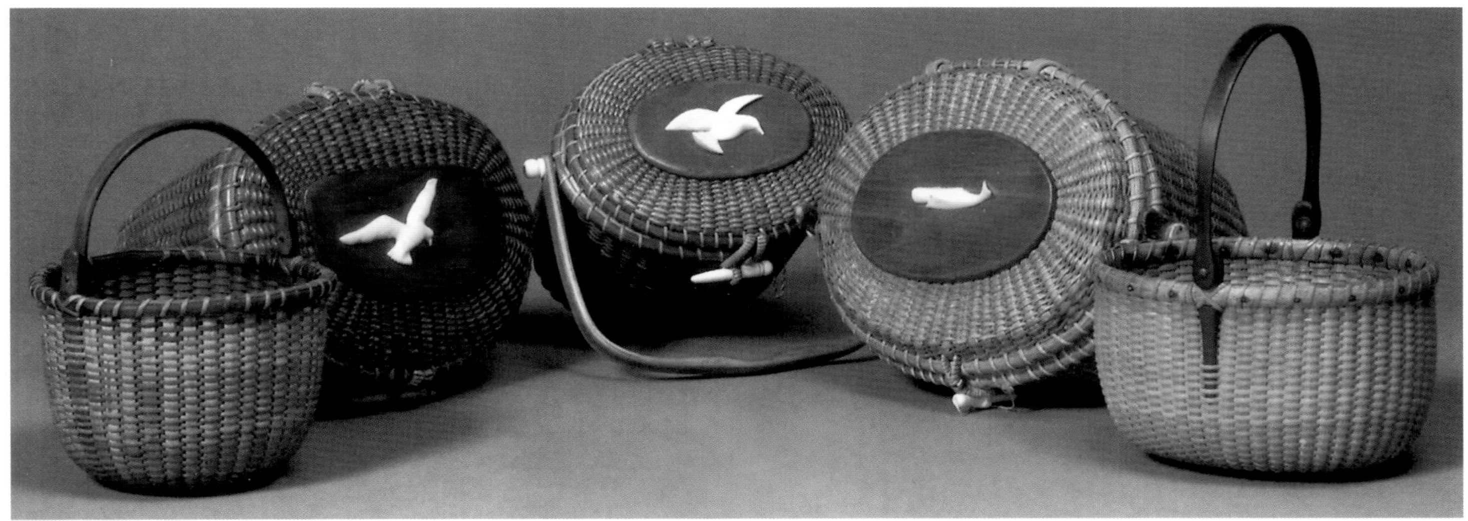

A-NH Aug. 2004 **Northeast Auctions**
Nantucket Baskets
152 **Swing Handle Basket** w/pinned & raised ribs, dated 1946, dia. 5½in. **$1,000**
153 **Early Purse Basket** w/ivory seagull mount & dark patina by José Formoso Reves, ht. 6, lg. 8¾in. **$1,900**
154 **Early Reves Purse Basket,** ca. 1950s, w/shaped swing handle secured by ivory buttons, peg fastener & dec. w/carved ivory seagull, ht. 6¾, lg.8 ¼in. **$2,200**
155 **Oval Purse Basket** dec. w/carved ivory whale mounted plaque, ht. 7in. **$300**
156 **Oval Basket** w/shaped swing handle. The exterior of bottom is inscribed F.G., lg. 6¾in. **$2,800**

BOTTLES

The "golden era" of bottle collecting escalated during the 1960s and well into the 1980s. It was a time when there was a steady supply of unusual new finds being discovered, either privately or through auctions which fueled collectors' demands. Bottle price guides were published, and eastern and mid-western auction houses began offering more bottles in their auctions. And it was at this time that major auction houses added specialists to their staff, as they moved into this "new" collectible field which became a major hobby for many collectors. The most desirable and pricy bottles are historic flasks, bitters, ink, figural and perfume.

A-ME Apr. 2004 James D. Julia, Inc.
Ink Bottles
372 **Umbrella Ink** w/eight sides w/open pontil, ht. 2¾in. **$345**
373 **Umbrella Ink** w/eight sides, open pontil & roll lip, ht. 2½in. **$345**
374 **Igloo Ink** w/lip chip, ht. 2in. **$488**
375 **Harrison Columbian Ink** w/eight sides, ht. 1½ in. **$603**

A-ME Apr. 2004 James D. Julia, Inc.
382 **Snuff Bottle,** rectangular, dark green, free blown w/open pontil, ht. 7in. **$86**
383 **Square Snuff Bottle** w/contents & Lorillard label, free blown, ht. 4½in., **$460**

A-ME Apr. 2004
James D. Julia, Inc.
339 **Stoddard Flag Historical Flask,** pint w/pontil mark & tiny flake on top of edge of lip. **$7,762**

A-ME Apr. 2004
James D. Julia, Inc.
335 **Franklin-Dyott M.D. pint** w/pontil mark & minor stain. **$517**

338 **Sunburst Flask** w/pontil mark & sheered mouth. **$1,380**

A-OH April 2004 Garth's Arts & Antiques
First Row
493 **Olive Blown Flask** w/Washington & Taylor in uniform w/minor blisters, ht. 6½in. **$258**
495 **Dark Olive Flask,** pint w/cornucopia & urn of fruit. **$115**
496 **Ribbed Double Bellflower Decanter,** 2nd period, ht. 9⅝in. **$172**
497 **Dark Amber Blown Flask,** scroll pint w/minor wear, ht. 7in. **$345**
Second Row
498 **Green Blown Flask,** pint w/cornucopia & urn of fruit, imper., ht. 7¼in. **$230**
499 **Railroad & Eagle Flask,** pint w/no inscriptions, ht. 6⅝in. **$402**
500 **Amber Blown Flask,** double eagle pint, roughness inside neck, ht. 7in. **$230**
501 **Olive Amber Blown Bottle** w/applied lip, surface wear, ht. 8½in. **$230**

186

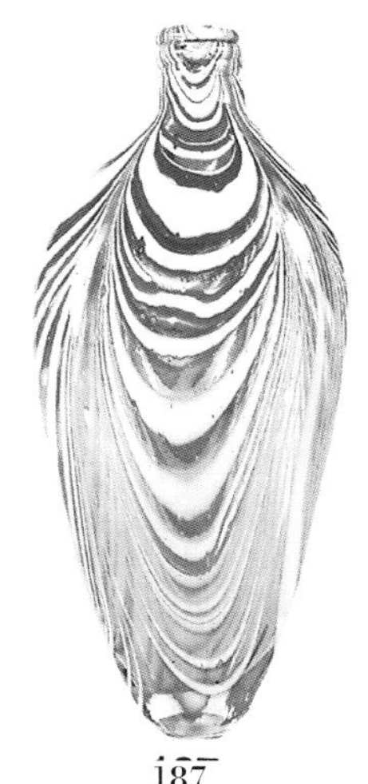
187

332

452

454

A-PA Mar. 2004 **Glass Works Auctions**
186 **Nailsea Flask,** ca. 1860-1885 w/scarred base, tooled mouth, ht. 7½in. **$275**
187 **Nailsea Flask,** ca. 1860-1885 w/pontil scarred base & tooled mouth, ht. 8¾in. **$250**

A-PA Mar. 2004 **Glass Works Auctions**
332 **Dr. C.W. Robacks Stomach Bitters,** Cincinnati, OH, ca. 1865 w/minor crack in neck, ht. 9½in. **$650**

A-PA Mar. 2004 **Glass Works Auctions**
452 **Cologne Bottle,** ca. 1850-1880, 12 sided w/sloped shoulders, ht. 6in. **$325**
454 **Cologne Bottle,** ca. 1860-1880, 12 sided, ht. 4⅛in. **$140**

501

507

59

631

632

A-PA Mar. 2004 **Glass Works Auctions**
501 **Harden Star Fire Extinguisher,** fire grenade, English, ca. 1884-1895 w/Reg. No. 10490 & orig. contents, ht. 6½in. **$200**
507 **Hazelton's High Pressure Chemical Fire Keg,** ca. 1880, ht. 11in. **$375**

A-PA Mar. 2004 **Glass Works Auctions**
59 **Brown's Celebrated Indian Herb Bitters,** Pat. 1867, Indian Queen w/chip on side of lip, polished, ht.12¼in. **$450**

A-PA Mar. 2004 **Glass Works Auctions**
631 **Barber Bottle,** ca. 1880-1925 w/white enamel dec., ht. 7½in. **$120**
632 **Barber Bottle,** ca. 1880-1925 w/white, blue & orange enamel, ht. 7⅛in. **$130**

523

524

A-PA Mar. 2004 **Glass Works Auctions**
523 **B.W. & Co., NY, Soda Water,** ca. 1840-1860 w/applied blob type mouth & open bubble at edge of base, ht. 7¼in. **$130**
524 **E.S. & H Hart, Superior Soda Water** by Union Glass Works, ca. 1840-1860, w/iron pontil, not a drug soda, ht. 7½in. **$325**

A-PA Mar. 2004 **Glass Works Auctions**
271 **Union Clasped Hands Eagle Flask** ca. 1860-1870, crude glass w/swirls of opalescent striations spiraling around body. **$1,900**
275 **Spring Garden Flask** by Anchor Glass Works, ca. 1865-1875, pint w/bubbles throughout. **$1,600**

271

275

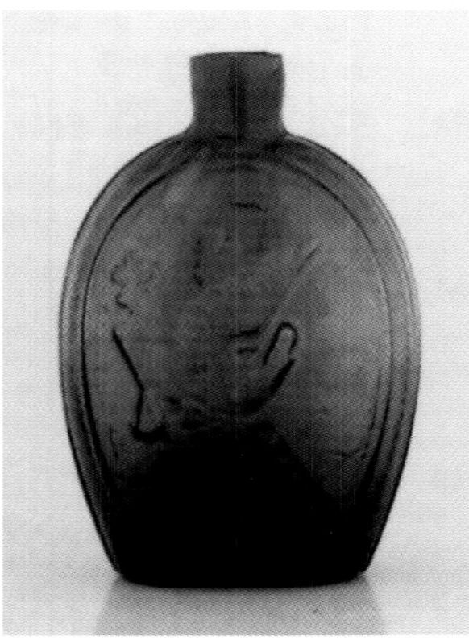

A-ME Apr. 2004
James D. Julia, Inc.
359 **Lowell Railroad Historical Flask,** half pint w/pontil mark, imper. **$402**

A-PA Mar. 2004
Glass Works Auctions
377 **Warner's Safe Nervine,** Rochester, NY, ca. 1880-1895, ht. 7½in. **$140**

A-ME Apr. 2004
James D. Julia, Inc.
399 **Star Whiskey** w/applied lip, handle, pouring spout & mkd. Star Whiskey, New York, H.B. Crowell Jr., size 8. **$747**

A-ME Apr. 2004
James D. Julia, Inc.
369 **Keene Blown Inkwell,** three mold, black glass, ht. 2½in. w/tiny chip on disk. **$4,312**

377

299

A-PA Mar. 2004 Glass Works Auctions
299 **St. Drake's 1862 Plantation Bitters** w/manuf. flaws, ht. 10⅛in. **$650**

375 376

A-ME Apr. 2004
James D. Julia, Inc.
395 **National Bitters Bottle** w/smooth base, applied top, ht. 12½in. **$517**

A-PA Mar. 2004 Glass Works Auctions
375 **L.Q.C. Wishart's-Pine Tree Tar Cordial,** Philadelphia Pat. 1859, Am. ca. 1860-1865, ht. 7½in. **$900**
376 **Tippecanoe-H.H. Warner & Co.,** ca. 1883-1895, amber figural log, ht. 9in. **$130**

313

313 **Greeley's Bourbon Bitters,** ca.1855-1870, unusual color, ht. 9¼in. **$2,750**

380 **Warner's Safe Diabetes Cure** w/motif of safe on bottle, English, ca. 1885-1900, yellow shading to amber, ht. 9½in. **$200**

380

A-PA Mar. 2004
Glass Works Auctions
Teakettle Ink Bottles
395 **Deep Amethyst,** ca. 1875-85, 8-sided w/hinged lid, ht. 2in. **$700**

396 **Dark Grape,** ca. 1875-1895, 8-sided w/vertical ribs, orig. brass neck ring & hinged lid, ht. 2⅛in. **$750**

397 **Amber** w/smooth base, 6-sided w/ground lip, lid missing, ht. 2in. **$475**

400 **Emerald Green**, 8-sided w/round lip & orig. brass neck ring, ht. 2⅛in. **$475**

152

153

154

A-PA Mar. 2004 Glass Works Auctions

152 **The Leader Jar,** quart, ca. 1890-1900 w/correct lid & metal closure. **$160**

153 **Trade Mark Lightning Jar,** ca. 1885-1895, mkd. Putnam 401 on base, w/orig. glass lid & Lightning closure. **$425**

154 **Trade Mark Lightning Quart,** 1882-1890, mkd. Putnam 127 on base w/orig. glass lid & Lightning closure. **$600**

A-PA Mar. 2004 Glass Works Auctions

166 **A.G. Smalley & Co. quart jar,** Pat. 1896, Boston & New York, together w/ The Vacuum Seal fruit jar, Pat. 1904 in clear glass, not illus. **$110**

171 **Cathedral Peppersauce Bottle,** ca. 1850-1860, 6-sided w/double collar mouth, ht. 8¾in. **$425**

A-PA Mar. 2004 Glass Works Auctions

155 **Trade Mark Lightning,** mkd. Putnam 196 on base & orig. lid. **$150**

156 **Trade Mark Lightning,** ca. 1882-1890, pint, mkd. Putnam 109. **$80**

157

158

159

A-PA Mar. 2004\ Glass Works Auctions

157 **Trade Mark Lightning,** ca. 1882-1890, half-gallon jar, mkd. Putnam 98 on smooth base. **$300**

158 **Unmarked Lightning Style Jar,** ca. 1882-1890, mkd. Putnam 197. **$90**

159 **Trade Mark Lightning Jar,** ca. 1882-1890, half-gallon, mkd. HWP 267. **$160**

160

161

163

164

A-PA Mar. 2004 Glass Works Auctions

160 **Putnam Quart Jar** ca. 1915-1925 w/trademark, Lightning U.S.Pat., smooth base, cornflower blue w/orig. lid & Lightning closure. **$250**

161 **Mason's Pat.,** Nov. 30th 1858, ca. 1875-1890, quart w/smooth base & zinc screw lid. **$150**

162 **Mason's Pat.,** Nov. 30th, 1858, half gallon, w/seed bubbles. **$600**

163 **Mason's Pat.,** Nov. 30th, 1858, ca. 1875-1890, w/zinc lid, quart. **$200**

164 **Mason's unlettered cross,** ca. 1880-1895, quart w/smooth base. **$200**

BOXES

Boxes are fascinating collectibles. They come in a variety of shapes, sizes and materials, and have been used for various purposes throughout our recorded history. Finding two early examples exactly alike is almost an impossibility, except for those that were made on molds or in wood factories during the 1800s.

Wooden boxes are favorites of the country collector. Wood used for making these containers are generally pine, birch, maple, ash or beech. For assembling the earliest boxes, short wooden pegs were used to fasten the bottom to the side and top to the rim. Later examples were fastened with copper or iron nails. Round boxes were the most common shape. These were used in pantries and in kitchens for storage, and rarely decorated.

Spice boxes – metal or wooden – are especially favored by collectors, in addition to candleboxes with their sliding covers, salt, pipe, sewing, writing, trinket, and interesting Bible boxes, oftentimes embellished with carving.

Bright and delightfully colorful boxes became popular during the late 1800s. These were common in the Pennsylvania German areas. And the interesting band box, oftentimes covered with colorful printed papers depicting well-known sights or historical events, have remained popular. These were used for storage as well as transporting clothing and personal effects.

Many boxes used in American homes were not originally of American manufacture. Before and after the Revolution, many commercially produced items were imported in exchange for domestic goods sent overseas. Among the 18th and early 19th centuries imports were snuffboxes made of china, silver, tortoiseshell, tin, papier-mâché and leather. Decorative Battersea enamel patch boxes were advertised during the 1760s. Elegant mahogany knife boxes became popular in England during the George III period (ca.1765), and are still available but very pricey. From the late 18th and early 19th centuries, a period without equal in the history of tea caddies, many rare and exciting examples were made in a wide range of shapes, sizes and decorative finishes. During the last decade, tea caddies made in England and Germany in the form of fruits and vegetables during the second half of the 18th century have literally set auction records. This may aptly be referred to as "The Golden Age of the Tea Caddy".

A-SC Dec. 2003
Charlton Hall Galleries, Inc.
017 **English Silver-Mounted Game Box,** walnut w/fitted interior & silverplate fittings, ht. 8¼, wd. 15½, dp. 9½in. **$850**

017

008 009 010

A-SC Dec. 2003
Charlton Hall Galleries, Inc.
008 **Tea Caddy,** Regency style, ca. 1840, w/hinged lid, inlaid lacewood, int. w/two fitted compartments & mixing bowl, ht. 6, wd. 12in. **$450**
009 **Tea Caddy,** George III style, mahogany w/hinged lid w/covered compartments, ht. 5⅛, wd. 4¾in. **$250**
010 **English Tea Caddy,** walnut w/brass mounts, ca. 1860, opening to divided & covered interior, ht. 6, wd. 7¾in. **$375**

A-IA Nov. 2003
Jackson's International Auctioneers
894 **Jewelry Box,** satinwood, mid-19th C., w/leather padded lid interior, lg. 8¾in. **$316**
895 **Sewing Box,** Anglo-Indian micromosaic & ivory, lg. 10in. **$460**
896 **Jewelry Box** w/burlwood veneer & interior divided tray, lg. 7½in. **$201**
897 **Glove Box,** lacquerware & bronze dec., & lined w/tufted satin, lg. 12in. **$230**
898 **Papier Mâché Lacquer Box,** Russian, ca. 1880 w/int. painted dec. in faux tortoiseshell, wd. 11¼in. **$805**
900 **Watch Box,** 19th C., French MOP & bronze inlay w/colorful fitted interior, lined, lg 4in. **$57**
899 **Burlwood & Tortoiseshell lined boxes** incl. a patch, snuff & a double stamp & inkwell box. **$201**
901 **Pocket Containers,** three, 19th C., burlwood & tortoiseshell lined. **$172**

A-NH Nov. 2003 **Northeast Auctions**
1615 **Dome-Top Box,** Lancaster Co., PA, mini. & dec. w/ compass rose & flowerheads overall & tinned iron lock, ht. 4¼, top 3¾ x 5in. **$6,500**

A-PA Jun. 2004 **Conestoga Auction Co., Inc.**
1027 **Lehnware Box** w/pegged const. & brown grain painted w/red, yellow & black highlights. Sgn. & dated on base 1898, wear & paint flaking, ht. 6½, lg. 10¾in. **$1,980**

A-PA Nov. 2003 Conestoga Auction Co., Inc.
244 **Oval Bent Wood Bucher Band Box** w/polychrome floral & foliate dec., & minor paint & wood wear, ht. 6½, wd. 15½, dp. 10 ½in. **$2,200**

A-PA Nov. 2003 Conestoga Auction Co., Inc.
268 **Sewing Box** attributed to Joseph Lehn w/salmon ground & applied floral dec., turned feet & key, ht. 6½, lg. 11in. **$11,550**

A-IA Nov. 2003
Jackson's International Auctioneers
886 **Tea Caddy** mah., w/satin wood & MOP scrolled florals & green stained tortoiseshell borders, int. complete, lg. 9¼in. **$1,035**
887 **Walnut Box,** 19th C., w/maple wood int., ht. 7, lg. 11in. **$201**
888 **Jewelry Box,** Regency, burlwood w/red satin lining & silver bail handle, losses, lg. 10in. **$287**
889 **Glove Box,** late 19th C., burl yew wood w/MOP & brass inlay, lg. 12in. **$287**
890 **Glove Box,** 19th C. French, rosewood w/ebony, ivory & satinwood honeycomb design, bird's-eye maple interior, mkd., lg. 10¼in. **$318**
891 **Trinket Box,** 19th C., mah. w/burlwood veneer & satinwood inlay, lg. 7in. **$86**
892 **Trinket Box** w/satinwood inlay & silvered ring handle, lg. 7in. **$230**
893 **Trinket Boxes,** pair, French, 19th C. w/MOP geometric designs, some losses, lg. 3 & 3¼in. **$144**

A-NH Aug. 2004 **Northeast Auctions**
Pennsylvania Toleware Boxes
612 **Dome Document Box** w/floral band of red flowers & green leaves on gray ground, lg. 7in. **$200**
613 **Dome Top Box** w/rose-red band below lid & embellished w/mustard stylized leaves at edge of lid & base, lg. 9in. **$450**
614 **Document Box** w/stylized floral & berry decoration, lg. 8in. **$800**

A-PA Nov. 2003 **Conestoga Auction Co., Inc.**
246 **Miniature Chest** w/paint dec., attributed to Jonas Weber, ca. 1835-1855, Lancaster Co., PA, w/scratches. **$4,950**

A-PA Jun. 2004 **Conestoga Auction Co., Inc.**
1031 **Seed Wall Box** attr. to Henry Lapp,ca. 1880s, w/ square nail const.,red & yellow graining, ht. 14½, wd.4¾in. **$18,150**

A-NE Nov. 2003 Northeast Auctions
Bandboxes

1690 **Water Spaniel Flushing Ducks** w/companion lid, ht. 10¼, lg. 16in. **$1,100**

1691 **Two Boxes** w/floral dec. & matching lids, one w/pineapple variation & foliage, ht. 10½in. The second w/yellow flowerheads on blue ground w/interior lined w/1876 PA newspaper, ht. 14in. **$600**

1692 **Buildings** w/unidentified chapel. has a matching cover, unlined. **$2,400**

1693 **Squirrels** w/matching lid, interior covered w/1831 PA newspaper, ht. 10in. **$900**

1694 **Coach Scene** on yellow ground w/stylized floral covered lid, ht. 14in. **$700**

1695 **Long-tailed Bird** & floral vines on blue ground w/matching lid. Each lined w/1831 NH newspaper, underside of base w/1824 Concord, NH paper, ht. 6in. **$700**

1696 **Port of Buffalo On Lake Erie box** w/lid & leather military hat w/NY label, ht. 10in. **$700**

1697 **Two Bandboxes** w/floral dec.,one w/stylized bouquets in white on blue ground, ht. 9½in. The second w/mustard ground & floral rosettes, ht. 13½in. **$700**

A-NH Aug. 2004 Northeast Auctions
Hat Boxes
571 **Two Pale Blue Floral Boxes,** wallpaper covered, oblong, lg. of one 13½in, the second w/brown leaves & floral border includes remnants of a lace bonnet, lg. 5¾in. **$500**
572 **Two Floral Wallpaper Covered Boxes** w/pink predominant. The largest w/pink drapery swag & bouquet, lg. 15in.; the smaller example w/pink bouquets on tan ground & an 1857 Philadelphia newsprint on base, lg. 4⅝in. **$700**
573 **Two Blue Oblong Hatboxes.** The largest w/bittersweet lid, & lined with Philadelphia Record newsprint, lg. 13½in.; the second floral w/teal & orange colors, & newsprint dated 1844 w/Baltimore & West Chester references lg. 5in. **$600**
574 **Blue Wallpaper Covered Box** depicting Deaf & Dumb Asylum, NYC, lg 16in., **$1,400**

A-NH Aug. 2004 Northeast Auctions
530 **Dome-Top Decorated Chest,** possibly Schoharie Co., NY, ca. 1820. The borders are red & yellow scrolling dec., ht. 13, lg.34½in. **$2,400**

Opposite
A-NH Aug. 2004 Northeast Auctions
Band Boxes
568 **Tall Hat-Form yellow ground wallpaper covered box.** The brim w/orange band is lined w/book print, & the underside w/label of owner, Haddonfield, N.J., ht. 8¾in. **$3,200**
569 **Tall Hat-Form wallpaper covered box** w/floral dec. & lined with 1833 Lancaster County newspaper, ht. 10in. **$1,200**
570 **Tall Hat-Form brown ground wallpaper covered box** w/mustard leaf dec. & a beaver top hat stamped w/name, address & Phila., ht. 9½in. **$3,400**

The earliest clocks came to America with the first settlers. At that point in our history, a clock had more prestige than practical value because time meant very little to the colonist who spent his daylight hours building a homestead or tilling the soil.

Over the years, America has added its fair share of illustrious names to the world's great clockmakers. Some craftsmen were working here as early as the 17th century and, during the 18th century, every colony had a clockmaker. It took months to produce a single clock because each of its innumerable parts was carefully made by hand.

The two main district communities producing clocks during the 18th century were Philadelphia and Boston. The early craftsmen – English, Dutch and German descendants – followed the traditional styles they had learned while apprentices; therefore, at first sight it was oftentimes difficult to distinguish the colonial tall-case clock from its progenitor in Europe. But, with the passage of time, American clockmakers developed their own recognizable styles. They chose for their cases the finest of hardwoods – walnut, mahogany and cherry preferred, with satinwood and other exotic hardwoods used.

Clocks did not become common in American homes until after the 1800s. Their manufacture in quantity began in 1840, fathered by Chauncey Jerome, a Waterbury clockmaker. His new methods of manufacture quickly replaced wooden movements with rugged interchangeable brass-geared works which eventually led to mass production. Surviving examples of the early tall case clocks, wall and shelf in addition to watches, are very collectible these days... and those in fine original condition and in good running order are very much in demand.

A-MA Nov. 2003 Fontaines Auction Gallery
278 **Royal Bonn Mantel Clock,** open escapement, porcelain w/floral dec. ht. 12in. **$900**

A-MA Nov. 2003 Fontaines Auction Gallery
279 **Royal Bonn Mantel Clock,** open escapement, Ansonia porcelain w/floral dec., ht. 13in. **$1,200**

A-NH Nov. 2003 Northeast Auctions
1549 **Banjo Presentation Clock** by Aaron Willard, w/floral eglomisé panel depicting the battle between the Constitution & Guerrière. Framed in ropetwist gilt molding. **$6,000**

A-MA June 2004 Skinner, Inc.
121 **Classical Carved Lyre Banjo Clock,** mahogany, MA., ca. 1825 w/eight-day weight-driven movement, ref. w/minor imp., ht. 39in. **$3,125**

1857 1858 1859 1860

1861 1862 1863 1864

1865 1866 1867 1868

A-IA Mar. 2004

Jackson's International Auctioneers, Inc.

1857 **"Bruno" Clock,** Waterbury, in black iron case w/ormolu mounts, 19th C., ht. 13in. **$230**

1858 **Ginger Bread Clock,** Ingraham, in oak case w/gilt door panel, ht.23in. **$161**

1859 **Ansonia Ginger Bread Clock** in oak case w/gilt door panel, ht. 22in. **$184**

1860 **Newhaven Ginger Bread Clock** in oak case, ht. 22¼in. **$115**

1861 **Victorian Walnut Shelf Clock** w/alarm mechanism & gilt dec. door, ht. 21in. **$126**

1862 **Walnut Shelf Clock** w/alarm, cameo pendulum & silvered dec., ht. 21in. **$172**

1863 **Victorian Walnut Shelf Clock** w/reverse paneled door, ht. 21in. **$172**

1864 **Walnut Shelf Clock** w/elaborately decorated door front, ht. 21in. **$184**

1865 **Victorian Walnut Shelf Clock,** as found original condition, ht. 22in. **$80**

1866 **German Regulator Clock,** ca. 1920, in oak case w/beveled glass door, ht. 33in. **$316**

1867 **Walnut Vienna Style Regulator Clock** w/turned dec., ht. 26in. **$316**

1868 **Waterbury Shelf Clock,** ca. 1845, in mahogany faced ogee case, ht. 26in. **$149**

A-NH May 2004 R.O. Schmitt Fine Arts
456 **Ithaca Calendar Clock,** ca. 1880, No. 6½ Belgrade, w/time, strike & perpetual calendar, walnut case, w/minor finish loss, ht. 32in. **$5,350**

111 112 113 114 115

A-MA June 2004 Skinner, Inc.
111 **Mirror Clock,** probably NH, ca. 1825, w/brass eight-day rack & snail movement, imper. & repl. tablet, ht. 29½in. **$1,763**
112 **Banjo Clock,** MA, ca. 1820, mahogany case w/painted iron dial & brass eight-day weight-driven movement, imper., ht. 33¾in. **$2,115**
113 **Banjo Clock** by Aaron Willard, Jr., Boston, ca. 1820 w/eight-day weight-driven movement, imper., ht. 28½in. **$1,645**
114 **Banjo Clock** attributed to William Grant, Boston, ca. 1820, w/alarm & eight-day weight-driven movement, imper., ht. 32in. **$2,468**
115 **Classical Carved Lyre Banjo Clock** by Aaron Willard, Jr., Boston, ca. 1825, w/eight-day weight-driven movement, old refinish & old replaced tablets, ht. 40½in. **$10,515**

A-MA June 2004 Skinner, Inc.
110 **Mahogany Shelf Clock** by Aaron Willard, Grafton, MA, ca. 1775-1825, framed by a ropetwist bezel w/brass weight-driven thirty-hour movement, imper., ht. 18in. **$4,700**

A-NH May 2004 R.O. Schmitt Fine Arts
310 **Pillar & Scroll Clock** by Eli Terry, ca. 1816 in restored condition w/orig. dial & label. ht. 32in. **$11,000**

A-NH May 2004 R.O. Schmitt Fine Arts
551 **Mantel Clock** by William L. Gilbert Co., porcelain case w/gilt dial, eight-day time & strike, ht. 10½in. **$200**

A-NH May 2004 R.O. Schmitt Fine Arts
271 **Royal Bonn Mantel Clock,** ca. 1901, eight-day time & strike, ht. 12in. **$1,100**

A-PA May 2004 Pook & Pook, Inc.
759 **Philadelphia Bracket Clock,** Chippendale, mahogany, late 18th C., backplate engraved Thos. Parker, Philadelphia, w/painted face & sgn. by retailer John Hall Philad., ht. 18½in. **$6,325**

A-NH Mar. 2004 Northeast Auctions
1053 **Mantel Clock,** English, George III, by Thomas Clare, Bedford, w/white enameled dial & brass ball feet, ht. 16in. **$2,500**

A-MA June 2004 Skinner, Inc.
104 **Acorn Shelf Clock,** Gothic, rosewood by Forestville Mfg. Co., J.C. Brown, Bristol, CT, ca. 1850, eight-day time & strike w/reverse painted tablet, ht. 20¼in. **$5,581**

A-June 2004 Skinner, Inc.
105 **Gothic Acorn Shelf Clock,** rosewood by Forestville Mfg. Co., J.C. Brown, Bristol, CT, ca. 1849 w/eight-day fusee movement & reverse painted tablet, ht 20¼in. **$6,463**

A-MA June 2004 Skinner, Inc.
102 **Gothic Shelf Clock** w/double steeple fusee by Birge & Fuller, Bristol, CT, ca. 1845-50 w/painted tablets, ht. 25in. **$3,173**

A-MA June 2004 Skinner, Inc.
103 **Gothic Shelf Clock** w/double steeple wagon spring clock by Birge & Fuller, Bristol, CT, ca. 1845 w/30 hour J.Ives Patent Accelerating Lever Spring Movement, ht. 24¼in. **$3,290**

A-NH Mar 2004 Northeast Auctions
475 **Pillar & Scroll Shelf Clock** w/label of E. Terry & Sons, Plymouth,CT, mahogany w/eglomisé panel depicting Mount Vernon w/gilt border, brass urn finials, ht. 31in. **$5,250**
367 **Banjo Clock** by Simon Willard, Boston, mahogany & giltwood case w/ American eagle & shield eglomisé dec. panel depicting a naval battle, ht. 40in. **$9,250**

A-IA Nov. 2003 Jackson's International Auctioneers, Inc.
857 **French Mantel Clock,** Louis XVI, gilt bronze, ca. 1800 & mkd. Lepaute Paris, raised on white marble plinth, ht. 16¾in. **$1,495**

A-IA Nov. 2003
Jackson's International Auctioneers, Inc.
858 **French Portico Clock,** burlwood & gilt bronze, ca. 1830 w/engine turned center & porcelain chapter ring, sgn. Vauguelin Paris, ht. 19¼in. **$1,610**

A-MA June 2004
Skinner, Inc.
106 **Lyre Acorn Wall Clock,** Forestville Mfg. Co., Bristol, CT, ca. 1850, rosewood w/tablet showing the Merchant's Exchange, Philadelphia, eight-day spring movement, minor imper., ht. 28¼in. **$15,275**

A-Nov. 2003
Northeast Auctions
394 **Gothic Double Steeple Shelf Clock,** mahogany w/wagon spring mechanism, w/floral dec. on upper door & feathery leaf dec. on lower door, opening to maker's label Birge & Fuller, Bristol, CT, ht. 26in. **$4,750**
395 **Brass Skeleton Clock,** English, fitted beneath glass dome w/circular open dial on circular base & knopped dome, ht. 15in. **$1,500**
396 **Gothic Double Steeple Shelf Clock** w/wagon spring mechanism by Daniel Pratt, Jr., Boston, w/frosted glass panel & ball feet, ht. 27in. **$2,250**

A-NH May 2004
R.O. Schmitt Fine Arts
457 **Ithaca Calendar Clock Co.,** Shelf Kildare, 30 day time & perpetual calendar in mahogany w/orig. cut glass pendulum, hands & hardware, ht. 26¼in. **$5,500**

A-NH May 2004
R.O. Schmitt Fine Arts
510 **Calendar Clock** by Southern Calendar Clock Co., St. Louis, MO, ca.1880 Fashion No. 4, 30 day, ht. 32in. **$1,650**

A-NH May 2004
R.O. Schmitt Fine Arts
347 **Regulator Clock** by Seth Thomas No. 5, mahogany case w/orig.lock, key & handle crank, ht. 50in. **$15,000**

A-PA May 2004
Pook & Pook, Inc.
546 **Federal Tall Case Clock,** MA, ca. 1805 w/arched bonnet, brass ball finials & open fretwork enclosing brass works, ht. 91in.
$10,350

A-NH Mar. 2004
Northeast Auctions
357 **Philadelphia Tall Case Clock,** walnut, dial inscribed "Jos. Wills" 1700-1759, w/brass & silvered dial w/moon phases & maker's name. ht. 106in.
$20,000

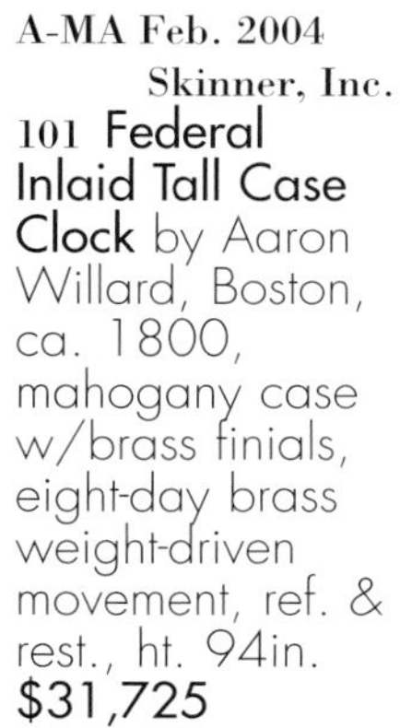

A-MA Feb. 2004
Skinner, Inc.
101 **Federal Inlaid Tall Case Clock** by Aaron Willard, Boston, ca. 1800, mahogany case w/brass finials, eight-day brass weight-driven movement, ref. & rest., ht. 94in.
$31,725

A-NH Mar. 2004
Northeast Auctions
673 **Georgian Inlaid Tall Case Clock,** mahogany, inscribed "Joshua Hewlett, Bristol." Brass dial w/second dial & calendar below an arch w/marine painted scene, ht. 96in. **$3,750**

A-MA June 2004
Skinner, Inc.
83A **Federal Tall Case Clock,** mahogany w/inlay, MA, ca. 1810-20, w/painted metal face w/flower-head spandrels & portrait of Washington & flags in arch, having a two-train movement. Inlaid w/checked banding throughout, rest., ht. 95in.
$9,988

A-MA Feb. 2004 Skinner, Inc.

102 **Federal Inlaid Tall Case Clock** attributed to Isaac Brokaw, Bridgetown, NJ, 1800-10, mahogany case w/brass rosettes & painted iron dial, ref. & imper., ht. 91in. **$7,638**

103 **Federal Cherry Tall Case Clock,** possibly NJ, ca. 1805-10, w/painted dial face & calendar aperture. The waist w/inlaid crossbanding & stringing above & below tombstone door, ref. & imper, ht. 97¼in. **$7,638**

104 **Classical Carved Tall Case Clock**, by James Rogers, NY, ca. 1825, mahogany w/Gothic arch panels & acanthus-carved columns, painted dial & hairy paw carved feet, old finish, imper., ht. 94in. **$7,638**

A-NH Mar. 2004 Northeast Auctions

360 **New Jersey Federal Tall Case Clock** with dial inscribed "Isaac Brokaw, Bridge Town," ca. 1770-1810, mahogany w/painted dial & moon phase, ht. 90in. **$12,000**

A-NH Mar. 2004 Northeast Auctions

359 **New Jersey Flat-Top Tall Case Clock** by "Jos. Hollinshead, Burlington." Cherry case w/brass & silvered dial & signed medallion, ht. 86in. **$11,000**

A-MA Feb. 2004 Skinner, Inc.
245 **Federal Tiger Maple Tall Case Clock,** probably MA, ca. 1810-15, w/ iron polychrome & gilt dial showing a flower in arch w/Am.shield spandrels. Eight-day brass weight-driven movement, ref. & rest. ht. 84in. **$11,163**
246 **Federal Tall Case Clock** by John Osgood, Haverhill, MA, ca. 1810 w/ polychrome & gilt iron dial, ref. & imper., ht. 93½in. **$11,163**
247 **Federal Inlaid Tall Case Clock** inscribed "Aaron Willard Boston," ca. 1815-20, mahogany w/eight-day brass weight-driven movement, rest., ht. 92in. **$14,685**

A-PA Dec. 2003 Pook & Pook, Inc.
202 **Pennsylvania Federal Tall Case Clock,** walnut, ca. 1800 w/eight-day works & face signed "Daniel Oyster, Reading", ht. 89½in. **$7,705**

A-NH Nov. 2003 Northeast Auctions
1561 **Rhode Island Chippendale Tall Case Clock** w/block & shell carving, mah., inscribed "Marm (aduke) Storr 1760-1774, London" fronting brass works. A number of American tall case clocks featured imported dials by Marmaduke Storr. Ht. 9in. **$60,000**

A-NH Mar. 2004 Northeast Auctions
365 **Boston Federal Eglomisé Shelf Clock** by Aaron Willard, mah. w/dished dial & brass paw feet, ht. 30½in. **$3,800**

DECOYS

Decoys are choice items of collectors and decorators these days. They diligently search for these pieces of floating and sitting sculpture, realizing that many have found their way into antique shops, or are still roosting quietly in old abandoned sheds, waterfront shacks and barns. Floaters are the most popular, followed by shorebird stickups which were never widely made beyond the Atlantic coastal area. In 1918 a Federal law prohibited shooting these diminutive shorebirds; therefore, early stickups are rare. Fish decoys have also become choice collectibles. They are used for ice fishing during the winter months, especially around the Great Lakes.

Many producers of decoys claimed that the most effective decoy was a realistic one, carved and painted to resemble a particular type of bird, while others believed that details didn't really matter; so the difference of opinions resulted in a great variety of decoy styles made from wood, metal, papier mâché, canvas and rubber. Most found today were made during the late 19th and 20th centuries. Wooden and tin decoys were produced by small manufacturers such as the Mason and Dodge factories.

Most professional carvers marked their birds and examples of their work is extremely valuable. Although many decoys are unsigned, carvers can oftentimes be identified by their style, while others will remain anonymous. Serious collectors prefer to collect the early hand-carved varieties which have become very scarce and expensive.

A-YE July 2004 Guyette & Schmidt, Inc.
Shorebirds
141 **Robin Snipe** in spring plumage, by Harry V. Shourds, 19th C., w/replaced bill, shot marks present & small chunk of wood is missing from tail. **$3,750**

142 **Black Bellied Plover** in full plumage by Shourds, w/orig. paint showing wear. The head has been broken off and reattached, showing fracture to the bill & shot marks. **$4,250**

143 **Yellowlegs** by Shourds, w/orig. paint, shows wear & the bill is a prof. repl. **$5,000**

523-524-525

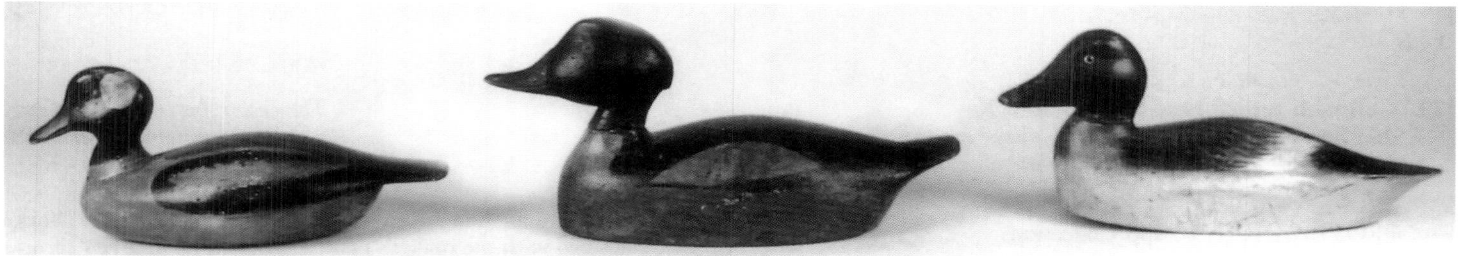

526-527-528

A-ME July 2004
Guyette & Schmidt, Inc.
523 **Canvasback Drake,** Chauncy Wheeler, Alexandria Bay, NY, w/old repaint, small dents & small crack in neck. **$440**
524 **Mallard Drake,** Harvey Stevens, Weedsport, NY, last qtr. 19th C., w/orig. worn paint & small dents. **$800**
525 **Black Duck,** Harvey Stevens, Weedsport, NY, last qtr, 19th C. w/minor roughness to tail. **$500**
526 **Bufflehead Drake** by Harvey or George Stevens, NY, w/good old paint, wear & small dents. **$700**
527 **Merganser Drake** attributed to M.C. Wedd, Rochester, NY, last qtr. 19th C., old paint, dents, small cracks & wear. **$1,000**
528 **Goldeneye** by Chauncey Wheeler, Alexandria Bay, NY, w/orig. paint, minor wear & chipping to paint. **$2,100**

A-MA Aug. 2004 Skinner, Inc.

441 **Pintail Drake Duck Decoy,** Am., ca. 1950, w/inset glass eyes, incised & painted details, ht. 7⅜, lg. 22¼in. **$300**

442 **Factory-Made Decoys,** Am., three incl. a merganser hen w/inset eyes & mkd. Joeckel on base, & two black ducks w/painted eyes, ht. 6, lg. 17½, 15½in. **$2,233**

443 **Curlew Shorebird Decoy,** Buzz Buzzanco, Mt. Kisco, NY, w/inset eyes & mounted on driftwood, sgn. under tail, ht. 15¼in. **$147**

444 **Carved Duck Decoys,** Am., 20th C., a white-winged scooter, mkd.Bieber on base, together w/a bluebill drake by Hanson, Osakis, MN, w/imper. **$264**

445 **Cork & Wood Curlew Decoy,** Am., mid-20th C., w/glass eyes, cork body, wood bill & mounted on wood base. Cracks to paint & losses, ht. 12¼, lg. 17½in. **$264**

446 **Shorebird Decoys,** five carved, possibly Bruce Bieber, Cape May, NY, 20th C. The decoys are lashed together on a rope, one marked Bieber, others impressed w/letter B. **$499**

447 **Carved & Painted Shorebird** by Harry V. Shourds, Seaville, NJ, 20th C., w/inset eyes & mounted on weathered slab, sgn. ht. 11in. n/s

448 **Three Painted Duck Decoys,** Am., early to mid-20th C.,including a black duck w/glass eyes, a bluebill hen & another unknown, ht. 6-7in. **$588**

449 **Four Carved & Painted Decoys,** Am., late 19th/20th C.,including a bluebill, pintail drake, an oldsquaw, and one unidentified decoy w/paper label mkd. #3 Ed Phillips, w/wear. **$441**

A-ME July 2004 Guyette & Schmidt, Inc.
266 **Mason Decoys,** Black Duck & Bluebill Drake, both standard grade w/glass eyes, restored paint & repairs. $350

267 **Mallard Drake,** Mason Factory, standard grade w/glass eyes, dry orig. paint, chips & cracks in neck filler, $325

268 **Bluebill Hen,** Peterson Decoy Factory, Detroit, MI, last qtr. 19th C., w/orig. paint, moderate wear, cracks, & shot marks. $300

269 **Pair of Mallards,** Hays Decoy Factory, Jefferson City, MO, ca. 1930s, w/orig.paint, minor wear & partial crack at neck filler. $1,250

270 **Pair of Carved Wing Mallards,** Herters Decoy Factory, Waseca, MN, w/minor wear & orig. paint. $2,100

A-ME July 2004 Guyette & Schmidt, Inc.
271 **Redhead Drake,** Mason Factory, hollow premier grade w/orig. paint, thin crack & slight separation at body seam. $2,000

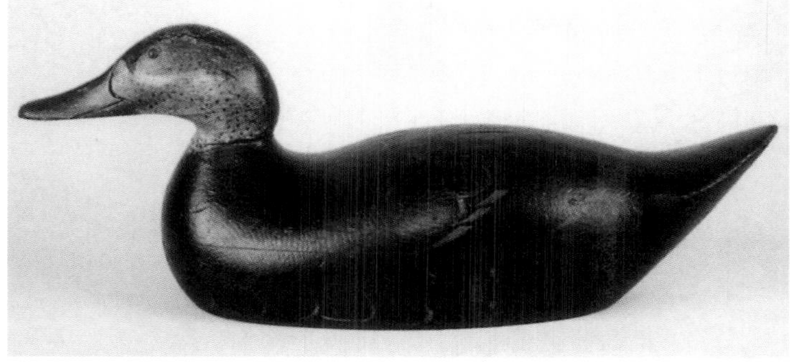

272 **Black Duck,** Mason Factory, first qtr. 20th C., premier grade w/orig. paint & old repair to chip in tail, dents. $800

A-ME July 2004 Guyette & Schmidt, Inc.
253 **Mallard Drake,** Mason Decoy Factory, ca. 1900-1905, premier grade w/orig. paint, never rigged & reglued crack in neck. $7,000

A-ME July 2004 Guyette & Schmidt, Inc.
254 **Bluebill Hen,** Mason, premier grade w/slight wear, shot mark & repair to bill w/touch up. $3,000

247A

248

249

250

251

252

A-ME July 2004 Guyette & Schmidt, Inc.
Mason Decoys 1896-1924
247A **Bluebill Drake,** premier grade w/snaky head & wide bill w/orig. paint showing moderate wear, small cracks & shot marks. **$1,400**
248 **Bluewing Teal Drake,** 1st qtr. 20th C., premier grade w/orig. paint, moderate wear & small defect in wood under tail. **$3,250**
249 **Redhead Hen,** 1st qtr. 20th C., w/orig. paint & minor wear & hairline crack in back. **$1,900**
250 **Canvasback Drake,** ca. 1900, premier grade, w/orig. paint w/moderate wear, bill strengthened slightly, small dents & shot marks. **$1,250**
251 **Hollow Bluebill Drake,** premier grade w/dry orig. paint, thin fractures to bill & crack to base of neck. **$2,650**
252 **Bluewing Teal Drake,** standard grade w/glass eyes, orig. paint & small crack at neck filler. **$2,200**

A-ME July 2004 Guyette & Schmidt, Inc.
255 **Mallard Hen,** Mason, premier grade w/orig. paint & repair to tail & crack in one side & several tiny dents. **$3,100**

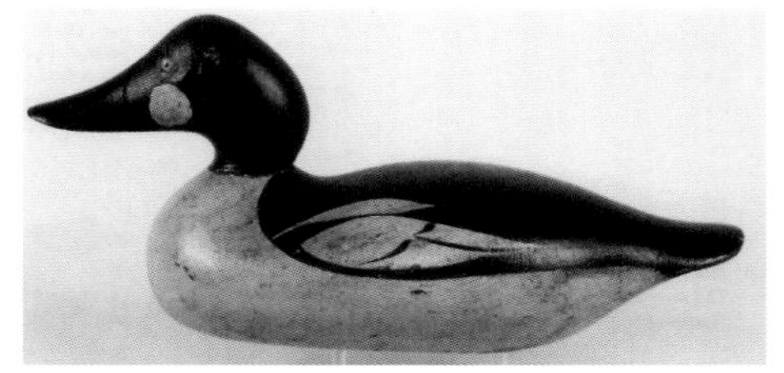

A-ME July 2004 Guyette & Schmidt, Inc.
256 **Goldeneye Drake,** Mason, Challenge grade w/orig. paint, minor wear & several tiny dents & shot marks. **$4,700**

A-PA June 2004 Conestoga Auction Co., Inc.
417 **Canvas Back Decoy,** Susquehanna River working drake w/minor use, lg. 17in. **$495**

A-OH July 2004 **Garth's Arts & Antiques**
Fish Decoys, Wood
228 **Carved S Curve Decoy** w/tin fins & tail made from tobacco tin, orig. paint, wear & rust, lg. 10⅝in. **$230**
229 **Frog Shaped Decoy** w/orig. paint & tin appendages, wear & rust, lg. 11in. **$201**
230 **Slender Decoy** w/orig. silver/green paint & stenciled black scales, tin fins & glass eyes. Carved by Andy Trombley, 1919-1975, lg. 11½in. **$316**
231 **Large Fish** by Chub Buchman, w/orange, green, yellow & white paint, large tin fins & glass eyes, lg. 12in. **$345**
232 **Mouse Fish Decoy** w/tin paws, wire tail & glass eyes. Some wear & minor touch-up to tail, lg. 7¾in. **$316**
233 **Turtle Decoy,** carved wood w/scalloped edge shell, tin legs, glass eyes & minor wear, lg. 9in. **$460**
234 **Large Catfish,** carved wood w/tin fins, glass eyes, wire whiskers & orig. paint. Minor wear & rust from use, lg. 12½in. **$287**
235 **Two Carved Wood Fish Decoys,** one w/silver & red repaint & brass fins, lg. 10in., together w/ an old decoy w/green & yellow paint w/copper fins & tail, lg. 7¼in. **$230**

A-ME July 2004 **Guyette & Schmidt, Inc.**
Fish Decoys by Oscar Peterson, ca. 1950
236 **Large Spear Fishing Decoy,** mid-1950s, w/3 weights, orig. paint, wear, hairline crack & tiny chip under tail, lg. 22in. **$600**

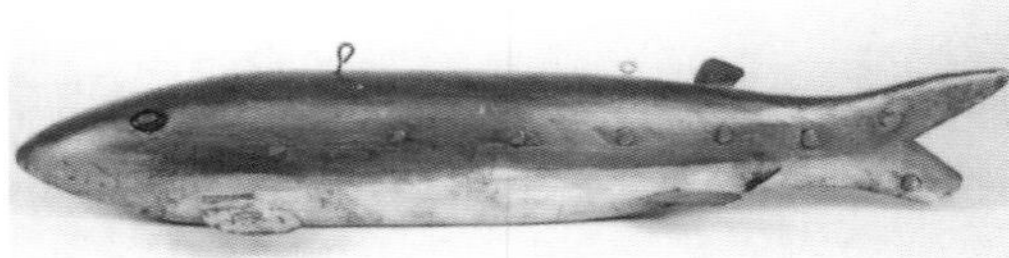

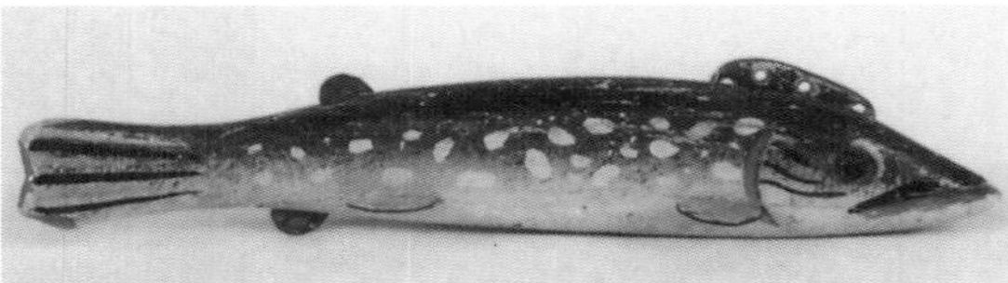

A-ME July 2004
Guyette & Schmidt, Inc.
237 **Pike** w/tack eyes, by Peterson, orig. paint w/minor flaking & wear, lg. approx. 7in. **$800**

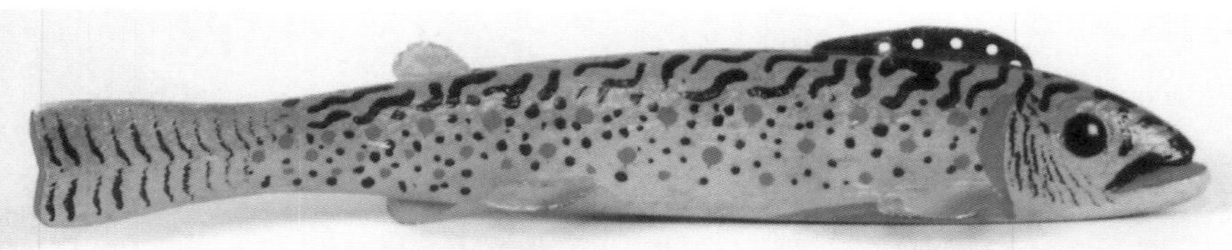

A-ME July 2004 **Guyette & Schmidt, Inc.**
Fish Decoys by Oscar Peterson, ca. 1950
223 **Trout Spear Fishing Decoy** w/metal fins, lg. 7⅞in. **$3,500**

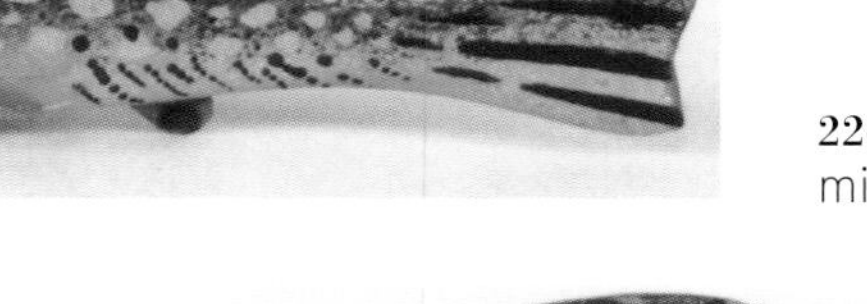

224 **Shiner Spear Fishing Decoy** w/paint flakes missing from metal fins, lg. 8in. **$2,350**

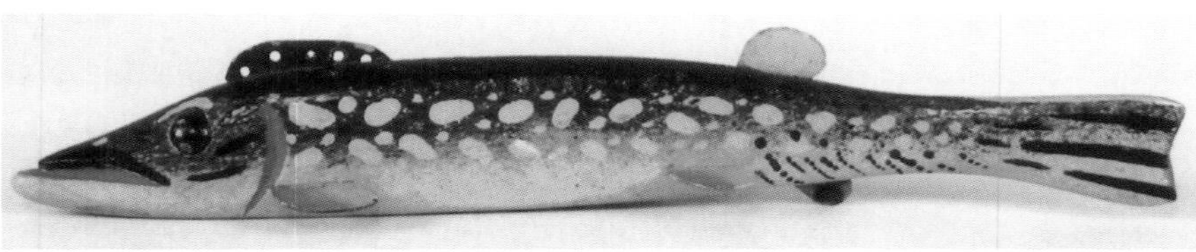

226 **Pike Spear Decoy** w/tiny flakes of paint missing from metal fins, lg. 8¼in. **$2,900**

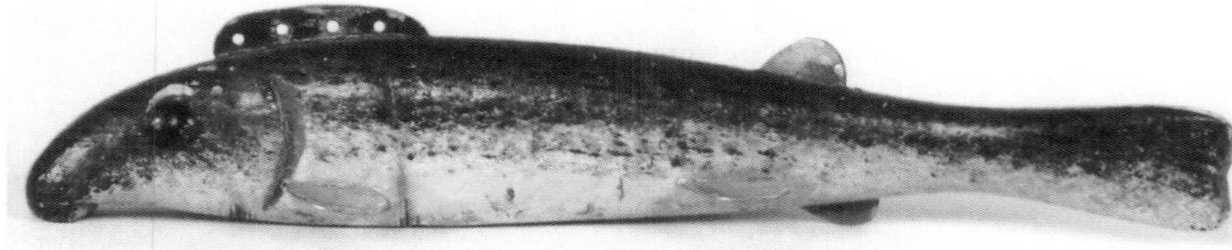

231 **Sucker Fish Decoy**, w/orig. paint & slight flaking to fins, lg. 7⅛in. **$1,700**

DOLLS & DOLL-HOUSES

Dolls come in an incredible variety ranging from the exquisitely dressed French fashion dolls to the fine German bisque dolls made in Meissen, Germany, to humble American folk dolls. Only in recent years have collectors' tastes broadened to include these charming old whimsical dolls which have a timeless quality.

Most dolls sold in America from 1900 to 1910 came from Europe. The First World War practically halted the production of French and German dolls and again during the Second World War dollmaking was disrupted. It wasn't until 1949 that a breakthrough invigorated the doll industry with the invention of hard plastic which quickly solved many problems that had plagued dollmakers. By the 1950s the introduction of soft vinyl resulted in the production of even more realistic dolls.

Modern and vintage dolls, like many toys these days, are throwbacks to dolls made years ago. Trends have a tendency to become fashionable again, only to lose their popularity after a few years and then reappear years later, different but reminiscent of the originals. An example would be cloth advertising dolls that became popular during the early 1900s.

Dolls delight children, but they serve primarily as a very gentle friend on whom they can project their fantasies and to whom they can turn in times of adversity. Today these childhood memories literally set records at auctions across America. Pristine condition contributes significantly to their value.

The earliest doll-houses were made in Germany and Holland. American doll-houses date from the late 1800s and were generally modeled after popular contemporary styles of architecture. The invention of lithography during the mid-19th century supplied manufacturers of doll-houses with an inexpensive means of mass-producing these toys. The R. Bliss Manufacturing Co., Pawtucket, RI, became a major manufacturer round 1904, and the Morton E. Converse Co, Winchendon, MA, one of America's largest manufacturers of toys during the early 1900s, produced a few doll-houses which appeared in the company's 1913 catalog. During the late 1920s A. Schoenhut & Co., Philadelphia, offered an array of colorful doll-houses in various styles and sizes, all of which are prized collectibles these days.

A-ME Nov. 2003 James D. Julia, Inc.
4 **Character Doll,** German bisque, Bruno Schmidt, w/orig. wig, possibly orig. clothes & period leather shoes. One finger tip missing, and light wear to body. ht. 11in. **$7,475**

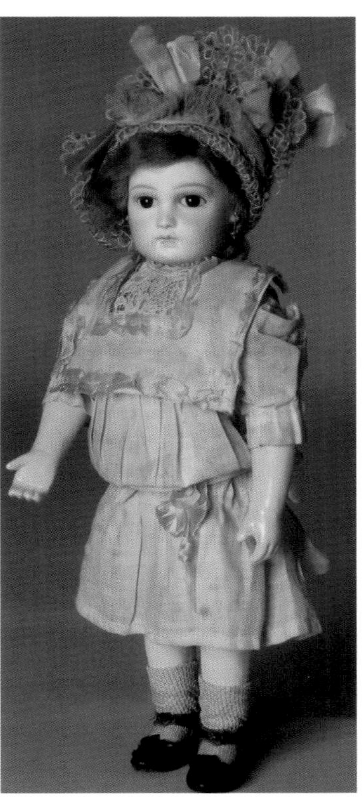

A-ME Nov. 2003 James D. Julia, Inc.
20 **Jumeau Portrait Doll,** first series, mkd., jointed w/repl. mohair wig, shoes mkd. Jumeau Bébé Deposé, ht. 15in. **$8,050**

37 **Queen Anne Type Wooden Doll,** 18th C., w/inset glass pupil-less eyes. Has had paint rest. to face & limbs, ht. 26in. **$2,874**

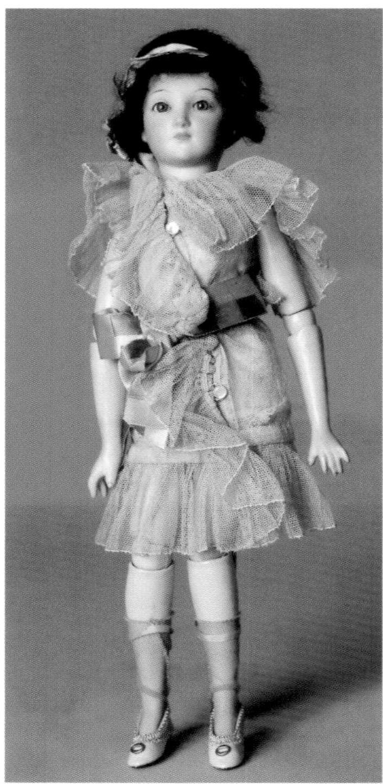

A-ME Nov. 2003 James D. Julia, Inc.
178 **Flapper Lady,** COD 1469, example of 20s. Clothing possibly orig, shoes are repl., ht. 14in. **$1,944**
178A **Simon & Halbig Flapper Lady,** w/20s style dress & some crazing to upper legs, ht. 14in. **$3,162**

A-ME Nov. 2003
James D. Julia, Inc.
216 **Tête Jumeau,** fully jointed & mkd. composition body & repl. wig. Dress is an old replacement, but undergarments are antique, no shoes, ht. 12in. **$4,255**

A-ME Nov. 2003
James D. Julia, Inc.
217 **Petit & Dumontier Bébé** w/French jointed composition body & metal hands. Extensive rest. to forehead & eyes, ht. 22in. **$1,725**

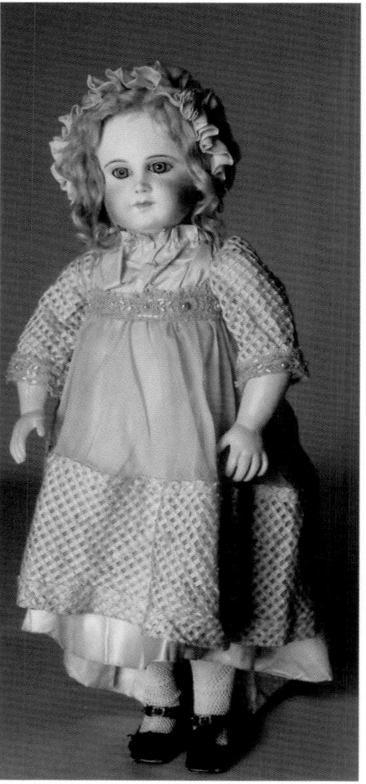

A-ME Nov. 2003
James D. Julia, Inc.
58 **French Bisque Bru Jne Bébé Doll** w/some moth damage to orig. clothing. Rub on right wrist, ht. 19.in. **$33,350**

A-ME Nov. 2003
James D. Julia, Inc.
110 **Schmitt Bébé** w/paperweight eyes, wig repl., orig. clothes & minor scuffs to left cheek, ht. 24in. **$ 11,500**

A-ME Nov. 2003 James D. Julia, Inc.
145 **Schmitt Bébé** w/blue threaded paperweight eyes, antique dress & repainted body, ht. 25in. **$20,075**
146 **Halopeau Bébé,** French jointed wood body & antique Bébé dress. The doll has a tiny mold flaw to her nose, and the bisque has some kiln dust throughout, ht. 16in. **$14,950**

A-ME Nov. 2003 James D. Julia, Inc.
199 **Steiner Bébé,** jointed & retains orig. mohair wig, unmarked, ht. 10½in., **$6,267**
200 **Jumeau Portrait Doll,** second series w/jointed body, mohair wig, antique clothing & shoes. Minor wear to joints, ht. 11in. **$3,162**

A-ME Nov. 2003 James D. Julia, Inc.
111 **French Jullien Bébé** w/fully jointed composition body, in fine orig. cond., ht. 19in. **$3,910**

A-ME Nov. 2003 James D. Julia, Inc.
193 **Kestner Doll,** closed mouth w/chunky straight-wristed body, ht. 24in. **$2,520**

A-PA June 2004
Noel Barrett Antiques & Auctions, Ltd.
64 **Jumeau Doll** w/early composition body, period clothing, repl. wig & marked Déposé shoes, ht. 26in. **$15,400**

A-ME Nov. 2003 James D. Julia, Inc.
149 **Déposé Doll** w/blue paperweight eyes, eight ball-jointed Jumeau body, unmarked, in orig. condition, ht. 19in. **$9,200**

A-ME Nov. 2003 James D. Julia, Inc.
148 **Steiner Bébé** w/original satin dress w/blond wig & gauze hat. Trunk includes some original clothing & newer added, ht. 8in. **$3,565**

A-PA June 2004
Noel Barrett Antiques & Auctions Ltd.
62 **Simon Halbig Bisque Doll** w/original brown wig, 5 piece comp. body dressed in white baby clothing, antique socks & leather baby booties, ht. 26in. **$1,320**

A-PA June 2004
Noel Barrett Antiques & Auctions, Ltd.
76 **Bébé Bru Jne Doll** w/wood legs, bisque arms & kid body. Three fingers have been re-attached, ht. 25in. **$13,200**

A-PA June 2004
Noel Barrett Antiques & Auctions, Ltd.
78 **Tête Jumeau,** mkd., w/human hair braided wig, jointed comp. body mkd. Jumeau Médaille D'Paris. Minor scuffing on body & finger tips, ht. 24in. **$7,150**

A-ME June 2004 James D. Julia, Inc.
2005 **Portrait Jumeau** w/blue threaded paperweight eyes on an eight jointed body, & original clothing, ht. 13½in. **$16,100**

A-ME June 2004 James D. Julia, Inc.
2012 **Bru Jne Bébé,** French bisque w/original clothing, incl. shoes. Small firing crack to shoulder, ht. 19in.
$34,500

A-ME June 2004 James D. Julia, Inc.
2050 **Bru Jne,** w/blond mohair wig & dressed in antique white cotton nightgown. Leather body has wear & wood legs have chipping paint. Both bisque hands have rest. to fingers, head & shoulder plate mkd., ht. 22in.
$10,925

A-ME June 2004 James D. Julia, Inc.
2022 **Tête Jumeau Bébé** w/orig. French style dress, German shoes & replaced wig, ht. 26in. **$2,702**

A-ME June 2004
James D. Julia, Inc.
1377 **Tiny Tête Jumeau Bébé** w/trunk & clothing, including fancy shoes w/rosettes & matching socks. Toes on left foot re-glued,normal wear to composition & wood body.
$6,325

A-ME June 2004 James D. Julia, Inc.
1351 Seth Doll by John Wright, an early creation w/orig. wrist tag, near mint. $780
1352 John Wright Doll, the mate to Seth, w/orig. clothing & wrist tag, mint. $780

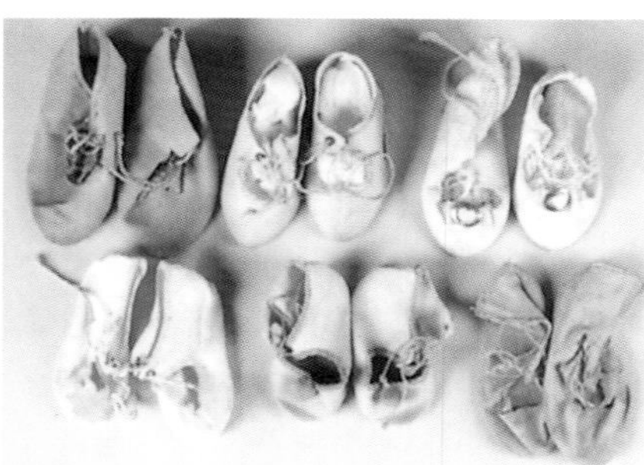

A-ME June 2004 James D. Julia, Inc.
2097 German Doll Shoes, 4 pair, antique, lg. 2 to 3in. $178
2098 German Cloth Doll Shoes, 6 pair, lg. 2½ to 3¼in. $287

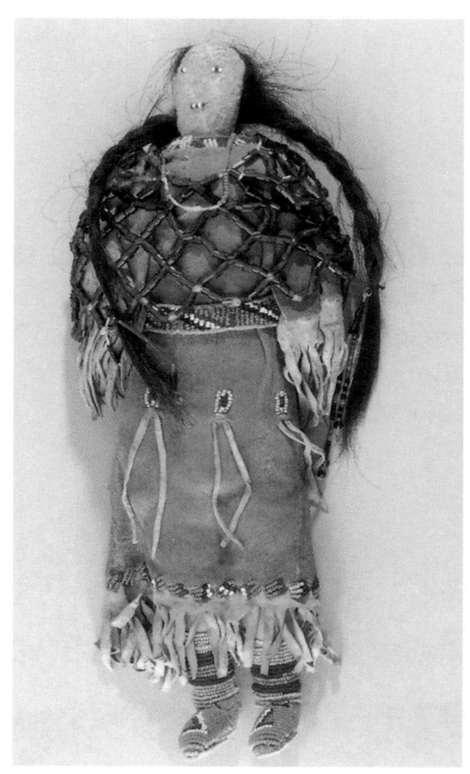

A-PA May 2004 Pook & Pook, Inc.
382 Plains Indian Doll wearing a hide dress w/beaded shoes, belt, face & trim, ht. 14in. $3,910

A-ME June 2004 James D. Julia, Inc.
2093 Bru Doll Shoes, black leather w/buckles, mkd. on soles & white fish net socks. $747

A-ME JUne 2004 James D. Julia, Inc.
194 Simon & Halbig Doll & Trunk w/several outfits. Doll w/mohair wig, jointed German composition body & straight wrists. Ht. 9in. $1,322

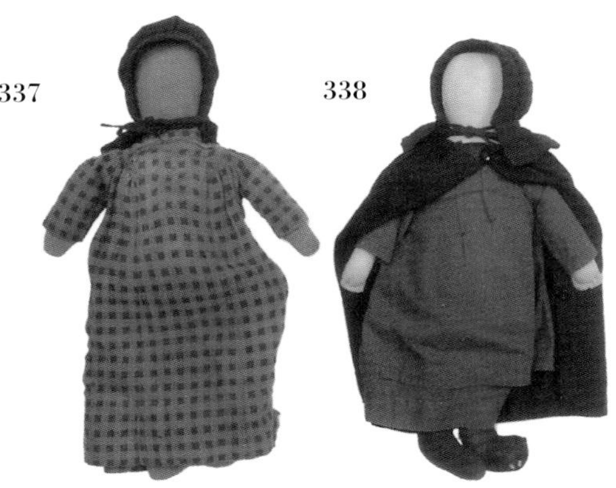

337 338

A-PA Apr. 2004 Conestoga Auction Co., Inc.

337 **Mennonite Doll,** hand sewn w/red & black checkered dress & black bonnet, ca. early 1900s, fading & holes to cloth, ht. 17½in. **$962**

338 **Amish Doll,** Lancaster County PA, in green dress w/black cape & bonnet, hand sewn, ht. 16in. **$687**

339 **Ohio Amish Doll,** hand sewn. Arms & legs made from corn cobs, staining, ht. 15in. **$341**

340 **Amish Teddy Bear,** hand sewn w/felt clothing & glass eyes. Old repairs to face, ht. 22in. **$1,980**

340 339

A-ME June 2004
James D. Julia, Inc.
1687 **Shirley Temple Composition Doll,** w/original box, clothes & pin. Needs to be re-strung. ht. 22in. **$1,380**

A-ME June 2004
James D. Julia, Inc.
1327 **French Clockwork Phaeton & Lady Driver.** A clockwork car w/wind-up mechanism, made of wood & dec. in a multitude of colors, ht. 10½, lg. 9½in. **$3,450**

A-MA Oct. 2003 Skinner, Inc.
275 **Shaker Miniature Doll House Furniture,** 20th C., some signed, & a non-Shaker doll. **$1,880**

A-ME June 2004 James D. Julia, Inc.
1424B **Character Doll,** Simon & Halbig, mkd., w/fully jointed composition body. Little touch-up to joints, ht. 37in. **$4,312**

A-ME June 2004 **James D. Julia, Inc.**

German Bisque Kewpie Dolls

2054 **Soldier** w/molded clothing w/partial label on chest, neck re-glued & tip of gun damaged, ht. 3¾in. $345

2055 **Thinker,** sign on bottom, ht. 4½in. $230

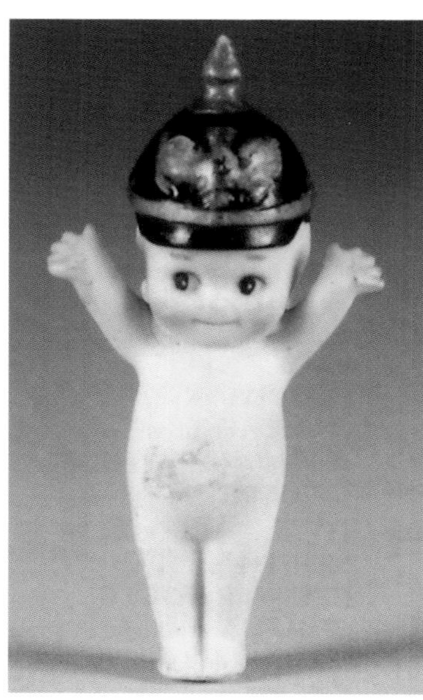

2027 **Governor,** sitting in chair, mkd. on bottom of chair. $230

2028 **Kewpie** wearing Russian Helmet, ht. 2¾in. $345

Lot 2029

Lot 2030

2029 **Kewpie** Playing Mandolin, ht. 2in. $172

2030 **Three Kewpies,** a guitar player & pair of salt & pepper shakers. $210

2053 **Two Kewpies,** one w/cat & one w/sled, ht. 2in. $210

2032 **Three Huggers,** ht. 3½in. $287

2033 **Two Kewpies,** one w/book and one w/sweeper, ht. 2 & 2½in. $390

A-MA Oct. 2003 Skinner, Inc.

159 **Shaker-style Wooden Doll House** w/miniature Shaker furnishings, 20th C. The exterior is a replica of a Shaker Trustees' Office w/painted sign, ht. 34, wd. 36, dp. 24in. **$7,050**

A-PA June 2004 Noel Barrett Antiques & Auctions, Ltd.

205 **Moritz Gottschalk Red roofed Bungalow,** two tone masonry exterior, original wall & floor papered two room interior, complete w/glass windows & curtains. ht. 15, wd. 13in. **$3,300**

206 **Whitney Reed New Practical House,** made in Leominster, MA, & advertised in Reed 1902-3 catalogue. House opens from back, has 4 glass windows w/orig. curtains, in brick red on stained wood w/painted roof portico, faux brick facade & solid gray roof, ht. 14in., wd. 24in. **$880**

A-PA June 2004

Noel Barrett Antiques & Auctions, Ltd.

447 **Bliss Fire Station,** early lithographed paper on wood w/bell tower & silver painted bell, ca. 1890s, ht. 12¼, wd. 10in. **$1,650**

448 **R. Bliss Modern Jack's House,** lithographed paper on card & wood construction w/numerous figures, animals & accessories. Opens from back & held together w/removable lathe turned wooden pegs, ca. 1898, ht. 13, wd. 10¼in. **$4,400**

The furnishings of America's past had a particular flair... functionalism that was the natural design expression of a country where practicality meant survival. The bulk of the early furniture was utilitarian and commonplace, made to serve a useful purpose. The earliest cabinetmakers were generally itinerant craftsmen who borrowed their ideas from several periods, oftentimes adding a bit of individuality of their own. Therefore, furniture produced in America was a combination of Yankee ingenuity in adopting revered Old World styling to New World materials, resulting in furniture having a timeless appeal in uniqueness that is purely American, with simplicity of line being its most characteristic feature.

As our population increases and collectors become more knowledgeable, no other field has attracted more attention than furniture from all periods. This chapter includes a variety of case pieces... that is furniture that encloses a space such as cabinets, chests of drawers, cupboards, desks, sideboards and the linen press. In addition, a variety of many other furnishings are included. Each illustrated entry describes the object, its condition and provides historical background information when available. Surprisingly, even restoration and repairs have become more acceptable these days. However, when the original finish or decoration has been removed from a period – or just an elderly – piece of furniture, it reduces the value substantially.

Because of the quality of much mass-produced furniture today, combined with the demand for and unavailability of quality, there has become an increased demand for custom-made furniture from all periods by well recognized cabinetmakers. Many of these pieces will become the sought-after antiques of tomorrow.

A-NH Mar. 2004 **Northeast Auctions**
722 **N. Eng. Federal Tester Bed,** maple, probably CT, includes side & foot rails, ht. 86, lg. 78, wd. 54in. **$4,000**

A-MA June 2004 **Skinner, Inc.**
86 **Federal Canopy Bed & Chamber Stand,** cherry, attributed to Abner Toppan, Newburyport, MA, ca. 1810, w/old red stained surface, ht. 83, wd. 49, lg. 72in.; the chamber stand w/square pierced top on beaded square legs w/ beaded drawer has been refinished, ht. 31, top 12 x 12in. **$9,400**

A-MA June 2004 **Skinner, Inc.**
17 **Federal Canopy Bed,** maple w/red stain, N. Eng., ca. 1815, old surface w/minor imper., ht. 80, wd. 51, lg. 70in. **$4,994**

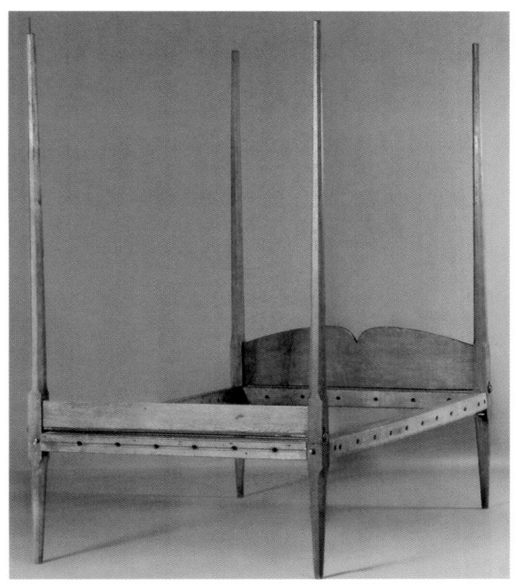

A-NH Mar. 2004 Northeast Auctions
809 Sheraton Large Tester Bed, mid-Atlantic, birch w/heart shaped headboard & narrow rectangular footboard, ht. 79, lg. 73, wd. 46in. **$800**

A-SC Dec. 2003 Charlton Hall Galleries, Inc.
305 Tester Bed, pine & maple, ca. 1850 w/turned posts & pegs for a rope platform. Old repairs, wear consistent w/age, ht. 82, wd. 49, lg. 78in. **$800**

A-MA June 2004 Skinner, Inc.
308 Federal Tall Post Bed, carved mah., probably Salem, MA, ca. 1810-15, w/vase & ring turned swelled & reeded foot posts, & maple square tapering head posts, old ref. & imper., ht. 80, wd. 49, lg. 71in. **$4,113**

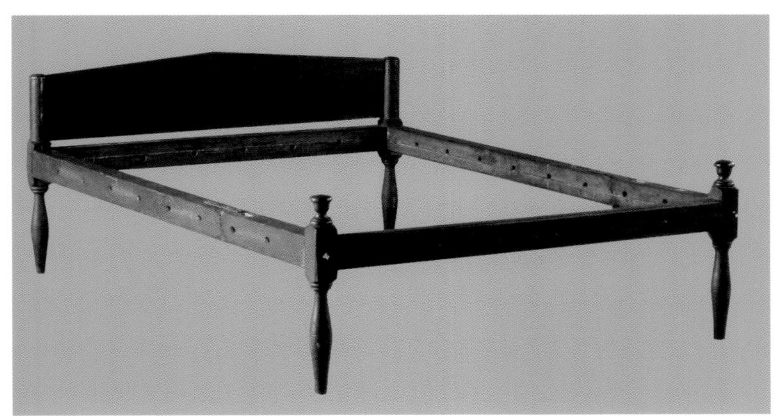

A-NH Mar. 2004 Northeast Auctions
820 Sheraton Low-Post Bed, oak & poplar in green paint & swelled footposts w/mushroom finials, ht. 29, wd. 55., lg. 79½in. **$1,600**

A-PA Apr. 2004
Conestoga Auction Co., Inc.
1174 Rope Bed w/turned posts, headboard w/molding arched gable w/orange paint dec. including brushwork highlights, ht. 54½, wd. 53½, lg. 79in. **$550**

A-PA Apr. 2004
Conestoga Auction Co, Inc.
1105 Canopy Rope Bed, Sheraton, Berks Co., PA w/orig. red paint & elaborately carved headboard w/central basket of fruit & flanked by rosettes & acanthus leaves, ht. 92, wd. 54½, lg. 79in. **$7,150**

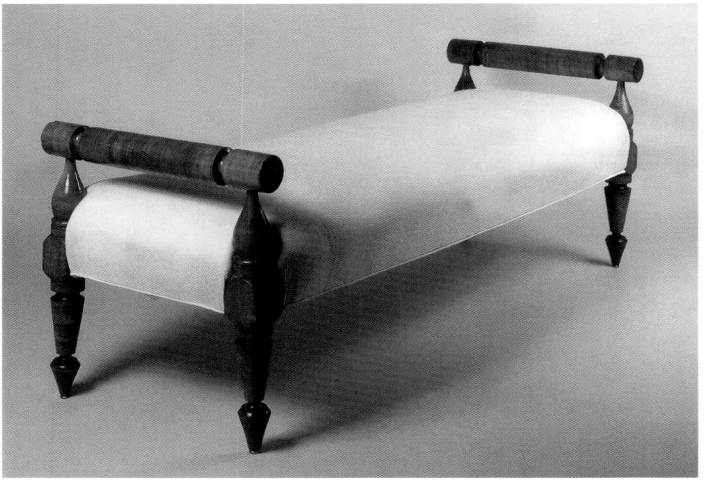

A-Aug. 2004 Northeast Auctions
581 **Sheraton Figured Maple Day Bed,** Lancaster Co., PA w/cylindrical rails at each end & turned legs ending in tulip feet, ht. 26, lg. 72in. **$4,000**

A-PA Oct. 2004 Pook & Pook, Inc.
696 **William & Mary Maple Daybed,** ca. 1730, PA w/rush seat & boldly turned legs & stretchers, ht. 36, lg. 72in. **$16,100**

A-PA Oct. 2004 Pook & Pook, Inc.
799 **N. Eng. William & Mary Maple Daybed,** ca. 1720 w/carved arch, turned & blocked legs joined by stretchers, lg. 72in. **$2,070**

A-PA Jan. 2004 Conestoga Auction Co., Inc.
543 **Plank Seat Half Spindle-back Settee,** PA w/maker's label under seat, Brown's Chair Mfg., Reading, Pa. Dec. w/bold orig. green ground paint w/black & yellow lined highlights in addition to three gilt stenciled urns of fruit on crest rail, seat ht. 17½, 36 overall, lg. 75in. **$9,900**

A-NH Nov. 2003 Northeast Auctions
1655 **Bow-back Windsor Settee,** Phil. PA w/bamboo turnings, painted black w/gold highlights, ht. 38½, lg. 79in. **$26,000**

A-PA Jan. 2004 Conestoga Auction Co., Inc.
520 Half Spindle-back Settee w/black & red striped paint decoration including gilt floral & foliate designs w/ an incredible orig. surface, seat ht. 18, 35½ overall, lg. 82in. $23,100

A-PA May 2004 Pook & Pook, Inc.
380 Pine Settle Bench/Bed, ca. 1800 w/carved lollipop arm rests & orig. overall yellow & ochre grain dec., ht. 48, lg. 73in. $1,955

A-ME Apr. 2004 James D. Julia, Inc.
636 Windsor Settee w/dark green re-paint, plank seat & 26 spindle-back w/plain crest & bamboo style turned back legs. ht. 35½, lg. 61½in. $2,645

A-NH Nov. 2003 Northeast Auctions
1422 N. Eng. Spindle-Form Cradle, rosewood w/painted dec., lg. 39in. $600
1423 Double Comb-back Mammy Rocking Bench w/landscape dec., lg. 48in. $1,200

A-PA Dec. 2003 Pook & Pook, Inc.
240 **Decorated Dower Chest,** ca. 1820, possibly York Co. PA, w/date 1820 in bold script, feet rest., ht. 28½, wd. 41in. **$3,450**

A-MA June 2004 Skinner Inc.
103 **Cherry Blanket Chest,** attributed to Jeremiah Stahl (1830-1907), Soap Hallow, Sommerset Co., PA, 1868, dec. w/stenciled fruit, floral designs & initials S.H. w/date. Base dec. w/gold stenciled eagles & foliage, ht. 23½, wd. 48in. **$9,400**

A-PA Dec. 2003 Pook & Pook, Inc.
300 **Lancaster Co. PA Dower Chest** dated 1787 by Johannes Ranck (1763-1828) w/cutout bracket feet & retaining inscriptions on the flower pots, ht. 22¼, wd. 50in. **$19,550**

A-PA Nov. 2003 Conestoga Auction Co., Inc.
573 **Step-back Dower Chest** w/diamond dec. border w/triple tombstone & putty dec. above three split lip molded drawers. Pine & poplar w/dov. const., int. till & wrought iron jaw lock & strap hinges, ht.28½, wd. 53¾in. **$21,100**

A-PA May 2004 Pook & Pook, Inc.
252 **Dower Chest,** ca. 1800 & inscribed painted by D.Y. Ellinger 1938, ht. 26½, wd 46½in. **$3,450**

A-PA May 2004 Pook & Pook, Inc.
249 **Schwenkfelder Dower Chest** w/overall vibrant feather grained dec., & inscribed Jacob Hubner 1815, ht, 27½, wd. 49in. **$43,700**

A-MA June 2004 Skinner, Inc.
44 **Chest-Over-Drawers,** N. Eng., 18th C., w/two graduated false drawers & two working drawers, turned wooden pulls & orig. red painted surface, ht. 45½, wd. 37¾in. **$8,813**

A-PA Apr. 2004 Conestoga Auction Co., Inc.
1172 **N. Eng. Pine Blanket Chest** w/painted dec., pegged & nailed const., & wire hinges, ht. 29⅞, wd. 39¼in. **$2,950**

A-NH Nov. 2003 Northeast Auctions
1563 **Pilgrim Carved Oak Blanket Chest** w/ebonized details, probably Boston. The upper section w/divided raised panels flanked by split panels over two drawers w/recessed panels, ht. 41½, top 41½ x 24in. **$13,000**
1564 **N. Eng. Blanket Chest,** joined oak w/ebonized details & int. till, ht. 32, top 50 x 22¼in. **$3,000**

A-PA Mar. 2004 Pook & Pook, Inc.
491 **Pine & Poplar Blanket Chest,** PA, ca. 1820 w/lift lid, three short drawers w/orig. glass pulls & retains the orig. red painted surface, ht. 31¼, wd 49¾in. **$4,600**

A-NH Mar. 2004 Northeast Auctions
910 **English Q.A. Blanket Chest,** oak w/two drawers, raised arched panels & sides w/single square raised panel, molded skirt & bracket feet, ht. 36, lg. 60in. **$3,100**

A-NC Sep. 2004 Brunk Auction Services, Inc.
0086 **Walnut Blanket Chest,** dov. const. w/applied thumb molding, lidded till w/secret drawer behind, orig. iron lock, hasp & strap hinges, shaped skirt & extensive double line inlay, probably Kentucky. Old ref. & minor repairs, ht. 26, wd. 46½in. **$11,000**

A-PA Oct. 2004 Pook & Pook, Inc.
596 **Blanket Chest,** PA, early 19th C. w/orig. ochre grain dec. surface, ht. 25, wd. 36in. **$2,990**

A-PA Oct. 2004 Pook & Pook, Inc.
631 **Dower Chest,** ca. 1800, Berks Co. PA, boldly dec. w/floral motifs, all on red ground, ht. 26¾, wd. 50in. **$36,800**

A-NH Mar. 2004 Northeast Auctions
929 Carved Walnut Dining Chairs, English Chippendale, set of four w/slip seats, cabriole legs, leaf carved knees & ball & claw feet. $8,000

A-PA Dec. 2003 Pook & Pook, Inc.
198 Chippendale Dining Chairs, walnut, pair, Philadelphia, ca. 1770 w/shell carved crest w/incised scrolling ears, slip seat resting on shell carved frame w/carved knees, ball & claw feet. $41,000

A-PA Dec. 2003 Pook & Pook, Inc.
471 Q.A. Dining Chairs, set of six, late 19th C., in the Boston tradition w/oxbow crest, solid vasiform splat, compass seat & cabriole front legs w/pad feet. $6,900

A-PA May 2004 Pook & Pook, Inc.
826 Q.A. Corner Chair, walnut, Delaware Valley, ca. 1740. $4,500

A-NH Mar. 2004 Northeast Auctions
685 Q.A. Carved Armchair, Philadelphia, w/shaped arched crest w/carved volutes & central carved shell, balloon seat fitted to a rounded seat & carved cabriole legs, ball & claw feet. $8,500

A-PA Dec. 2003 Pook & Pook, Inc.
105 **Mah. Dining Chairs,** set of six George III w/cupid's bow crest, pierced splat & slip seats, ca. 1790. **$6,900**

A-MA Nov. 2003 Skinner, Inc.
45 **Walnut Side Chair,** Q.A., ca. 1740-60, MA, w/slip seat, ring-turned swelled stretchers, ref. & minor rest. **$4,406**
46 **Q.A. Side Chair,** walnut, PA, ca. 1740-60 w/scratchbeaded crest, slip seat, shaped stretchers & chamfered rear legs, ref. **$5,288**
47 **Walnut Side Chair,** Q.A., MA, ca. 1740-60 w/over-upholstered compass seat, swelled stretchers, ref. & imper. **$2,350**

A-NH Mar. 2004 Northeast Auctions
783 **Library Armchairs,** pair, Chippendale, mah., on square fluted legs joined by pierced carved rectangular stretchers, ht. 39in. **$14,000**

A-NH Nov. 2003 Northeast Auctions
817 **Spindle-back Side Chairs** w/sausage turned legs, set of six, Fairfield, CT, black painted surface & splint seat. **$2,600**

A-NH Nov. 2003 Northeast Auctions
1498 **Hitchcock Decorated Chairs,** set of ten, limited edition Christmas chairs dated 1980-1989. **$4,250**

A-NH Aug. 2004 Northeast Auctions
1349 **Chippendale Wing Chair,** Boston, carved mah., w/conical rolled arms & loose seat. **$10,000**

A-NH Mar. 2004 Northeast Auctions
726 **N. Eng. Lolling Chair,** mah., w/square tapered reeded legs joined by box stretcher. **$7,500**

A-MA Feb. 2004 Skinner, Inc.
490 **Fan-back Windsor Side Chairs,** two similar, N. Eng., ca. 1790, black paint w/gilt highlights & saddle seats. **$940**
491 **Sack-back Windsor Chair,** CT or RI, 18th C., w/knuckled handholds & shaped seat, imper. incl. cracks. **$940**
492 **Fan-back Windsor Side Chair,** N. Eng., ca. 1780-90 w/seven spindles, serpentine crest rail, saddle seat & painted white over earlier black & red. **$1,116**
493 **Bow-back Windsor Armchair,** ash, pine & maple, N. Eng., ca. 1780. **$1,293**

A-MA Nov. 2003 Skinner, Inc.
292 **Windsor Comb-back Armchair,** N. Eng., late 18th C. w/shaped saddle seat, ref., ht. 37in. **$1,763**
293 **Windsor Writing Armchair,** N. Eng., late 18th C.w/a shaped backrest, carved knuckle handhold & writing surface, old ref. & imper. **$3,525**
294 **Brace-back Windsor Side Chair,** RI, late 18th C. w/shaped seat, old ref., imper. **$264**

A-NH Aug. 2004 Northeast Auctions
770 **Bootjack Dining Chairs,** set of six, PA, brown painted & floral dec. w/a matching oversized armchair. Each w/red flowers, mustard & black outlines, ht. of rocker 39¾in. **$1,400**

A-ME Jan. 2004
James D. Julia, Inc.
1148 **Steer Horn Armchair & Foot Stool,** late 19th C., upholstered in repl. black leather w/brass upholstery tacks, ht. of chair 40in. **$3,450**

A-MA June 2004 Skinner, Inc.
332 **Classical Carved & Turned Side Chairs,** set of six, N. Eng., ca. 1825, w/rush seats, ref. & imper. , ht. 34½in. **$1,763**

A-PA Dec. 2003 Pook & Pook, Inc.
270 **Bow-back Windsor Chairs,** set of six, w/bamboo turned legs & retaining red wash surfaces, ca. 1820. **$10,350**

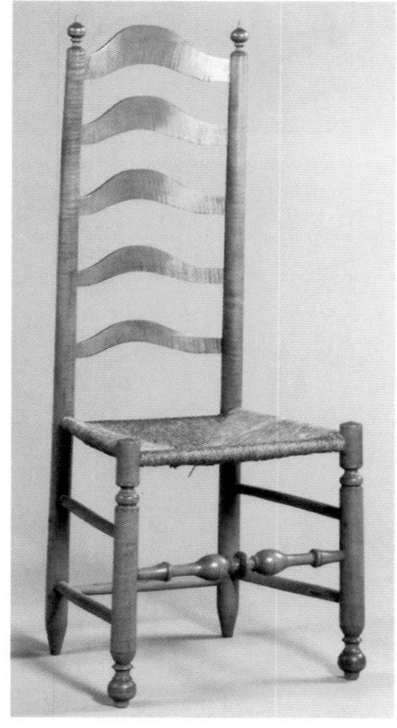

A-NH Nov. 2003
Northeast Auctions
1634 **Tiger Maple Ladder-back Side Chair,** PA or NJ w/trapezoidal rush seat, cylindrical turned legs & ball feet. **$2,250**

A-NH Aug. 2004
Northeast Auctions
688 **Five-Slat Maple & Ash Armchair** in red finish, Delaware Valley, w/five graduated arched slats, disk & spire feet & rush seat, ht. 47in. **$9,000**
689 **Delaware Valley Five-Slat Armchair** in brown finish, the frontal stretcher w/ball & ring turning, ht. 45½in. **$4,500**

A-MA June 2004 Skinner, Inc.
490 **Highchair,** turned maple & birch, N. Eng., late 18th C., w/old finish, ht. 40in. **$1,058**
491 **Child's Armchair,** ash, late 17th C., w/old finish & imper., ht. 21½in. **$2,820**
492 **Child's Potty Chair,** oak, Am. or Eng., 18th C. w/old surface, ht. 24½in. **$235**
493 **Child's Shaker Production Rocking Armchair,** Mt. Lebanon, NY, w/an incised 0 & decal, old varnished surface , repl. tape seat & imper., ht. 24in. **$3,290**
494 **Children's Chair,** N. Eng., 18th C. Chippendale, cherry & birch w/a shaped crest & arms, old ref. & imper., ht. 20½in; together w/ a Chippendale black painted ladder-back side chair, ht. 23¾in. **$646**

A-MA Feb. 2994 Skinner, Inc.
547 **Shaker Production No. 3 Armless Rocking Chair,** Mount Lebanon, NY, late 19th/early 20th C., w/old varnished surface & trademark decal. **$176**
548 **Shaker Cherry Armed Rocking Chair,** mid-19th C, old ref. & imper. **$118**
549 **Shaker Production No. 3 Rocking Chair,** Mt. Lebanon NY, late 19th/early 20th C. **$176**
550 **Child's Armed Rocking Chair,** Shaker Production No. 0, Mount Lebanon, NY, late 19th C. w/old dark stain. **$1,645**
551 **Shaker Production No. l Child's Armed Rocking Chair,** Mount Lebanon w/red wash & trademark decal. **$558**
552 **Low-back Dining Chair,** Shaker Production No. 2, Mount Lebanon, w/dark stain & decal. **$558**
553 **Child's Armless Rocking Chair,** Shaker Production No. 0, Mount Lebanon, w/dark brown stain & trademark decal. **$646**

A-MA Feb. 2004 Skinner, Inc.
208 **Braced Bow-back Windsor Side Chairs,** N. Eng., an assembled set, ca. 1780 w/old brown paint over earlier gray-green paint, imper. **$2,115**

A-NH Nov. 2003 Northeast Auctions
499 **Side Chairs,** pair of George III, carved mah., w/slip-seats. **$3,800**
500 **George II Footstool,** walnut w/losses to finish, ht. 17in. **$2,600**
501 **George II Side Chairs** w/losses & one seat missing. **$15,500**

52

A-NY Dec. 2003 Fontaines Auction Gallery
52 **Wicker Wing-back Armchair,** Bar Harbor style, ca. 1890 w/orig. finish, ht. 45in. **$300**

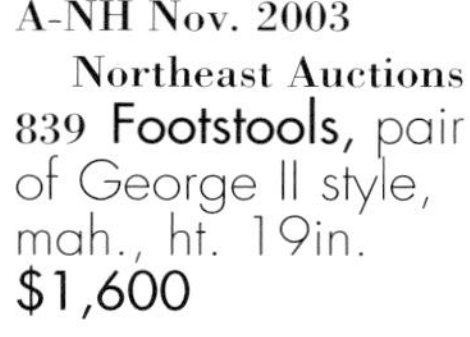

A-NH Nov. 2003 Northeast Auctions
839 **Footstools,** pair of George II style, mah., ht. 19in. **$1,600**

A-MA June 2004 Skinner, Inc.
9 **Fan-back Windsor Side Chair,** N. Eng. w/old black/brown paint over green & red paints, ht. 36in. **$7,638**

A-OH Oct. 2004 Garth's Arts & Antiques
78 **Windsor Bow-back Highchair,** attributed to Delaware Valley w/traces of red over blue paint w/black highlights in the bamboo turnings, seat ht. 22, overall ht. 37½in. **$9,487**

A-OH July 2004 Garth's Arts & Antiques
199 **Sack-back Windsor Armchair** w/old reddish brown surface w/rest. splits on bow & seat, ht. 38½in. **$1,495**

53

A-NY Dec. 2003 Fontaines Auction Gallery
53 **Wicker Glider Rocker** in orig. finish, ca. 1885. **$400**

A-NH Nov. 2003 Northeast Auctions
1533 **Chippendale Chest on Chest,** MA, mah., w/swan's neck, blocked bracket feet & shaped returns, ht. 80, wd. 30in. **$10,000**

A-MA Nov. 2003 Skinner, Inc.
77 **Q.A. High Chest of Drawers,** probably Salem, MA, ca. 1740-60, maple w/orig. brasses, cabriole legs w/arris knees & pad feet on platforms, ref., ht. 71, wd. 35¾in. **$22,325**

A-MA June 2004 Skinner, Inc.
94 **Q.A. Walnut High Chest** w/inlay, MA, 1725-50 w/cabriole legs ending in pad feet, old ref. & rest., ht. 84 incl. finial, wd. 36in. **$44,063**

A-MA Feb. 2004 Skinner, Inc.
69 **Q.A. High Chest,** maple, probably Hampden, MA area, 1760-80 w/carved pinwheels flanking the central plinth, flame-carved finial, and two carved fans, repl. brasses, ref. & imper., ht. 84, wd.37½in. **$29,375**

A-PA Dec. 2003 Pook & Pook, Inc.
355 **Mah. High Chest,** Philadelphia, mah., ca. 1770, w/a broken arch bonnet w/carved rosettes flanked by flame finials & knees terminating in bold ball & claw feet, ht. 96½, wd. 42½in. **$46,000**

A-OH Jan. 2004
Garth's Arts & Antiques
99 Q.A. High Chest of Drawers, walnut & walnut flame veneer, ref., two parts, old repl. brasses & rest. to case, ht. 84, wd. 42in. $17,250

A-OH Nov. 2003 Garth's Arts & Antiques
91 English Chest on Chest w/inlay, Hepplewhite, ref. mah. & mah. veneer w/pine & oak secondary wood, rest. to trim, glued splits to feet, ht. 75¾, wd. 42in. $4,140

A-PA Mar. 2004 Pook & Pook, Inc.
376 Q.A. Tiger Maple Highboy, Delaware Valley, ca. 1760 w/squared cabriole legs, Spanish feet & orig. batwing brasses. With family provenance, & bears an 18th C. paper label identifying the orig. owner. ht. 73½, wd. 38in. $142,500

A-MA June 2004
Skinner, Inc.
49 Chippendale Carved Tiger Maple Chest on Chest, Rhode Island, 1750-96, w/flame carved side finials, graduated drawers, molded base w/ogee feet, some orig. brass, imper. & feet repairs, ht. 87, wd. 38½in. $23,500

A-PA Dec. 2003
Pook & Pook, Inc.
100 Chippendale Walnut High Chest, PA, ca. 1780, w/matchstick cornice, carved frieze over case & resting on ogee bracket feet, ht. 72, wd. 42¾in. $8,050

A-OH Jan. 2004 Garth's Arts & Antiques
165 **Sheraton Six-Drawer Chest** w/inlay, ref. cherry w/walnut secondary wood. The dov. drawers have repl. eagle brasses & minor rest., ht. 42, wd. 42¾in. **$1,265**

A-OH Jan. 2004 Garth's Arts & Antiques
49 **Chippendale Transitional High Chest,** Chippendale to Hepplewhite, in cherry w/old ref., orig. brasses, reeded quarter columns & cove molded cornice, ht. 63¾, wd 42½in. **$5,200**

A-OH Nov. 2003 Historic Americana Auctions
954 **New York Chippendale Tiger Maple Tall Chest,** ca. 1770-90 w/int. red wash throughout, repl. brasses & old ref., ht. 53, wd. 40in. **$7,475**

A-NH Nov. 2003 Northeast Auctions
834 **George III Mah. Chest on Chest** w/cockbeaded graduated drawers & ogee bracket feet, ht. 68, wd. 41in. **$5,500**

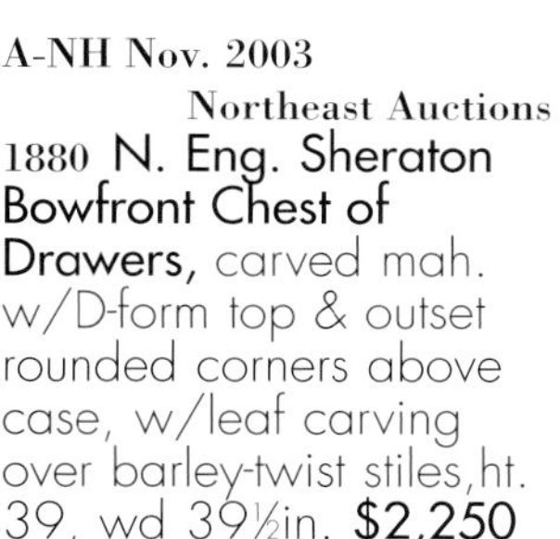

A-NH Nov. 2003 Northeast Auctions
1880 **N. Eng. Sheraton Bowfront Chest of Drawers,** carved mah. w/D-form top & outset rounded corners above case, w/leaf carving over barley-twist stiles,ht. 39, wd 39½in. **$2,250**

A-NH Mar. 2004 Northeast Auctions
720 **N. Eng. Chippendale Oxbow Chest of Drawers,** mah., w/serpentine front, stepmolded skirt & cabriole legs w/scalloped returns terminating in ball & claw feet, ht. 34½, wd. 43in. **$22,000**

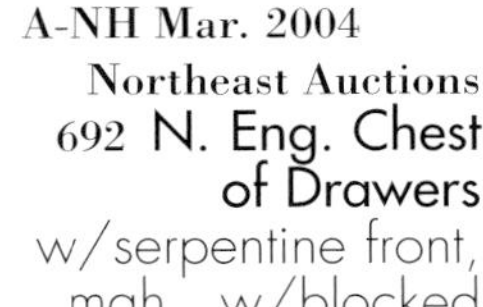

A-NH Mar. 2004
Northeast Auctions
692 **N. Eng. Chest of Drawers** w/serpentine front, mah., w/blocked ends, on angular ogee feet, ht. 31, wd. 33½in. **$85,000**

A-PA Apr. 2004
Conestoga Auction Co., Inc.
383 **Wm. & Mary Chest over Drawers,** cherry w/molded lift-lid, cotter-pin hinges, two upper false drawer fronts & two full lower drawers & repl. pulls, ht. 44½, wd. 42½in. **$2,750**

A-PA May 2004
Pook & Pook, Inc.
827 **Chest of Drawers,** Philadelphia Chippendale, ca. 1770 w/fluted quarter columns, bracket feet & original brasses, ht. 33½, wd. 37¾in. **$11,500**

A-SC Dec. 2003
Charlton Hall Galleries, Inc.
266 **Chest of Drawers,** Georgian Style, inlaid mah., ca. 1850, w/stringing on graduating drawers & bracket feet, ht. 41⅞, wd. 43⅛in. **$1,300**

A-PA Nov. 2003 Conestoga Auction Co., Inc.
572 **Soap Hollow Chest of Drawers** w/original red & black paint, gilt highlights, foliate & floral motifs & scrolled backboard sgn. M.B. & dated 1870, ht. 53, wd. 39in. **$28,600**

A-MA June 2004 Skinner, Inc.
28 **Federal Cherry Chest of Drawers,** MA, early 19th C., w/rectangular top & crossbanded edge overhangs case, repl. brass & ref., ht. 35½, wd. 40¼in. **$2,703**

29 **Federal Chest of Drawers,** cherry, N. Eng., w/string-inlay, quarter fans & central paterae above a shaped skirt & glaring French feet, repl. brass, old ref.& reprs. ht. 36¾, wd 42¾in. **$3,055**

A-NH Nov. 2003 Northeast Auctions
1467 N. Eng. Chest of Drawers, yellow painted & decorated w/spoon turned columns, ht. 43½in., wd. 40in. $2,400

A-OH Jan. 2004 Garth's Arts & Antiques
401 Sheraton Chest, KY, cherry w/old finish, ring turned legs, dov. drawers & orig. brass, ht. 41½, wd. 42in. $3,105

A-MA June 2004 Skinner, Inc.
405 Chippendale Maple Chest of Drawers, N. Eng., late 18th C., w/orig. brasses, ref. & minor rest., ht. 42, wd. 36in. $4,113
406 N. Eng. Chest of Drawers, Chippendale, maple w/orig. brass, ref. & imper., ht. 47, wd. 35in. $3,055
407 Chippendale Cherry Chest of Drawers, N. Eng., late 18th C., w/graduated thumb-molded drawers on base w/ogee feet, repl. brass & rest. ht. 34¾, wd. 36¾in. $2,350

A-MA Nov. 2003 Fontaine's Auction Gallery
63 Chippendale Centennial Chest on Chest w/block front & full bonnet top, flame finials, ball & claw feet, ca. 1870, ht. 85, wd 39¼in. $8,500

A-PA Jan. 2004 Conestoga Auction Co., Inc.
519 **Chippendale Chest,** walnut, PA w/fluted quarter columns, molded top & base, & ogee bracket feet, ht. 39, wd. 37¾in. **$4,950**

A-NH Mar. 2004 Northeast Auctions
799 **Chippendale Chest,** walnut, PA w/fluted quarter columns, graduated drawers, ogee bracket feet w/scalloped returns, ht. 34, wd. 38in. **$6,800**

A-NC Jan. 2004 Brunk Auction Services, Inc.
0337 **Dressing Table,** walnut, PA, w/cusped corners, dov. drawers, 3rd qtr. 18th C., old ref. & later brass pulls, ht. 36in. **$14,000**

A-NH Mar. 2004 Northeast Auctions
696 **Q.A. Cherry Dressing Table** w/arcaded skirt & drops on cabriole legs, ht. 32½in. **$9,500**

A-MA Nov. 2003 Skinner, Inc.
52 **Q.A. Walnut Dressing Table,** ca. 1740-60, N. Eng. w/cockbeaded case, fan carved concave short drawer, old finish & some old brasses, imper., ht. 29in. **$22,325**

A-MA Feb. 2004 Skinner, Inc.
66 **Tiger Maple Dressing Table,** Delaware River Valley, ca. 1770 w/orig. brasses & lock, ref. & imper., ht. 29¾in. **$15,275**

A-MA Nov. 2003 Skinner, Inc.
116 **Federal Dressing Bureau,** Boston, ca. 1820, mah. & tiger w/bird's eye maple veneer, cockbeaded drawers, reeded posts & legs, repl. pulls, old finish & minor imper. Attributed to John & Thomas Seymour, ht. 72, wd. 36in. **$38,188**

A-PA Dec. 2003 Pook & Pook, Inc.
94 **French Walnut Panetière,** late 18th C. w/carved crest & base, ht. 31, wd. 31in. **$4,370**
95 **French Walnut Dough Box on Stand,** late 18th C., ht. 39, wd. 49in. **$1,840**

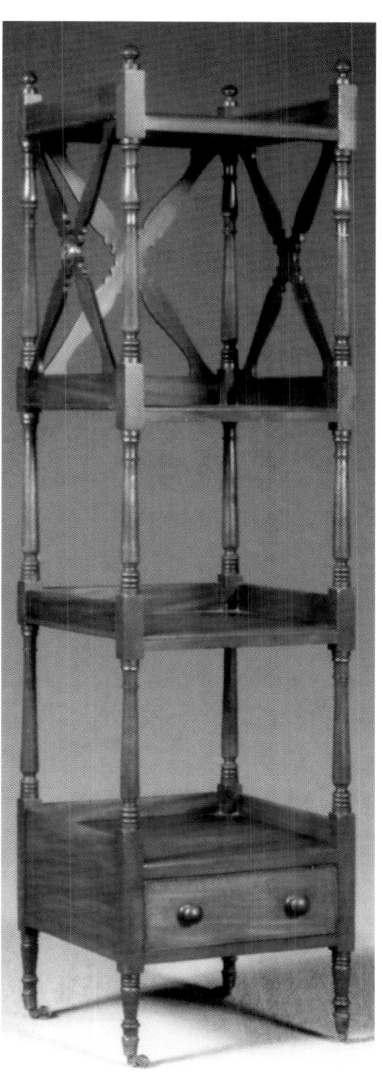

A-NC Jan. 2004
Brunk Auction Services, Inc.
0101 **English Etagère,** mah. w/turned supports, dov. drawer, orig. brass casters, old ref., surface scratches & early 19th C., ht. 62½in. **$2,500**

A-NC Jan. 2004
Brunk Auction Services, Inc.
0141 **Cherry Sugar Chest** w/dov. case, lift top, breadboard ends, orig. lock & wooden pulls. Int. w/three compartments, minor imper., ht. 40in. **$8,000**

A-NC Jan. 2004 Brunk Auction Services, Inc.
0631A **Sugar Chest,** cherry w/breadboard lift top, dov. drawer, frame & panel const., old finish & probably KY, ht. 36½in. **$2,500**

A-NC Jan. 2004 Brunk Auction Services, Inc.
0316 **Cherry Cellaret on Stand,** dov. const., w/double string & bellflower inlay, old ref. & repl. brass. **$14,000**

A-PA June 2004
Conestoga Auction Co., Inc.
1103 **Corner Cupboard,** PA, two-part w/orig. painted dec. White coat of paint removed in 1961, to the orig. painted surface, ht. 95, wd. 46in. **$71,500**

A-MA June 2004 Skinner, Inc.
16 **N. Eng. Federal Cupboard,** 2nd qtr. 19th C., two-part w/orig. red surface & pulls w/minor repairs, ht. 85, wd. 57½in. **$6,463**

A-OH Jan. 2004 Garth's Arts & Antiques
70 **Corner Cupboard,** one-piece, walnut & poplar w/dov. drawer, sq. nail const., ref. & old repl., ht. 82, wd. 48in. **$2,185**

A-PA June 2004 Conestoga Auction Co. Inc.
1101 **Mahantonga Valley,** PA, two part Dutch Cupboard w/orig. red, green & black paint, dov. drawers, one of three known cupboards by this maker, ht. 82½, wd. 67, dp.20in. **$264,000**

A-PA Dec. 2003 Pook & Pook, Inc.
540 **Cherry & Poplar Dutch Cupboard,** PA, dated 1851 & dec. w/stenciled stylized roosters centering the date & trailing star decoration over the pie shelf. The stencil dec. is typical of the Soap Hollow School. Retains its original red wash surface, ht. 81, wd. 50in. **$16,000**

A-MA Aug. 2004 Skinner, Inc.
51 **Pine Pewter Dresser,** N. Eng., 18th C. w/old ref., reprs. & imper., ht. 76, wd. 55in. **$1,058**

A-NC Sep. 2004 Brunk Auction Services, Inc.
023A **Walnut Jelly Cupboard,** drawer fronts w/crotch figure & curly walnut, mid-19th C., old ref. w/stains, chips & surface abrasions, ht. 54, wd. 47in. **$1,800**

A-PA Jan. 2004 Conestoga Auction Co., Inc.
516 **Chippendale Dutch Cupboard,** walnut, PA, two-part w/fluted quarter columns & ogee bracket feet, ht. 88, wd. 58in. **$6,050**

517 **Corner Cupboard,** PA, walnut, two-part w/dov. doors & bracket base, ht. 87, wd. 45in. **$9,900**

518 **Blind Door Cupboard,** walnut single part w/molded bracket base, ht. 80, wd. 41in. **$3,575**

A-MA Nov. 2003 Skinner, Inc.
208 Federal Pine Corner Cupboard, PA, early 19th C. w/beaded carved arch, shaped glazed door, all flanked by reeded & molded pilasters on turned feet, old finish, ht. 89, wd.47in. $6,463

A-NH Mar. 2004 Northeast Auctions
525 Chippendale Walnut Corner Cupboard w/swan's neck crest above geometric glazed doors, on molded base w/bracket feet, ht. 85, wd. 37in. $3,000

A-PA Dec. 2003 Pook & Pook, Inc.
305 Corner Cupboard, PA, two-piece, painted poplar, ca. 1820 w/molded stepped cornice over a carved match-stick frieze & retains overall painted surface, ht. 88, wd. 45in. $8,050

A-PA Jan. 2004 Conestoga Auction Co., Inc.
536 Blind Door Dutch Cupboard, PA, w/pie shelf, paneled doors & dov. drawers, molded base & ogee bracket feet, ht. 87, wd. 54in. $2,200

A-PA Jan. 2004 Conestoga Auction Co., Inc.
521 Bucket Bench, PA, softwood w/peaked splash-back, dov. drawers, cut-out supports above paneled doors & cut-out feet, ht. 56½, wd. 42in. $2,200

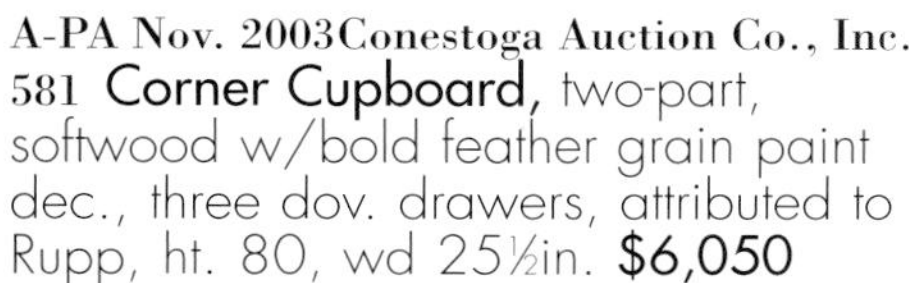

A-PA Nov. 2003 Conestoga Auction Co., Inc.
581 **Corner Cupboard,** two-part, softwood w/bold feather grain paint dec., three dov. drawers, attributed to Rupp, ht. 80, wd 25½in. **$6,050**

582 **PA Federal Dutch Cupboard,** walnut w/a red finish, pie shelf surface, turned column styles & ring turned feet, ht. 89, wd. 53in. **$6,050**

583 **PA Federal Tiger Maple Corner Cupboard** w/blind doors,two-part w/cove molded cornice, arch paneled doors, shaped int. shelves & scalloped skirt, ht. 96, wd. 53, dp. 27in. **$13,200**

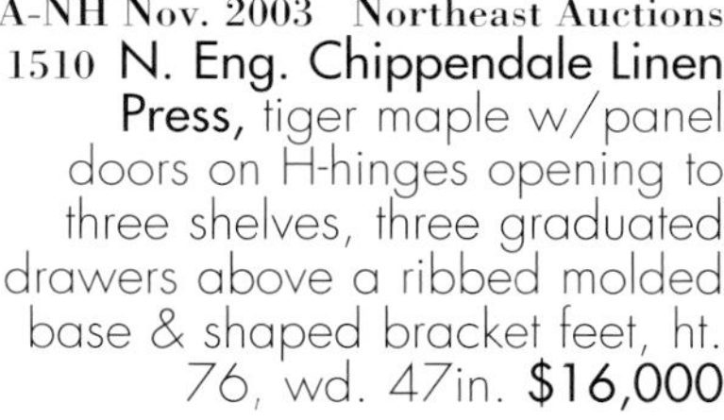

A-NH Nov. 2003 Northeast Auctions
1510 **N. Eng. Chippendale Linen Press,** tiger maple w/panel doors on H-hinges opening to three shelves, three graduated drawers above a ribbed molded base & shaped bracket feet, ht. 76, wd. 47in. **$16,000**

A-NC Jan. 2004
Brunk's Auction Services, Inc.
0356 **Pie Safe,** walnut & cherry, Wythe Co. VA, attrib. to the Rich family shop 1830-1880, w/cut-nail const., w/punched tin panels, each w/grapes, urns & star corners, old ref. & traces of old blue paint, ht. 51, wd. 50in. **$6,000**

A-PA May 2004 Pook & Pook, Inc.
840 **PA Pie Safe,** poplar w/punched tin eagle panels flanked by sides w/similar panels, ht. 53, wd. 39¾in. **$4,140**

A-PA Mar. 2004 Pook & Pook, Inc.
597 **PA Dutch Cupboard,** Lancaster Co., ca. 1770 w/rattail hinges over matchstick molding, ogee bracket feet & retains a later red painted surface w/black, white & blue highlights, ht. 95, wd. 56½in. **$11,500**

A-PA Nov. 2003 Conestoga Auction Co., Inc.
1174 **Walnut Two-Part Dutch Cupboard,** ca. 1770 w/brass H hinges & candle drawer reeded stiles & three split lip-molded drawers, ht. 86, wd. 75in. **$16,500**

A-NH Mar. 2004 Northeast Auctions
464 **Chippendale Walnut Stepback Cupboard,** PA, w/candle drawers & ogee bracket feet, ht. 81, wd. 48in. **$7,000**

A-MA Feb. 2004

Skinner, Inc.

91 **Chippendale Maple Slant-lid Desk,** N. Eng., late 18th C., w/thumb molded drawers, on bracket feet, orig. finish w/imper. & the brass pulls appear to be original, ht. 41¾, wd. 36in. **$3,408**

92 **Maple Slant-lid Desk,** MA, Chippendale, late 18th C., w/thumb molded drawers on bracket feet & orig. brasses. Minor imper., ht. 42½, wd. 38¾in. **$3,819**

A-MA Nov. 2003

Skinner, Inc.

215 **Q.A. Tiger Maple & Maple Slant-lid Desk,** ca. 1740-60 w/cabriole legs ending in pad feet on platforms, repl. brasses, imper. & ref., ht. 43, wd. 35½in. **$6,463**

A-NC Jan. 2004

Brunk Auction Services, Inc.

0402 **Cherry Butler's Desk & Chest,** secondary wood poplar, ca. 1850, glass pulls orig., ht. 46, wd. 42in. **$1,300**

A-MA Nov. 2003

Northeast Auctions

1767 **Oxbow Slant-Lid Desk,** Chippendale, mah., probably North Shore of MA., all drawers w/beaded dividers, on ball & claw feet w/shaped return, ht. 44½, wd. 42, dp. 22½in. **$7,000**

A-PA May 2005
Pook & Pook, Inc.
72 **Chippendale Birch Slant Front Desk,** ca. 1780, CT, w/oxbow case supported by ogee feet, ht. 44½,wd. 41¼in. $2,875

A-MA June 2004 Skinner, Inc.
99 **Chippendale Oxbow Serpentine Slant-lid Desk,** MA, late 18th C., w/graduated drawers on cabriole legs ending in claw & ball feet centering a shell & scroll carved pendant, repl. brasses, ref. & imper., ht. 44in. $5,875

A-MA Mar. 2004
Northeast Auctions
418 **Chippendale Slant-lid Desk,** NH, carved & painted maple, sgn. Samuel Dunlap. The case w/four graduated drawers, grained dec. & painted line borders. The flowered carved ogee base molding & ball & claw feet are typical Dunlap tradition, ht. 45, lg. 38¼in. $175,000

A-NC Jan. 2004 Brunk Auction Services, Inc.
0097 **Plantation Desk,** yellow pine, top w/14 int. compartments & two drawers behind two frame-and-pane1 doors, wooden gallery & slant-front base. The drawers have orig. leather pulls, cut nails throughout, old ref., ht. 64, wd. 37in. $1,000

A-PA May 2004 Pook & Pook, Inc.
373 **George III Hepplewhite Cylinder Roll Desk,** mah., ca. 1790 w/fitted int. w/satinwood inlaid drawers & an adjustible inlaid writing surface flanked by inlaid panels. The tapering legs have banded cuffs, ht. 41¾in., wd. 44¾in. $7,475

A-PA Oct. 2004 Pook & Pook, Inc.
580 **Tiger Maple Secretary Desk,** CT, ca. 1780 w/fall front enclosing a fitted int., on bracket feet, ht. 63, wd. 38in. **$9,200**

A-NH Mar. 2004 Northeast Auctions
506 **Hepplewhite Cherry Secretary,** Springfield, MA, in two parts w/inlay & flaring French feet, ht. 85, wd. 42in. **$4,500**

A-PA May 2004 Pook & Pook, Inc.
823 **New England Secretary,** mahogany, ca. 1810, in two parts w/tambour doors over a fall front writing surface, overall double line & barbel inlay & French feet, ht. 83, wd. 42½in. **$3,220**

A-NH Nov. 2003 Northeast Auctions
1524 **Blockfront Secretary Desk,** New England, Chippendale, mah. w/broken arch pediment, fitted interior, two parts, lower case has blocked serpentine drawers w/pine tree brasses, ht. 94½, wd. 41½in. **$30,000**

A-NH Mar. 2004 Northeast Auctions
671 **Cherry Secretary,** Chippendale, w/molded bonnet top & broken arch pediment, blind doors open to an interior fitted for shelves, two pieces, ht. 98, wd. 39in. **$15,000**

A-PA May 2004 Pook & Pook, Inc.
207 **Baltimore Federal Secretary Desk,** mah., ca. 1795 w/lattice glazed doors w/oval mirror panels & inlays on satinwood reserve & French bracket feet, ht. 99, wd. 45in. **$20,700**

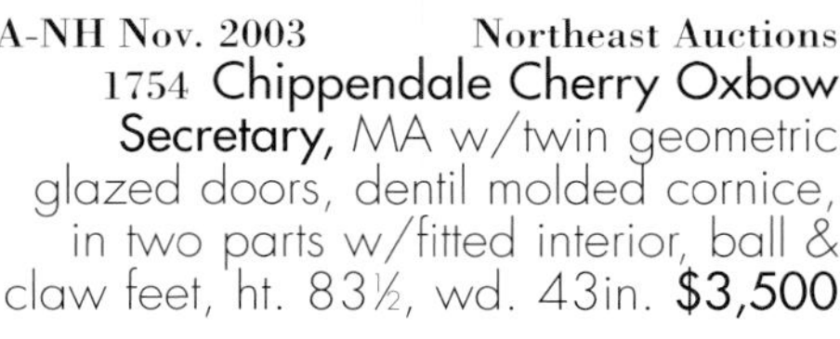

A-NH Nov. 2003 Northeast Auctions
1754 **Chippendale Cherry Oxbow Secretary,** MA w/twin geometric glazed doors, dentil molded cornice, in two parts w/fitted interior, ball & claw feet, ht. 83½, wd. 43in. **$3,500**

A-ME Jan. 2004 James D. Julia, Inc.
75 **George III Breakfront Bookcase,** inlaid mah., w/removable flat top, bookcase section having four glazed doors w/silk lined interior. Lower section w/desk has tooled green leather writing surface w/drawers & cubby holes, ht. 94½, wd. 71in. **$12,075**

A-Mar. 2004 Northeast Auctions
724 **Federal Mahogany & Flame Birch Secretary,** New England, w/hinged writing surface & skirt supported by French feet, ht. 73, wd. 33½in. **$7,500**

A-OH Apr. 2004
Garth's Arts & Antiques
706 **Chippendale Mirror** w/orig. mirror & backboard, mah. & figured mah. veneer w/minor rest., ht. 44½, wd. 22in. **$2,760**

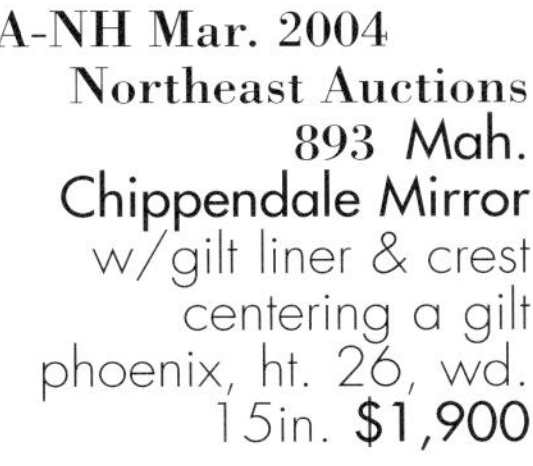

A-NH Mar. 2004
Northeast Auctions
893 **Mah. Chippendale Mirror** w/gilt liner & crest centering a gilt phoenix, ht. 26, wd. 15in. **$1,900**

A-OH Apr. 2004
Garth's Arts & Antiques
108 **Chippendale Scroll Mirror,** mah. w/molded liner, gilded gesso trim, pierced & carved acanthus leaf scroll medallion at top, 20th C., ht. 38, wd. 21in. **$690**

A-NH Mar. 2004
Northeast Auctions
834 **Chippendale Mah. Mirror** w/pierced & scrolled crest w/a central gilt phoenix. The ribbed molded frame has a gilt inner liner, ht. 24½, wd. 14½in. **$1,800**

A-OH Apr. 2004

Garth's Arts & Antiques

133 **Q.A. Scroll Mirror** w/urn carving, mah. veneer w/fine scrolling, molded liner & gilded gesso inner liner. Minor ear rest., ht. 40, wd. 21in. **$690**

A-OH Apr. 2004

Garth's Arts & Antiques

776 **Adams Style Gilt Mirror** w/relief molded gesso, split on crest & a few small chips, rest., ht. 42, wd. 23½in. **$460**

A-NH Mar. 2004

Northeast Auctions

590 **Empire Giltwood & Ebonized Split-Spindle Mirror,** Boston, w/reeded columns, gilt acanthus leaves & corner blocks w/rosettes, ht. 72, wd. 46in. **$11,000**

249 **Federal Two-Part Mirror** w/orig. reverse painting, raised floral corner blocks & mirror wear, repainted, ht. 39¾, wd. 18¾in. **$546**

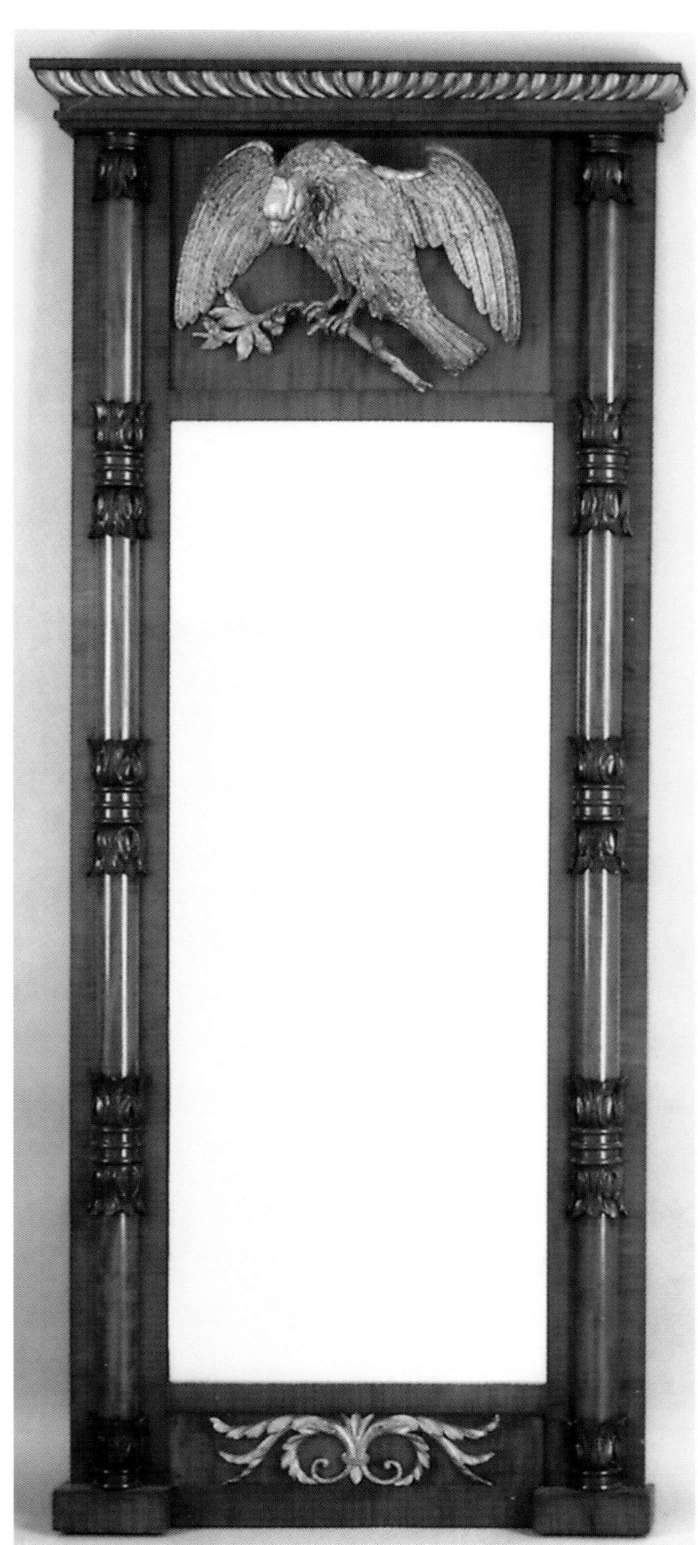

A-PA Dec. 2003 Pook & Pook, Inc.
529 **Federal Mah. & Mah. Veneer Mirror,** ca. 1810, w/a giltwood gadrooned cornice, above a panel w/carved & gilded spread winged eagle. The mirror is flanked by acanthus carved half column, ht. 77½, wd. 31in. **$5,060**

A-NE. Mar. 2004 Northeast Auctions
725 **Gilt Federal Mirror** w/molded flat cornice, pendants & a pale blue panel w/house & trees, flanked by gilt corbels over mirror plate, ht. 53½, wd. 28in., **$2,200**

A-MA Mar. 2004
Northeast Auctions

1043 **Q.A. Walnut Dressing Mirror** w/inlaid burl, resting on bracket feet, ht. 28, wd. 17½in. **$800**

1044 **Q.A. Walnut Dressing Mirror** w/beveled mirror plate within a shaped gilt liner, ht. 26, wd. 17½in. **$700**

A-MA Dec. 2003 Skinner, Inc.

107 **Gilded Wood & Marble Veneer Bilboa Mirror,** probably Spain or Portugal, ca. 1790-1810, w/imper. & rest., ht. 33, wd. 14¾in. **$2,585**

108 **Bilboa Mirror,** gilded wood & marble veneer, probably Spain or Portugal, w/imper., ht. 35, wd. 16in. **$9,988**

109 **Neo-classical Giltwood, Gesso & Wire Looking Glass,** probably N. Eng., early 29th C., w/imper., ht. 22, wd. 9¾in. **$705**

A-MA June 2004 Skinner, Inc.
309 Federal Mah. Inlaid Sideboard, Baltimore, MD, 1790-1810 w/veneered top, ovolo corners, all doors embellished w/ovals outlined in banding & cuff inlays. Old surface, imper., & repl. brass, ht. 39, lg. 75in. $14,000

A-NH Aug. 2004 Northeast Auctions
1606 Federal Inlaid Mah. Sideboard w/double contrasting stringing, the alternating stiles w/elm panels inlaid w/large diamonds & the tapering legs inlaid w/bellflower & loop inlay over cuffs, ht. 39½, lg. 73in. $20,000

A-NH Mar. 2004 Northeast Auctions
512 Hepplewhite Mah. Inlaid Sideboard, MA, rectangular top w/shaped bow front, concave drawers w/string inlay & square tapering legs, ht. 43, lg. 67in. $6,500

A-NH Mar. 2004

Northeast Auctions

781 **English Sideboard,** Hepplewhite, Mah. w/cross-banded rectangular top & serpentine front on square tapered legs terminating in spade feet, ht. 36, lg. 72in. **$8,500**

A-NH Nov. 2003

Northeast Auctions

1860 **Federal Inlaid Sideboard,** MA, mah. w/serpentine front & string inlay, ht. 39¾, lg. 68½in. **$10,000**

A-NH Nov. 2003

Northeast Auctions

1812 **George III Bird's-Eye Maple & Mah. Sideboard** w/shaped outset top & inlayed w/displayed fans, ht. 35¾, lg. 61¾in. **$1,500**

A-ME Apr. 2004 James D. Julia, Inc.
25 **Federal Carved Sideboard** w/10in. fully carved back splash, right door has orig. removable six bottle divided insert, center & left have shelves. Top has some veneer chipping & pieces missing from left side, ht. 54, wd. 53½in. **$4,830**

A-NH Nov. 2003 Northeast Auctions
328 **Hepplewhite Huntboard,** Mid-Atlantic w/line inlay, two short drawers on left & fitted deep drawer on right, ht. 40, lg. 53in. **$9,000**

A-NC Sep. 2004 Brunk Auction Services, Inc.
0065 **Mah. Sideboard,** Wilmington, NC, w/string inlaid edges & panels of alternating light & black vertical elements, dov. drawers, original brasses. Left rear leg partially repl., some buckling & separations to veneer on drawer fronts, old ref., ht. 43, lg. 70in. **$15,000**

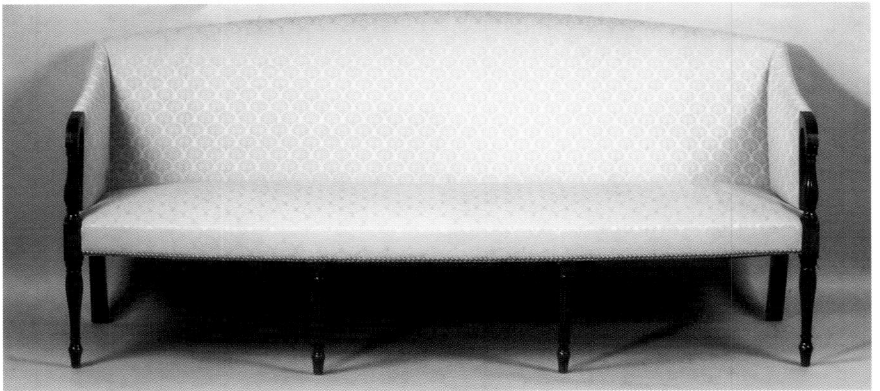

A-MA Nov. 2003 **Skinner, Inc.**
125 **Federal Sofa,** mah., probably MA, ca. 1810-15 w/vase & ring-turned reeded legs joined by an overupholstered slightly swelled seat, ref., **$3,290**

A-MA Nov. 2003 **Fontaines Auction Gallery**
34 **Sofa,** laminated rosewood in the Hawkins patt., attrib. to J & JW Meeks, ca. 1855, ht. 78, lg. 53in. **$6,000**

A-OH Nov. 2003 **Garth's Arts & Antiques**
772 **Empire Sofa,** mah. & mah. flame veneer w/old ref., rolled crest on back, relief carving on frame & paw feet, ht. 36, lg. 95in. **$1,955**

A-NH Nov. 2003 **Northeast Auctions**
736 **Louis XV Carved Beech Sofa** w/continuing armrests, bow-fronted fluted seat & fluted legs, lg. 6ft. **$3,500**

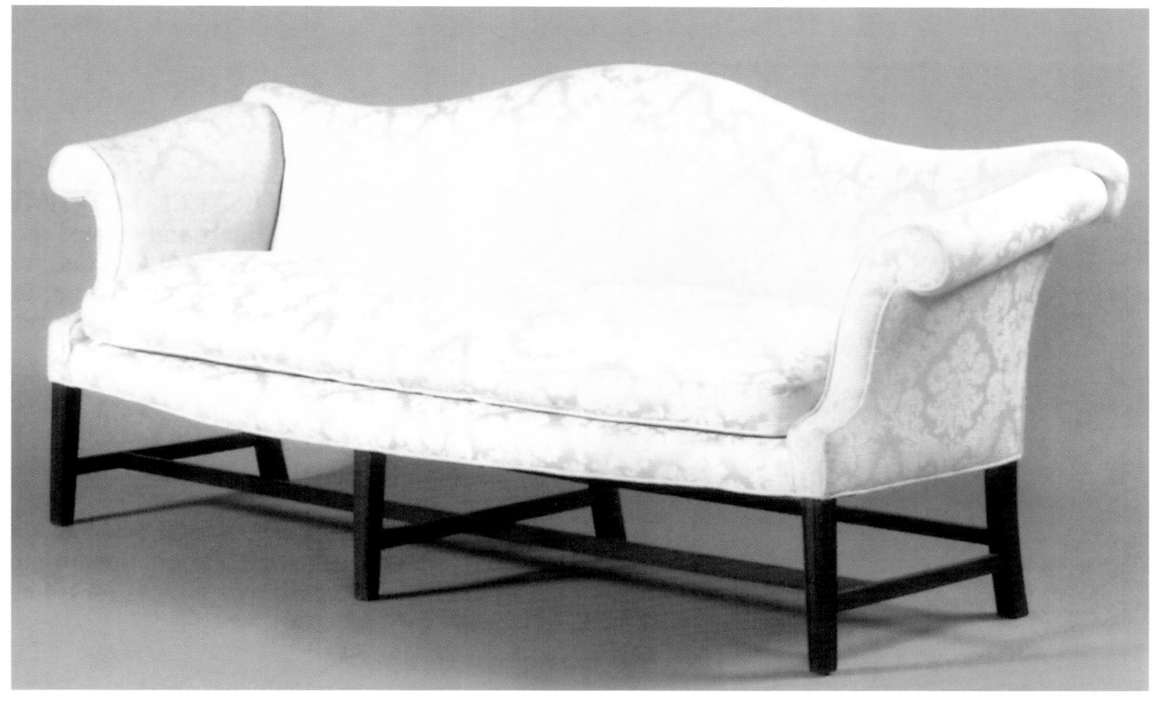

A-NH Nov. 2003
Northeast Auctions
816 **George III Camelback Sofa,** mah., w/serpentine back above outscrolled arms & loose seat cushion & square legs joined by boxed stretcher, lg. 84in. **$3,250**

A-PA May 2004
Pook & Pook, Inc.
534 **Federal Sofa,** NY, ca. 1815, w/swag & bow carved crest above reeded arms, & supported by turned & reeded legs w/brass casters, lg. 77½in. **$2,070**

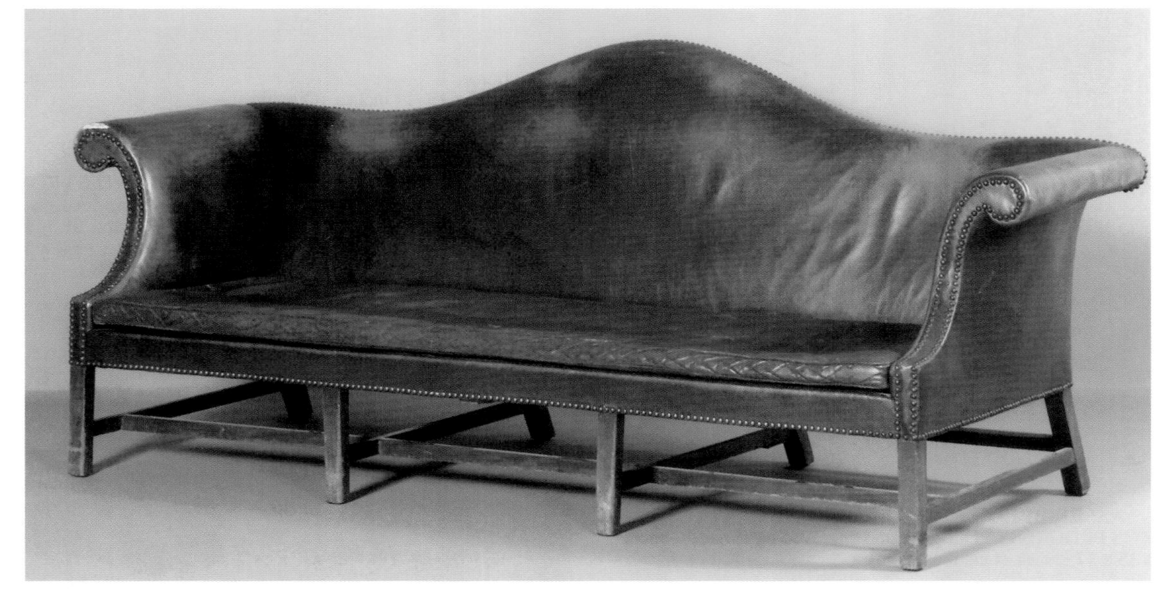

A-NH Mar. 2004
Northeast Auctions
706 **English Camelback Sofa,** mah., Chippendale w/leather upholstery & square legs, lg. 88in. **$13,000**

A-MA Nov. 2003
Fontaines Auction Gallery
45 **Rosewood Laminated Sofa** w/triple back, ca. 1855, and attributed to J & JW Meeks, ht. 46, lg. 84in.
$10,000

A-PA Oct. 2004
Pook & Pook, Inc.
303 **George III Chippendale Camel-back Sofa,** mah., ca. 1760, ht. 37, lg. 89in.
$4,370

A-NH Aug. 2004
Northeast Auctions
640 **Federal Sofa,** N. Eng., mah. & maple in old surface, ca. 1815-1820, retains orig. stuffing & webbing w/scrolling terminals ending in volutes on swelled reeded baluster supports continuing to legs, ht. 36, lg. 72in.
$2,750

A-MA Nov. 2003
Northeast Auctions
1811 Sheraton Three-Part Mah. Dining Table, probably VA w/two D-form ends & rectangular center section, tapering legs & ringed cuffs, ht. 22½in. $3,500

A-NH Nov. 2003 Northeast Auctions
1605 Q.A. Drop-Leaf Dining Table, walnut, PA w/arcaded skirt on cabriole legs & pad feet on platforms, ht. 29½in. $5,000

A-MA Nov. 2003 Skinner, Inc.
182 Classical Extension Banquet Table, mah. & mah. veneer, ca. 1885, probably Boston & sold w/four leaves, imper. ht. 29, dia. 45, w/leaves 121in. $10,575

A-NH Nov. 2003
Northeast Auctions
833 Regency Banquet Table, mah. w/three-section top, reeded legs terminating in brass caps, ht. 28, wd. 50, lg. 90in. together w/three leaves. $15,000

A-NH Aug. 2004 Northeast Auctions
1351 **Hepplewhite Three-Part Dining Table,** Maryland, w/inlay, square tapering legs w/cuffs on steel buttons, ht. 28, wd. 48, lg.open, 142in. **$30,000**

A-MA June 2004 Skinner, Inc.
396/397 **Neo-classical Mah. Dining Table** w/two pedestals, reeded legs, brass paw feet on casters & one removable leaf, ref. & rest, ht. 27¾, wd. 46, dp. w/leaf 76¼in. **$3,408.** Chairs **$4,348**

A-MA Feb. 2004 Skinner, Inc.
325 **Q.A. Dining Table,** maple, N. Eng., last half 18th C. w/circular drop-leaf top, ref. & imper., ht. 27, wd. 42in. **$2,500**
326 **Q.A. Dining Table,** N. Eng., 18th C. on shaped skirt, ref. & imper., ht. 27in. **$1,998**
327 **Chippendale Tiger Maple Table,** N. Eng., 1760-90 w/hinged drop leaves, old finish & minor imper., ht. 27in. **$1,410**

A-NH Mar. 2004 Northeast Auctions
909 **English Gate-Leg Dining Table,** mah. & chestnut w/Spanish feet joined by square stretchers, ht. 29, lg. 42, wd. open 49in. **$5,250**

A-NH Mar. 2004 Northeast Auctions
705 **Philadelphia Chippendale Dish-Top Tea Table** w/a birdcage & columnar pedestal, ht. 29, dia. 36in. **$13,000**

A-MA June 2004 Skinner, Inc.
360 **Federal Work Stand Table,** bird's eye maple & oak veneer, ca. 1815-25 w/ hinged leaves, old ref. & imper. **$2,703**
361 **Tiger Maple Work Table,** late Federal, NYS, ca. 1820 w/hinged top, drawers have divided int., brasses repl., ref. ht. 32in. **$2,820**

A-PA May 2004 Pook & Pook, Inc.
687 **Federal Sewing Stand,** MA, mah. & bird's eye maple, early 19th C., w/sewing bag, ht. 30in. **$2,530**
688 **Federal Work Table,** MA, mah., mid 19th C., w/ovolo corners, barber pole inlaid edges & reeded tapering legs, ht. 28in. **$3,220**

A-NH Nov. 2003 Northeast Auctions
1764 **Federal Tilt-Top Candlestand,** flame mah. w/oval top tilting above a flaring pedestal on tripod spider legs & spade feet, ht. 29in. **$1,200**
1765 **Federal Cherry Cut-Corner Tilt-Top Candlestand,** w/center leafy floral inlay on arched tripod spider legs,ht. 28in. **$2,200**
1766 **Q.A. Cherry Tilt-Top Candlestand,** CT w/tripod arched cabriole legs on slipper feet w/pads, ht. 28in. **$700**

A-PA May 2004
Pook & Pook, Inc.
803 **Hepplewhite Pembroke Table,** ca. 1800, NY, w/demilune drop leaves, square tapered legs inlay & banded cuffs, ht. 28in. **$9,775**

A-NH Nov. 2003
Northeast Auctions
1331 **Mah. Pembroke Table,** NY w/rectangular top, bowed ends & border of stringing inlay, the styles have oval sunburst inlay over square tapering legs w/bellflower drops, ht. 27in. **$4,000**

A-NH Nov. 2003 Northeast Auctions
1593 **New York Classical Trick-Leg Card Table,** mah., attrib. to Duncan Phyfe or one of equal rank. The treble elliptical hinged top w/banded border above pedestal w/reeded urn on tripod splayed acanthus carved legs that end in brass paw casters, ht. 28½in. **$12,000**

A-NH Nov. 2003 Northeast Auctions
1594 **New York Federal Breakfast Table,** attrib. to Duncan Phyfe, w/twin hinged leaves on baluster turned pedestal w/acanthus leaf carving & hairy paw feet, ht. 28¾, lg. 37¾in. **$2,900**

A-MA June 2004 Skinner, Inc.
24 **Q.A. Figured Walnut Drop-leaf Table,** ca. 1740-50 w/hinged leaves that flank the serpentine shaped skirts above cabriole legs ending in pad feet, old surface & imper., ht. 28, wd. 42in. **$11,163**

A-MA June 2004 Skinner, Inc.
22 **Chippendale Tilt-top Candlestand,** mah., late 18th C. The molded top tilts on a vase & ring-turned post on tripod cabriole leg base, old finish & minor imper., ht. 28¾, top 28x27¾in. **$7,638**

A-NH Nov. 2003 Northeast Auctions
1816 **Sheraton Mah. Work Table,** N. Eng. w/bag drawer, lion's head pulls & fitted for a bag, ht. 30in. **$3,250**

A-MA June 2004 Skinner, Inc.
178 **Federal Tilt-top Candlestand,** MA, mah., late 18th C. w/oval top on vase & ring turned post w/tripod base, cabriole legs & pad feet, old surface & minor imper., ht. 28, top 23x17¼in. **$8,813**

A-NH Nov. 2003 **Northeast Auctions**
1831 **Sheraton Games Table,** N. Eng., inlaid mah. & birch w/hinged top, flame birch panels & reeded legs, ht. 29½in. **$6,500**

A-NH Mar. 2004 **Northeast Auctions**
928 **Nest Of Four Regency Tray Top Tables,** rosewood w/bamboo trestle legs on shoe feet, ht. 29½in., top of largest 23x12¼in. **$4,600**

A-NH Nov. 2003 **Northeast Auctions**
840 **George III Folding Top Games Table,** mah. w/rectangular top & outset corners opening to a baize-lined playing surface, ball & claw feet, ht. 29, wd. 35., dp. 17in. **$3,000**

A-SC Dec. 2003 **Charlton Hall Galleries, Inc.**
502 **Regency Games Table,** late 19th C., w/bookmatched top, lobed corners & turned tapering legs, chips to mah. veneer, ht. 30in. **$500**

A-NH Aug. 2004 Northeast Auctions
591 **PA Federal One Drawer Stand,** 19th C. w/brown & russet painted dec., w/starflower motif, splayed legs, swelled cuffs & button feet w/rings., ht. 29¾, top 24x25¼in. **$6,000**

A-OH Jan. 2004
Garth's Arts & Antiques
340 **Q.A. Tavern Table,** maple w/old red finish, pegged const., single board oval top, slightly warped, age splits & minor repairs, ht. 27½, wd. 29¼in. **$6,036**

A-PA Oct. 2004 Pook & Pook, Inc.
568 **Chippendale Walnut Drop Leaf Table,** PA, ca. 1760 w/rectangular top over a scalloped skirt, cabriole legs, ball & claw feet, ht. 29, wd. 49in. **$2,990**

A-NH Mar. 2004 Northeast Auctions
819 **Q.A. Walnut Tavern Table W/Drawers** w/rectangular top, chamfered edges pinned to base & supported by tapered legs terminating in pad feet, ht. 29½, wd. 59, dp. 33in. **$4,500**

353

A-PA Apr. 2004 Conestoga Auction Co., Inc.
353 **Pin Top Tavern Table,** walnut, Moravian w/three board thumb molded top & dov. drawer. Horizontal stretchers attached to boldly turned legs & pegged const., rest. to feet, ht. 30, wd. 61, dp. 34in. **$6,050**

A-PA Oct. 2004 Pook & Pook, Inc.
502 **William & Mary Tavern Table,** early 18th C. w/single drawer, bold turned legs & joined by a box stretcher, ht. 31½, wd. 61in. **$5,060**

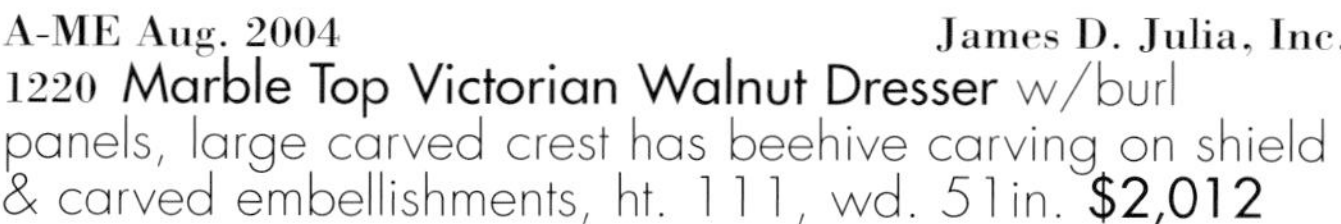

A-ME Aug. 2004 James D. Julia, Inc.
1220 Marble Top Victorian Walnut Dresser w/burl panels, large carved crest has beehive carving on shield & carved embellishments, ht. 111, wd. 51in. $2,012

1221 Walnut Victorian Bed w/burl panels, diamond carved dec. & five petal shell type carving at top, ht. 114, wd. 55in. $1,955

A-ME Aug. 2004 James D. Julia, Inc.
1149 Laminated Rosewood Carved Parlor Set attributed to Charles Boudoine, NYC. The set consists of large three-part sofa, armchair & two side chairs all upholstered in green velvet. Sofa has carved face w/leaf and tongue w/similar carvings on each chair. Legs are carved in French style w/caster front feet & solid backs. $29,900

A-MA Nov. 2003
Fontaines Auction Gallery
197 **Triple-back Renaissance Revival Sofa,** rosewood w/maiden head arms & oval back w/crested medallion, ca. 1875, attrib. to John Jellif, ht. 47, lg. 7in. **$3,050**

A-MA Nov. 2003
Fontaines Auction Gallery
198 **Victorian Walnut Marble Top Parlor Table** w/shaped inset, maiden head skirt & elaborate carved base, Ca. 1875, ht. 30, wd. 46in. **$2,250**

199 **Renaissance Revival Burled Walnut Lamp Table** w/marble top, ca. 1875. **$750**

A-MA Nov. 2003 Fontaines Auction Gallery
202 **Rosewood Rococo Marble Top Console Table,** mah., w/floral carved apron & legs, ht. 35, wd. 51in. **$2,200**

A-MA Nov. 2003 Fontaines Auction Gallery
169 **Carved Mahogany Fireside Bench** w/open mouth lions & claw feet, ca. 1885, ht. 39, wd. 73in. **$1,350**

A-NH Mar. 2004
Northeast Auctions
1172 **Victorian Rococo Walnut Bookcase-Secretaire** w/inscrip. Emancipation Jan 1 1863, w/fitted int. & writing surface above two cupboard doors, ht. 105, wd. 50in.
$8,750

A-MA Nov. 2003
Fontaines Auction Gallery
306 **Mirrored Etagère,** ornately carved w/winged griffins, figural crest, single door w/beveled mirrors, ca. 1890, ht. 67, wd. 47in.
$1,100

A-MA Nov. 2003 Fontaines Auction Gallery
266 **Walnut Renaissance Revival Marble Top Bedroom Set** w/round burled panels & carved crests, ca. 1870. **$4,250**

A-NH Mar. 2004 Northeast Auctions
1176 **Renaissance Revival Walnut Gentleman's Chair,** Am., w/gilt highlights. **$700**

A-ME Apr. 2004 James D. Julia, Inc.
716 **Eastlake Marble Top Bedroom Set** w/orig. rails & chest lock key. **$1,150**

A-MA Nov. 2003 Fontaines Auction Gallery
30 **Rosewood Rococo Double Door Armoire** w/bonnet top & shaped mirrors, ca. 1880, ht. 104, wd 60in. **$6,000**

A-MA Nov. 2003 Fontaines Auction Gallery
11 **Oak China Cabinet** w/serpentine front, carved lion heads & claw feet, crest shows swirling leaf patterns & a maiden's head, ca. 1895, ht. 77, wd. 45in. **$2,650**

A-OH Nov. 2003 Garth's Arts & Antiques
151 **Rococo Revival Carved Armchair,** attributed to John H. Belter, Fountain Elms patt., laminated rosewood, old dark ref. w/finely carved & pierced framework. Arm restorations & edge chips, ht. 43in. **$10,925**

A-MA Nov. 2003
Fontaines Auction Gallery
304 Hunzinger Lollipop Rocker, mah., w/stick & ball const. $550

A-MA Nov. 2003 Fontaines Auction Gallery
8 Walnut Victorian Shaving Stand w/block front & swivel mirror, ca. 1875, ht. 55in. $1,100
9 Empire Dressing Table, crotch grained mah. w/pedestal base, ca. 1850, $1,800

1718

1719

1720

1721

1722

1723

1724

1725

A-IA Jan. 2004
Jackson's Auctioneers International
1718 Victorian Gentleman's Chair, heavily carved. $489
1719 Balloon-back Armchair in walnut. $207
1720 Louis XV Style Armchair w/balloon back. $218
1721 Louis XV Style Chair w/medallion back. $184
1722 Art Nouveau Etagère, ca. 1910. $431
1723 Balloon-back Chair, walnut. $126
1724 Late Victorian Side Chair w/carved crest. $103
1725 Victorian Center Table w/marble top & turned center post. $374

A-MA Nov. 2003 Fontaines Auction Gallery
305 **Victorian Oval Marble Top Center Table,** ca. 1870, ht. 29in. **$375**

A-MA Nov. 2003 Fontaines Auction Gallery
302 **Victorian Piano Lamp** w/onyx tops & orig. shade, ca. 1885. **$800**

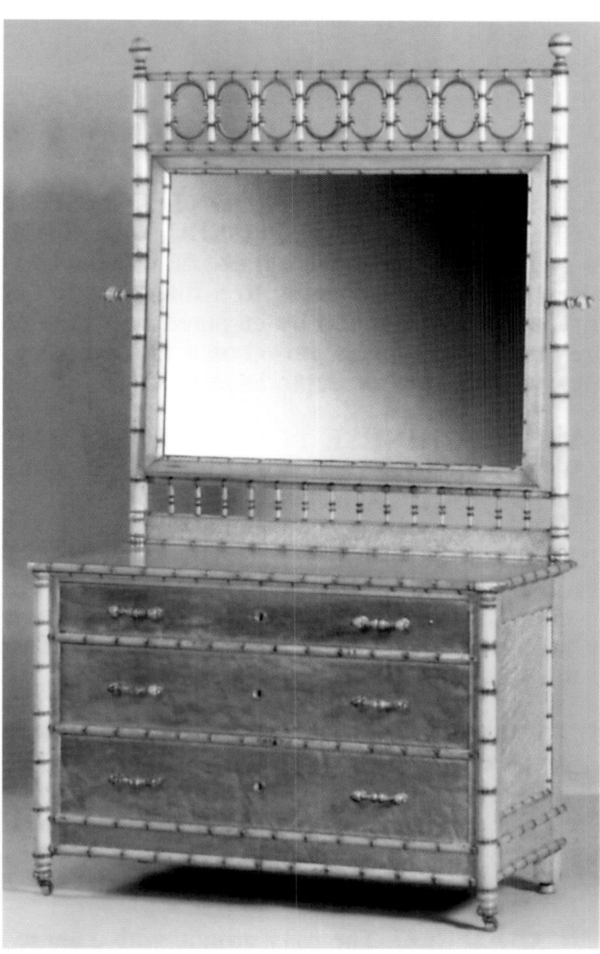

A-NH Mar. 2004
Northeast Auctions
1189 **Bird's Eye Maple & Faux Bamboo Bedroom Set,** five pcs., 19th C., incl. a drop-center chest of drawers, chest of drawers, each w/attached mirror, half-commode, night-stand & chair. Height of center chest w/mirror, 7ft.3in. **$11,000**

A-IA Nov. 2003 **Jackson's International Auctioneers**

757 **Louis XV Bombé Commode,** ca. 1740, in geometric marquetry w/foliate handles & lockplates, minor losses, cracked pull & locks missing, ht. 33, lg. 50in. **$1,810**

758 **Louis XVI Commode,** ca. 1800 w/ring pulls & wreath escutcheons, marquetry design on oak body w/losses to veneer & gray marble top, ht. 35, lg. 42in. **$2,530**

759 **Louis XVI Bonheur du Jour,** veneered mah., ca. 1800 w/mirrored doors & folding leather covered writing surface & pull-out supports w/shelf drawer ht. 44, wd. 31in. **$1,495**

1729

1730

1731

1732

1733

A-IA Mar. 2004 **Jackson's International Auctioneers**

1729 **Corner Washstand** w/splashback, ht. 45in. **$316**

1730 **Walnut Sewing Stand,** Empire style w/two lift lids & two drawers, ht. 30, wd. 21in. **$460**

1731 **Victorian Fireplace Screen** w/needle point & beaded insert, ht. 43in. **$402**

1732 **Lift Lid Writing Desk** w/sloping top outlined in brass, ht. 32in. **$259**

1733 **Victorian Commode** w/brass & aluminum mounts & pulls, ht. 34in. **$184**

Opposite
A-IA Nov. 2003
Jackson's International Auctioneers

797 **Victorian Center Table,** mah. w/round beveled top on baluster turned column, w/carved splayed legs, ht. 29, dia. 46in. **$345**

798 **Empire Chairs,** mah. veneer, matched pair w/slip seat, ht. 33in. **$230**

799 **Oak Wine Cabinet,** ca. 1920, ht. 62, wd. 39in. **$345**

800 **Oriental Plant Stand,** 20th C., heavily carved, ht.32in. **$143**

801 **Victorian Side Chairs** w/carved crest & balloon backs,ht. 34in. **$431**

802 **Walnut Lectern,** Gothic style, late 19th C, ht. 37in. **$431**

803 **Oak Lectern,** Eastlake style w/burl front & side panels, ht. 36in. **$287**

804 **Oriental Carved Chairs,** pair, 20th C. Entwined dragons form the back. **$690**

805 **Oak Commode & Washstand,** 19th C. w/marble top, ht. 30in. **$517**

806 **Victorian Commode,** walnut w/white marble top. **$517**

807 **Victorian Entry Table,** 19th C., walnut, Gothic style, lg. 48in. **$373**

808 **Eastlake Writing Table** w/burl front, ht. 30, lg. 36in. **$316**

809 **Victorian Center Table,** walnut w/marble top, ht. 30in. **$460**

797

799

800

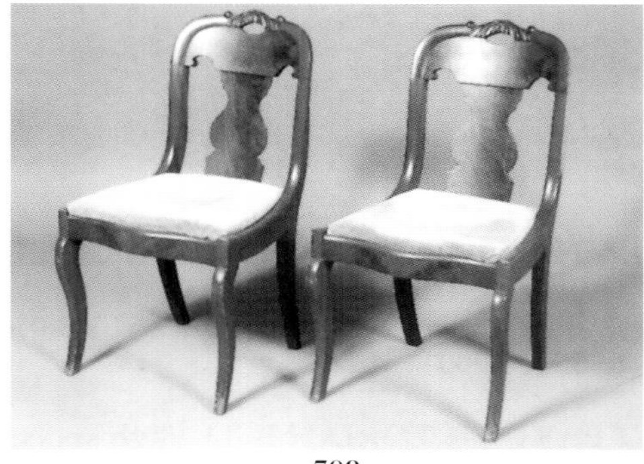
798

802

803

801

804

805

806

807

808

809

1758 1759 1760 1761

1762 1763 1764

1765 1766 1767

1768 1769 1770

Opposite
A-IA Mar. 2004
Jackson's International Auctioneers
1758 **Pine Corner Cupboard,** two piece w/double barrel front, ht. 85in. **$1,265**
1759 **Pine Corner Cupboard,** single door opens to four shelves, ht. 52in. **$402**
1760 **Pine Wall Cabinet,** opens to three shelves w/drawer in base, ht. 44in. **$218**
1761 **Pine Wall Cupboard,** 19th C. w/porcelain pulls, ht. 83, wd. 44in. **$977**
1762 **Dry Sink,** 19th C. w/rollers, small size, ht. 30, wd. 28in. **$345**
1763 **Pine Settle Bench in knotty pine,** ht. 55, lg. 82in. **$207**
1764 **Combination Chair & Table,** pine, ht. 29, wd. 38in. **$115**
1765 **Pine Wood Box** w/divider & lift lid, ht. 24, wd. 29in. **$138**
1766 **Drop Leaf Table** w/turned legs, pine, ht. 28, wd. 39in. **$161**
1767 **Bench** w/two shelves, pine w/hand hold, ht. 23, lg. 36in. **$103**
1768 **Pine Wash Bench,** lg. 30in., & two plank seat chairs. **$103**
1769 **Maple Rope Bed,** ht. 40, wd. 52in. **$138**
1770 **Pine Trunk** w/strapped pinch waist, ht. 17, lg. 34in. **$345**

749

750

751

752

753

754

755

A-IA Sept. 2004
Jackson's International Auctioneers
749 **Walnut Corner Cupboard** w/four blind doors & int. shelves, ht. 72in. **$747**
750 **Walnut Kitchen Cupboard** w/glazed doors, ht. 77in. **$690**
751 **Oak Secretary/Bookcase** w/curved glass door & orig. finish, ht. 75in. **$1,092**
752 **Victorian Oak Secretary/Bookcase** w/drop front desk, ht. 77in. **$575**
753 **Oak Cabinet** w/glass display, ht. 60in. **$488**
754 **Maple Kitchen Cupboard,** possum belly style, includes nine glass canisters, ht. 70in. **$488**
755 **Maple Kitchen Cupboard,** possum belly style & the original canisters embossed Hoosier on lids, ht. 63in. **$575**

756

757

758

759

A-IA Sept. 2004
Jackson's International Auctioneers
756 **Oak Bookcase,** two doors & five adjustable shelves, ht. 58, wd. 39in. **$517**
757 **Victorian Walnut Dresser** w/hankie boxes, ht. 45, wd. 38in. **$517**
758 **Walnut Dresser,** Victorian w/swivel mirror, ht. 78in. **$575**
759 **Oak Bookcase** w/carved backrest & four adjustable shelves, ht. 65in. **$287**

1726

1727

1728

A-IA Mar. 2004
Jackson's International Auctioneers
1726 **Walnut Chest Of Drawers** w/raised veneered panels on drawers & pillars on each side, ht. 41, wd. 40in. **$259**
1727 **Victorian walnut marble top commode** w/backsplash & candle stands, ht. 36, wd. 29in. **$259**
1728 **Victorian Walnut Center Table** w/marble top & spoon carved frame, ht. 30in. **$316**

Opposite
A-IA Sept. 2004
Jackson's International Auctioneers
762 **Mah. Dining Set** incl. breakfront, six shield-back chairs & a six legged table not shown, mkd. Bernhart Furniture, in average cond. **$517**
763 **Mah. Bookcase/Secretary** w/serpentine drawer front, ht. 80in. **$575**
764 **Mah. Chest of Drawers,** ht. 47in. **$230**
765 **Mah. Four Post Single Beds,** matching pair, one illus., ht.36in. **$230**
766 **Victorian Walnut Chair** w/balloon back, needlepoint floral seat, front & back, 20th C., ht. 38in. **$258**
767 **Victorian Style Armchair** w/tapestry weave floral upholstery, ht. 44in. **$287**
768 **Victorian Revival Armchair,** walnut w/balloon back w/needlepoint seat & back. **$258**
769 **Walnut Side Chairs,** set of six w/burled panel backs & cane seats, ht. 33in. **$546**
770 **Oak Side Chairs,** set of four w/press backs, ca. 1900, ht. 40in. **$201**
771 **Oak Side Chairs,** set of six w/press backs & woven cane seats, ht. 39in. **$287**
772 **Maple Bed Frame,** spool turned, 19th C., full size. **$258**
773 **Oak Dining Table,** ca. 1900 w/five twist legs, 42in. sq. **$143**
774 **Oak Sideboard** w/back mirror & carved dec., ht. 42, wd. 57in. **$316**

762

763

764

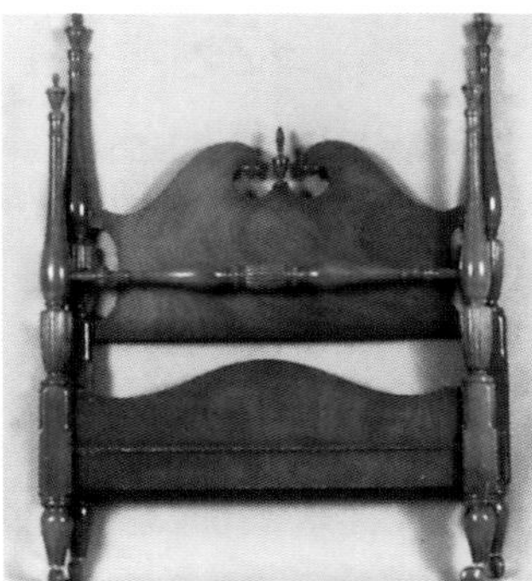

765

766

767

768

769

770

771

772

773

774

A-MA Nov. 2004 Skinner, Inc.
72 **Shaker Ministry Dining Table,** Harvard. MA community, ca. 1830 w/old finish. A horizontal stretcher, now removed, was a later addition. Ht. 28⅛, wd. 34, lg. 96in. **$64,624**

A-MA Nov. 2004 Skinner, Inc.
302 **Federal Card Table,** N. Eng., ca.1800, mah. w/inlay & bird's-eye maple reserve, stringing & cuff inlays, minor imper. & old ref., ht. 30, wd. 36in. **$3,055**
303 **Federal Card Table,** mah. & bird's-eye maple veneer, Boston, ca. 1800, w/string-inlaid legs ending in cuffs, w/old ref. & minor imper., ht. 31, wd. 35½in. **$5,581**

A-MA Nov. 2004 Skinner, Inc.
262 **Federal Cherry Inlaid Stand,** N. Eng., ca. 1800 w/drawer, stringing & cuffs of crossbanding, ref. & top slightly reduced in size, ht. 28¾in. **$1,058**
263 **Federal Birch Stand** w/red stain, ca. 1810 w/bird's-eye maple drawer, old surface & minor imper., ht. 28¾in. **$1,116**
264 **Federal Tiger Maple Inlaid Candlestand,** early 19th C., w/octagonal top centering an inlaid diamond, minor imper., ht. 29½in. **$3,290**
265 **Federal Worktable,** mah. w/mah. veneer, ca. 1810, ref., ht. 28½in. **$1,410**

A-MA Nov. 2004 Skinner, Inc.

157 **Mahogany Tea Table,** Chowan Co., NC., ca. 1750-80 w/tilt top, old ref. & minor repr., ht. 28in. **$4,700**

158 **Chippendale Shell-Carved Walnut Dressing Table,** Phil. PA, 1750-60 w/orig. finish & hdw., minor repr., ht. 27½, wd. 33½in. **$16,450**

103 104 105 106 107

A-MA Nov. 2004 Skinner, Inc.

103 **Q.A. Walnut Tilt-top Candlestand,** last half 18th C., w/old finish & minor imper., ht. 28in. **$940**

104 **Cherry Candlestand w/Drawer,** early 19th C. w/minor imper. & ref., ht. 27¾in. **$1,880**

105 **Federal Candlestand,** Cherry, N.Eng. c.1800 w/old ref., ht. 27¼in. **$1,058**

106 **Q.A. Cherry Candlestand,** last half 18th C., w/square top & applied edge, minor imper. & old surface, ht. 28in. **$940**

107 **Federal Mahogany Candlestand,** N. Eng., c.1800 w/rectangular top & ovolo corners, minor imper. & old surface, ht. 27in. **$940**

Agata Glass was patented by Joseph Locke of the New England Glass Company of Cambridge, Massachusetts, in 1877. The application of a metallic stain left a mottled design characteristic of agata, hence the name.

Amber Glass is the name of any glassware having a yellowish-brown color. It became popular during the last quarter of the 19th century.

Amberina Glass was patented by the New England Glass Company in 1833. It is generally recognized as a clear yellow glass shading to a deep red or fuchsia at the top. When the colors are opposite, it is known as reverse amberina. It was machine-pressed into molds, free blown, cut and pattern molded. Almost every glass factory here and in Europe produced this ware, but few pieces were ever marked.

Amethyst Glass – The term identifies any glassware made in the proper dark purple shade. It became popular after the Civil War.

Art Glass is a general term given to various types of ornamental glass made to be decorative rather than functional. It dates primarily from the late Victorian period to the present day and, during the span of time, glassmakers have achieved fantastic effects of shape, color, pattern, texture and decoration.

Aventurine Glass The Venetians are credited with the discovery of aventurine during the 1860s. It was produced by various mixes of copper in yellow glass. When the finished pieces were broken, ground or crushed, they were used as decorative material by glassblowers. Therefore, a piece of aventurine glass consists of many tiny glittering particles on the body of the object, suggestive of sprinkled gold crumbs or dust. Other colors in aventurine are known to exist.

Baccarat Glass was first made in France in 1756, by La Compagnie des Cristelleries de Baccarat – until the firm went bankrupt. Production began for the second time during the 1820s and the firm is still in operation, producing fine glassware and paperweights. Baccarat is famous for its earlier paperweights made during the last half of the 19th century.

Bohemian Glass is named for its country of origin. It is ornate, overlay, or flashed glassware, popular during the Victorian era.

Bristol Glass is a lightweight opaque glass, often having a light bluish tint, and decorated with enamels. The ware is a product of Bristol, England – a glass center since the 1700s.

Burmese – Frederick Shirley developed this shaded art glass at the now famous old Mt. Washington Glass Company in New Bedford, Massachusetts, and patented his discovery under the name of "Burmese" on December 15, 1885. The ware was also made in England by Thomas Webb & Sons. Burmese is a hand-blown glass with the exception of a few pieces that were pattern molded. The latter are either ribbed, hobnail or diamond quilted in design. This ware is found in two textures or finishes: the original glazed or shiny finish, and the dull, velvety, satin finish. It is a homogeneous single-layered glass that was never lined, cased, or plated. Although its color varies slightly, it always shades from a delicate yellow at the base to salmon-pink at the top. The blending of colors is so gradual that it is difficult to determine where a color ends and another begins.

Cambridge glasswares were produced by the Cambridge Glass Company in Ohio from 1901 until the firm closed in 1954.

Cameo Glass can be defined as any glass in which the surface has been cut away to leave a design in relief. Cutting is accomplished by the use of hand-cutting tools, wheel cutting and hydrofluoric acid. This ware can be clear or colored glass of a single layer, or glass with multiple layers of clear or colored glass.

Although cameo glass has been produced for centuries, the majority available today dates from the late 1800s. It has been produced in England, France and other parts of Europe, as well as the United States. The most famous of the French masters of cameo wares was Emile Gallé.

Carnival Glass was an inexpensive, pressed iridescent glassware made from about 1900 through the 1920s. It was made in quantities by Northwood Glass Company, Fenton Art Glass Company and others, to compete with the expensive art glass of the period. It was originally called "taffeta" glass during the 1920s, when carnivals gave examples as premiums or prizes.

Chocolate Glass, sometimes mistakenly called caramel slag because of its streaked appearance, was made by the Indiana Tumbler & Goblet Company of Greentown, IN, from 1900 to 1903. It was also made by the National Glass Company factories, and later by Fenton from 1907 to 1915.

Consolidated Lamp & Glass Co. of Coraopolis, PA, was founded in 1894 and closed in 1967. The company made lamps, art glass and tablewares. Items made after 1925 are of the greatest interest to collectors.

Coralene – The term coralene denotes a type of decoration rather than a kind of glass – consisting of many tiny beads, either of colored or transparent glass, decorating the surface. The most popular design used resembled coral or seaweed, hence the name.

Crackle Glass – This type of art glass was an invention of the Venetians which spread rapidly to other countries. It is made by plunging red-hot glass into cold water, then reheating and reblowing it, thus producing an unusual outer surface which appears to be covered with a multitude of tiny fractures, but is perfectly smooth to the touch.

Cranberry Glass – The term "cranberry glass" refers to color only, not to a particular type of glass. It is undoubtedly the most familiar colored glass known to collectors. This ware was blown or molded, and often decorated with enamels.

Crown Milano glass was made by Frederick Shirley at the Mt. Washington Glass Company, New Bedford, Massachusetts, from 1886-1888. It is ivory in color with a satin finish, and was embellished with floral sprays, scrolls and gold enamel.

Crown Tuscan glass has a pink-opaque body. It was originally produced in 1936 by A.J. Bennett, president of the Cambridge Glass Company of Cambridge, Ohio. The line was discontinued in 1954. Occasionally referred to as Royal Crown Tuscan, this ware was named for a scenic area in

Italy, and it has been said that its color was taken from the flash-colored sky at sunrise. When trans-illuminated, examples do have all of the blaze of a sunrise – a characteristic that is even applied to new examples of the ware reproduced by Mrs. Elizabeth Degenhart of Crystal Art Glass, and Harold D. Bennett, Guernsey Glass Company of Cambridge, Ohio.

Custard Glass was manufactured in the United States for a period of about 30 years (1885-1915). Although Harry Northwood was the first and largest manufacturer of custard glass, it was also produced by the Heisey Glass Company, Diamond Glass Company, Fenton Art Glass Company and a number of others.

The name custard glass is derived from its "custard yellow" color which may shade light yellow to ivory to light green glass that is opaque to opalescent. Most pieces have fiery opalescence when held to the light. Both the color and glow of this ware came from the use of uranium salts in the glass. It is generally a heavy type pressed glass made in a variety of different patterns.

Cut Overlay – The term identifies pieces of glassware usually having a milk-white exterior that have been cased with cranberry, blue or amber glass. Other examples are deep blue, amber or cranberry on crystal glass, and the majority of pieces have been decorated with dainty flowers. Although Bohemian glass manufacturers produced some very choice pieces during the 19th century, fine examples were also made in America, as well as in France and England.

Daum Nancy is the mark found on pieces of French cameo glass made by August and Jean Daum after 1875.

Durand Art Glass was made by Victor Durand from 1879 to 1935 at the Durand Art Glass Works in Vineland, New Jersey. The glass resembles Tiffany in quality. Drawn white feather designs and thinly drawn glass threading (quite brittle) applied around the main body of the ware, are striking examples of Durand creations on an iridescent surface.

Findlay or Onyx art glass was manufactured about 1890 for only a short time by the Dalzell Gilmore Leighton Company of Findlay, Ohio.

Flashed Wares were popular during the late 19th century. They were made by partially coating the inner surface of an object with a thin plating of glass of another, more dominant color – usually red. These pieces can readily be identified by holding the object to the light and examining the rim, as it will show more than one layer of glass. Many pieces of "rubina crystal" (cranberry to clear), "blue amberina" (blue to amber), and "rubina verde" (cranberry to green), were manufactured in this way.

Francisware is a hobnail glassware with frosted or clear glass hobs and stained amber rims and tops. It was produced during the late 1880s by Hobbs, Brockunier and Company.

Fry Glass was made by the H.C. Fry Company, Rochester, Pennsylvania, from 1901, when the firm was organized, until 1934, when operations ceased. The firm specialized in the manufacturing of cut glassware. The production of their famous "foval" glass did not begin until the 1920s. The firm also produced a variety of glass specialties, oven wares and etched glass.

Gallé glass was made in Nancy, France, by Emile Gallé at the Gallé Factory, founded in 1874. The firm produced both enameled and cameo glass, pottery, furniture and other art nouveau items. After Gallé's death in 1904, the factory continued operating until 1935.

Greentown glass was made in Greentown, Indiana, by the Indiana Tumbler and Goblet Company from 1894 until 1903. The firm produced a variety of pressed glasswares in addition to milk and chocolate glass.

Gunderson Peachblow is a more recent type of art glass produced in 1952 by the Gunderson-Pairpoint Glass Works of New Bedford, Massachusetts, successors to the Mt. Washington Glass Company. Gunderson pieces have a soft satin finish shading from white at the base to a deep rose at the top.

Hobnail – The term "hobnail" identifies any glassware having "bumps" – flattened, rounded or pointed – over the outer surface of the glass. A variety of patterns exists. Many of the fine early examples were produced by Hobbs, Brockunier and Company, Wheeling, West Virginia, and the New England Glass Company.

Holly Amber, originally known as "golden agate," is a pressed glass pattern which features holly berries and leaves over its glossy surface. Its color shades from golden brown tones to opalescent streaks. This ware was produced by the Indiana Tumbler and Goblet Company for only 6 months, from January 1 to June 13, 1903. Examples are rare and expensive.

Imperial Glass – The Imperial Glass Company of Bellaire, Ohio, was organized in 1901 by a group of prominent citizens of Wheeling, West Virginia. A variety of fine art glass, in addition to carnival glass, was produced by the firm. The two trademarks which identified the ware were issued in June 1914. One consisted of the firm's name, "Imperial," by double-pointed arrows.

Latticino is the name given to articles of glass in which a network of tiny milk-white lines appear, crisscrossing between two walls of glass. It is a type of filigree glassware developed during the 16th century by the Venetians.

Legras Glass – Cameo, acid cut and enameled glasswares were made by August J.F. Legras at Saint-Denis, France, from 1864-1914.

Loetz Glass was made in Austria just before the turn of the century. As Loetz worked in the Tiffany factory before returning to Austria, much of his glass is similar in appearance to Tiffany wares. Loetz glass is often marked "Loetz" or "Loetz-Austria".

Lutz Glass was made by Nicholas Lutz, a Frenchman, who worked at the Boston and Sandwich Glass Company from 1870 to 1888, when it closed. He also produced fine glass at the Mt. Washington Glass Company. Lutz is noted for two different types of glass – striped and threaded wares. Other glass houses also produced similar glass, and these wares were known as Lutz-type.

Mary Gregory was an artist for the Boston and Sandwich Glass Company during the last quarter of the 19th century. She decorated glassware with white enamel figures of young children engaged in playing, collecting butterflies, etc., in white on transparent glass, both clear and colored. Today the term "Mary Gregory" glass applies to any glassware that remotely resembles her work.

Mercury Glass is a double-walled glass that dates from the 1850s to about 1910. It was made in England as well as the United States during this period. Its interior, usually in the form of vases, is lined with flashing mercury, giving the items an all over silvery appearance. The entrance hole in the base of each piece was sealed over. Many pieces were decorated.

Milk Glass is an opaque pressed glassware usually of milk-white color, although green, amethyst, black, and shades of blue were made. Milk glass was produced in quantity in the United States during the 1880s, in a variety of patterns.

Millefiori – This decorative glassware is considered to be a specialty of the Venetians. It is sometimes called "glass of a thousand flowers" and has been made for centuries. Very thin colored glass rods are arranged in bundles, then fused together with heat. When the piece of glass is sliced across, it has a design like that of many small flowers. These tiny wafer-thin slices are then embedded in larger masses of glass, enlarged and shaped.

Moser Glass was made by Ludwig Moser at Karlsbad. The ware is considered to be another type of art nouveau glass, as it was produced during its heyday – during the early 1900s. Principal colors included amethyst, cranberry, green and blue, with fancy enameled decoration.

Mother-of-Pearl, often abbreviated in descriptions as M.O.P., is a glass composed of two or more layers, with a pattern showing through to the other surface. The pattern, caused by internal air traps, is created by expanding the inside layer of molten glass into molds with varying designs. When another layer of glass is applied, this brings out the design. The final layer of glass is then acid dipped, and the result is mother-of-pearl satin ware. Patterns are numerous. The most frequently found are the diamond quilted, raindrop and herringbone. This ware can be one solid color, a single color shading light to dark, two colors blended or a variety of colors which include the rainbow effect. In addition, many pieces are decorated with colorful enamels, coralene beading, and other applied glass decorations.

Nailsea Glass was first produced in England from 1788 to 1873. The characteristics that identify this ware are the "pulled" loopings and swirls of colored glass over the body of the object.

New England Peachblow was patented in 1886 by the New England Glass Company. It is a single-layered glass shading from opaque white at the base to deep rose-red or raspberry at the top. Some pieces have a glossy surface, but most were given an acid bath to produce a soft, matte finish.

New Martinsville Peachblow Glass was produced from 1901-1907 at New Martinsville, Pennsylvania.

Opalescent Glass – The term refers to glasswares which have a milky white effect in the glass, usually on a colored ground. There are three basic types of this ware. Presently, the most popular includes pressed glass patterns found in table settings. Here the opalescence appears at the top rim, the base, or a combination of both. On blown or mold-blown glass, the pattern itself consists of this milky effect – such as Spanish lace. Another example is the opalescent points on some pieces of hobnail glass. These wares are lighter weight. The third group includes opalescent novelties, primarily of the pressed variety.

Peking Glass is a type of Chinese cameo glass produced from the 1700s well into the 19th century.

Phoenix Glass – The firm was established in Beaver County, Pennsylvania, during the late 1800s, and produced a variety of commercial glasswares. During the 1930s the factory made a desirable sculptured gift-type glassware which has become very collectible in recent years. Vases, lamps, bowls, ginger jars, candlesticks, etc., were made until the 1950s in various colors with a satin finish.

Pigeon Blood is a bright reddish-orange glassware dating from the early 1900s.

Pomona Glass was invented in 1884 by Joseph Locke at the New England Glass Company.

Pressed Glass was the inexpensive glassware produced in quantity to fill the increasing demand for tablewares when Americans moved away from the simple table utensils of pioneer times. During the 1820s, ingenious Yankees invented and perfected machinery for successfully pressing glass. About 1865, manufacturers began to color their products. Literally hundreds of different patterns were produced.

Quezal is a very fine quality blown iridescent glassware produced by Martin Bach, in his factory in Brooklyn, New York, from 1901-1920. Named after the Central American bird, quezal glassware has an iridescent finish, featuring contrasting colored glass threads. Green, white and gold colors are most often found.

Rosaline Glass is a product of the Steuben Glass Works of Corning, New York. The firm was founded by Frederick Carter and T.C. Hawkes, Sr. Rosaline is a rose-colored jade glass or colored alabaster. The firm is now owned by the Corning Glass Company, which is presently producing fine glass of exceptional quality.

Royal Flemish Art Glass was made by the Mt. Washington Glass Works during the 1880s. It has an acid finish which may consist of one or more colors, decorated with raised gold enameled lines separating into sections. Fanciful painted enamel designs also decorate this ware. Royal Flemish glass is marked "RF," with the letter "R" reversed and backed to the letter "F," within a four-sided orange-red diamond mark.

Rubina Glass is a transparent blown glassware that shades from clear to red. One of the first to produce this crystal during the late 1800s was Hobbs, Brockunier and Company of Wheeling, West Virginia.

Rubina Verde is a blown art glass made by Hobbs, Brockunier and Company, during the late 1800s. It is a transparent glassware that shades from red to yellow-green.

Sabino Glass originated in Paris, France, in the 1920s. The company was founded by Marius-Ernest Sabino, and was noted for art deco figures, vases, nudes and animals in clear, opalescent and colored glass.

Sandwich Glass – One of the most interesting and enduring pages from America's past is Sandwich glass produced by the famous Boston and Sandwich Glass Company at Sandwich, Massachusetts. The firm began operations in 1825, and the glass flourished until 1888, when the factory closed. Despite the popularity of Sandwich Glass, little is known about its founder, Deming Jarvis. The Sandwich Glass house turned out hundreds of designs in both plain and figured patterns in colors and crystal, so that no one type could be considered entirely typical – but the best known is the "lacy" glass produced there. The variety and multitude of designs and patterns produced by the company over the years is a tribute to its greatness.

Silver Deposit Glass was made during the late 19th and early 20th centuries. Silver was deposited on the glass surface by a chemical process so that a pattern appeared against a clear or colored ground. This ware is sometimes referred to as "silver overlay."

Slag Glass was originally known as "mosaic" and "marble glass" because of its streaked appearance. Production in the United States began about 1880. The largest producer of this ware was Challinor, Taylor and Company.

Spanish Lace is a Victorian glass pattern that is easily identified by its distinct opalescent flower and leaf pattern. It belongs to the shaded opalescent glass family.

Steuben – The Steuben Glass Works was founded in 1904, by Frederick Carder, an Englishman, and T.G. Hawkes, Sr., at Corning, New York. In 1918, the firm was purchased by the Corning Glass Company. However, Carder remained with the firm, designing a bounty of fine art glass of exceptional quality.

Stevens & Williams of Stourbridge, England, made many fine art glass pieces covering the full range of late Victorian ware between the 1830s and 1930s. Many forms were decorated with applied glass flowers, leaves and fruit. After World War I, the firm began producing lead crystal and new glass colors.

Stiegel-Type Glass – Henry William Stiegel founded America's first flint glass factory during the 1760s at Manheim, Pennsylvania. Stiegel glass is flint or crystal glass; it is thin and clear, and has a bell-like ring when tapped. The ware is quite brittle and fragile. Designs were painted free-hand on the glass – birds, animals and architectural motifs, surrounded by leaves and flowers. The engraved glass resulted from craftsmen etching the glass surface with a copper wheel, then cutting the desired patterns.

It is extremely difficult to identify, with certainty, a piece of original Stiegel glass. Part of the problem resulted from the lack of an identifying mark on the products. Additionally, many of the craftsmen moved to other areas after the Stiegel plant closed, producing a similar glass product. Therefore, when one is uncertain about the origin of this type of ware, it is referred to as "Stiegel type" glass.

Tiffany Glass was made by Louis Comfort Tiffany, one of America's outstanding glass designers of the art nouveau period, from about 1870 to the 1930s. Tiffany's designs included a variety of lamps, bronze work, silver, pottery and stained glass windows. Practically all items made were marked "L.C. Tiffany" or "L.C.T." in addition to the word "Favrile".

Tortoiseshell Glass – As its name indicates, this type of glassware resembles the color of tortoiseshell, and has deep, rich brown tones combined with amber and cream colored shades. Tortoiseshell glass was originally produced in 1880 by Francis Poh, a German chemist. It was also made in the United States by the Sandwich Glass Works and other glass houses during the late 1800s.

Val St. Lambert Cristalleries – The firm is located in Belgium, and was founded in 1825. It is still in operation.

Vasa Murrhina glassware was produced in quantity at the Vasa Murrhina Art Glass Company of Sandwich, Massachusetts, during the late 1800s. John C. Devoy, assignor to the firm, registered a patent on July 1, 1884, for the process of decorating glassware with particles of mica flakes coated with copper, gold, nickel or silver, sandwiched between an inner layer of clear or transparent colored glass. The ware was also produced by other American glass firms and in England.

Vaseline Glass – The term "vaseline" refers to color only, as it resembles the greenish-yellow color typical of the oily petroleum jelly known as Vaseline. This ware has been produced in a variety of patterns both here and in Europe – from the late 1800s. It has been made in both clear and opaque yellow, vaseline combined with clear glass, and occasionally the two colors are combined in one piece.

Verlys Glass is a type of art glass produced in France after 1931. The Heisey Glass Company, Newark, Ohio, produced identical glass for a short time, after having obtained the rights and formula from the French factory. French produced ware can be identified from the American product by the signature. The French is mold marked, whereas the American glass is etched script signed.

Wavecrest Glass is an opaque white glassware made from the late 1890s by French factories and the Pairpoint Manufacturing Company at New Bedford, Massachusetts. Items were decorated by the C.F. Monroe Company of Meriden, Connecticut, with painted pastel enamels. The name wavecrest was used after 1898 with the initials for the company "C.F.M. Co." Operations ceased during World War II.

Webb Glass was made by Thomas Webb & Sons of Stourbridge, England, during the late Victorian period. The firm produced a variety of different types of art and cameo glass.

Wheeling Peachblow – With its simple lines and delicate shadings, Wheeling Peachblow was produced soon after 1883 by J.H. Hobbs, Brockunier and Company at Wheeling, West Virginia. It is a two-layered glass, lined or cased inside with an opaque, milk-white type of plated glassware. The outer layer shades from a bright yellow at the base to a mahogany red at the top. The majority of pieces produced are in the glossy finish.

1354

1355

1356

1357

1358

1359

A-IA Mar. 2004

Jackson's International Auctioneers

1354 **Victorian Pattern Glass** incl. beaded grape, Colorado Priscilla & Croesus, 8 pcs. **$92**

1355 **Bohemian Etched Glass** in cranberry incl. a pair of lustres, ht. 13in., & bowl, 3 pcs. **$373**

1356 **Cranberry Flashed Glass,** Bohemian, incl. vase, pitcher & bottle, all late 20th C. **$172**

1357 **Bohemian Cut Glass,** ruby flashed, incl. 2 vases, pitcher & 2 tumble ups, all late 20th C. **$195**

1358 **Bohemian Etched Glass** incl. 12 pc. set, late 20th C. **$195**

1359 **Assorted Glass** incl. an Independence candy container, Bohemian goblet, bread plate, tumbler & amber pitcher w/blue handle. **$80**

1340

1341

1342

1343

1344

A-IA Mar. 2004

Jackson's International Auctioneers

1340 **Victorian Epergne** in green opal. glass w/lily vases & posy baskets, ht. 23in. **$1,265**

1341 **Pickle Castors,** pair, together w/an assembled condiment set. **$373**

1342 **Victorian Pickle Castors** in cranberry thumbprint & opal. swirl. The latter has a replaced lid. **$517**

1343 **Victorian Cut Glass Castor & Condiment Set,** together w/sgn. pickle castor w/replaced lid. **$373**

1344 **Victorian Brides' Baskets** in silvered frames. The first cased cranberry, the second w/enameled dec. **$575**

A-IA Oct. 2003
Jackson's International Auctioneers
797 **Center Piece Bowl,** in pink shaded glass cased over yellow w/mother-of pearl Herringbone patt., w/enameled florals on a silvered metal base mkd. Meriden, dia. 11in. **$1,840**

A-IA Oct. 2003
Jackson's International Auctioneers
798 **Satin Glass Epergne,** Eng. by Webb, mother-of-pearl Diamond Quilt patt., consisting of 4 posy vases & embossed clear leaf forms rising from a circular mirror plateau, ht. 10in. **$1,840**

1345

1346

1347

1348

1349

1350

1351

1352

1353

A-IA Mar. 2004
Jackson's International Auctioneers
1345 **Group of Victorian Glass & Silvered Pieces** incl. a matching sugar bowl & creamer, enameled bud vase & sugar bowl w/no handles. **$345**
1346 **Victorian Glass** incl. a Thousand Eye salt shaker & a Cone & Nine Panel Thumbprint muffineers. **$161**
1347 **Victorian Custard Glass Tankard** w/hand painted dec., ht. 11in. **$57**
1348 **Custard Glass** consisting of a Winged Scroll cream & sugar, Intaglio Flower tumbler & spooner w/reprs., a Geneva Shell cruet & three piece set w/beaded swags, 8 pcs. **$575**
1349 **Northwood Custard Glass** in Louis XV patt., incl. butter dish, 2 sugars, 2 creamers, covered butter & 2 waste bowls, 7 pcs. **$345**
1350 **Victorian Pattern Glass** in assorted patterns incl. Lacy Medallion, CO, & Croesus toothpick holder, 11 pcs. **$172**
1351 **Mary Gregory Style Glass** in various colors, 6 pcs. **$920**
1352 **Victorian Colored Glass** incl. a four pc. inkwell & five pc. enameled cordial set. **$149**
1353 **Cranberry Glass,** 3 of which are Victorian w/applied clear dec., 6 pcs. **$195**

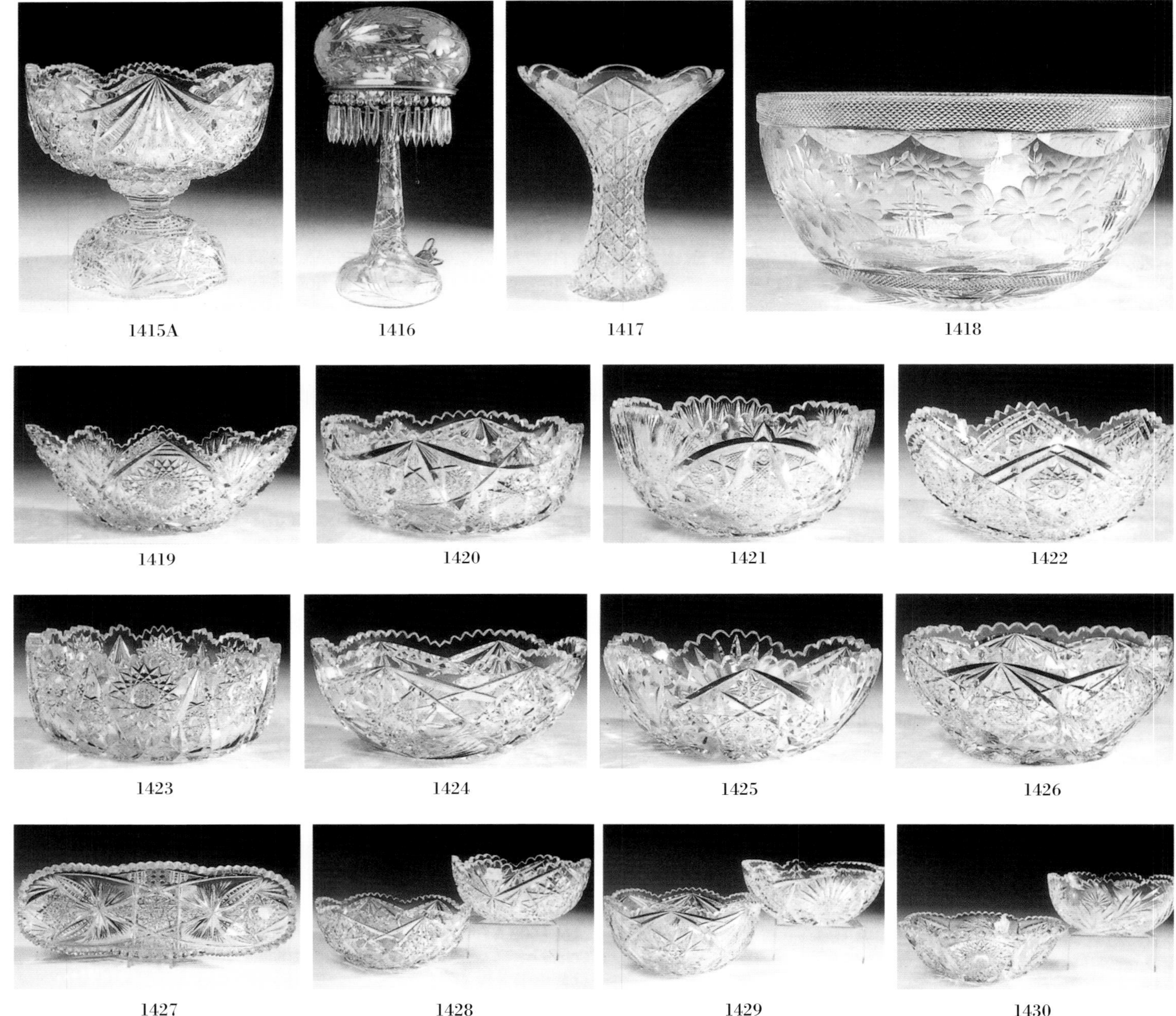
1415A 1416 1417 1418

1419 1420 1421 1422

1423 1424 1425 1426

1427 1428 1429 1430

A-IA Mar. 2004
Jackson's International Auctioneers
Cut Glass

1415 **Punch Bowl,** ca. 1900 w/cut hobstar & fan designs, raised on bell shape pedestal, unmarked, ht. 11, dia. 12in. **$920**

1416 **Table Lamp,** early 20th C., w/mushroom shade & cut prisms, ht. 23in. **$750**

1417 **Large Vase,** mid-20th C., w/paneled hobstar dec., ht. 11in. **$103**

1418 **Libbey Bowl,** sgn., ca. 1910 w/etched floral designs & diamond point bands, dia. 9in. **$258**

1419 **Bowl** of oval form w/large hobstar & fan designs, lg. 11in. **$184**

1420 **Bowl** w/hobstar & diamond patterns, dia. 8in. **$92**

1421 **Bowl** w/cut buttons, arches & fan designs, dia. 8in. **$57**

1422 **Brilliant Bowl** cut with buttons, hobstars & arches, dia. 9in. **$149**

1423 **Bowl** w/hobstar & arches throughout, dia. 8in. **$126**

1424 **Tuthill Bowl,** ca. 1910 w/hobstar & arches design, sgn. in base, dia. 8in. **$126**

1425 **Hawkes Bowl,** early 20th C., cut w/hobstars, diamonds & fans, sgn. in base, dia. 8in. **$161**

1426 **Libbey Bowl,** early 20th C., w/hobstar designs, sgn. in base, dia.8in. **$115**

1427 **Pitkin & Brooks Celery,** early 20th C., w/hobstar, fan & button designs, sgn. in base P&B, dia. 8in. **$103**

1428 **Pair of Bowls** w/hobstar & fan patterns, first sgn. Tuthill, second sgn. Hawkes, dia. 8in. **$287**

1429 **Pair of Bowls** w/sunburst designs, dia. 8in. **$161**

1430 **Pair of Bowls,** the first w/thistle designs sgn. Clark, the second is unmarked w/hobstar & buzzsaws, dia. 8 & 9¼in. **$103**

A-IA Nov. 2003

Jackson's International Auctioneers

Victorian Epergnes

1005 **Cranberry Glass,** ca. 1900 w/ruffled rigaree spirals & 2 hanging baskets, ht. 21in. **$747**

1006 **Cranberry Glass,** ca. 1900, highlighted by 4 crystal rimmed trumpets & clear baskets, ht. 23in. **$1,265**

1007 **Cranberry Glass,** ca. 1900 w/trumpets & baskets, some arms reset. **$977**

A-IA Nov. 2003

Jackson's International Auctioneers

1032 **Art Glass Basket,** ca. early 20th C., cased in white satin glass w/rose int., ht. 10in. **$345**

1033 **Cranberry Cut To Clear Bowl,** ca. 20th C., dia. 7in. **$46**

1034 **Cranberry Cruet,** ca. early 20th C., w/clear applied handle & faceted stopper, ht. 7in. **$92**

1035 **Opalescent Cruet,** ca. 20th C., translucent glass w/swirl patt. ht. 6in. **$57**

1036 **Francisware Cream Pitcher,** ca. 1880 by Hobbs Brockunier, ht. 6in. **$46**

1037 **Frosted Rubina Glass Pitcher** by Hobbs Brockunier w/overall hobnail dec. **$258**

1038 **Condiment Set** in silver plate caddy, ca. 1890, consisting of pair of shakers & a mustard, ht. 7in. **$86**

1039 **Vasa Murrhina Tumblers,** ca. 1890, pink w/silver flecks. **$92**

1040 **Hobnail Syrup Pitcher,** ca. 1900, ht. 6in. **$115**

1041 **Cranberry Ruffled Rim Basket** w/overshot finish, ca. 1900, dia. 11in. **$57**

1042 **New Martinsville Bride's Basket,** ca. 1900, w/ruffled rim, dia. 10in. **$218**

A-IA Oct. 2003
Jackson's International Auctioneers
Burmese Decorated Satin Glass

821 **Fairy Lamp,** mkd. Thomas Webb & Sons w/Clarke's insert, Eng., ht. 6in. **$2,070**

822 **Biscuit Jar,** Am., Mt. Washington w/embossed silvered lid & handle, mkd. Crown Milano w/paper label, ht. 8in. **$1,035**

823 **Mt. Washington Vases,** matched pair, late 19th C., ht. 6in. **$1,092**

824 **English Webb Vase,** late 19th C., unmarked, ht. 4in. **$345**

825 **English Webb Vase** w/flared fluted rim & Webb Patent etched mark, ht. 3in. **$460**

826 **Webb Rose Bowl,** unmarked, late 19th C., ht. 2¼in. **$316**

827 **Webb Vases,** unmarked, matched pair, ht. 3¼in. **$546**

828 **Webb Vases,** one w/enameled florals, the other w/acorns, unmarked. **$546**

829 **English Webb Vase,** late 19th C. w/gilt berries, unmarked. ht. 5in. **$373**

A-IA Nov. 2004
Jackson's International Auctioneers

1016 **Northwood Rubina Glass,** ca. 1900, incl. a Royal Ivy frosted pitcher, covered jar, translucent tumbler, toothpick & pair of Royal Oak shakers. **$258**

1017 **Pigeon Blood Water Pitcher,** ca. 1920 w/clear handle, ht. 9in. **$230**

1018 **Amberina Tumblers,** five, Inverted Thumbprint patt. **$172**

1019 **Amberina Water Pitcher** in a diagonal ribbed form w/reeded handle, ht. 8in. **$172**

1020 **Reverse Amberina Pitcher** in Coin Spot patt, ht. 6in. **$172**

1021 **Amberina Fingerbowl & Under Plate,** dia. 6in. **$57**

A-IA Oct. 2003
Jackson's International Auctioneers
Mother-of-Pearl Satin Glass

802 **Continental Vases,** first half of 20th C., in Diamond Quilt patt., ht. 7in. **$201**

803 **Satin Glass Handled Vases,** first half of 20th C., in Herringbone patt., **$431**

804 **Fairy Lamp,** late 19th C., in 2 parts, in Diamond Quilt patt., ht. 7in. **$431**

805 **Vase,** ca. 1900 w/Diamond Quilt patt., ht. 7in. **$172**

806 **Vase,** late 19th C., in Flower & Acorn patt., ht. 6in. **$891**

807 **Bowl,** late 19th C., w/ Peacock Feather design. **$632**

A-IA Nov. 2003
Jackson's International Auctioneers

993 **Mt. Washington Burmese Vase,** ca. 1890, in Hawthorn patt. ht. 4in. **$316**

994 **Burmese Sugar Bowl,** Eng. by Webb, dia. 4in. **$230**

995 **Burmese Fairy Lamp**, ca. 1890, insert mkd. Trademark Cricklite Clark's, ht. 5in. **$1,150**

996 **Mt. Washington Burmese Cup** w/a later bird dec. **$80**

997 **Reverse Amberina Water Pitcher,** ca. 1900 in Diamond patt. **$115**

998 **Two Victorian pcs.,** ca. 1900, End of Day tumbler & an Amberina bowl. **$80**

A-IA Nov. 2003
Jackson's International Auctioneers

999 **Mt. Washington Biscuit Jar,** ca. 1890 w/repl. lid, sgn. C.F. Monroe, ht. 6in. **$230**

1000 **Wave Crest Letter Holder** by Monroe, in blown pillow design & dec. w/ flowers, ht. 4in. **$402**

1001 **Mt. Washington Flower Frog,** ca. 1890 in opal glass, dia. 5in. **$345**

1002 **Wave Crest Ferner** by Monroe & dec. w/enameled flowers, w/orig. insert, dia. 7in. **$201**

1003 **Wave Crest Dresser Box** by Monroe, in Helmschmeid form. **$316**

1004 **Mt. Washington Salt Shakers,** ca. 1890, incl. two tomato & one egg. **$230**

A-OH Nov. 2003
Early Auction Company
519 **English Cameo Rose Jar** by Thomas Webb & Sons, ht. 8¾in. **$19,500**

A-OH Nov. 2003 Early Auction Company
479 **English Cameo Pitcher** w/applied gold handle sgn. GLF, ht. 3¾in. & matching pink fish scale cameo bowl, cased in white, dia. 4¼in. **$900**

A-OH Nov. 2003 Early Auction Company
Scent Bottles
483 **Textured Blue & Frosted Cameo Glass** w/sterling mounted cap chased in floral relief, ht. 3¾in. **$375**
485 **English Cameo Perfume,** flattened ovoid shape in citron, carved front & back, ht. 3¼in. **$650**
486 **Prussian Blue Perfume** by Thomas Webb & Sons, Eng. w/hallmarked cap & monogram, lg. 8in. **$1,250**

A-IA Oct. 2003 Jackson's International Auctioneers
1033 **Set of McKee Croesus,** 32 pcs., ca. late 19th C., in deep purple glass w/gold highlights. **$2,645**

A-OH July 2004 Early Auction Company
Rainbow Mother of Pearl

555 **Footed Bowl** w/Diamond Quilted patt, mkd. Patent w/berry pontil & rests on clear glass feet w/roughness. ht. 6¼in. **$3,400**

554 **Rose Bowl** w/Diamond Quilted design, mkd. Patent, ht. 4in. **$1,900**

551 **Vase** w/crimped fold down rim w/Diamond Quilted design, ht. 7in. **$800**

553 **Circular Bowl** w/Diamond Quilted design, mkd. Patent, ht. 2¾in. **$1,100**

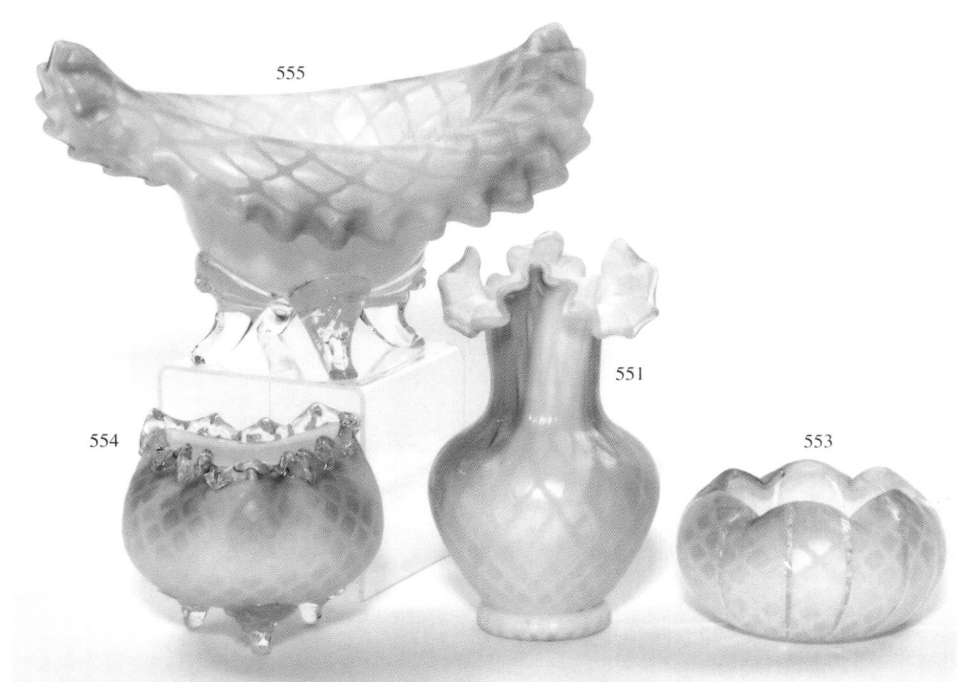

A-OH Nov. 2003 Early Auction Company
Pomona Glass

351A **Center Bowl** in Cornflower patt., w/petaled base, ht. 2½in. **$500**

351B **Finger Bowl,** 2nd ground, Cornflower patt., ht. 2½, dia. 5in. **$50**

351 **Finger Bowl,** first ground in gold over frosted body, dia. 5in. **$50**

351C **Toothpick,** Quilted patt., w/tricon inverted top, ht. 2in. & a punch cup in Quilted patt., ht. 2½in., both first ground pcs. **$275**

349 **Water Pitcher,** second ground w/frosted inverted coinspots, ht. 7¼in. **$70**

350 **Tumblers,** two are first ground, one w/Diamond Optic patt., & the other Diamond Optic & Leaf patt. The other two are second ground, one w/blueberries & gold bands at top & bottom, the second one w/cornflower dec. **$125**

A-IA Nov. 2003 Jackson's International Auctioneers
French Cameo Enameled Glass
564 **Scenic Vase** w/a summer lake scene, sgn. in black enamel Daum Nancy w/cross of Lorraine, ht. 4¼in. **$2,070**
565 **Vase,** cut & enameled w/red berries on green leafy stems, sgn. in cameo Daum Nancy w/cross, ht. 4¼in. **$2,300**

664 **Burgun Schverer Vase** sgn. BX Co., Verrerie, D'art Delorraine Déposé, ht. 4in. **$1,800**

A-ME May 2004 James D. Julia, Inc.
665 **Daum Nancy Landscape Vase,** sgn. w/Cross of Lorraine, & France, ht. 10⅜in. **$8,625**

A-IA Nov. 2003 Jackson's International Auctioneers
Daum Nancy French Cameo Glass
560 **Enameled Glass Vase,** ca. 1910, footed form, sgn. in green enamel on foot Daum Nancy w/cross of Lorraine, ht. 12½in. **$3,450**
561 **Monumental Vase** w/winter scene, ca. 1900, sgn. in black w/cross, ht. 13in. **$4,830**
562 **Cameo Enameled Vase,** ca. 1910, ovoid form & signed w/cross of Lorraine, ht. 7¼in. **$4,140**
563 **Vase,** ca. 1900, of ovoid pillow form w/enameled scene & sgn. in black enamel w/cross, ht. 4¼in. **$4,025**

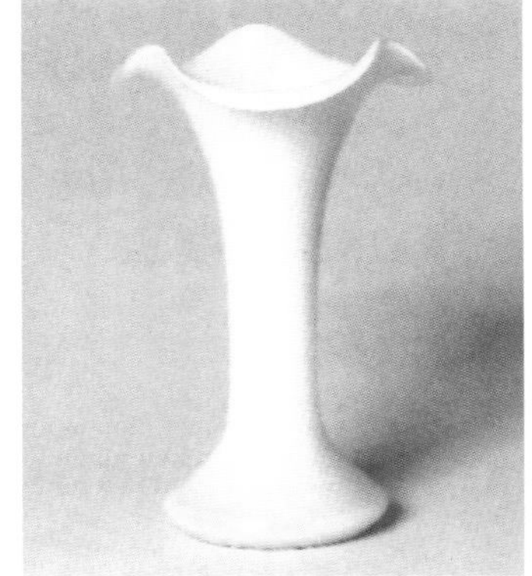

A-ME Nov. 2003 James D. Julia, Inc.
667 **Steuben Tree Trunk Vase,** sgn., small trunk has crack, ht. 5⅞in. **$201**
668 **Steuben Tree Trunk Vase,** sgn. w/Fleur-de-Lis mark, ht. 6in. **$230**
669 **Candlestick,** Steuben, sgn. Aurene w/iridescence, ht. 8in. **$920**
670 **Steuben Perfume,** jade w/alabaster stopper, unsgn., ht. 4½in. **$517**
671 **Steuben Perfume,** Rosaline glass w/alabaster foot, ht. 8in. **$805**
673 **Centerbowl,** sgn. Aurene F. Carder, ht. 2¾, dia. 12in. **$230**
675 **Gold Aurene Vase,** sgn. Steuben Aurene, w/six sided top & pedestal foot applied, ht. 8in. **$690**
676 **Steuben Celeste Vase** w/applied foot, unsgn. ht. 6in. **$172**
701 **Steuben Vase** w/swirl ribbing & flared top, ht. 5½in. **$172**
702 **Steuben Trumpet Vase,** Ivrene color w/purple highlights, open bubble on rim & chips to pontil, ht. 9¼in. **$143**
743 **Jean Beck Vases,** in rich red crystal w/faceted band near foot & fluted design dec. the body of each vase, sgn., ht. 5¼ & 6in. **$57**
748 **Durand King Tut Vase,** sgn. on base Durand, ht. 5¼in. **$1,035**

A-ME Nov. 2003 James D. Julia, Inc.
671A **Aurene Footed Bowl** w/applied feet & stretched rim, sgn. dia. 7in. **$258**

A-ME Nov. 2003 James D. Julia, Inc.
769 **Loetz Bowl** in Bronze Holder, bowl has rolled lip & all over swirls of blue, purple, green & gold iridescence, overall ht. 8, wd. 10in. **$780**

A-ME Nov. 2003 James D. Julia, Inc.
703 **Steuben Bristol Vase** w/inverted thumbprint design & white threading around rim, unsgn. ht. 6¼in. **$86**
766 **Loetz Vase** in gold iridescent w/applied knobs, ht. 4¾in. **$2,070**
767 **Vase,** sgn. Loetz Austria, dec. w/swirling silver-blue iridescent lines against a bronze background, ht. 7¼in. **$2,520**
730 **Imperial Vase** w/cobalt blue ground & orange vine dec., ht. 7in. **$977**

A-IA Oct. 2004
Jackson's International Auctioneers
Cut Glass Unless Noted
606 **Tray,** North Star patt. by Hawkes w/some chips, dia. 15in. **$2,645**
607 **Vase,** early 20th C., cut w/stars & horizontal bars, sgn. Hawkes, ht. 12in. **$195**
608 **Water Pitcher,** early 20th C., cut w/diamonds, bars, & stars, ht. 8in. **$184**
609 **Vase,** sgn. Hawkes, cut w/diamonds & ribbed panels, ht. 9in. **$230**
610 **Bowl,** sgn. Hawkes, cut w/diamonds, stars, fans & arches, dia. 9in. **$258**
611 **Mayonnaise Bowl,** cut w/diamonds, bars & fans, together w/a nappy. **$34**
612 **Sabino Figure,** early 20th C. of two birds, mkd. Sabino France. **$492**
613 **Carafe,** early 20th C. w/rim chips, cut w/bars & stars, ht. 7in. **$34**
614 **Salts,** set of four, cut w/panels, incl. 4 sterling spoons. **$40**
615 **Bottle,** cut w/diamonds in attached panels, ht. 9in. **$103**
616 **Lalique Crystal Ashtray** w/embossed designs, sgn. dia. 6in. **$46**
617 **Celery** w/buzzsaw & fan designs, lg. 10in. **$34**
618 **Compote** by Wright, sgn., cut w/diamonds, arches & fans, dia. 6in. **$69**
619 **Silver Mounted Bottle,** mid-20th C., cut w/buttons, stars & diamonds, w/Continental hallmarks, ht. 9in. **$115**

A-ME Nov. 2003 James D. Julia, Inc.
705 **Steuben Swirl Vase,** sgn. w/Fleur-de-Lis mark, ht. 7in. **$230**

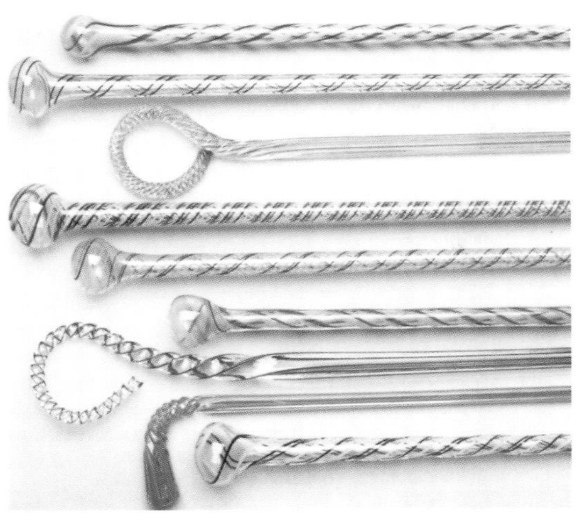

A-OH June 2004Garth's Arts & Antiques
835 **Three Glass Canes,** two have knob ends, either yellow, blue & red swirls, lg. 53, 63½in.; third is aqua ribbed w/round shepherd handle w/minor end damage, lg. 48in. **$316**
836 **Four Glass Canes,** three w/knob ends w/swirls, lg. 53, 57 & 61in.; the fourth has blue swirls & twisted detail w/shepherd handle & edge damage. **$546**
837 **Three Canes,** one w/knob end & white swirls, lg. 45in., & two w/crook handles, clear lg. 50½in., & clear w/red, lg. 48in. **$373**

A-IA Oct. 2004
Jackson's International Auctioneers
620 **Victorian Cake Stand,** late 19th C., dia. 12in. **$28**
621 **Compote** by Thompson Glass Co., ca. 1890, pattern glass in Summit patt. **$23**
622 **Victorian Pattern Glass Compote,** ht. 14in. **$34**
623 **Compote,** Log Cabin patt, ca. 1875, w/chip on lid, ht. 10in. **$5**
624 **Compote,** late 19th C., w/embossed rope design,lg. 10in. **$46**
625 **Cut Glass Wine Jug,** w/star, diamond & fan designs, ht. 8in. **$125**
626 **Square Bowl** by Sinclaire w/monogram & chip on corner, 7in. **$316**
627 **Cut Glass Tumblers,** Newport patt., by J.D. Bergen, ht. 4in. **$80**
627A **Heisey Crystal Compote** in Tudor patt. w/monogram, ht. 6in. **$40**
628 **Cut Glass Jug,** w/button & diamond patt., ht. 7in. **$86**
629 **Cut Glass Decanter** w/button & diamond patt, ht. 9in. **$46**
630 **Crystal Candlesticks,** mid-20th C., ht. 6in. **$17**
631 **Victorian Pressed Glass Pickle Castor** in silvered frame, ht. 11in. **$161**
632 **Heisey Cologne Bottles,** Hexagon Stem #487 w/enameled flowers, ht. 7in. **$34**
633 **Orrefors Vase** w/etched doves, sgn., w/minor flake, ht. 6in. **$74**
634 **Cut Glass Low Bowls** w/diamond & ribs dec., sgn. Libbey. **$80**
635 **Lalique Frosted Knife Rest,** mid-20th C., lg. 5¼in. **$34**
636 **Crystal items,** early 20th C., consisting of a syrup, cut glass muffineer w/silvered top & a small syrup w/cut designs. **$69**
637 **Cut Glass Nappy,** mid-20th C., w/hobnail star & diamonds, lg. 7in. **$17**
638 **Crystal Humidor,** ca. 1900 w/embossed silver lid, ht. 7in. **$46**

709 710 711 712
714 715 720 731

A-IA Mar. 2004
Jackson's International Auctioneers

709 **Stemware,** 29 pcs. of crystal incl. Meadow Rose, Woodland, Chantilly & other patterns, partially illus. lot. **$207**

710 **Crystal Stemware** in assorted patterns including Buttercup, Manor & other patterns, 19 pcs., partially illus. lot. **$80**

711 **Crystal Stemware** in various patterns incl. Fountain, Willow, Romance & other Fostoria, 26 pcs., partially illus. **$149**

712 **Assortment of Stemware** incl. Heisey Titania, Daffodil & other patterns, 31 pieces, partially illus. **$195**

714 **Amber Depression Glass,** partially illus., 11 pcs. incl. Patrician. **$34**

715 **Blue Dinnerware,** 28 pieces incl. Fostoria Priscilla & Capri patterns. Partially illus. **$126**

720 **Colored Etched Stemware** in various patterns incl. Fostoria, partial lot of 32 pcs. **$126**

731 **Assortment of Fenton glass** incl. bowls & baskets, assortment of 11 pcs. **$161**

757 758 759 760
761 762 763 764

A-IA Mar 2004
Jackson's International Auctioneers

757 **Pink & Blue Depression Glass** w/Heisey, Old Sandwich & Cambridge Georgian patt., 84 pcs. **$195**

758 **Crystal** incl. Fostoria Contour patt. & Federal Heritage., 67 pcs. **$69**

759 **Opaque Glass,** group of 120 pcs. incl. petal ware, cremax & ovoid. **$195**

760 **Assorted Glass & Ceramic Dinnerware** incl. opaque varieties & carnival glass, 68 pcs. **$218**

761 **Assorted Glass** incl. Heisey, Depression & various table accessories, 61 pcs. **$126**

762 **Etched & Satin Glassware** w/enameled Fenton, 26 pcs. **$161**

763 **Cape Cod, Kings Crown & Depression glass,** 22 pcs. **$184**

764 **Crystal Group,** 12 pcs. incl. an Irena whiskey, Wedgwood ice bucket & perfume w/sterling top. **$195**

A-ME Nov. 2003
James D. Julia, Inc.

768 **Loetz Vase,** iridescent gold w/orange oil spots, ht. 6½in. **$460**

A-IA Mar 2004
Jackson's International Auctioneers
Partially Illustrated Lots

737 **Fostoria Century Crystal** incl. four plates, 2 sherbets, candy dishes, a footed bowl & ladles. **$115**

738 **Pattern Glass,** 5 pcs., 19th C. pattern glass incl. footed dish, compote, vase & domed butters. **$57**

739 **Blue Dress Lamps** together w/2 figural bottles & 2 lamp shades. **$103**

740 **Crystal Glassware** incl. mostly trays & platters, 11 pcs. **$92**

741 **Collection of 11 Pitchers,** incl. pink Adam, amber Cambridge, Heisey & later pcs. **$207**

742 **Fostoria Console Bowls** incl. Versailles & a 3 pc. Duncan console set. **$103**

743 **Depression Era Glass,** 17 pcs. incl. vases & bowls. **$184**

744 **Cremax Dinnerware i**n two different decorations, 95 pcs. **$172**

745 **Bowls & Trays,** group of 7, incl. Lattice & Rose patt. w/other pieces in color. **$126**

746 **Depression Era Glass,** 34 pcs. in a variety of patterns, shapes & colors. **$172**

747 **Group of Mid Century Glass,** 32 pcs. incl. two beverage sets. **$57**

748 **Crystal,** 27 pcs. incl. Navarre, Provincial & Romance patterns. **$184**

749 **Trays & Platters** in various colors & etched patterns, incl. 15 pcs. **$80**

750 **Depression & earlier period glass** incl. 33 pcs. w/4 pcs. of Akro Agate glass & various cruets. **$115**

751 **Table Shakers,** assortment of 28 pcs. **$230**

752 **Depression Kitchenware,** 39 pcs., incl. Fireking ovenware. **$138**

753 **Depression Era Crystal i**ncl. 67 pcs. w/large variety of Pineapple & Swirl patt. glass. **$138**

754 **Assortment of Mostly Tumblers** incl. Heisey, cut glass, enameled, cups & saucers, 53 pcs. **$103**

755 **Collection of Depression Glassware** in various patterns, 72 pcs. **$195**

756 **Depression Glassware,** 85 pcs. in various colors & patterns. **$258**

A-IA Mar. 2004
Jackson's International Auctioneers
1034 **Rose Bowl,** Westmoreland, Louisa patt., in amethyst, together w/an Imperial Glass grape carafe in amethyst. **$126**
1035 **Creamer,** Colorado patt. in green, ht. 4in. **$92**
1036 **Carnival Glass Bowl** by Millersburg in Nesting Swan patt., dia. 9in. **$92**
1037 **Carnival Glass Bowl** by Northwood in Grape & Cable patt., amethyst, **$103**
1038 **Consolidated Oil Lamp,** ca. 1900, in Cosmos patt., w/floral dec., chips to fitters, ht. 8in. **$195**
1039 **Covered Butter** in Cosmos patt., w/floral dec., w/slight chips around lid. **$69**
1040 **Consolidated Lamp** in Cosmos patt. w/flower dec., ht. 8in. **$172**
1041 **Cosmos Glass,** tumbler w/ pair of salt & peppers. **$23**

A-OH Nov. 2003 Early Auction Company
New England Peachblow Unless Noted
111 **Lily Vase** w/ruffled top which sits atop raised opal disc, ht. 12in. **$550**
114 **Gunderson Peachblow** w/bulbous stopper, ht. 11¾in. **$350**
117A **Rose Bowl** w/crimped top in satin finish, ht. 3½in. **$200**
119 **Jack-in-the Pulpit Vases,** pair, L&R, w/wide mouth on yellow ribbed & cased standards & raised discs, ht. 14¼ & 14¾in. **$450**
108 **Gunderson Peachblow Lily Vase** w/tapering standard on tinted circular base, ht. 9in. **$200**
116 **Wild Rose Lily Vase** w/tapering stem & circular disc, ht. 6in. **$650**
112 **Lily Vase** w/ruffled top shading from fuchsia to opal, ht. 5in. **$375**
115 **Wild Rose Lily Vase** shading to opal w/circular disc, ht. 9in. **$650**
113 **Jack-in-the Pulpit Vase** w/glossy finish, ht. 6¾in. **$750**
117 **Wild Rose Tumbler** w/glossy finish, ht. 3¾in. **$150**
118 **Wild Rose Sauce Dish,** shades from deep fuchsia to cream, dia. 4in. **$125**
110 **Gunderson Peachblow Jack-in-the Pulpit Vase,** ht. 9¼in. **$150**
108 **Gunderson Peachblow Lily Vase** w/tinted circular disc, ht. 9in. **$200**

Opposite
A-OH July 2004 Early Auction Company
Amberina
244 **Water Pitcher & Tumbler,** Inverted Thumbprint, w/reeded handle. **$370**
245 **Water Pitcher** w/applied reeded handle, Optic Ribbed patt. **$400**
247 **Footed Water Pitcher** w/reeded handle & tumbler in Thumbprint patt. n/s
248 **Spooner,** Diamond Quilted patt., ht. 4¾in. **$475**
256 **Bottle,** attributed to Libbey, in Coin Spot patt., ht. 8in. **$450**
254 **Libbey Finger Bowl,** Diamond Quilted patt., together w/underplate. **$170**
250 **Toothpick** w/squared mouth, ht. 2¼in. **$95**
252 **Shot Glass** attributed to Brayden Pairpoint, ht. 2¼in. **$175**
251 **Tumbler,** Inverted Thumbprint patt. ht. 3¾in., together w/Reverse Amberina Punch Cup, ht. 2¾in. **$75**
253 **Libbey Toothpick,** barrel shaped in Diamond Quilted patt., ht. 2½in. **$450**
257 **Stemmed Wine** in Optic Ribbed patt., ht. 4¾in. **$450**
246 **New England Ribbed Lemonades** w/applied amber handles, ht. 5in. **$50**
255 **Finger Bowl** w/crimped rim, wd. 5½in., together w/punch cup in the Optic Ribbed patt. **$250**

A-ME May 2004 James D. Julia, Inc.
556 **Gallé Cameo Vase** w/frosted background, sgn. **$632**

A-ME May 2004 James D. Julia, Inc.
454 **Loetz Titanium Vase** w/sterling silver overlay, unsgn., marked Sterling, ht. 8¼in. **$4,945**

A-ME May 2004 James D. Julia, Inc.
558 **Cameo Vase** sgn. Gallé w/frosted background, ht. 11½in. **$5,175**

A-IA Oct. 2003
Jackson's International Auctioneers
841 **Victorian Vase,** Jack-in-the-Pulpit shape, ht. 9in. **$69**
842 **Art Glass Vase,** late 19th C., Jack-in-the Pulpit shape, ht. 9in. **$92**
843 **Underplate,** mother-of-pearl w/spiral ribbed design, dia. 6in. **$46**
844 **Peachblow Basket** w/amber coralene dec., applied amber handle & feet. **$977**
845 **Kralik Peloton Art Glass Bowl,** late 19th C., satin finish w/colored ribbons on opal under clear threading & petal feet, dia. 8in. **$375**
846 **Kralik Peloton Vase** w/ruffled rim dec. w/glass ribbons on opal vertical ribs. ht. 5in. **$143**
847 **Bohemian Stopper Bottle,** ca. 1920, in clear & ruby flashed glass dec. w/grape vines & leaves, ht. 7in. **$115**
848 **Satin Glass Vase** w/coralene decoration, ht. 8in. **$258**
849 **Victorian Basket** w/applied thorny glass handle, ht. 5in. **$92**
850 **Amberina Vase,** ca. 1900 in Thumbprint patt. ht. 9¼in. **$69**
851 **Victorian Cologne Bottle** in blue glass w/floral dec., ht. 5in. **$46**

1

2

3

4

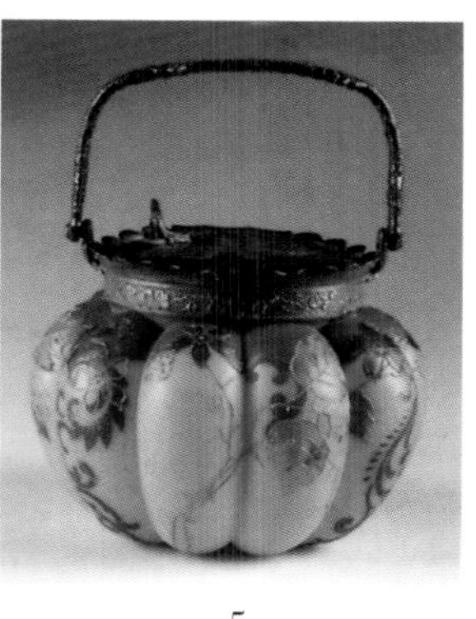

5

6

7

57

58

59

A-ME May 2004 James D. Julia, Inc.

01 **Satin Glass Sugar Shaker,** Peacock Eye patt., sgn. Webb. ht. 5in. **$718**

02 **Biscuit Jar,** Diamond Quilted patt., w/silver collar mkd. Tiffany & Co., overall ht. 9in. **$1,035**

03 **Mt Washington Cracker Jar,** cut velvet patt. w/white cased lining & silver plated collar w/wear to silver & tiny dent., ht. 11in. **$1,020**

04 **Burmese Biscuit Jar,** attributed to Webb w/pinecone design, ht. 6in. **$1,020**

05 **Crown Milano Melon Rib Jar** w/leaf & berry dec., sgn. CM & artist sgn. Top dec. w/embossed crab design, ht. 5¼in. **$1,320**

06 **Crown Milano Melon Rib Biscuit Jar,** w/body dec. of flowers, leaves & raspberries. Silver lid mkd. Pairpoint, overall ht. 9in. **$575**

07 **Wave Crest Cracker Jar** w/hand dec. on all sides, overall ht. 11in., **$460**

57 **English Cameo Vase** w/white floral design & a dragonfly, unsgn. **$1,782**

58 **English Cameo Vase** w/white floral dec., cameo cut on blue ground, ht. 7¼in. **$805**

59 **Webb Cameo Vase** w/white floral & foliage design overall, unsgn., ht. 9½in. **$2,530**

563

575

A-OH July 2004 Early Auction Company

563 **Burmese Sociable** by Thomas Webb & Sons, comprised of 7 pcs., ht 8¾in. **$9,000**

575 **Burmese Epergne** w/metal footed base & holder separated w/insert dec., in the Hawthorn patt., w/small chip to one side flower holder, ht. 11½in. **$900**

A-NH Aug. 2004 Northeast Auctions

175 **Sandwich Glass Crucifix Candlesticks,** the first is deep amethyst, ht. 11½in., the second & third in deep emerald & citrine, ht. 9¾in. **$600**

176 **New England Glass Co. canary yellow Caryatid candlestick,** ht. 9¾in. **$1,400**

A-NH Aug. 2004 Northeast Auctions

Sandwich Glass

177 **Deep Amethyst Plate in** Pressed Plume & Acorn patt. dia. 5¼in. **$225**

178 **Candlesticks,** two similar sapphire blue & an amethyst hexagonal candlestick, probably New England Glass Co., hts. 7 & 7¾in. **$600**

179 **Sandwich Plate,** deep amber, Pressed Plume & Acorn patt., dia. 6in. **$100**

180 **Cobalt Blue Candlestick,** hexagonal, ht. 9¼in. **$500**

181 **Electric Blue Dolphin Candlestick** & a clear example w/each petal candle cup & standard raised on a single-step base, 1st illus. ht. 10in. **$350**

182 **Sandwich Jars,** one black amethyst & clambroth bear, & a cavalier opaque blue pomade w/clambroth plumed hat. Pomade mkd ETS & Co, NY, hts. 3¾ & 4in. **$2,000**

183 **Amber Hexagonal Candlestick,** ht. 9in. **$750**

184 **Pressed Gothic Arch Footed Sugar Bowl & Cover,** ht. 5¼in. **$450**

185 **Clambroth Match Box & Cover** stamped Matches, together w/lavender blue Match Holder, lengths 3¾ & 5in. **$300**

186 **Cobalt Blue Pressed Glass Boat** w/sixteen-point star on stern, lg. 4in. **$1,000**

A-NH Aug. 2004 Northeast Auctions

Sandwich Glass

195 **Pressed Three-Printie Vase** w/gauffered rim, ht. 9¼in. **$225**

196 **Pair of Hexagonal Candlesticks** & a single example, ht. 10¾in. **$750**

197 **Candlestick,** Petal & Loop patt. in pale green, ht. 7in. **$500**

198 **Candlesticks,** pair, each petal candle cup raised on a columnar standard & stepped square base, ht. 9¼in. **$100**

199 **Candlesticks,** three, Sandwich & other makers. First Petal & Loop patt., ht. 7in.; second w/flared standard & sq. base w/outset corners, ht. 4¾in; the third w/petal socket & hexagonal base, ht. 7½in. **$325**

200 **Sugar Bowl,** Pressed Gothic Arch patt.,ht. 5¼in. **$550**

201 **Cologne Bottle,** Star & Punty patt., blown molded, ht. 6¾in. **$275**

A-ME May 2004 James D. Julia, Inc.

600 **Blue Aurene Bowl,** Steuben, slightly ribbed sides. Interior has bright blue iridescence w/flashes of gold, dia. 7in. **$1,092**

602 **Tiffany Vase,** organic form w/Favrile finish, sgn. & numbered, ht. 5¼in. **$1,552**

A-NH Aug. 2004 **Northeast Auctions**
Sandwich Glass
188 **Candlesticks,** pair, translucent blue w/each petal candle cup raised on a columnar standard & stepped square base, ht. 9¼in. **$2,400**
189 **Dolphin Candlesticks,** pair, clambroth w/each petal candle cup & standard raised on a double stepped base, ht. 10in. **$225**
190 **Dolphin Candlestick,** opaque blue & clambroth w/petal candle cup & double stepped base, ht. 10in. **$325**
191 **Candlestick,** opaque blue & clambroth w/petal candle cup & stepped square base, ht. 9¼in. **$125**
192 **Blue Sanded & Clambroth Candlestick** w/petal candle cup, ht. 9¼in. **$100**
193 **Blue Sanded Candlestick,** probably Sandwich on hexagonal base, ht. 7½n. **$50**
194 **Brilliant Opaque Blue Sanded Candlestick** on stepped square base, ht. 9¼in. **$125**

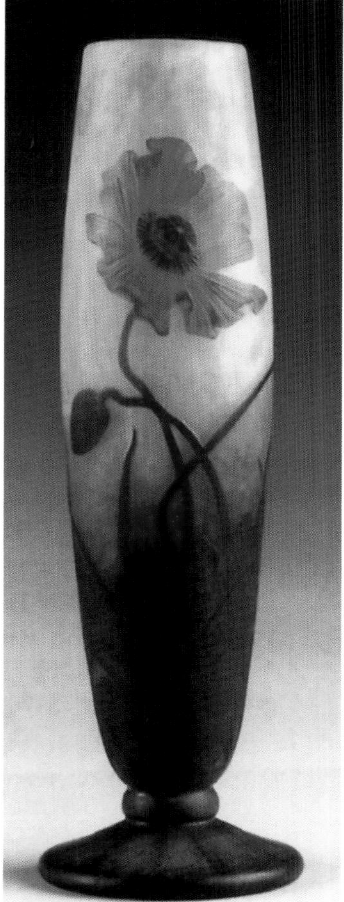

A-May 2004 **James D. Julia, Inc.**
522 **Daum Nancy Wheel Carved Vase** w/poppy dec, sgn. ht. 11½in. **$6,900**

A-NH Aug. 2004 **Northeast Auctions**
Sandwich Spoon Holders
204 **Deep Amethyst,** Pressed Inverted Diamond & Thumbprint patt, ht. 4½in. **$500**
205 **Two Canary Yellow Holders** in above pattern, ht. 4½in. **$300**
206 **Clambroth Holder** in clambroth Horn of Plenty patt., ht. 4½in. **$150**
207 **Fiery Opalescent Holder** in Pressed Punty & Ellipse patt., together w/ an opalescent Excelsior patt. holder, ht. 5in. **$375**
208 **Electric Blue Holder** in Star Diamond patt., ht. 5¼in. **$850**
209 **Electric Blue Holder** in Star Diamond patt, ht. 5¼in. **$200**
210 **Clambroth Holder** in Sandwich Star patt, ht. 5in. **$45**
211 **Opaque White Holder** in Pressed Grape Vine patt., ht. 4½in. **$50**
212 **Canary Yellow Holder,** Pressed Star & Punty patt., ht. 4¾in. **$425**
213 **Canary Yellow Holder,** Pressed Star & Diamond patt., ht. 5¼in. **$275**
214 **Green Spoon Holder** in Prism & Flattened Sawtooth patt., ht. 5in. **$75**

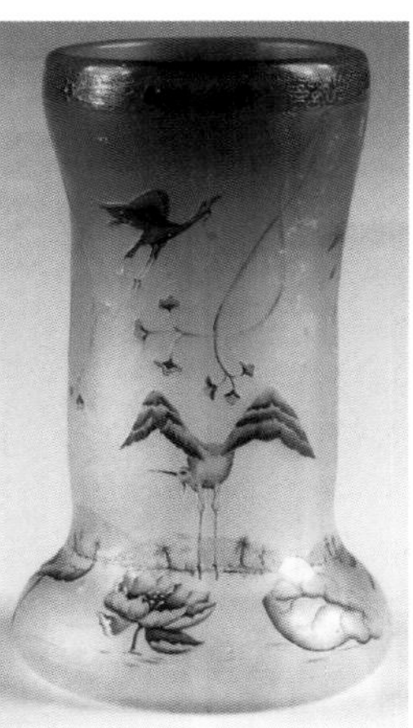

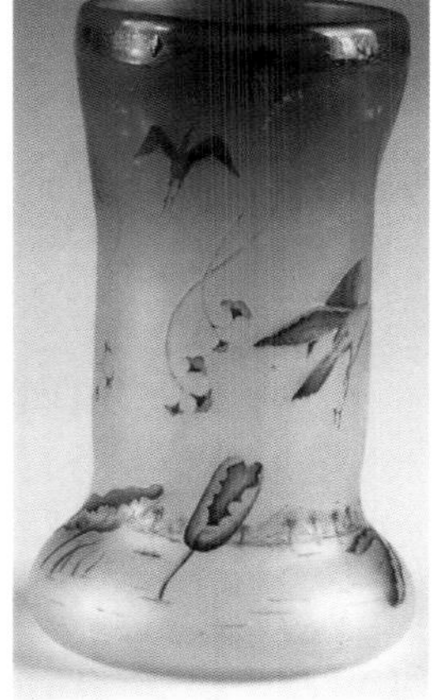

A-May 2004 **James D. Julia, Inc.**
523 **Daum Nancy Vase** w/oriental mystical scene depicting enameled cranes, water lilies, floral design & scenic background, sgn. Daum Nancy w/Cross of Lorraine on bottom, front & reverse shown, ht. 8in. **$4,427**

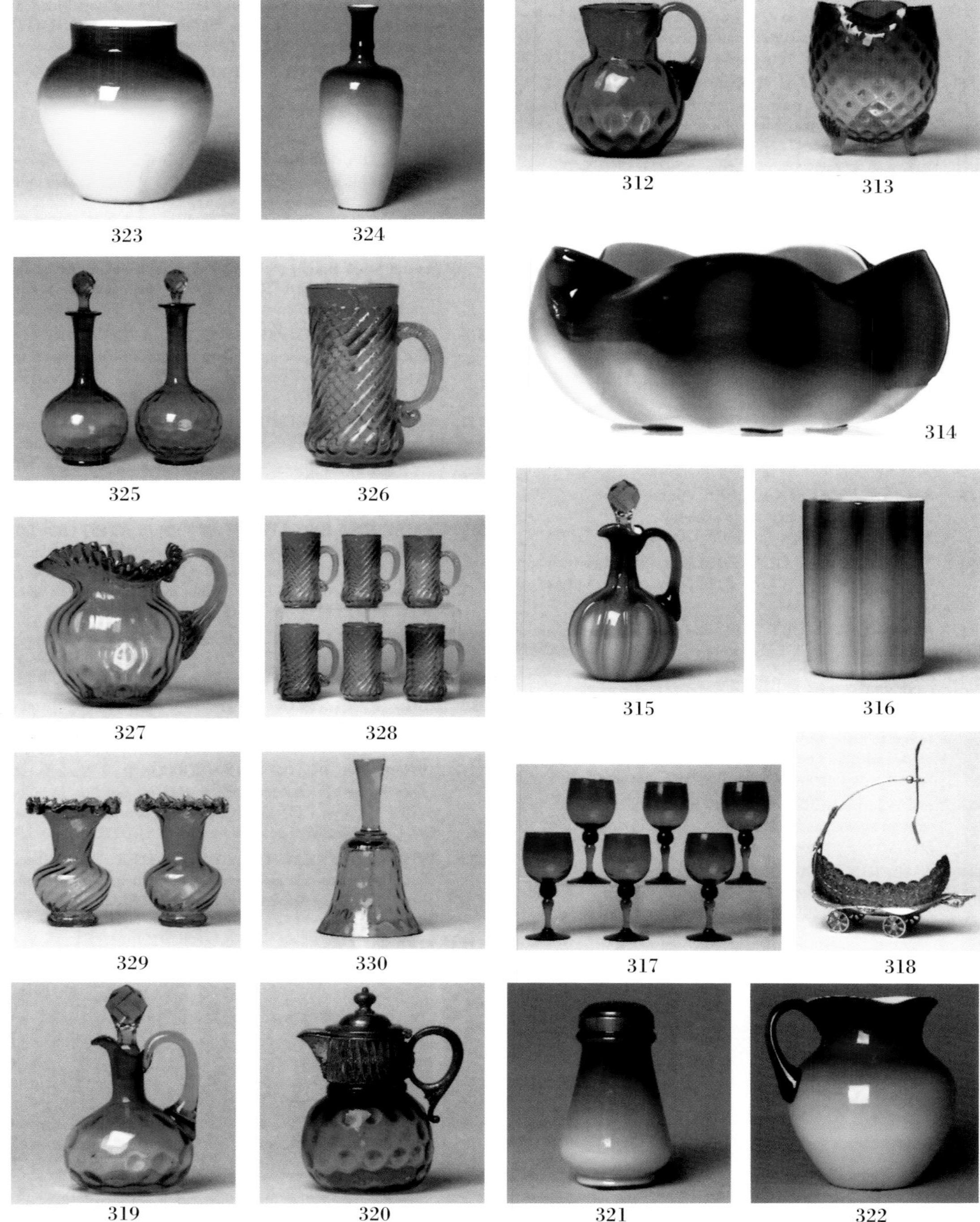

323 324 312 313 325 326 314 327 328 315 316 329 330 317 318 319 320 321 322

A-ME Nov. 2003 James D. Julia, Inc.

323 **Wheeling Peachblow Vase,** cased in white, ht. 6½in. **$1,200**
324 **Morgan Vase,** Wheeling Peach Blow, does not have griffin base, ht. 7¾in. n/s
312 **Amberina Pitcher** w/Inverted Thumbprint patt., ht. 4¾in. **$164**
313 **Amberina Egg Shaped Vase** w/ Diamond Quilted patt., ht. 5½in. **$460**
325 **Decanters,** amberina w/Inverted Thumbprint patt., ht. approx. 11¾in. **$287**
326 **Amberina Mug,** blown-out swirl glass w/applied gold enamel dec. of leaves & branches w/applied amber rope handle, ht. 5½in. **$57**
314 **Plated Amberina Bowl** w/white cased interior, dia. 7½in. **$7,187**
327 **Amberina Pitcher,** Moire patt. w/ applied reeded handle, ht. 5¾in. **$120**
328 **Amberina Mugs,** blown-out Swirl patt. w/applied reeded handles, ht. 5¼in. **$115**
315 **Plated Amberina Cruet** w/creamy lining, amber lapidary stopper & handle w/heat crack, ht. 7in. **$1,437**
316 **Plated Amberina Tumbler,** New England Glass Co., w/creamy white lining, ht. 3¾in. **$1,897**
329 **Amberina Vases,** pair in Swirl patt., w/applied rigaree around the top, ht. 7in. **$115**
330 **Amberina Art Glass Bell** w/Inverted Thumbprint patt., ht. 6in. **$28**
317 **Amberina Goblets,** set of six, attributed to New England Glass Co., ht. 8½in. **$460**
318 **Amberina Boat,** canoe shaped in Daisy & Button patt., w/silver-plated holder & fork, unsgn., overall ht. 9¼in. **$632**
319 **Amberina Cruet,** Inverted Thumbprint patt., w/applied amber handle & lapidary stopper, ht. 5¾in. **$86**
320 **Amberina Syrup** w/orig. metal top, Inverted Thumbprint patt. & minor exterior scratches, ht. 5½in. **$2,242**
321 **Wheeling Peach Blow Sugar Shaker** w/dent & wear to lid, ht. 5¼in. n/s
322 **Wheeling Peach Blow Pitcher** w/ applied amber handle, ht. 7½in. **$1,437**

A-OH Oct. 2004 Early Auction Company, LLC
561 **Tiffany Favrile Vase,** ca. 1919, sgn., ht. 5¼in.
$6,500

A-OH Oct. 2004 Early Auction Company, LLC
743 **Loetz Pitcher,** green iridescent w/applied handle & internally dec. w/stemmed patt., ht. 5in. **$100**
744 **Loetz Vase,** pinch sided w/overall blue iridescent finish, ht. 8in. **$250**

A-OH Oct. 2004 Early Auction Company, LLC
568 **Punch Bowl** w/12 matching cups, ca. 1896, dec. w/flowing freeform designs & sgn. on base Louis C. Tiffany.
$8,250

A-ME Nov. 2004 James D. Julia, Inc.
869 **Muller Frères Luneville Vase,** sgn. in cameo, ht. 13in. **$2,587**

A-OH Oct. 2004
Early Auction Company, LLC
598A **Mosaic Vase** by Fenton w/overall threading, ca. 1926, ht. 11in. **$2,300**

A-ME Nov. 2004 James D. Julia, Inc.
799 **Gallé Scenic Vase** depicting mountains & lake, sgn. in cameo, ht. 17in. **$10,925**

A-ME Nov. 2004 James D. Julia, Inc.
484 **Amberina Berry Set** by Hobbs w/bowl & 10 matching saucers. **$650**

A-ME Nov. 2004 Early Auction Company, LLC
801 Cameo Vase w/floral dec. & applied embossed overlay, sgn. Bergen & Schverer, ht. 4in. $4,370

A-ME Nov. 2004 James D. Julia, Inc.
863 Damon Enameled Vase w/an acid texture chipped ice ground & cameo enamel dec., sgn. Damon Paris, ht. 18¾in. $2,587

633 632 631

A-OH Oct. 2004 Early Auction Company, LLC
Wedgwood
633 Dragon Lustre Vase w/turquoise interior & stamped in gold, ht. 9in. $775
632 Dragon Lustre Bowl, stamped Wedgwood in gold, wd. 9in., $850
631 Bulbous Stick Vase w/rampant gold dragon & gold stamp, ht. 9in. $625

A-ME Nov. 2004 James D. Julia, Inc.
720 **Favrile Wine Glasses,** set of four, each sgn. LCT & two are numbered, ht. 7¼in. **$2,300**

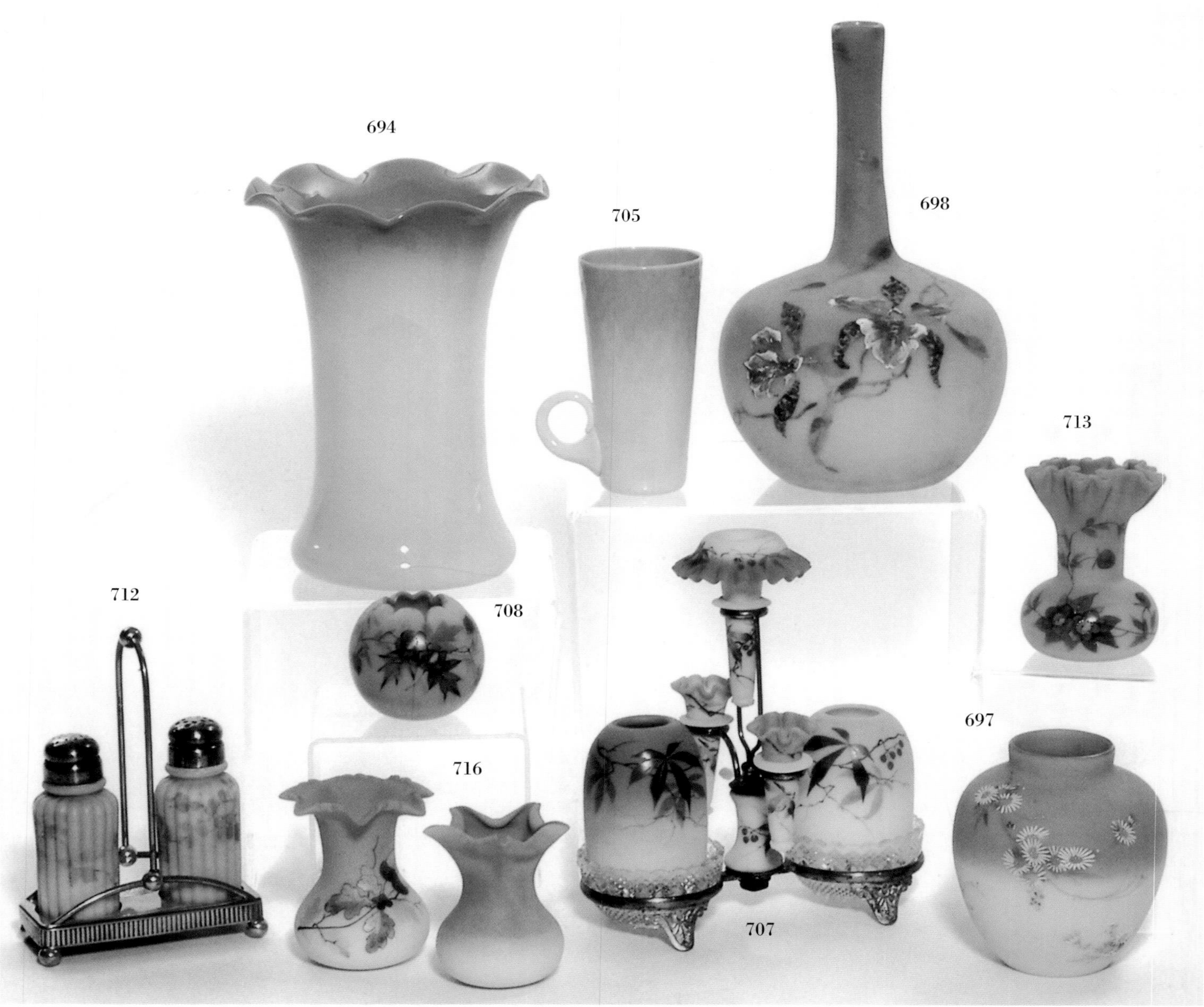

A-OH Oct. 2004
Early Auction Company, LLC
Burmese Glass

694 **Pairpoint Cylindrical Vase** w/shiny finish & ruffled rim, ht. 8in. **$150**

705 **Mt. Washington Lemonade,** ht. 4¾in. **$500**

698 **Stick Vase,** Mt. Washington w/leaf dec., ht. 9½in. **$800**

712 **Mt. Washington Salt & Pepper Shakers,** ribbed & dec. w/pastel florals. **$500.**

708 **Rose Bowl** by Webb w/floral dec. , ht. 2½in. **$225**

716 **Vases by Webb,** one w/ dec., & one w/line crack, ht. 3½in. **$550**

707 **Webb Fairy Lamp Epergne** w/floral dec. & brass holder mkd. Clark, ht. 8¼in. **$2,500**

713 **Vase by Webb** in Hawthorn patt., ht. 4in. **$125**

697 **Mt. Washington Vase** dec. w/daisies, ht. 4½in. **$300**

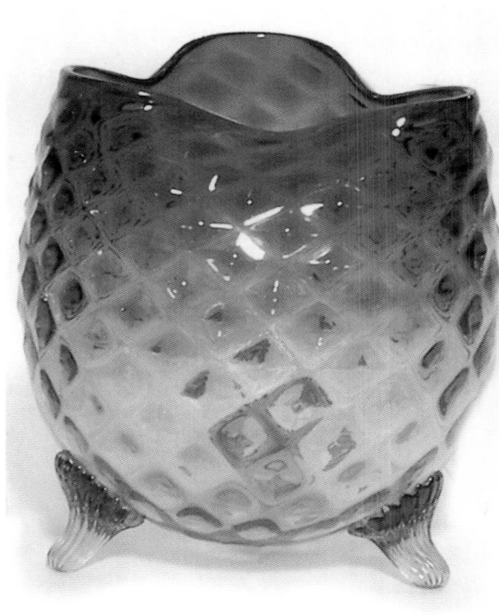

A-Oh Oct. 2004
Early Auction Company, LLC
488 **Amberina Pinch Sided Vase** w/inverted rim, optic ribbed body & rigaree collar, ht. 6in. **$100**

486 **Libbey Amberina Compote,** optic ribbed body, ht. 4in. **$500**

492 **Amberina Footed Vase,** diamond quilted patt., w/three applied reeded feet, ht. 6in. **$350**

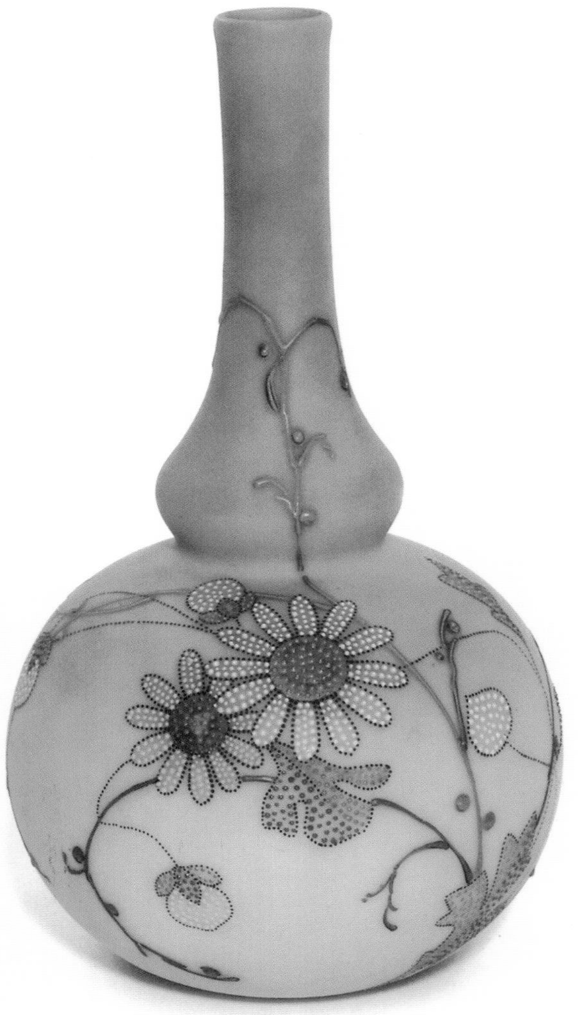

A-Oh Oct. 2004 Early Auction Company, LLC
709 **Mt. Washington Burmese Stick Vase,** Queen's patt., ht. 8in. **$1,950**

A-Oh Oct. 2004
Early Auction Company, LLC
583 **Steuben Aurene Vase** w/gold interior & bright red exterior, dec. w/random gold heart & vines, sgn. , ht. 12¼in. **$25,000**

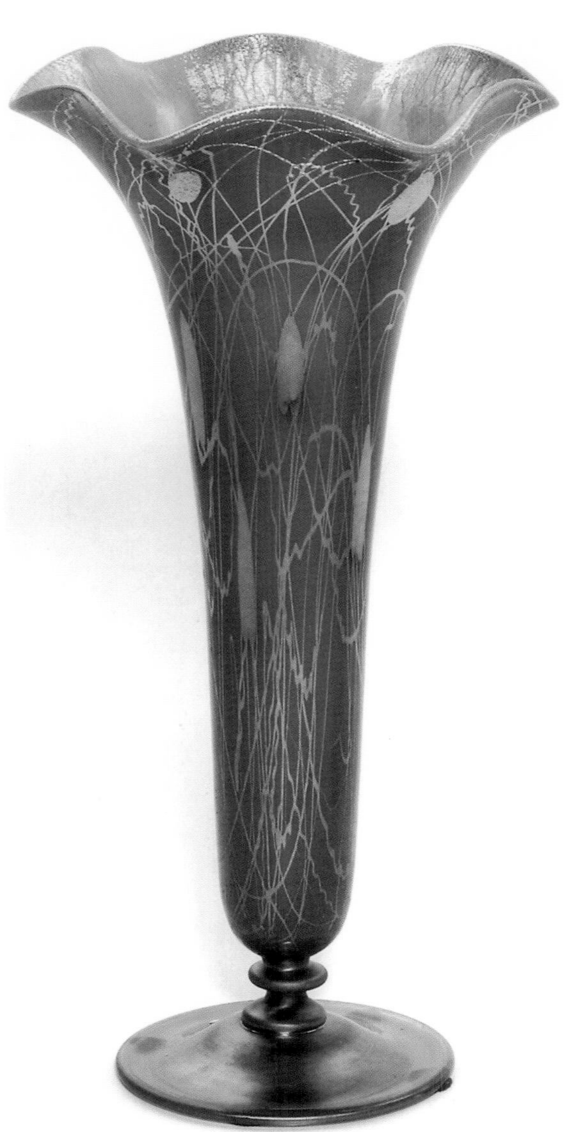

Opposite
A-OH Oct. 2004
Early Auction Company, LLC
160 **Compote, Mt. Washington/Pairpoint glass** w/6in. opal glass plate dec. w/red roses attached to a cherub figural Pairpoint stem, sgn. ht. 5½in. **$275**
154 **Covered Sugar,** melon ribbed & dec. w/raised flowers & leaves, Smith Bros., sgn w/rampant lion trademark, ht. 4in. **$200**
152 **Cracker Jar** w/orig. lid, faceted body dec. w/flowers & mkd. w/Pairpoint diamond mark. **$150**
157 **Smith Brothers Dresser Jar,** melon ribbed & dec., sgn. w/rampant lion trademark, ht. 3½in. **$175**
156 **Mt. Washington Flip Lid Dresser Box,** dec. w/pansies, ht. 4½in. $250
159A **Cracker Jar** w/metal lid signed Pairpoint & body dec. w/waves framing a sailboat, ht. 6in. **$650**
171 **Mt. Washington Crown Milano Atomizer,** w/floral enamel dec., ht. 6½in. **$300**
159 **Rose Bowl,** oversized, Mt. Washington & dec. w/blue daisies & foliage, ht. 5in. **$150**
153 **Cracker Jar, Pairpoint,** dec. w/large pink flowers, mkd. **$150**
167 **Mt. Washington Crown Milano Biscuit Jar,** dec. w/gilt flowers, bugs & leafy stems, sgn. Pairpoint & lid initialed MW, ht. 6in. **$400**
161 **Crown Milano Biscuit Jar** w/Burmese body dec. w/gold leafy budding branches, sgn. w/CM under crown mark, missing lid, ht. 6¼in. **$175**

A-OH Oct. 2004 **Early Auction Company, LLC**
747 **Loetz Vase,** deep amethyst to green glass dec. w/a platinum internal stemmed flower design, ht. 9¾in. **$1,700**

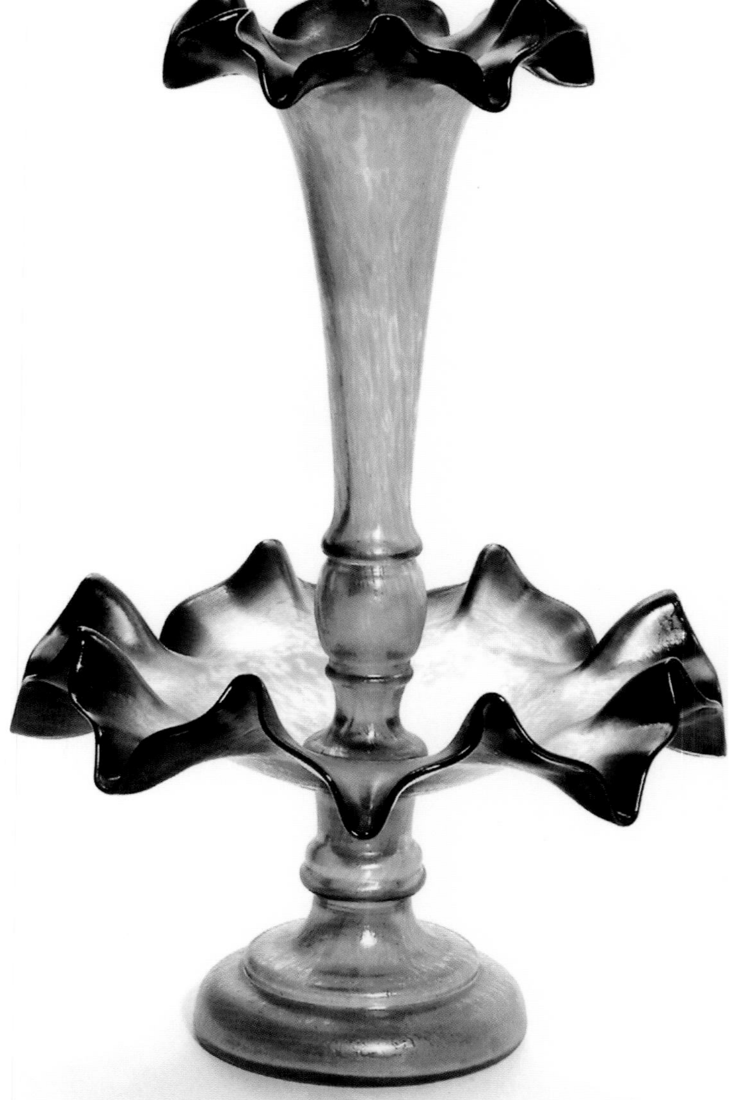

A-OH Oct. 2004 **Early Auction Company, LLC**
738 **Bohemian Epergne** w/single arm lily vase, attributed to Rindskopf, ht. 18in. **$600**

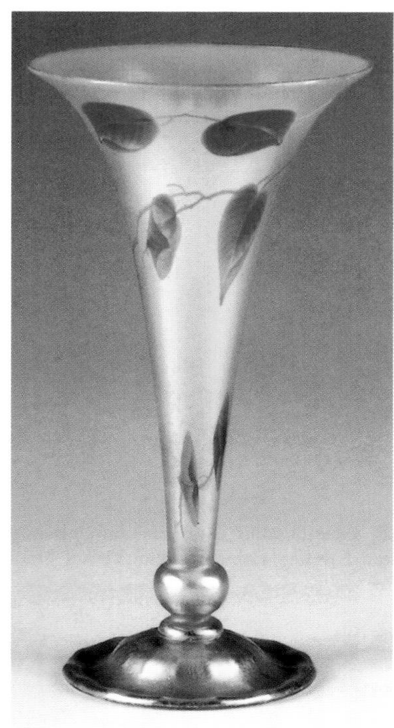

A-ME Nov. 2004
James D. Julia, Inc.
716 **Tiffany Intaglio Carved Trumpet Vase** w/iridized ribbed foot, sgn. ht. 13¼in. **$3,737**

A-OH Oct. 2004
Early Auction Company, LLC
367 **Phoenix Umbrella Stand** w/blown out thistle patt. in opal to mauve glass ht. 17¼in. **$250**

A-ME Nov. 2004 James D. Julia, Inc.
722 **Tiffany Favrile Vase,** corset shaped, sgn. w/interior staining, ht. 5¼in. **$1,840**

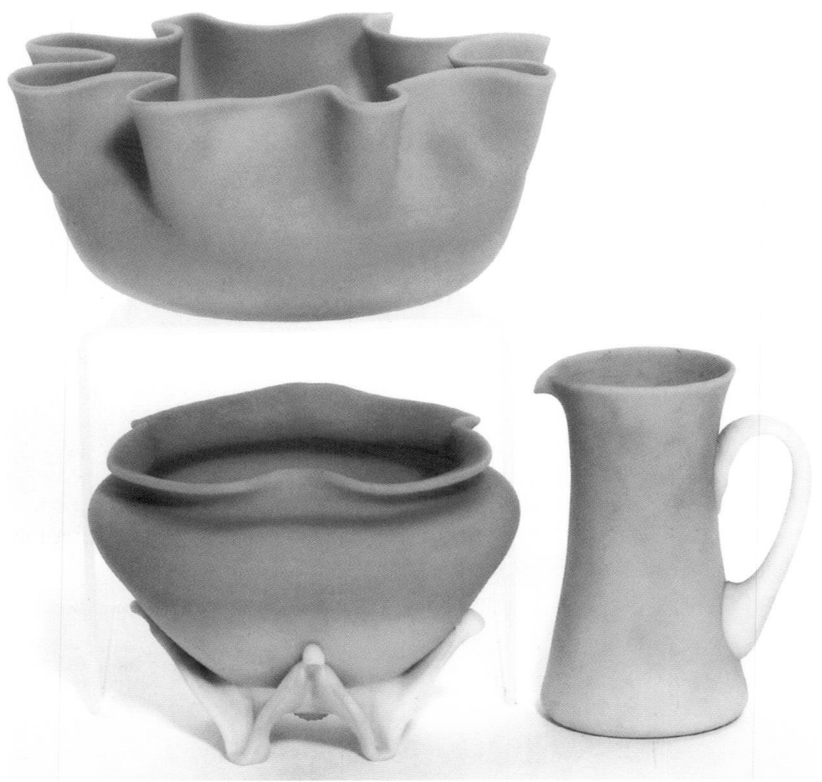

A-Oh Oct. 2004 Early Auction Company, LLC
Mt. Washington Peachblow
659 **Finger Bowl,** dia. 5½in. **$2,000**
658 **Sugar Bowl** w/four applied wishbone feet & berry pontil, ht. 3½in. **$3,000**
657 **Cream Pitcher** w/acid finish, shades from soft pink to pearl blue, ht. 3⅝in. **$2,600**

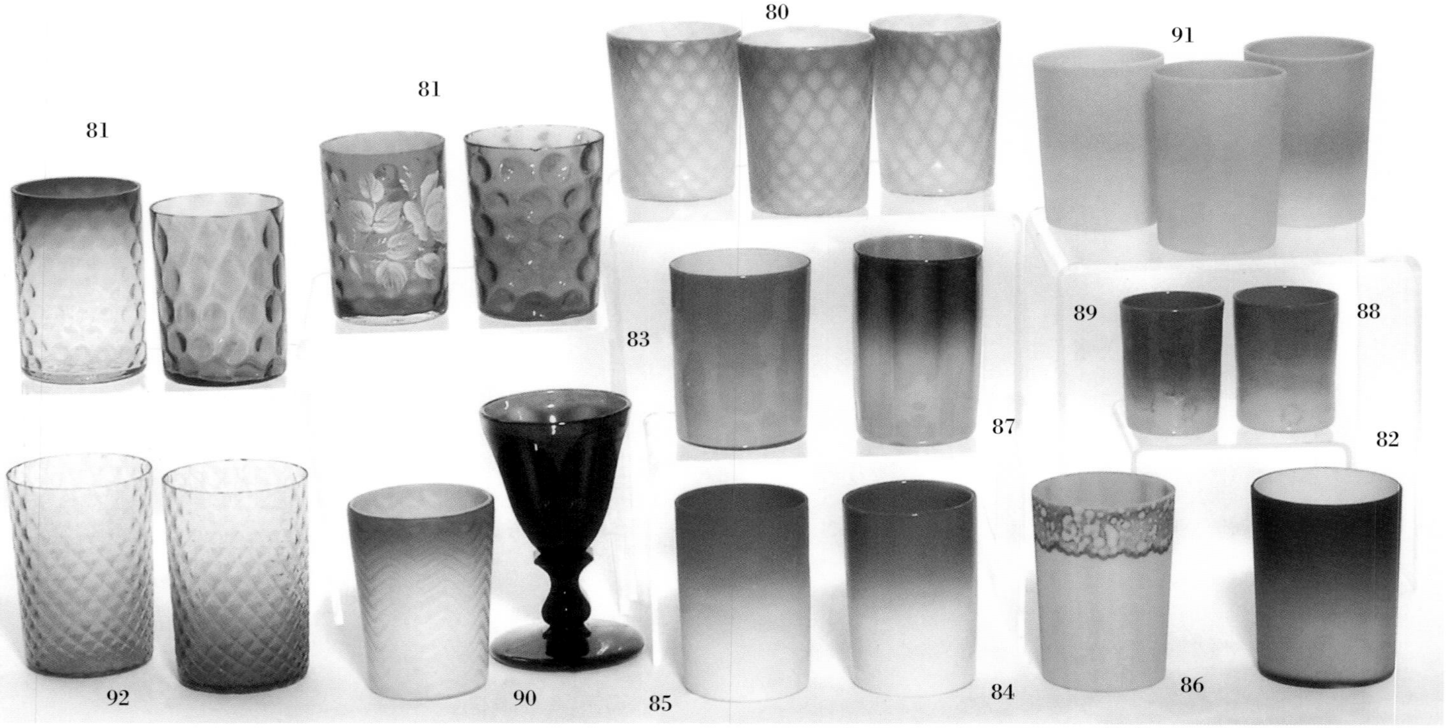

A-OH Oct. 2004
Early Auction Company, LLC
81 **Tumblers,** lot of four including bluerina, inverted coin spot, enamel floral dec. tumbler & a cranberry inverted thumbprint. **$75**
80 **Three Diamond Quilted MOP Tumblers** w/white interiors. **$100**
91 **Three Mt. Washington Burmese Tumblers** w/acid finish. **$140 ea.**
83 **Wheeling Peachblow Tumbler** w/glossy finish. **$125**
87 **New England Plated Amberina Tumbler** w/vertical ribs. **$1,900**
89 **New England Agata Whiskey,** wear & staining. **$120**
88 **New England Agata Whiskey** w/overall mottling. **$150**
92 **Reverse Amberina Tumblers,** diamond quilted patt. **$60**
90 **MOP Tumbler,** Herringbone patt. w/a Sandwich Glass Goblet. **$110**
85 **New England Tumbler,** Wild Rose patt. w/acid finish & scratch to body. **$175**
84 **New England Tumbler,** Wild Rose patt. w/glossy finish. **$300**
86 **New England Green Opaque Tumbler** w/gilt highlights & ribbed body. **$375**
82 **Wheeling Peachblow Tumbler** w/acid finish & white opaque interior. **$125**

Interest in American Indian crafts has attracted collectors from the late 19th century, but it has only been within the latter half of the 20th century that the demand reached the present fever pitch. The major areas of Indian collectibles are rugs, blankets, pottery, beadwork, basketry, wood carvings, leather work and jewelry. Each tribe has its own distinctive designs.

Blankets and rugs have had a great attraction for collectors. The Hopi and Zuni tribes have produced some very appealing examples. However, many collectors search for examples made by Navajo weavers. They worked on an upright loom of their own invention, using natural dyes and wool from their sheep. Today, examples of their early creations are considered art forms.

Perhaps the best known pottery is the black-on-black pieces that were made at the San Ildefonso pueblo, near Santa Fe, New Mexico, by the Martinez family. Julian and Maria signed pieces are especially sought by collectors. Other fine examples of pottery were made at the pueblos of Santo Domingo, Santa Clara and Acoma in New Mexico. And the Hopi Indians in Arizona made fine pottery.

The finest baskets, and the one most sought by collectors are those of the Southwest. Their light and durable Indian baskets were made in large quantities, for both personal use and as something to be sold to tourists.

This chapter also includes interesting kachinia dolls of the Southwestern pueblos. Because several hundred known examples were made, many great dolls can still be found. Kachinias represent figures from the Indian spirit world.

A-MA May 2004 Skinner, Inc.
459 **California Pictorial Coiled Basketry Jar,** Yokuts, ca.1900 w/remnant top-knot feathers & possibly wool at shoulder, ht. 5¼in., dia. 9in. **$10,575**
460 **California Coiled Pictorial Basketry Bowl,** ca.1900, w/eight human forms, all but one w/unusual framing device, ht. 3¼in, lg., 8¾in. **$3,760**

A-MA May 2004 Skinner, Inc.
497 **SW Coiled Basket Olla,** Apache, ca.1900, dec. in an overall diagonal grid patt. w/human forms & animals. Some res. to rim & stitch loss, ht. 24 in. **$8,225**

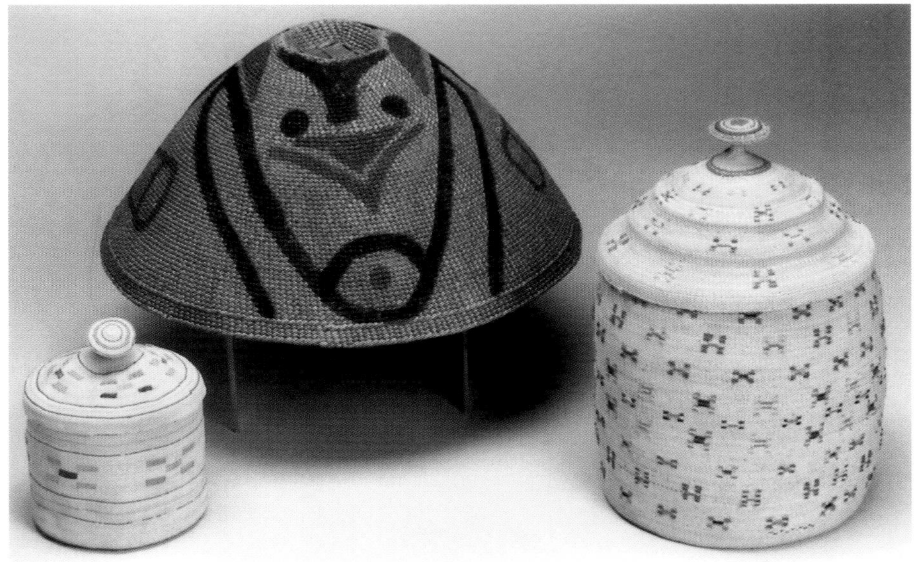

A-MA May 2004 Skinner, Inc.
568 **Lidded Basket,** Attu, NW polychrome twined, ca.1900, minor damage, ht. 5in., dia. 4in. **$2,233**
567 **Twined Basketry Hat,** NW Coast, Nootka, ca. late 19th C. w/polychrome dec. & minor damage to inner headband, ht. 5in., dia. 12in. **$2,350**
566 **Twined Lidded Basket,** NW Attu, dec. w/embroidered polychrome yarn, ht. 9¾in., dia. 12in. **$4,700**

A-MA May 2004 Skinner, Inc.
458 **Western Pictorial Coiled Basket Bowl,** Havasupai. The selvage finished with a tight herringbone weave, ht. 5½in., dia. 12¼in. **$23,500**

A-MA May 2004 Skinner, Inc.
383 **SW Polychrome Painted Olla,** Acoma, ca.1900 w/rest., ht. 11in, dia.12½in. **$23,500**

A-OH Apr. 2004 Garth's Arts & Antiques
412 **Pueblo Pottery Jar,** Acoma or Laguna w/polychrome dec., rest. ht. 6½in., dia. 7in. **$805**
413 **Aoma Pueblo Bowl** w/polychrome dec.,ca.1930-40, ht. 4in., dia. 8in. **$143**
414 **Zia Pueblo Jar** w/polychrome dec. of bird on Pole slip ground, ht. 2⅞in., dia. 3½in. **$115**
415 **SW Pueblo Pottery,** 2 pcs., jar w/avian & geometric design in muted orange & amber, ht. 5in. & Zia plate by Candelaria Gauchupin, w/ centered bird, wear & soil, dia. 4¾in. **$258**
416 **Hopi Shallow Bowl,** possibly by Nampeyo, CA, ca.1900, sm. crack & chip at rim, wear, ht. 2½in., dia. 9¼in. **$1,495**

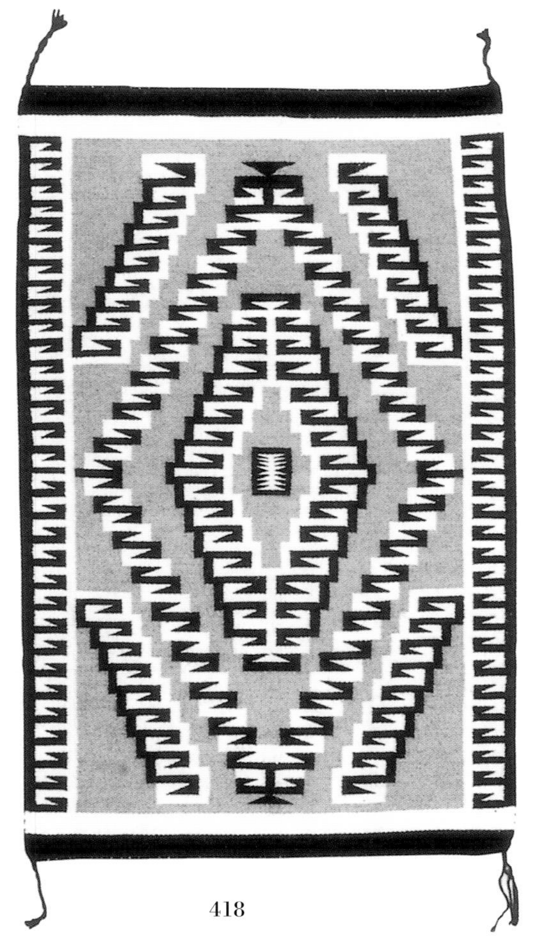

418

417

A-OH Apr. 2004 Garth's Arts & Antiques
417 **Navaho Yeibechai Tapestry Weaving** depicting male dancers led by talking god, on wool ground, 25 x 24in. **$460**

A-OH Apr. 2004 Garth's Arts & Antiques
418 **Navaho Rug,** Two Gray Hills w/intricate intertwining hook design, 2ft.2in. x 3ft.7in. **$345**

A-MA May 2004 Skinner, Inc.
264 **William Spratling Solid Silver Spurs,** ca.1930s, Spanish Colonial-style w/large rowels, dogs on shanks & single bell jingle-bobs. Leather is orig., lg. 8½in. **$11,163**

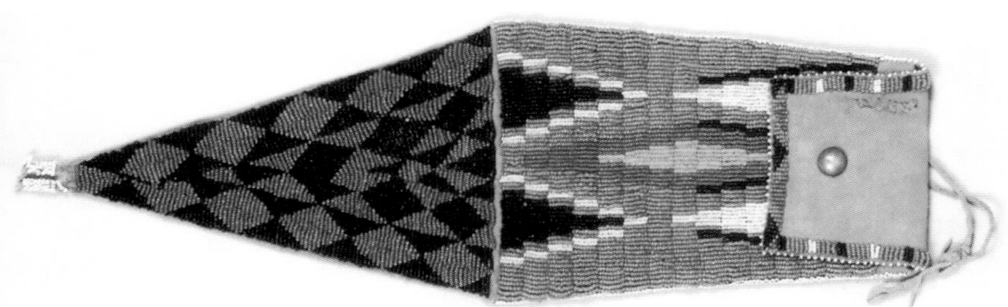

A-MA May 2004 Skinner, Inc.
440 **Beaded Tail Bag,** late 19th C., Ute in form of style, fringe below dangles missing, lg. 19in. **$1,380**

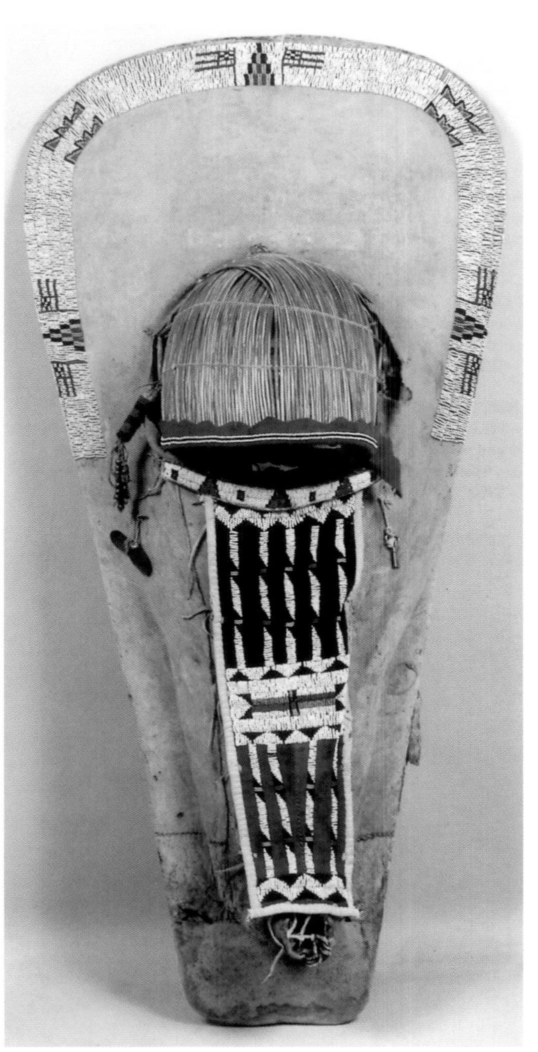

A-MA May 2004 Skinner Inc.
441 **Cradleboard,** ca. 1875-1890 w/flag motifs around curvature of top, stained yellow for a girl. Attached are an umbilical fetish bead wrapped in white heart reds and blue w/brass bead drops, a weasel claw amulet for safety in travel & strength, a mini.brass shoe sole & a small Victorian key, lg. 39in. **$6,900**

A-MA May 2004 Skinner, Inc.
231 **NW Coast Carved Wood Totem Pole** w/polychrome dec., early 20th C., w/stylized eagle & animal forms, ht. 20in. **$558**

A-MA May 2004 Skinner, Inc.
109 **Ute Wood & Beaded Hide Cradle** w/suspended doll, ca. late 19th C., some loss & damage to cradle, ht. 44in. **$12,925**
110 **Kiowa Beaded Cloth & Wood Model Cradle,** late 19th C.,containing a cloth doll w/bead detailed hide head w/some rest., mkd. Geronimo's granddaughter, made this, Lawton, OKLA, ht. 22in. **$8,813**

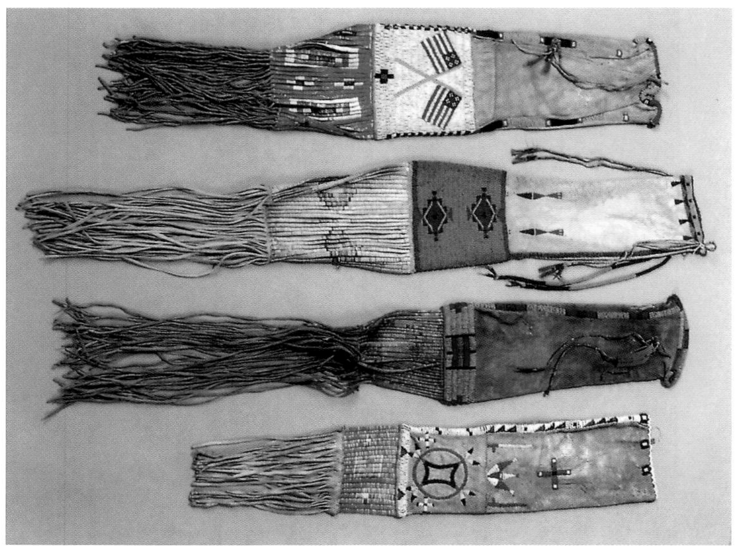

A-MA May 2004 Skinner, Inc.
76 **Quilled Hide Pipe Bag,** beaded, Central Plains, Lakota, late 19th C., w/fringe, minor damage, lg. 32in. **$2,820**
77 **Lakota Beaded & Quilled Hide Pipe Bag,** late 19th C., w/minor quill loss, lg. 39in. **$2,938**
78 **Northern Plains Hide Pipe Bag,** Lakota, ca. 1870s w/polychrome quilled rawhide slats & fringe from bottom,quill loss, lg. 37in., **$4,994**
79 **Lakota Pipe Bag,** beaded & quilled, early 20th C., w/polychrome quilled rawhide slats & fringe from bottom, lg. 27in. **$1,645**

A-OH Apr. 2004 Garth's Arts & Antiques
546 **Sioux Child's Beaded Bonnet** w/red silk ribbon lining, ca. 1890, ht. 5½in. **$2,070**
547 **Sioux Doll** w/finely detailed costume including moccasins w/legging strips. Dress has yoke w/Morning Star design, multicolor beading & beaded leather belt. ca.1880, ht. 13in. **$3,162**
548 **Beaded Awl Case,** found throughout the Plains, topped by the lid w/a Morning Star design dec. w/beads & wooden needle inside, lg. 10½in. **$920**
549 **Lady's Beaded Tobacco Bag,** Crow, w/letter of authentication inside, lg. 10in. plus fringe. **$690**
550 **Eastern Woodlands Carved Pipe,** burl w/carved figure of a man, ca.1830s, w/old damage, lg. 4in. **$287**
551 **Sioux Catlinite Pipe,** smoothly formed w/bowl showing much use, **$86**

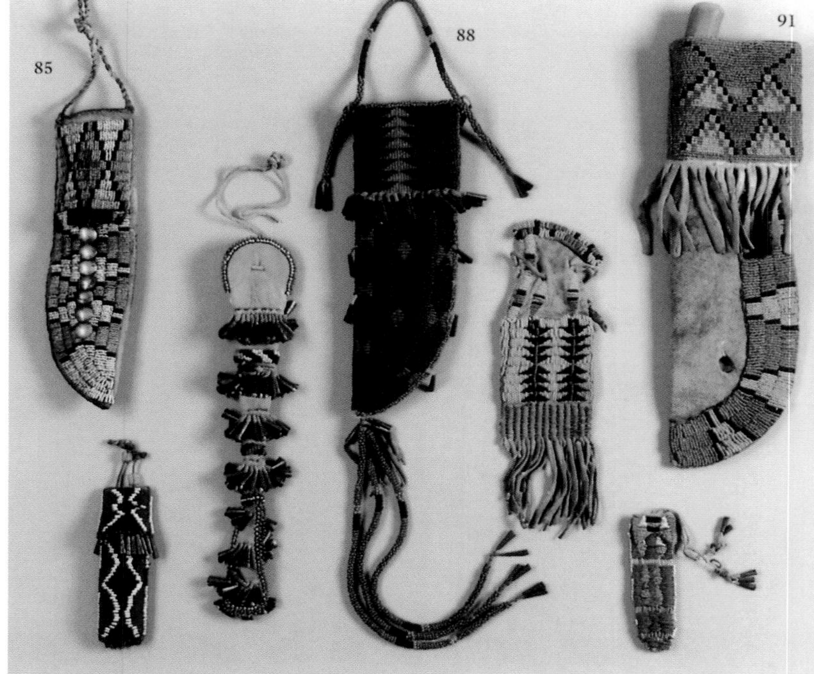

A-MA May 2004 Skinner, Inc.
85 **Plains Beaded Hide Knife Sheath,** Cheyenne, late 19th C., stiff rawhide liner covered w/buckskin, beaded on one side, & dec. w/tin cones & German silver discs, tin cone loss, lg. 8¾in. **$5,288**
86 **Whetstone Case,** Southern plains, Kiowa,late 19th C., dec. w/remnant tin cone danglers & beads, ht. 4¼in. **$2,938**
87 **SW Beaded Hide Awl Case,** Apache, late 19th C., dec. w/multicolored geometric beadwork & tin cones, lg. 11in. **$1,998**
88 **Northern Plains Beaded Hide Knife Case,** Yankton Sioux, late 19th C., buffalo hide dec. w/multicolored beads & tin cones, minor rest., lg. 20in. **$7,050**
89 **Central Plains Beaded Hide Pouch,** Arapaho, late 19th C., dec. w/ multicolored geometric devices on a greasy yellow ground, lg. 9in. **$7,050**
90 **Plains Beaded Hide Pouch,** late 19th C., dec. w/multicolored devices in small seed beads w/tin cone danglers, bead loss, lg. 3¾in. **$558**
91 **Blackfeet Beaded Hide Knife Case,** late 19th C., sinew sewn buffalo hide form beaded w/multicolored elements on light blue ground & partially stitched w/metal wire. Includes an old antler-handled knife. Minor bead loss, lg. 21½in. **$8,813**

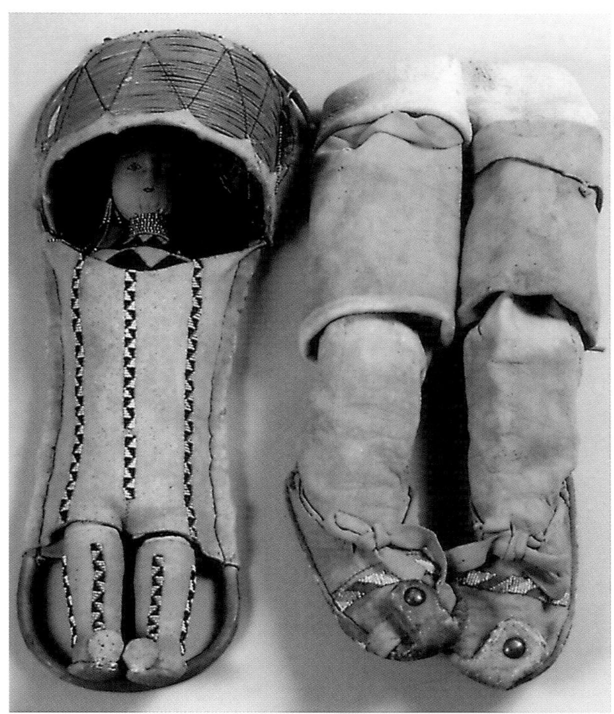

A-OH Apr. 2004 — **Garth's Arts & Antiques**

452 **Apache Model Cradleboard w/Doll,** noses are on leather moccasins, two bead rows missing, ht. 21¾in. **$2,012**

453 **Western Apache Moccasins,** White River area, w/turned up noses dec. w/metal conchos and loom beaded strips, ht. 16in. **$575**

A-MA May 2004 — **Skinner, Inc.**

594 **Navajo Pictorial Weaving,** early 20th C., woven in natural & commercial dyed homespun wool depicting Yei figures, lizards, fish, feathers, square faced lighting corner devices & central avian figure w/minor damage & one side faded, 89 x 63in. **$8,225**

A-MA May 2004 — **Skinner, Inc.**

228 **Dance Skirt,** Northern CA, last quarter of 19th C., heavily fringed buckskin wrap folded laterally & dec. w/vegetal wrapped strips & strands of cut glass beads terminating in brass thimbles, wd. 34in. **$21,150**

A-MA May 2004 — **Skinner, Inc.**

443 **California Coiled Basket Bowl,** Pomo, ca.1900, compressed globular form w/gold zigzag devices, clamshell & top-knot accents, minor stitch, shell & feather loss, ht. 2¾in., lg. 11½in. **$7,050**

444 **California Coiled Gift Basket,** Pomo, ca.1900 w/dark brown & black zigzag & further dec. w/red tuft feathers & spot-stitched w/colored glass seed beads, clamshell & abalone pendants, ht. 3in., dia. 8in. **$5,581**

445 **California Coiled Gift Basket,** Pomo, ca.1900, tightly woven w/stepped grid patt., red tuft feathers, string & clamshell hanging strap, dia. 7⅜in. **$2,585**

A-MA May 2004 Skinner, Inc.

372 **SW Painted Pottery Olla,** Acoma, ca. 1934, sgn. M. Aragon, w/concave base & abstract dec., hairline cracks, ht. 12½in., dia. 15½in. **$9,400**

373 **SW Pottery Pitcher,** Acoma, 20th C., w/abstract foliate dec., & reglued spout, ht. 8½in. **$646**

374 **SW Painted Pottery Olla,** Acoma, ca. 1900 w/crimped rim & concave base painted red & inner rim, rest. chip at rim, ht. 9½in., dia. 11in. **$4,700**

A-MA May 2004 Skinner, Inc.

453 **Coiled Basketry Bowl,** CA, Yokuts, ca. 1900 w/classic red & black polychrome rattlesnake patt., ht. 5½in., lg. 11in. **$3,408**

454 **Coiled Basket Bowl,** CA, 19th C.,Panamint w/row of two-colored joined human figures, wear & stitch loss, ht. 2¾in., dia. 8in. **$2,350**

455 **Coiled Basket Jar,** Panamint ca. 1900 w/two bands of black concentric diamonds bordered in dark red, ht. 3½in., dia. 6in. **$3,818**

A-MA May 2004 Skinner, Inc.

456 **Great Basin Coiled Basketry Bowl,** possibly Washo, ca. early 20th C., dec. w/vertical stacked concentric diamond devices alternating w/a vertical patt. of seven diamonds, minor stitch loss, ht. 6¼in., dia. 9¾in. **$16,450**

457 **Great Basin Coiled Basketry Bowl,** possibly Washo, globular form & tightly woven w/zigzag band of arrowhead devices, ht. 3¾in., dia. 6¾in. **$2,468**

A-MA May 2004 Skinner, Inc.

Katsina Dolls With Polychrome Decoration

327 **Zuni Carved Wood,** early 20th C., w/bent articulated arms, wearing a cloth & yarn kilt, painted face mask w/feathered collar, shell & abalone necklace, minor damage, ht. 12½in. **$8,813**

328 **SW Carved Wood,** Hopi, ca. early 20th C., w/cottonwood form, large case mask & kilt w/painted sash, wood loss, ht. 10½in. **$1,116**

329 **SW Carved Wood Owl,** Hopi, carrying a bow w/hide cape & anklets, carved by Jimmie Kewanwytewa, w/detailed mask & old repair, ht. 12½in. **$5,581**

330 **SW Carved Wood Cow,** Hopi, early 20th C., w/highly detailed clothing & case mask, ht. 8¼in. **$3,055**

331 **SW Carved Wood Katsina,** Hopi, ca. mid-20th C., cottonwood form w/ large case mask & projecting snout. Arms are carved away from the body w/fiber attachments, ht. 11in. **$558**

332 **SW Carved Wood Aya,** Hopi, ca. first half of 20th C., w/elongated case mask, Maltese cross design & painted sash hanging below kilt, ht. 10in. **$1,410**

333 **SW Carved Cottonwood form,** Malo, Hopi, mid-20th C., w/large case mask dec. w/dyed horsehair, detailed sash & kilt, holding a staff, old repair. ht. 9½in. **$2,468**

KITCHEN COLLECTIBLES

Of all the many types of kitchen collectibles, woodenware has the greatest appeal. It has been produced in America from the earliest times. From the Indians the colonists learned the art of making utilitarian objects such as trenchers, porringers, noggins and bowls. The completely hand-shaped pieces are prized by collectors, as no two were ever alike. Oftentimes cutting lines, copper, pewter and iron, left by the craftsman are clearly evident on the surface of an object. Even vessels may bear signs of crude decoration, having an incised geometric design, wiggle work, initials, a date or name... which, of course, enhances the value.

Although numerous kinds of wood were available to the colonists, it was the bulgy growth scar tissue found at the base of certain trees that was favored. This is known as "burl". Its grain, instead of running in the usual parallel lines, was twisted and coiled and produced an unusually attractive grain. In this field, it is the interesting early burl examples that fetch the highest prices when sold.

There are almost countless examples of many types of early kitchen utensils and gadgets... from the hearth to the cookstove... still available for a price, because "waste not, want not" was a favorite maxim. Recycling was simply a natural way of life for our ancestors. Objects were well made and designed to be functional. During the mid-1800s, when mass production was in full gallop, every imaginable device for the refinement of the culinary art was patented. Therefore, most of us have a few old or inherited items in our modern-day kitchens, and these old "classics" are treasured.

Because of the scarcity of early objects, many collectors have become interested in collecting not only gadgets but utensils dating from the second half of the 20th century, including appliances.

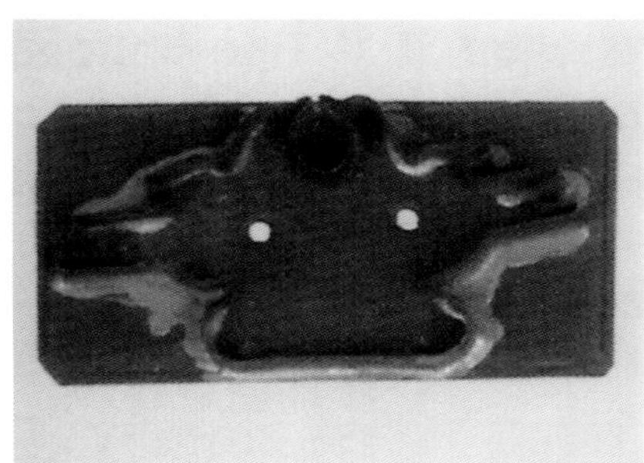

A-PA Jan. 2004
Conestoga Auction Co., Inc.
Cookie Cutters
269 **Kissing Birds on nest** form w/backing & applied handle, oxidation, lg. 6in., wd.3in. **$742**
275 **Large Bird** w/fan tail on flat back, 6½ x 5½in. **$495**

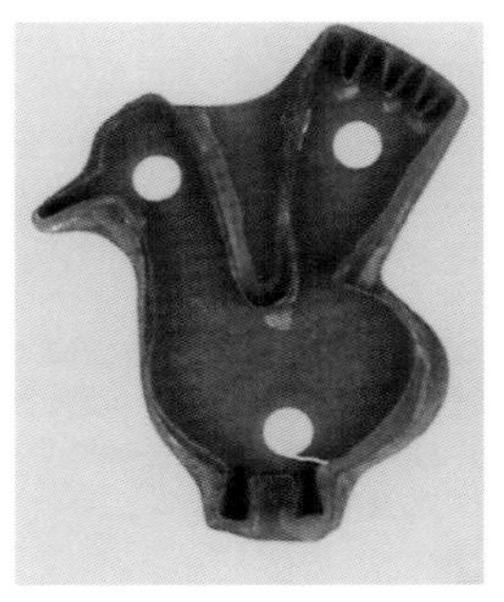

A-IA Sep. 2003
Jackson's International Auctioneers
263 **Burl Bowl,** 19th C., w/small mottled grain, dia. 14in. **$1,207**

A-OH Nov. 2003
Pease Jars, First Row
146 **Five Graduated Jars,** assembled set w/varying degrees of damage, one missing bale & largest has age splits, ht. 2½in.to 5¼in. **$1,178**
147 **Two Covered Jars,** one w/pedestal base, both w/urn finials, larger w/warped lid, ht. 7in. The other has slightly worn varnish & warped lid. **$603**
Second Row
148 **Two Jars,** one w/light varnish finish, ht. 5½in. The other is darker revarnished, wear, ht. 4¾in. **$345**
149 **Three Covered Jars** w/varnish finish, smallest has age split, ht. 2½in. One w/good patina, ht. 4in. The other has wear and a replaced lid, ht. 4in. **$258**
150 **Two Large Covered Jars,** one w/glued split in lid, ht. 6in. The other has worn varnish & dark patina, ht. 4½in. **$316**

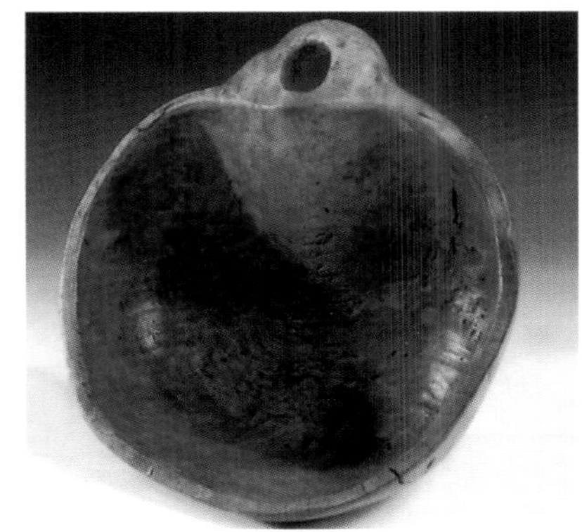

A-IA Sep. 2003
Jackson's International Auctioneers
264 **Burl Bowl,** 19th C., w/carved finger ring handle, ht. 9½in. **$632**

A-NH Mar .2004
Northeast Auctions
646 **Copper Dessert Molds,** four, English, incl. one w/two parts, dia. 5 & 5¼in., wd. 4¾ & 7in. **$2,800**

A-OH Nov. 2003 Garth's Arts & Antiques
Butterprints
First Row
253 **Lollipop** w/sunburst design & starflower center, lg. 9in. **$143**
254 **Lollipop,** elongated w/chip carved designs & center flower, Lg. 12in. **$80**
255 **Running Fox Print** w/one handle & age splits, dia. 3½in. **$86**
256 **Hen,** well carved w/long threaded handle & sm. chip, dia. 4in. **$575**
257 **Fish,** swimming through water plants w/long handle, dia.3in. **$670**
258 **Eagles,** Am., facing each other w/shields & arrows, dia. 3½in. **$287**
Second Row
259 **Ram** w/curled horns & double scalloped border & handle, dia. 2½in. **$345**
260 **Cow** named Doll w/old scratches & one piece handle, dia. 3⅛in. **$258**
261 **Game Bird** w/long legs, short beak & threaded handle, dia. 3¾in. **$258**
262 **Songbird** seated on flower w/one-piece handle, dia. 3½in. **$115**
263 **Songbird** seated on three leaves w/one piece handle, dia. 3¾in. **$172**
264 **Eagle** on branch w/one piece handle, dia. 2⅞in. **$575**
Third Row
265 **Stylized Eagle,** Am., w/shield & one piece handle, dia. 4⅛in. **$230**
266 **Sheaf of Wheat** w/threaded handle, one chip, dia. 4⅛in. **$86**
267 **Starflower** w/carved scalloped back & inset handle, dia. 3½in., together w/a tulip print w/one-piece handle, age splits, dia. 3in. **$86**
268 **Heart print** w/white stain & age splits, dia. 2¾in., together w/carved hearts, edge damage & a nailed handle, dia. 3¾in. **$143**

A-PA Dec. 2003 Pook & Pook, Inc.
525 **Wrought Iron Ladle & Flesh Fork,** ca. 1800, PA, each handle is dec. w/3 copper inlaid hearts, fork lg. 16¼in, ladle 19in. **$2,300**
526 **Wrought Iron Utensils,** ca. 1800, comprising an iron flesh fork, skimmer, iron & brass ladle, all mkd. L.G. Cunkle on handle. **$2,300**
527 **Wrought Iron & Brass Spoon,** ca. 1800, PA w/imp. mark, Lg.. 10in. **$460**
528 **PA Wrought Iron & Brass Ladle,** ca. 1800, mkd. DC, Lg.. 10½in. **$403**

A-PA Apr. 2004
Conestoga Auction Co., Inc.
157 **Pie Board** w/circular cut-out handle, minor splitting, ht. 26in. **$660**

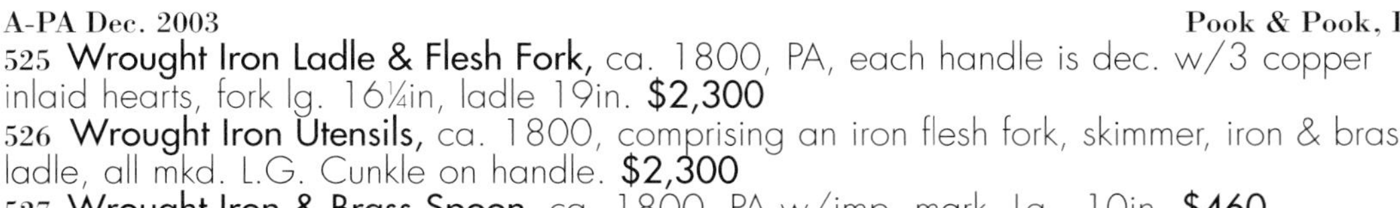

A-PA Dec. 2003 Pook & Pook, Inc.
505 **Pineapple Butterprints,** 19th C., together w/two other examples w/floral motif. **$575**
506 **Pineapple Half Round Butterprint,** 19th C., together w/three others w/ thistle, tulip & wheat design. **$920**
507 **Eagle Butterprint,** round, 19th C. **$460**
508 **Half Round Print** w/thistle design, together w/ two other butterprints & a group of miniature prints. **$460**
509 **Round Butterprint** w/carved cow design, 19th C. **$403**
510 **Horse Cookie Cutter,** tin, ca. 1900, Lg.. 9½in., together w/small lamb example. **$1,495**
511 **Tulip Butterprint,** small, early 19th C., together w/two others w/acorn and tulip carving. **$1,035**
512 **Double Sided Butterprint,** 19th C., w/tulip & pinwheel design, together w/three other examples. **$230**
513 **Lollipop Butterprint,** 19th C., together w/ a pineapple & floral example. **$690**
514 **Elephant Cookie Cutter,** tin, ca. 1900, Lg.. 14in., together w/a smaller example. **$1,725**

A-IA Oct. 2003 Jackson's International Auctioneers, Inc.
262 **Enterprise Coffee Mill,** cast iron w/orig. poly. dec., losses, ht. 12in. **$54**

A-PA Apr. 2004 Conestoga Auction Co., Inc.
584 **Coffee Pot,** dec. w/wriggle work depicting a spread wing Am. eagle holding a flag, perched on a vine & tulips. In addition, a dove, floral motifs on body & a snake on handle, ht. 11½in. **$4,125**

A-NH Mar .2004 Northeast Auctions
908 **Box Churn,** Delaware River Valley, pine w/wooden gears & hand-crank fitted to upright supports above fitted lids on sq. box base, ht. 25in. **$250**

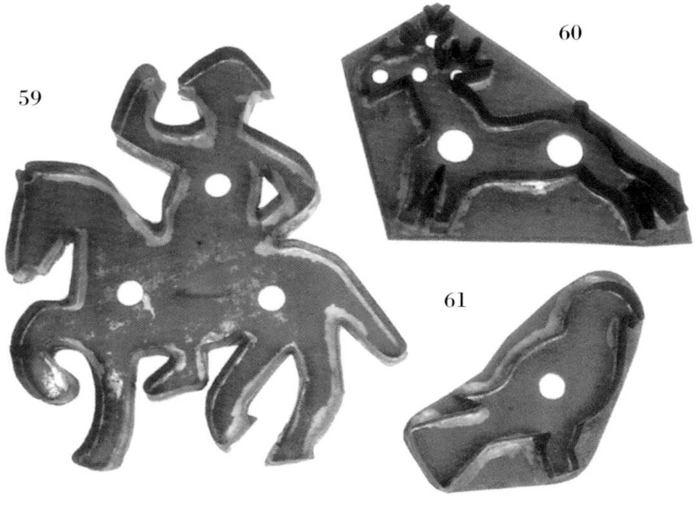

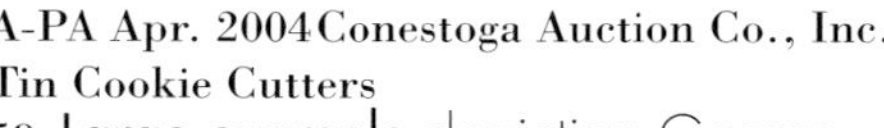

A-PA Apr. 2004Conestoga Auction Co., Inc.
Tin Cookie Cutters
59 **Large example** depicting George Washington on his horse, illegible stamp in center believed to be that of a Germantown, PA maker, ht. 12½ x 10½in. **$13,200**
60 **Large Moose,**mounted on back plate w/crimped edges, ht. 8in. **$1,210**
61 **Parrot,** mounted on flat back plate, ht. 8in. **$1,100**
62 **Swan,** mounted on flat back plate, ht. 6in. **$880**
63 **Man in the Moon** cutter,mounted on flat back plate, ht.4¾in. **$585**
64 **Profile of Uncle Sam,** on flat back plate w/unusual shaped handle & thumb rest, ht. 8in. **$770**
65 **Eagle on Nest,** mounted on back plate w/raised post for eye, ht. 5in. **$165**
66 **Crowing Rooster,** mounted on flat back plate w/crimped edges, ht. 6in. **$330**
67 **Standing Rooster,** mounted on flat back plate, ht. 5⅝in. **$1,320**

A-PA Apr. 2004 Conestoga Auction Co., Inc.
228 **Sugar Bowl** w/scrolled finial to lid & floral dec., ht. 3¾in. **$11,500**

A-PA Apr. 2004 Conestoga Auction Co., Inc.
229 **Cream Pitcher** w/lid & triangular spout & floral dec., ht. 4in. **$5,500**

A-PA Apr. 2004
Conestoga Auction Co., Inc.
231 **Hanging Match Holder** w/floral dec., crimped edges & triangular pocket, minor flaking to paint, ht. 7½in. **$412**

A-PA Apr. 2004
Conestoga Auction Co., Inc.
225 **Tray** w/eight sides & wire rim, dec. w/floral designs & green leaves on red ground, minor flaking, lg. 8¾, wd. 6¼in. **$990**
226 **Chamberstick** w/applied handle & floral dec., ht. 2in., dia. 6¼in. **$22,000**

A-PA Apr. 2004
Conestoga Auction Co., Inc.
223 **Red Dome-top Coffee Pot** w/goose-neck spout, & dec. w/an identical central medallion motif on each side, ht. 10½in. **$55,000**

224 **Dome-top Coffee Pot** w/goose-neck spout & dec. w/a central floral medallion on black ground, ht. 10½in. **$38,500**

A-PA May 2004 Conestoga Auction Co., inc.
253 **Cheese Mold,** heart shaped w/punched tin dec., ht. 4¾, Lg. 7¼in. **$495**
254 **Cheese Mold,** cylindrical form w/punched tin dec. ht. 6, dia. 4½in. **$192**

A-PA Apr. 2004
Conestoga Auction Co., Inc.
147 **Slaw Board,** maple w/hand forged blade & heart shaped handle, ht. 20¼, wd. 7½in. **$330**

280 **Slaw Board** w/stylized heart cut-out at top, outlined by incised carved dots & crowned by three six-pointed Germanic stars in field of snowflakes, dated 1887, York Co., PA, ht. 16½in. **$2,090**

A-PA Nov. 2003 Conestoga Auction Co., Inc.
Copper
126 **Tea Kettle** w/gooseneck spout, sgn. C. Kiefer, w/small repr. to spout, ht. 11½in. **$1,017**
128 **Tea Kettle** w/gooseneck spout & dated July 3, 1869, w/step-out bottom for stove top, ht. 11¾in. **$660**

A-IA Oct. 2003 Jackson's international Auctioneers
394 **Copper Candy Kettle,** dovetailed w/wrought iron handles, ht. 14, dia. 16in. **$225**

A-PA Nov. 2003 Conestoga Auction Co., Inc.
Copper
112 **Pitcher,** quart size w/riveted rolled spout rim, sgn. B. Budde, NY, ht, 8¼in. **$110**
113 **Gooseneck Tea Kettle** sgn. Thos. M. Hammett, Philad., w/stepped edge lid, copper finial & rolled edge collar, ht. 10¾in. **$2,970**
114 **Measures,** matched set w/brass collars & riveted brass handles. **$357**

A-PA Apr. 2004 Conestoga Auction Co., Inc.
53 **Pierced Tin Cheese Mold** w/geometric patt. & three feet, ht. 3 x 7in. **$2,420**

A-ME Apr. 2004 James D. Julia, Inc.
638 **Piggin** w/red paint & two wide fingered wood bands, ht. 6in. **$115**
639 **Wooden Bucket** w/swing handle, metal bands & painted red, ht. 9in. **$632**

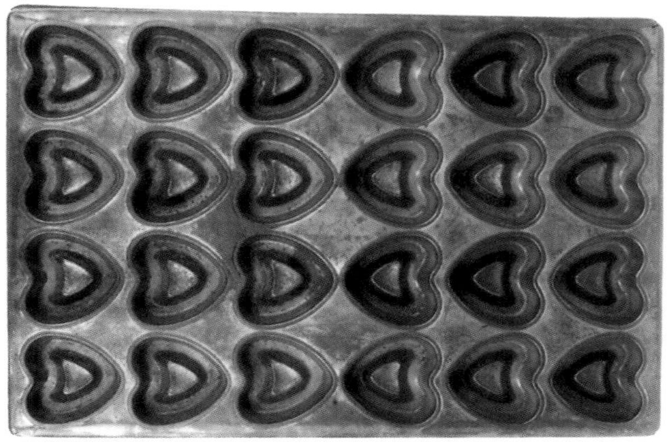

A-PA May 2004 Conestoga Auction Co., Inc.
498 **Muffin or Cake Mold,** Lockwood Tin, 24 heart form, 25 x 17in. **$605**

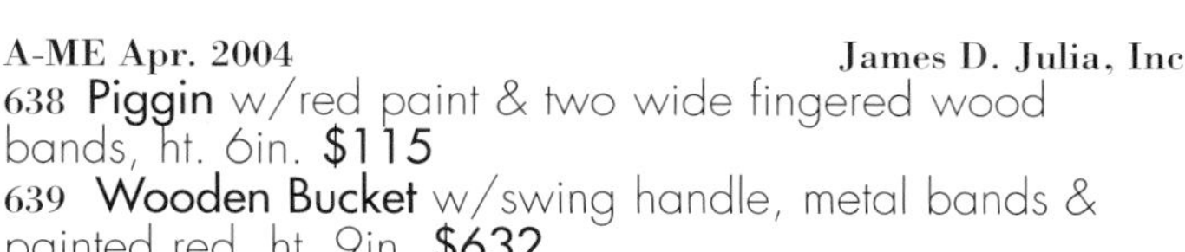

A-PA Nov. 2003 Conestoga Auction Co., Inc.
235 **Splint Market Basket** w/square style handle, ht. 14, wd. 14in. **$110**
236 **Splint Egg Basket,** ht. 11, dia. 12in. **$82**
237 **Circular Top Market Basket** w/tapered ribs, ht. 9½, dia. 10in. **$220**

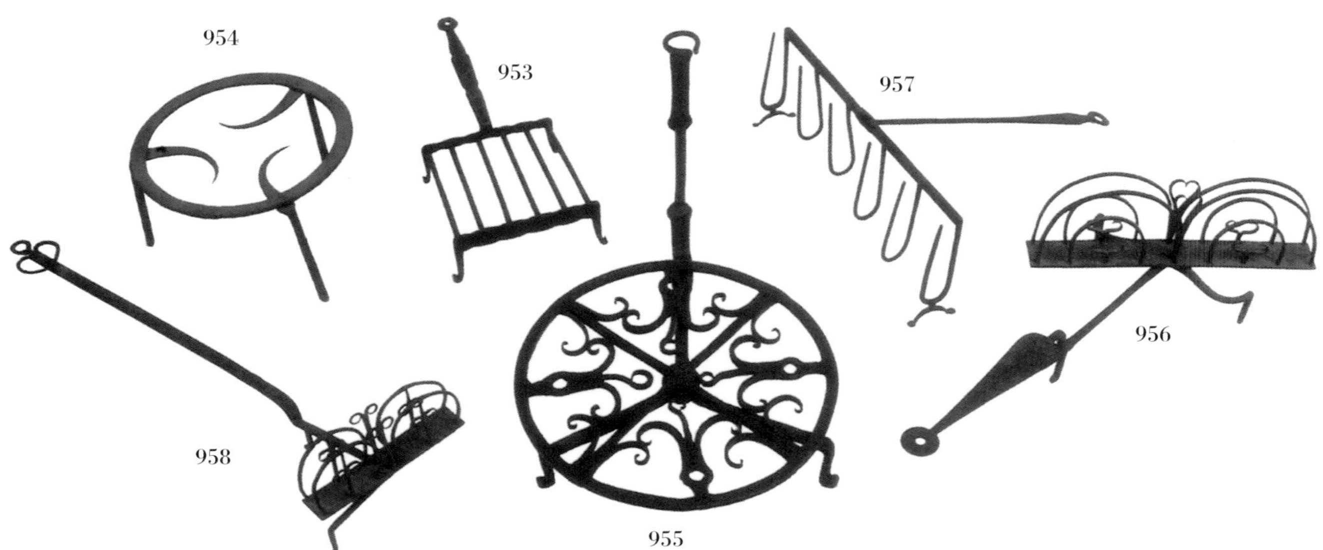

A-PA Nov. 2003 Conestoga Auction Co., Inc.
Wrought Iron
954 **Fireplace Trivet** w/C shaped bent center pieces & three feet, ht. 6½, dia. 10½in. **$137**
953 **Grid Iron** w/framing bars & flat handle, mkd. & dated July 4, 1834, lg. 16in. **$137**
957 **Footed Hearth Toaster** w/six U-shaped toaster racks & mkd. I.M. 1795, lg. 16¾in. **$165**
958 **Footed Toaster** w/swivel holder, arch & twist designs. Repr. to handle, lg. 23in. **$605**
955 **Grid Iron** w/moveable round form & stylized tulip designs, dia. 14in. **$1,650**
956 **Footed Toaster** w/T shaped frame & swivel holder & heart shaped designs, ht. 6¾, lg. 19½in. **$880**

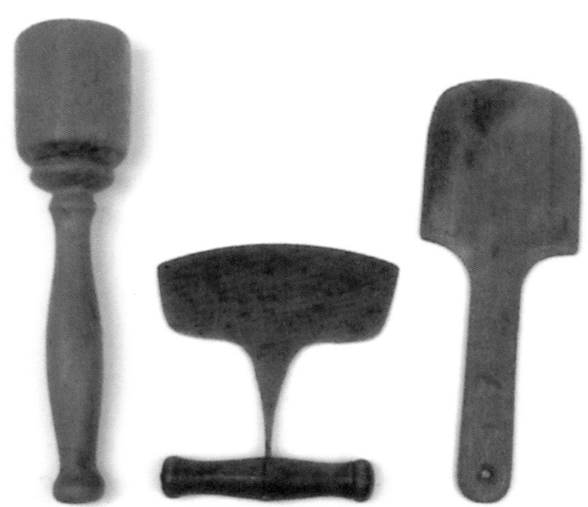

A-PA May 2004 Conestoga Auction Co., Inc.
502 **Steel Food Chopper** w/wooden handle, together w/a potato masher & oak butter paddle. **$38**

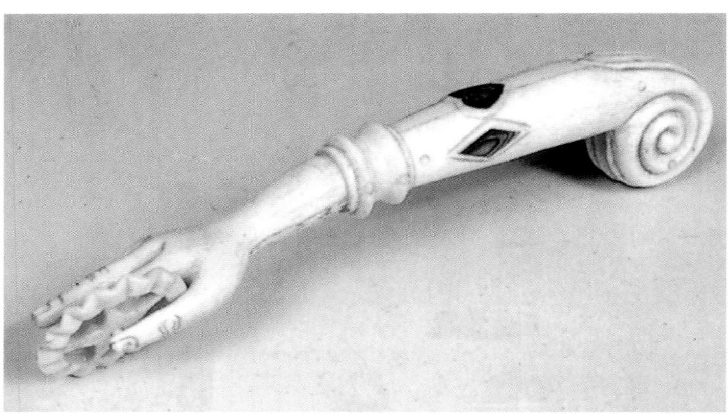

A-IA Mar. 2004 Jackson's International Auctioneers
937 **Pie Crimper or Jagging Wheel,** ivory w/diamond & heart shape inlay. Small chip on thumb, Lg.. 6¼in. **$300**

A-OH Jan. 2004 Garth's Arts & Antiques
Butterprints
First Row
219 **Tulip** w/stars, one-piece handle, dia. 4⅞in. **$287**
220 **Rooster** w/one-piece handle & scrubbed surface, dia. 4⅜in. **$172**
221 **Rabbit,** mini. w/one-piece handle & scrubbed surface, dia. 2in. **$172**
222 **Pheasant** w/old ref. & replaced inset handle, dia. 4⅜in. **$287**
223 **Songbird,** mini. surrounded by leaves, scrubbed surface, dia. 1⅞in. **$172**
Second Row
224 **Cow** w/two-part border, one-piece handle, scrubbed surface, chipped handle & few worm holes, dia. 3½in. **$230**
225 **Feathered Crosshatched Heart,** old ref. w/filled in age split, dia. 3⅜in. **$287**
226 **Deeply Carved Eagle & Star** w/one-piece handle, ref. w/filled in age split, dia. 4¼in. **$345**
227 **Songbird** w/one-piece handle, scrubbed finish, dia. 3⅜in. **$258**
Third Row
228 **Swan,** finely carved w/one-piece handle, dia. 2¾in. **$115**
229 **Stylized Tulip** w/wide one-piece handle w/scratch carved tulip, dia. 5½in. **$287**
229A **Basket of varying flowers,** scrubbed surface w/worm holes, dia. 3½in. **$143**

A-ME Jun. 2004 James A. Julia, Inc.
Coffee Grinders

2610 **Enterprise Model No. 7,** Pat. July 12, 1898 w/orig. stenciling & decals. **$747**

2612 **Lane Brothers Model No. 13,** The Swift Mill from Poughkeepsie, NY, w/repl. drawer & repainted. **$690**

2614 **Cha's Parker Co. Grinder,** pat. March 1898, all orig. **$920**

2607 **Enterprise Grinder No. 12,** large store model, Pat. July 1898, ht.37in. **$977**

A-ME Jun. 2004 James A. Julia, Inc.

2606 **Enterprise Floor Model Grinder** w/nickel plated brass hopper & eagle finial, Pat. Oct. 21, 1873 & retains orig. stenciling & decals. Broken hinge to hopper, ht. 68in. **$2,242**

LIGHTING

The commodities for producing light in colonial America were splints of wood, animal or vegetable oils, depending upon their availability. The oils were used for burning fluids in various forms of shallow flat grease lamps. Because domestic animals were not plentiful in America until the late 1600s, finding a substitute for beef tallow was a major difficulty. Substitutes included beeswax, found on stems of the bay shrub, and "spermaceti" from the head of the sperm whale.

An enormous variety of candlesticks were made of wood, tin and pewter. Candlemolds were made in quantity, as well as sconces with backplates of pewter and tin. Those made with bits of looking glass that reflected the candlelight are extremely desirable. Candlestands soon became fashionable which permitted height adjustments. But, it was not until the 1700s that lanterns, portable and fixed, and fitted with candles became popular.

The availability of whale oil transformed lamp designs during the late 1700s, and remained the most important type of fuel for lamps well into the 1800s. Camphene lamps came into use during the second quarter of the 19th century. They resemble the whale oil lamps, but their wick tubes are set at opposing angles… "V" … shape to compensate for the extreme combustibility of the fuel. From the 1830s until the 1860s the Argand whale oil burner dominated lamp designs. It was not until the 1860s that kerosene eventually replaced all fuels.

Between the rush light holders of the early settlers and the fancy kerosene lamps of the late Victorian era, to the very pricey colorful Art Deco creations, there still exists a seemingly endless variety of very fine lighting collectibles and accessories. Many are readily adaptable for modern decorative and functional usage.

A-ME Nov. 2003 James D. Julia, Inc.
943 **Cameo Art Deco Lamp** sgn.on foot, LeVerre Francis, overall ht. 15in., dia. of shade 8½in. **$6,325**
944 **Tiffany Linenfold Table Lamp** w/twelve panels of emerald green glass trimmed at top & bottom w/frosted borders. Crown of shade is pierced bronze & skirt w/bronze border, sgn.Tiffany Studios New York, shade dia. 19in., overall ht. 23in. **$24,150**

A-IA Oct. 1003
Jackson's International Auctioneers
816 **Reverse Painted Lamp,** early 20th C., w/painted roses on a Venice shade w/blown-out ribs, base sgn. Pairpoint B & No., ht. 21in. **$4,485**
817 **Reverse Painted Lamp,** early 20th C., w/hand painted shade sgn. Berkeley. Base sgn. Pairpoint D & No. Minor heat check in rim, ht. 27in. **$1,840**

A-May 2004 James D. Julia Inc.

254 **Quezal Hooked Feather Shades,** ht. 5in. **$1,725**

257 **Art Glass Shades** w/pulled feather design, one sgn. Quezal & one sgn. Steuben, ht. 5½in. **$345**

262 **Steuben Glass Shades,** gold Aurene, one sgn., ht. 4¼in. **$402**

829

830

831

834

835

836

A-IA Oct. 2003

Jackson's International Auctioneers

829 **Victorian Bronze Table Lamp,** ca. 1900 w/pink satin glass shades dec. w/ coralene & mkd. Victor Made In USA, ht. 24in. **$920**

830 **Cut Glass Table Lamp,** early 20th C., w/mushroom form shade & teardrop prisms, ht. 23in. **$700**

831 **Victorian Two-Arm Lamp,** ca. 1900 w/brass & onyx base, pink satin glass shades. Center accented w/three porcelain yellow roses, ht. 20in. **$345**

834 **Victorian Hanging Glass Chandelier,** ca. 1900 w/brass fixture. **$805**

835 **Figural Lamp,** ca. 1900 w/bronze base & Steuben aurene shades mkd. ht. 16in. **$1,380**

836 **Victorian Hanging Chandelier,** 20th C., w/brass holder, shade dia. 13¾in. **$862**

A-IA Oct. 2003
Jackson's International Auctioneers
826 **Table Lamp** w/reverse painted shade, early 20th C., by Jefferson, dia. of shade 18in., ht. 23in. **$1,955**

827 **Panel Shade Lamp** w/reverse painted repeating scenic designs, unsigned, ht. 22in. **$1,035**

A-MA Dec. 2003 Skinner, Inc.
232 **Tiffany Daffodil Lamp,** early 20th C., w/bronze base, shade sgn. Tiffany Studios New York on rim tag & base sgn. ht. 22¼in. **$28,200**

186 **Tiffany Pomegranate Table Lamp** w/leaded glass domed shade sgn. w/orig. metal tags Tiffany Studios New York, & bronze base sgn. Some cracked shade segments, dia. 15¾in, ht. 19½in. **$20,563**

A-MA Dec. 2003 Skinner, Inc.
139 **Moorish Bronze Chandelier** w/Tiffany gold Favrile shades sgn. L.C.T., fixture unsigned, drop ht. 34in. **$21,150**

A-IA Oct. 2003
Jackson's International Auctioneers
801 **Banquet Lamp,** late 19th C., w/font & shade in ribbed & shaded cranberry glass w/MOP diamond quilt design. Bronze mounts & base. ht. 16in. **$1,207**

A-MA Dec. 2003 Skinner, Inc.
145 **Tiffany Bronze Hanging Lamp,** early 20th C. w/geometric dome of green glass w/pomegranate border in yellow glass, shade sgn. Tiffany Studios NY, dia. 16in., drop ht. 27in. **$9,988**

A-ME Nov. 2003 James D. Julia, Inc.
978 **Favrile Glass Lamp** in bright gold iridescence w/all over green dec., shade sgn. on top LCT, dia. 12in., overall ht. 18in. **$7,187**
980 **Roycroft Lamps** w/dome hand hammered copper shades riveted w/acanthus leaf straps & inset on skirt w/mica panels. Lamps signed on base w/Roycroft Orb & Cross mark, ht. 14in. **$9,200**

A-IA Nov. 2003 Jackson's International Auctioneers
669 **Victorian Banquet Lamp,** 19th C., w/hand painted windmill scenes on three sections of opaque glass, ht. 35in. **$747**

A-ME Nov. 2003 James D. Julia, Inc.
969 **Lily Table Lamp** w/ribbed shades sgn. at upper rim Quezal, lg. 4¾in., overall ht. 15in. **$6,325**

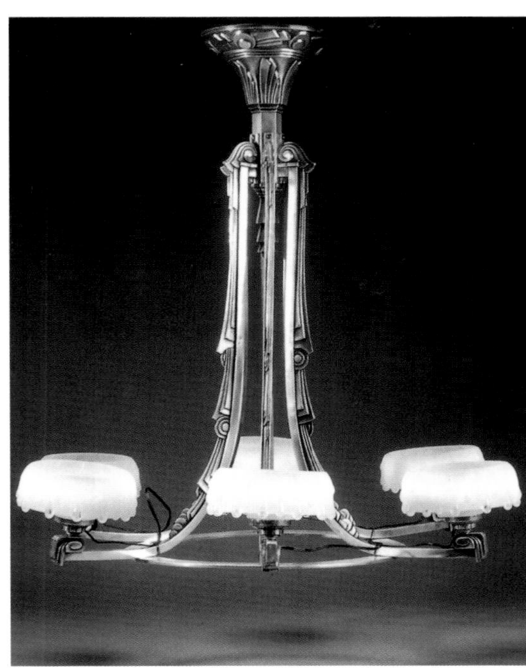

A-IA Nov. 2003
Jackson's International Auctioneers
French Chandeliers
663 **Art Deco,** ca. 1930, nickel plated bronze w/six scrolled arms w/raised step designs, each supporting an opalescent glass shade, ht. 29in. **$2,530**
664 **Art Deco,** ca. 1930, nickel plated bronze w/six blown out floral panels in frosted glass, attributed to Genet-Michon, ht. 39in. **$1,955**

A-IA Nov. 2003
Jackson's International Auctioneers
French Chandeliers
665 **Wrought Iron & Glass,** early 20th C. w/scrolled grape vines & gilt clusters suspending central fixture & four shades in mottled blue & red/yellow glass sgn. Muller Frères Luneville, ht. 34, dia. 31in. **$4,715**
666 **Gilt Iron Chandelier,** early 20th C., w/mottled blue, pink & yellow shades suspended from embossed gilt fittings, ht. 23, dia. 22in. **$1,495**

A-IA Nov. 2003
Jackson's International Auctioneers
910 **French Gilt Bronze Candlesticks** in form of classical man & woman holding urn-shape candle sockets on white marble bases, ht. 12¼in. **$1,380**

911 **Silvered Bronze Candelabra,** late 19th C., w/3-arm branches, fitted in candlestick base, unmarked, ht. 15in. **$862**

912 **French Empire Gilt Bronze Candlesticks** w/embossed dec., some wear to gilt, ht. 15in. **$1,035**

A-IA Nov. 2003 Jackson's International Auctioneers
917 **French Gilt Bronze Candle Sconces,** 19th C., w/urn finials, ht. 12in. **$920**

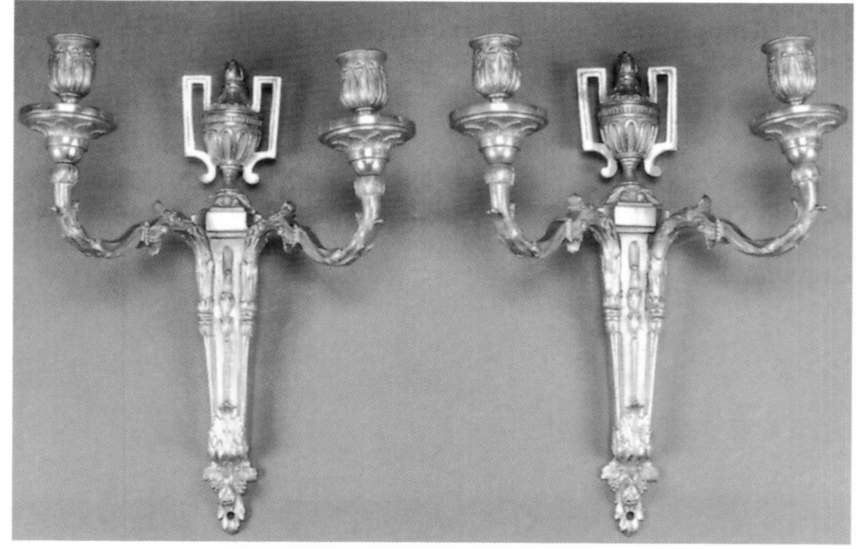

A-IA Nov. 2003
Jackson's International Auctioneers
913 **French Gilt Bronze Candlesticks,** late 19th C., each assembled from six sections, ht. 10in. **$977**

914 **French Gilt Bronze Candlesticks,** 19th C., w/scrolled bases & orig. bobeches, ht. 14in. **$3,565**

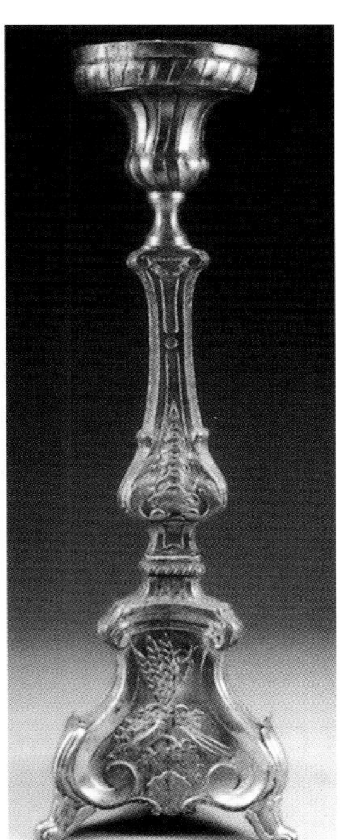

A-IA Nov. 2003 Jackson's International Auctioneers
915 **Large Brass Candle Pricket,** ca. 1800 w/repoussé & chased foliate dec., ht. 32in. **$373**

916 **French Bronze Candlesticks** assembled in six sections, ht. 11in. **$575**

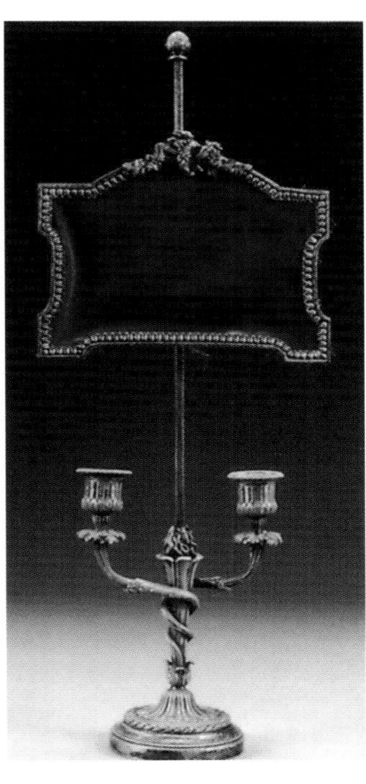

918 **Silvered Bronze Candlestand** w/two entwined candle arms & adjustable screen w/later fabric, ht. 22in. **$517**

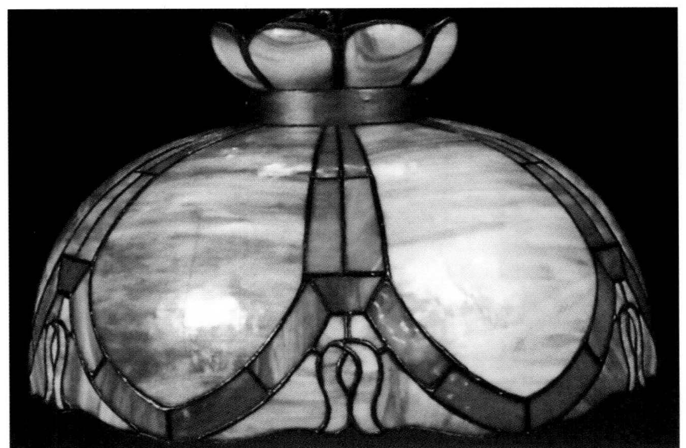

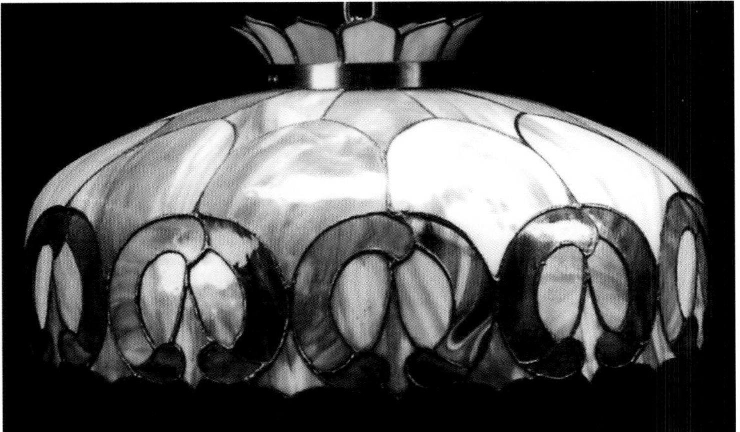

A-IA Nov. 2003 Jackson's International Auctioneers
1833 **Leaded Glass Hanging Lamp Shade,** ca. 1925, dia. 22in. **$218**
1834 **Leaded Glass Hanging Lamp Shade,** w/floral & scroll design, dia. 24in. **$316**

A-IA Nov. 2003

Jackson's International Auctioneers

727 **Lily Form Stained Glass Shades** w/pink & green glass panels, ht. 6in. **$201**

728 **Victorian Touchier Glass Shade** in translucent glass w/green hues, ht. 8in. **$115**

729 **Opal Iridescent Shade,** dec. w/green hearts & gold threading, sgn. Quezal, ht. 5in. **$230**

730 **Iridescent Shade** in white & dec. w/red, blue & gold coiled dec., attrib. to Durand, ht. 5in. **$488**

731 **Quezal Iridescent Glass Shades** w/pulled feather dec., sgn. ht. 5in. **$460**

732 **Lily Lamp Shades** in amber glass w/irid. gold finish, cont., ht. 5¼in. **$373**

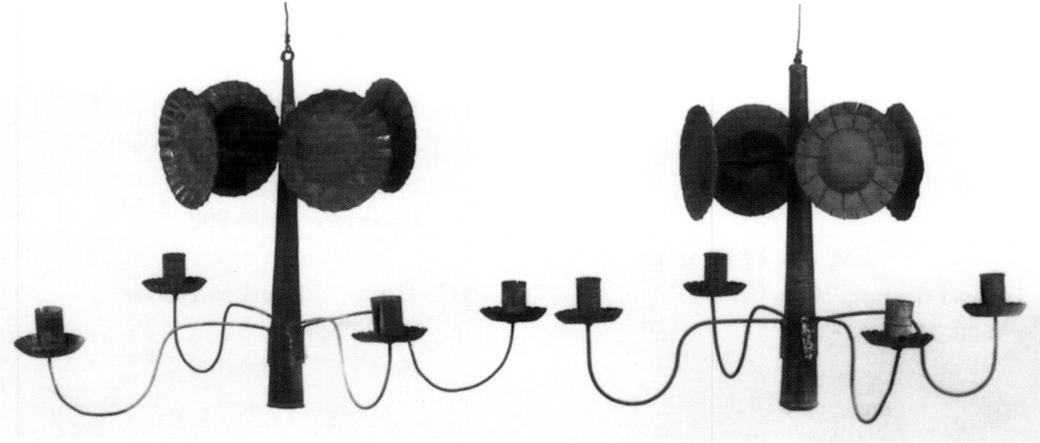

A-PA Mar. 3004

Pook & Pook, Inc.

503 **Tin Candelabra** w/four arms, matched pair, ca. 1800, ht. 14¼in. **$4,830**

Opposite

A-IA Nov. 2003

Jackson's International Auctioneers

1824 **Victorian Opalescent Cranberry Hobnail Lamp** in jeweled frame w/an inner rubina hobnail shade w/4in. fitter, motor complete, dia. 14in. **$1,725**

1825 **Hanging Parlor Lamp** w/dec. opal shade & font, dia. 14in. **$259**

1826 **Victorian Hanging Lamp** w/jeweled frame & hand painted shade & font, motor complete, dia. 14in. **$345**

1827 **Parlor lamp** w/dec. opal shade & font, motor complete, electrified, dia.13in. **$345**

1828 **Victorian Parlor Lamp** w/dec. opal shade & font, electrified, dia. **$218**

1829 **Victorian Hall Lamp** w/kerosene lamp insert, electrified, ht. 12in. **$316**

1830 **Victorian Cranberry Glass Hall Lamp** w/embossed frame, ht. 13in. **$345**

1831 **Leaded Glass Table Lamp** w/leaded glass shade & Handel base, cont. **$195**

1832 **Victorian Cranberry Glass Hall Lamp,** ht. 12**in. $218**

1824

1825

1826

1827

1828

1829

1830

1831

1832

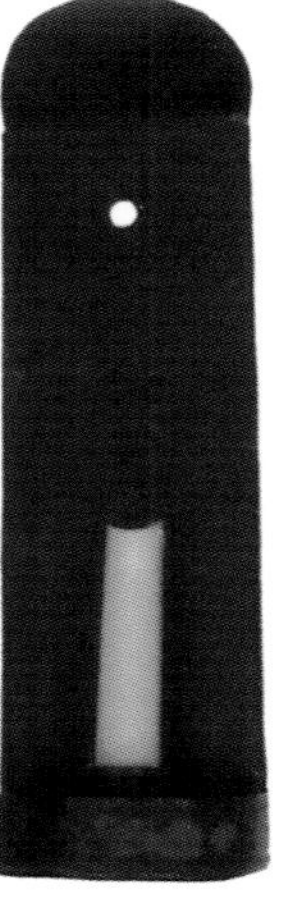

A-PA Nov. 2003
Conestoga Auction Co., Inc.
904 **Tin Candle Lantern** w/cylindrical punches, conical top, hanging ring & hinged door w/D-shaped hasp, 19th C., overall ht. 15in. **$330**
905 **Tin Candle Lantern** w/cylindrical punches, hanging ring & hinged door w/D-hasp, ht. 15in. **$385**

A-PA Apr. 2004
Conestoga Auction Co., Inc.
263 **Tin Candle Mold** w/12 tubes & ring handle, ht. 15¾in. **$1,650**

A-PA Apr. 2004 Conestoga Auction Co., Inc.
252 **Tin Wall Sconce** w/tapered back & dec. edges, ht. 9in. **$495**
253 **Rectangular Tin Wall Sconce,** japanned black w/half circle roof & candle holder base, ht. 12¼in. **$110**
254 **Oval Tin Sconce** w/scalloped edges & crimped edge reflector, ht. 11in. **$1,045**

A-PA Jun.2004 Conestoga Auction Co., Inc.
246 **Tin 12-tube Candle Mold** w/strap handle & arched footed base, w/oxid., ht. 10¾in. **$385**
247 **Tin 24-tube Candle Mold** w/arched base & oxid., ht. 9½in. **$385**

A-PA Jan 2004 Conestoga Auction Co., Inc.
59 **Tin Triangular Base Candlestick** w/push-up. Remnants of japanned finish, ht. 3½in. **$577**

A-OH Apr. 2004 Garth's Arts & Antiques
Skaters' Lamps
406 **Tin w/deep amethyst globe,** mkd. Jewel, w/usual rust, ht. 7in. **$1,092**
407 **Tin w/amethyst globe,** mkd. Jewel w/rust, ht. 7in. **$833**
408 **Tin w/cobalt blue globe,** scratches & rust, ht. 7in. **$517**
409 **Brass w/green globe,** ht. 7in. **$546**
410 **Brass w/peacock blue globe** w/short crack & split in top. **$172**

A-PA Jun. 2004 Conestoga Auction Co., Inc.
241 **Tin Betty Lamp & Base** w/hanging hook, chained wick pick, hinged lid & wick holder. The base is weighted w/attached handle, ht. 4¾in. **$412**
242 **Iron & Brass Oil Lamp** w/brass container, incised banding, swivel hinged to iron stand, baluster post & round base. By Peter Derr, Berks Co., PA, & stamped P.D. 1856. **$8,250**

A-PA Apr. 2004 Conestoga Auction Co., Inc.
52 **Tin Pierced Conical Candle Lantern** w/removable base & banded pierce work, PA, rare form, PA, ht. 10in. **$5,390**
55 **Tin Wall Sconce** w/scalloped roof & D-shaped base, ht. 12in. **$330**

A-PA Jan. 2004 Conestoga Auction Co., Inc.
56 **Tin 12-Tube Candle Mold** w/applied handle, hanger ring & two wick holders. Orig. old wicking in place, ht. 10in. **$247**

A-PA Jan. 2004 Conestoga Auction Co., Inc.
486 **Wrought Iron Hog Scraper Candlesticks** w/adjustable push rods, ht. 5½, 6½ & 8in. **$319**
487 **Brass Saucer Base Candlesticks** w/adjustable push rods,ht. 16¾in. **$550**

A-PA Jun. 2004 Conestoga Auction Co., Inc.
1081 **Brass & Wrought Iron Fat Lamp** w/hinged lid, iron hanger, brass chain & iron wick pick, stamped P.D. 1851, missing wick holder, ht. 5½in. **$3,300**

The number of small objects made of metal and used in American households that were treated in such a way to attract collectors in this field is enormous. The pleasure of pewter lies not only in its softly rounded forms, but in its glowing surface. Copper has been used essentially for utilitarian articles since the 18th century. Pots, pans, molds and kettles for example are difficult to identify as American, because few were marked and American styles closely resemble European styles. Iron was the most commonly used metal because it was low in cost and high in strength. Early brass pieces, especially candlesticks, are very decorative and are becoming scarcer and more expensive with each passing year. Because tin-plate was a cheap and flexible medium, a tremendous variety of objects were produced. It is the early custom-made objects produced by tinsmiths that are sought after by collectors... such as decorative little cookie cutters and unusual candlemolds and sconces. It is the gaily decorated tinware known as "toleware" that is so popular among collectors. (Examples of toleware are included in the Kitchenware Chapter.) Although it dates from the 19th century, a great number of decorated pieces were produced by talented artists.

A century after America was settled, every center of population had a number of silversmiths to supply the needs of the wealthier colonist. Therefore, early American silver is understandably very rare, but on occasion a fine piece will surface. The majority of objects included in this chapter include silver plate, sterling and English old Sheffield plate. Silver plate is not solid silver, but a ware made of metal such as copper or nickel. The objects are simply covered with a thin coating of silver, whereas the term "sterling" refers to an object of solid silver, conforming to the highest standard. The term "Sheffield" refers to fused plate (a thin sheet of silver fused by heat to a thicker copper ingot), a process discovered by a Sheffield (England) man. Sheffield plate was, however, also produced in Birmingham (England), France and Russia. Lastly, it should be included that between 1836 and 1838 the English firm of G.R. & H. Elkington, of Birmingham, are credited with the invention of electroplating. By the 1840s, the first successful plating techniques were achieved in America.

322 321 322

A-MA Feb. 2004 Skinner, Inc.

317 **Andirons w/Matching Tools,** brass & iron w/ball-top, sgn. John Molineux Boston, ca. 1800, andiron ht. 17½, wd., dp. 24½in. **$2,820**

318 **Folding Fire Fender,** Am., brass & wirework, Am. or Eng., late 18th/early 19th C., ht. 30, lg. 47in. **$3,525**

319 **Double Lemon-top Andirons** w/matching tools, brass & iron, NY, early 19th C. Andiron ht. 20¾, dp. 19¼in. **$1,763**

320 **Brass & Iron Acorn-top Andirons,** Am., ca. 1800 w/log stops, ht. 20½, dp. 25½in. **$1,528**

321 **Brass & Wirework Fire Fender,** Eng. or Am., late 18th/early 19th C., ht. 12¾, wd. 52⅝, dp. 19in. **$4,406**

322 **Brass & Iron Ball-top Andirons,** attrib. to Richard Wittingham, NY, first qtr. 19th C., ht. 15⅝, dp. 8½in. **$441**

A-PA Dec. 2003 Pook & Pook, Inc.

497 **Weather Vane,** full bodied copper eagle, Am., 19th C., w/spread wings & a cast head sitting atop a ball plinth, ht. 10, wd. 20in. **$5,060**

498 **Cut Tin Indian Weather Vane,** Am., late 19th C., retains its orig. red, yellow and green dec., ht. 24½in. **$2,070**

499 **Full Bodied Fox Weather Vane,** Am. copper, retains remnants of old gilt & yellow painted surface, ht. 16, wd. 30in. **$14,950**

A-IA Nov. 2003 Jackson's International Auctioneers

Russian Cloisonné

416 **Decanter** w/shaded enamel dec., second half of the 20th C., ht. 8¼, dia. 4¼in. **$632**

417 **Large Plique-à-Jour Enamel Egg,** second half of the 20th C. The egg opens into two halves &, when re-positioned, the pieces form two goblets, mkd., goblets ht. 6in. **$862**

418 **Silver-Gilt & Enamel Kovsh,** mid-1800s, embellished w/cabochons, lg. 12in. **$1,150**

419 **Tulip Shape Goblet** w/gilt metal & poly. enamel dec., ht. 4in. **$230**

420 **Tea Service,** three pcs., mid-20th C., silver & shaded enamel. **$977**

A-MA Jun. 2004 Skinner, Inc.
144 **Pewter Plates,** matched set of four by Boardman & Co., Hartford, CT, ca. 1805-50. Touchmarks include two oval eagles, one circular w/eagle & Boardman & Co. New York, dia. 9⅜in. **$940**

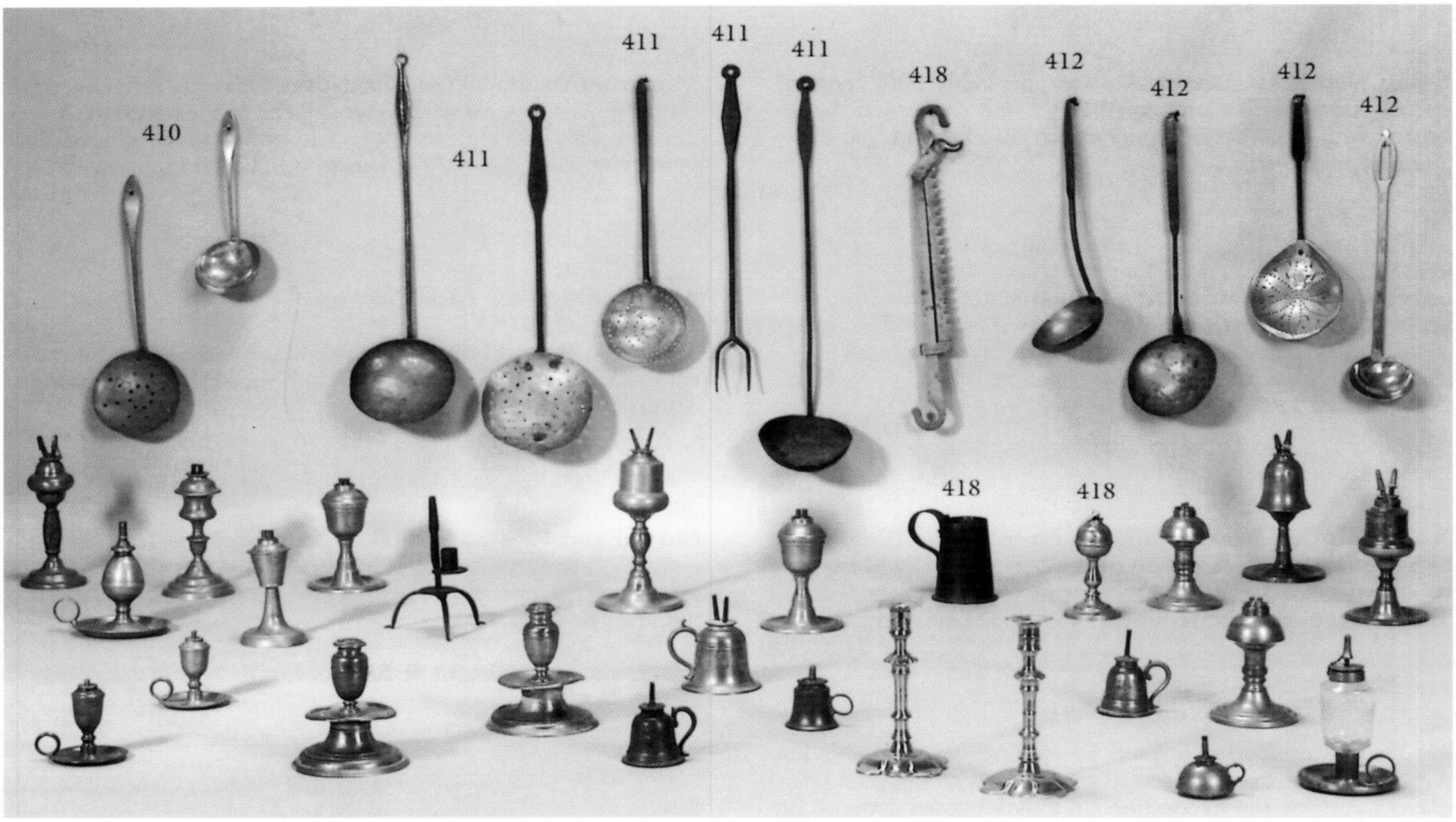

413 415 414 415 416 417 417 419

A-MA Feb. 2004 Skinner, Inc.
410 **Brass Skimmer & Ladle,** late 18th/early 19th C., by Richard Lee Jr., Springfield, VT, both w/R.LEE touchmark on handle, sm. loss on edge of skimmer, lg. 16⅛, 11½in. **$1,528**
411 **Hearth Tools,** Am. or Eng., 18th C., inc. two ladles & two skimmers, ea. w/wrt. iron handles & hammered brass bowl secured w/copper rivets, together: w/wrt. iron meat fork, wear to bowl edges, lg. 20¼, 24½in. **$499**
412 **Hearth Tools,** Am., Eng. or Cont., 18th C., two ladles, skimmer, bowl & brass ladle, wear & repair on ladle. **$705**
413 **Pewter Lamps,** seven assorted, Am., early to mid-19th C., one lamp by Geo. Norris, NY, w/whale oil burners, & one mkd. W.J. on base. **$999**
414 **Wrought Iron Rush Light & Candleholder,** Am., 18th/early 19th C., w/boot form tripod base, ht. 7in. **$881**
415 **Candlesticks,** brass, probably Spain, ca. 1625-50, ea. w/baluster-shaped candle cup w/drip pan, dents, ht. 5⅞ & 6in. **$705**
416 **Pewter Lamps,** six assorted, Am., early to mid-19th C., one by Capin & Molineux, NY, w/camphene burners, three bell-form hand lamps w/imper., one mkd. G. Norris, NY, w/whale oil burners. **$705**
417 **Queen Anne Brass Candlesticks,** pr., Eng., ca. 1750, ht. 7¾in. **$1,293**
418 **Brass Trammel, Copper Measure & Whale Oil Lamp,** 18th to 19th C. **$764**
419 **Pewter Lamps,** Am., seven, early 19th C., two w/brass camphene burners, a pair w/brass whale oil burners; one brass fluid burner on bell-shaped font; a small hand lamp & a peg lamp w/cut berry & vine motif. **$881**

A-MA Jun. 2004 Skinner, Inc.
126 **Pewter Flagon,** 3 qt. by Thomas E. & Sherman Boardman, Hartford, CT, ca. 1815-20, mkd. TDSB w/an eagle & an X, their quality mark, ht. 14in. **$3,819**

A-MA Jun. 2004 Skinner, Inc.
127 **Pewter Flagon,** 3 qt. by Boardman & Hart, Hartford, CT, ca. 1825-30, mkd. Boardman & Hart, N-York, & two round eagles, ht. 13in. **$3,055**

A-Jun. 2004 Skinner, Inc.
129 **Pewter Mug,** qt., by Samuel Hamlin, Hartford, CT, late 18th C. w/touchmark, minor wear, ht. 5⅞in. **$3,819**
130 **Pewter Mug,** qt., by Joseph, Danforth,Sr., Middletown, CT, 1780-88, w/touchmark, minor wear & pitting, ht. 6in. **$4,700**
131 **Pewter Mug,** qt., by Samuel Hamlin, Hartford, CT., late 18th C. w/touchmark, wear & pitting, ht. 5⅞in. **$4,113**

A-MA June. 2004 Skinner, Inc.
Pewter
145 **Plate** by Gershom Jones, Providence, RI, 1774-1809 w/two lion touchmarks and four hallmarks, dia. 8¼in. **$1,116**
146 **Plate** by Thomas Danforth II, Middleton, CT, ca. 1760-70 w/two lion touchmarks & hallmarks w/an X for quality, dia. 9½in. **$3,173**
147 **Plate** by Richard Austin, Boston, 1792-1817 w/oval touchmark, a dove & lamb, dia. 7⅞in. **$235**

A-Jun. 2004 Skinner, Inc.
Pewter
151 **Plates,** set of three by John Skinner, Boston, 1760-90. The plates w/hammered booge, have always been together & bear left facing lion touchmark and the same owner's marks. **$1,880**

A-MA Jun. 2004 Skinner, Inc.
Pewter
148 **Mug** by Boardman & Hart, w/touchmarks, minor wear, ht. 4in. **$1,880**
149 **Mug** w/touchmarks of CMS& CS, around rim, Boston, ht. 6¼in. **$7,050**
150 **Pint Mug** by T.D. & Sherman Boardman w/touchmarks, wear & small dent on base,ht. 4½in. **$1,538**

A-PA May 2004 Pook & Pook, Inc.
First Row, Pewter
422 **Flagon** w/strap handle & eagle touch marked Boardman New York, ht. 8in. **$920**
423 **Footed Beakers,** pair attributed to Israel Trask, 1807-1856, together w/a chalice ht. 6½in., and an E. Kauman chalice, ca. 1850, ht. 7¼in. **$316**
424 **Coffeepot** by Isaac C. Lewis, Meridian, CT, 1834-1852, w/touchmark, ht. 11½in. **$230**
425 **Flagon** w/strap handle by Thomas Boardman, mkd. BX on base, ht. 12¼in. **$460**
426 **Footed Bowl** w/eagle touch imp. Glennore Co., G. Richardson, Cranston, RI, ht. 2⅝, dia. 5½in. **$661**
427 **Flagon** w/strap handle by Israel Trask, Beverly, MA, w/I.Trask touchmark, ht. 10½in. **$489**
428 **Mugs,** three pint w/strap handles, w/Morey & Ober imp. mark, Boston, MA, 1852-1860, ht. 4⅝in. Third mug on second row. **$805**
429 **Pewter lamp** w/Dunham touchmark, ht. 9¾in., together w/a blown glass hour lamp, ht. 14in. not illus. **$345**
Second Row, Pewter
430 **Deep Bowls,** two w/imp. touch of Samuel Hamlin, Providence, RI, 1771-1801, dia. 7¾in. **$748**
431 **Teapot,** Q.A. style marked w/a B on base, ht. 5¾in. **$748**
432 **Basin** w/eagle touch of B. Barnes, Philadelphia, PA, 1812-1817, dia. 10in. **$805**
433 **Teapot,** Boardman & Hart w/impressed X Boardman & Hart, N. York, ht. 5¾in. **$920**
434 **Porringer** w/open work handle & tulip dec., attributed to Samuel Hamlin, ht. 5½in. **$115**
423 **Israel Trask Footed Beaker** not illus. on first row. Price of group. **$316**

A-MA Feb. 2004 **Skinner, Inc.**

132 **Porringer** by Samuel Hamlin, Jr., Providence, RI, 1801-1806, flowered handle engraved w/LAH monogram, dated 1820 w/round touchmark, eagle & anchor on handle, dia. 5⅝in. **$1,528**
133 **Porringer** by Samuel Hamlin, Jr., circular basin form w/boss bottom & touchmarks, dia. 4½in. **$1,058**
134 **Porringer** attrib. to Richard Lee, or Lee, Jr., Springfield, VT, 1788-1820, w/boss bottom, openwork handle w/crescents & hearts. The reversed letter R mark on handle back, dia. 3¾in. **$588**
135 **Porringer** by Gershom Jones, 1774-1809, w/boss bottom , flowered handle, circular lion touch & GI initials on handle, dia. 4¼in. **$2,350**
136 **Larger porringer** by Gershom Jones, w/boss bottom, flowered handle, & partial circular lion mark, dia. 5⅝in. **$2,115**

132 133 134 135 136

A-PA May 2004 **Pook & Pook, Inc.**
Silver
First Row
612 **English Lidded Tankard,** ca. 1785, by John Wren, ht. 8in. **$2,070**
613 **Irish Queen Anne Candlesticks,** ca. 1740, hallmarked John Moore, ht. 8¼in. **$10,925**
614 **Mint Julep Cups,** three, ca. 1850, by E.&.D. Kinsey, Cincinnati, OH, & Newport, KY. The first mkd. KY State Agl. Soc. 1856 Premium, the second Prem. B. Co. A.S. 1854, and the third McDonalds Premium, ht. 3½in. **$2,070**
615 **Coffeepot,** Am., ca. 1815 w/cut dec. resting on a circular plinth, ht. 13½in. **$863**
616 **Coin Silver Tea Service,** Ca. 1820, by John Crawford, NY, teapot ht.10in. Sugar bowl on second row. **$1,265**
Second Row
617 **Coin Silver Porringer,** ca. 1815, by Nichols, RI, ht. 2, dia. 5¼in. **$1,840**
618 **Centerpiece Bowl,** mid-19th C., by R.& W. Wilson, w/repoussé floral dec., dia. 12in. **$345**
619 **English Queen Anne Candlesticks,** pair, ca. 1745 w/indistinct marks, ht. 8½in. **$3,680**
620 **English Silver Lidded Tankard,** ca. 1752, by Fuller White, London, ht. 7in. **$2,300**

A-IA Jun. 2004 Jackson's International Auctioneers
339 **Sterling Silver Coffee & Tea Service,** late 19th C. Each piece chased w/bank of ivy leaves & topped w/pinecone finials, mkd. Tiffany & Co., together w/large silvered butler's tray, lg. 30in. not illus. **$7,475**

A-IA Jun. 2004 Jackson's International Auctioneers
341 **Caster Set** by Reed & Barton, ca. 1900, displaying cranberry glass cruets w/Egyptian styled silvered frame, ht. 18in. **$603**
342 **Silvered Ice Water Pitcher,** ca. 1870, by Jaccard & Co., w/embossed & chased dec., ht. 12¼in. **$201**

A-IA Jun. 2004 Jackson's International Auctioneers
343 **Tilting Ice Water Pitcher** by Rogers Smith & Co., ca. 1872, complete w/ stand & goblets, ht. 16¾in. **$546**

A-OH Jan. 2004 Garth's Arts & Antiques
471 **Rooster Weather Vane,** copper, full bodied & attrib. to J.W. Fiske, w/ old brown patina & areas of verdigris in recesses, a few dents & bullet holes, ht. 33in. **$11,202**

A-IA Jun. 2004 Jackson's International Auctioneers
371 **French Gilt Bronze Cage** w/life-sized feathered animated birds that sing in unison, early 20th C., ht. 21in. **$862**

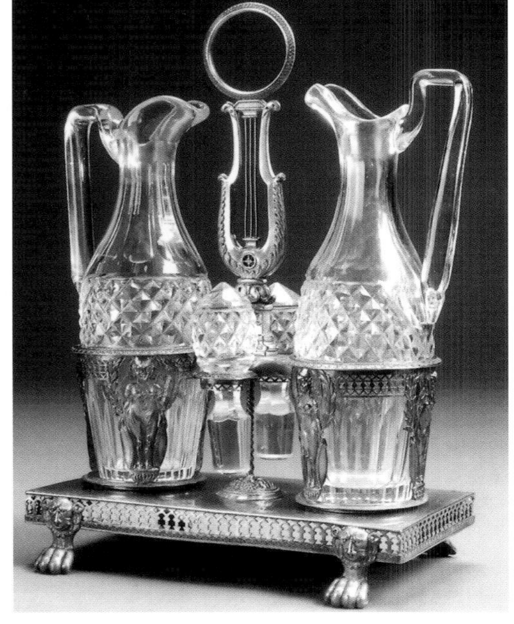

A-IA Nov. 2003 Jackson's International Auctioneers
734 **French Silver Cruet Stand,** early 19th C., w/two cut crystal handled bottles w/stoppers. Stamped French hallmarks include AM for maker, ht. 12in. **$1,035**

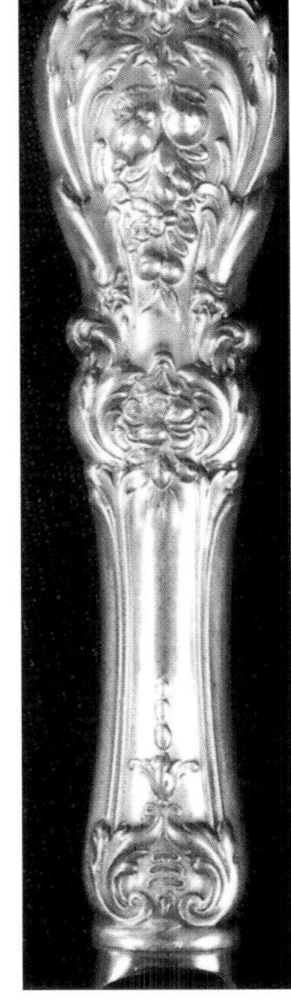

A-IA Jun. 2004 Jackson's International Auctioneers
340 **Sterling Flatware Service,** 100 pcs. by Reed & Barton, Francis I patt. **$2,530**

The market has remained strong and a remarkable number of exceptionally important original American artwork has sold. Although professional artists did flourish in the more populated areas, most of our early American paintings fall under the heading of amateur work, painted by itinerant artists during the 18th and 19th centuries. Their inability to create a cohesive composition, and their lack of skill in depicting a true likeness or correct perspective, resulted in many naïve paintings. No one speaks more eloquently for our heritage than the folk artist. Their portraits of sober-faced children – especially those with their favorite toy or dog – are very valuable these days because all serve as a surviving link to a vital and fascinating past. These paintings with juvenile quality are extremely appealing to collectors.

Today there are available to collectors many charming and beautiful paintings, drawings and prints, from all schools and periods of art. As with all fields of collecting, values vary greatly and many factors – quality, size, an artist's signature, and condition – determine value. But, in general, a beautiful original work of art can be found to fit almost every budget.

Many charming works of art are available, including portraits, still-life, historical, and religious paintings. However, folk art paintings and pictures are in a class all of their own. They include paper cuttings, tinsel pictures, theorems on velvet, cotton or paper, calligraphic drawings, needlework pictures and silhouettes.

Collectors should never overlook artwork by an unknown artist, or an unsigned work if it is good. It will not only bring the owner the aesthetic pleasure of owning something beautiful, but it also offers the practical quality of generally being a good investment. However, it is the signed and dated pieces that will fetch substantially high prices in the marketplace.

A-MA Feb. 2004 Skinner, Inc.

10 The Road – Winter by Nathaniel Currier, 1853, Am. Publisher 1813-1888, litho. w/hand-coloring on paper, w/ light toning & minor foxing, sheet- size 19¾x28⅜in. **$25,850**

A-MA Feb. 2004 Skinner, Inc.

Currier & Ives Prints, Am., 1857-1907

Identified in inscription in the matrix.

28 New England Winter Scene, 1861, litho. w/hand-coloring on paper, matted & framed, minor toning, sheet size 20x26⅞in. **$6,463**

30 Winter In The Country .. The Old Grist Mill, 1864, w/hand-coloring on paper, repair tear in title & light mat stain, sheet size 23x29in. **$8,813**

A-PA May 2004
Pook & Pook, Inc.
251 **Landscape** by Jacob Maentel, Am. 1783-1863, watercolor on paper, ht. 8, wd.6in. **$14,950**

A-MA Jun. 2004
Skinner, Inc.
353 **Portrait of Girl** holding doll, unsgn., oil on canvas in giltwood frame, relined in painting, 36 x 29in. **$8,813**

A-MA Jun. 2004 Skinner, Inc.
36 **Theorem,** unsgn., watercolor on velvet, 13½ x 16½in. **$4,113**

A-MA Feb. 2004 Skinner, Inc.
73 **Portrait,** Girl in a Red Dress, 1840s, attrib. to William W. Kennedy, known to have worked in New England. Oil on academy board w/slight warping, minor abrasions & minor paint loss, sight ht. 22, wd. 17½in. **$88,125**

A-PA May 2004 Pook & Pook, Inc.
299 **Landscape Painting** attrib. to George Henry Durrie, 1820-1863, oil on panel, 12x14½in. **$43,700**

A-MA Jun. 2004 **Skinner, Inc.**
134 **Portrait of the Ship Cherub of Boston.** Unsigned inscriptions below read: CHERUB of Boston, CHAS. JONES, Master, saving the Crew of the Jersey Schooner, WAR OAK. Oil on paper laid onto linen, unframed w/few losses to sky. The Cherub was built in Boston in 1816/1817. Charles Jones was Master in 1832. Sight 16½ x 21⅞in. **$4,406**

A-MA Feb. 2004 **Skinner, Inc.**
131 **Portrait of the Clipper Ship Great Republic,** sgn. Percy Sanborn l.r., oil on canvas. As rebuilt after the fire of Dec. 26, 1853. The background has been retouched, framed ht.26, wd. 40in. **$17,625**

A-NH Aub. 2004 **Northeast Auctions**
634 **Picking Apples,** Am. School watercolor, ca. 1830, depicting two girls & a boy in garden w/fruit tree. ht. 18, wd. 26in. **$29,000**

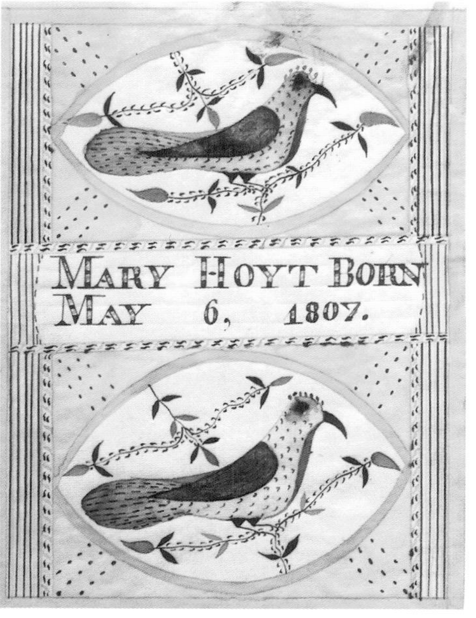

A-MA Jun. 2004 **Skinner, Inc.**
8 **Birth Record,** watercolor & ink on paper, reverse sgn. Henniker May 7,1829 by Moses Connor, minor staining, unframed, 9 x 7in. **$8,225**

A-NH Aug. 2004 **Northeast Auctions**
632 **Pen & Ink Drawings,** Peace & Plenty, ca. 1820, watercolors, w/labels on reverse Painted by Susan Phelps or Sophia Phelps, sisters, about 1820. Ht. 15, wd. 12in. **$3,750**

A-MA Feb. 2004 Skinner, Inc.
33 Snowed Up, Ruffed Grouse In Winter, 1867, litho. w/hand-coloring on paper by Currier & Ives. Sheet size 17⅞ x 23⅞in., matted, light toning, stains & small repaired tear. $6,463

A-MA Feb. 2004 Skinner, Inc.
23 Peytona And Fashion. In Their Great Match For $20,000., Nathaniel Currier litho. w/hand coloring on paper, repaired tears & subtle toning. Sheet size 20½ x 30⅝in. $4,700

2 (pair)
3
4
5 (partial)

A-MA jun. 2004 Skinner, Inc.
2 Hollowcut Portrait Silhouettes, pair, unsgn., mkd. Dudley, Oct. -1835. Watercolor, pen & ink, gouache, silk on paper, black silk backing, in brass & wood frame, 3½ x 2½in. $2,233
3 Portrait of Two Sisters, unsgn., watercolor on paper, dresses accented w/pinprick designs, framed, reprs, 9 x 7in. $1,410
4 Portrait Miniature of a Gentleman, unsgn., watercolor on paper, crease & minor foxing, dia. 4½in. $881
5 Silhouette Portraits, partial, ca. 1820, a hollowcut profile of a young man ca. 1820; a profile of a gentleman on the reverse not illus., & a profile portrait of a woman, light stains. $881
6 Pair of Hollowcut & Painted Silhouettes, possibly work of Wm. Chamberlain, ca. 1820 w/inscriptions on back. $764
7 Two Girls W/Kitten, unsgn., watercolor & gouache on ivory in molded gilt frame, paint loss on clothing, 3⅝ x 2¾in. $4,113

A-MA Feb. 2004 Skinner, Inc.
31 **American Winter Sports,** Deer Shooting On The Shattagee, 1855. Lithograph by Nathaniel Currier, w/hand-coloring on paper. Repaired tears, light toning & stains. Sheet size 20⅜ x 20⅝in. **$3,055**

A-NH Aug. 2004 Northeast Auctions
655 **Portrait,** Am., probably eastern New York, ca. 1825, oil on panel depicting a young woman in elaborate lace collared dress & cap, ht. 27½, wd. 21¼in. **$75,000**

A-MA Feb. 2004 Skinner, Inc.
14 **The Rocky Mountains,** Emigrants Crossing The Plains, 1866, w/hand-coloring on paper by Currier & Ives w/toning & stains, sheet size 22⅝ x 29¼in. **$21,150**

A-PA. Nov. 2003 Conestoga Auctions, Inc.
541 Reward of Merit in contemporary dec. frame, slight foxing to paper, image size ht. 5¾, wd. 3¼in. **$4,100**

A-NH Aug. 2004 Northeast Auctions
559 **American School Farm Landscape,** mid-19th C., New England, oil on canvas in orig. frame, ht. 40¾, wd. 50¾in. **$27,500**

A-PA Mar. 2004 Pook & Pook, Inc.
145 **Fraktur,** watercolor & ink on paper, PA, inscribed Jacob Leith, ht. 3¾, wd. 4in. **$2,990**

A-PA Mar. 2004 Pook & Pook, Inc.
139 **Fraktur,** watercolor on paper dated 1824 w/two panels, ht. 8, wd. 4½in. **$29,900**

143 **Fraktur**, watercolor & ink on paper, PA, w/imper., ht. 5½, wd. 3¼in. **$7,475**

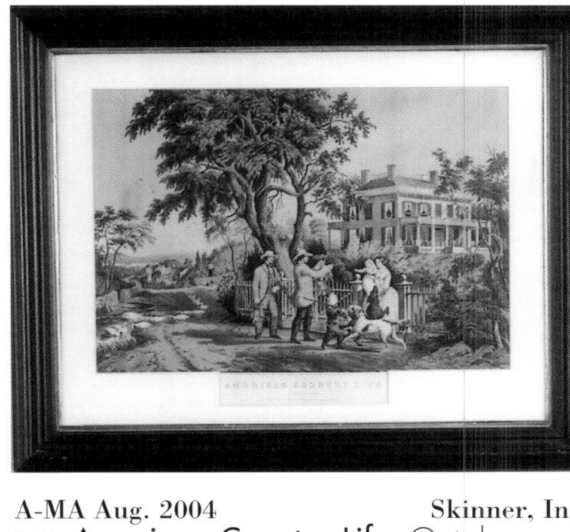

A-MA Aug. 2004 Skinner, Inc.
160 **American Country Life,** October Afternoon, 1885, lithograph w/hand-coloring on paper, published by Nathaniel Currier, 1855, w/toning & stains, sheet size 22 x 27in. **$1,410**

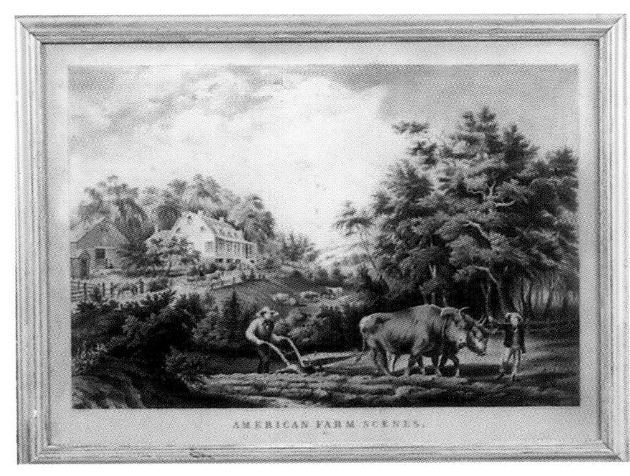

A-MA Aug. 2004
Skinner, Inc.
164 **American Farm Scenes,** No. I, 1853, published by Nathaniel Currier, 1853, lithographed w/hand coloring on paper, w/toning & stains, sheet size 20 x 26½in. **$1,293**

A-MA Aug. 2004 Skinner, Inc.
161 **Tobogganing On Darktown Hill,** An Untimely Move, 1890, published by Currier & Ives, lithograph w/hand-coloring heightened w/gum arabic on paper, sight size 11 x 13¾in. **$411**

A-NH Aug. 2004 Northeast Auctions
662 **Still-Life Painting,** oil on canvas w/watermelon & basket of fruit, ht. 19, wd. 26in. **$1,600**

A-NH Aug. 2004 Northeast Auctions
504 **Still-Life Painting** w/abundant fruit & vegetables on a gray marble table top. American School, oil on canvas, ht. 24, wd. 32in. **$6,000**

ABC Plates – Alphabet plates were made especially for children as teaching aids. They date from the late 1700s and were made of various material including porcelain, pottery, glass, pewter, tin and ironstone.

Amphora Art Pottery was made at the Amphora Porcelain Works in the TeplitzTum area of Bohemia during the late 19th and early 20th centuries. Numerous potteries were located there.

Anna Pottery – The Anna Pottery was established in Anna, IL, in 1859 by Cornwall and Wallace Kirkpatrick, and closed in 1894. The company produced utilitarian wares, gift wares and pig-shaped bottles and jugs with special inscriptions, which are the most collectible pieces.

Battersea Enamels – The name "Battersea" is a general term for those metal objects decorated with enamels, such as pill, patch, and snuff boxes, doorknobs, and such. The process of fusing enamel onto metal – usually copper – began about 1750 in the Battersea district of London. Today the name has become a generic term for similar objects – mistakenly called "Battersea".

Belleek porcelain was first made at Fermanagh, Ireland, in 1857. Today this ware is still being made in buildings within walking distance of the original clay pits, according to the skills and traditions of the original artisans. Irish Belleek is famous for its thinness and delicacy. Similar wares were also produced in other European countries, as well as in the United States.

Bennington Pottery – The first pottery works in Bennington, Vermont, was established by Captain John Norton in 1793, and for 101 years it was owned and operated by succeeding generations of Nortons. Today the term "Bennington" is synonymous with the finest in American ceramics because the town was the home of several pottery operations during the last century – each producing under different labels. Today items produced at Bennington are now conveniently, if inaccurately, dubbed "Bennington". One of the popular types of pottery produced there is known as "Rockingham". The term denotes the rich, solid brown glazed pottery from which many household items were made. The ware was first produced on the Marquis of Rockingham's estate in Swinton, England – hence the name.

Beswick – An earthenware produced in Staffordshire, England, by John Beswick in 1936. The company is now a part of Royal Doulton Tableware Ltd.

Bisque – The term applies to pieces of porcelain or pottery which have been fired but left in an unglazed state.

Bloor Derby – "Derby" porcelain dates from about 1755 when William Duesbury began the production of porcelain at Derby. In 1769 he purchased the famous Chelsea Works and operated both factories. During the Chelsea-Derby period, some of the finest examples of English porcelains were made. Because of their fine quality, in 1773 King George III gave Duesbury the patent to mark his porcelain wares "Crown Derby". Duesbury died in 1796. In 1810 the factory was purchased by Robert Bloor, a senior clerk. Bloor revived the Imari styles which had been so popular. After his death in 1845, former workmen continued to produce fine porcelains using the traditional Derby patterns. The firm was reorganized in 1876 and in 1878 a new factory was built. In 1890, Queen Victoria appointed the company "Manufacturers to Her Majesty" with the right to be known as Royal Crown Derby.

Buffalo Pottery – The Buffalo Pottery of Buffalo, New York, was organized in 1901. The firm was an adjunct of the Larkin Soap Company, which was established to produce china and pottery premiums for that company. Of the many different types produced, the Buffalo Pottery is most famous for its "Deldare" line, which was developed in 1905.

Canary Luster earthenware dates to the early 1800s, and was produced by potters in the Staffordshire district of England. The body of this ware is a golden yellow and decorated with transfer printing, usually in black.

Canton porcelain is a blue-and-white decorated ware produced near Canton, China, from the late 1700s through the 19th century and into the 20th. Its hand-decorated Chinese scenes have historical as well as mythological significance.

Capo-di-Monte, originally a soft paste porcelain, is Italian in origin. The first ware was made during the 1700s near Naples. Although numerous marks were used, the most familiar to us is the crown over the letter N. Mythological subjects, executed in either high or low relief and tinted in bright colors on a light ground, were a favorite decoration. The earlier wares had a peculiar grayish color as compared with the whiter bodies of later examples.

Carlsbad porcelain was made by several factories in the area from the 1800s and exported to the United States. When Carlsbad became a part of Czechoslovakia after World War I, wares were frequently marked "Karlsbad". Items marked "Victoria" were made for Lazarus & Rosenfeldt, importers.

Castleford earthenware was produced in England from the late 1700s until around 1820. Its molded decoration is similar to Prattware.

Celadon – Chinese porcelain having a velvet-textured greenish-gray glaze. Japanese and other Oriental factories also made celadon glazed wares.

Chelsea – An early soft paste porcelain manufactured at Chelsea in London from around 1745 to 1769. Chelsea is considered to be one of the most famous of English porcelain factories.

Chelsea Keramic Art Works – The firm was established in 1872, in Chelsea, MA, by members of the Robertson family. The firm used the mark CKAW. The company closed in 1889, but was reorganized in 1891, as the Chelsea Pottery U.S. In 1895, the factory became the Dedham Pottery of Dedham, MA, and closed in 1943.

Chinese Export Porcelain was made in quantity in China during the 1700s and early 1800s. The term identifies a variety of porcelain wares made for export to Europe and the United States. Since many thought the product to be of joint Chinese and English manufacture, it has also been known as "Oriental" or "Chinese Lowestoft".

As much of this ware was made to order for the American and European market, it was frequently adorned with seals of states or the coat of arms of individuals, in addition to eagles, sailing scenes, flowers, religious and mythological scenes.

Clarice Cliff Pottery – Clarice Cliff (1889-1972) was a designer who worked at A.J. Wilkinson Ltd.'s Royal Staffordshire Pottery at Burslem, England. Cliff's earthenwares were bright and colorful Art Deco designs which included squares, circles, bands, conical shapes and simple landscapes incorporated with the designs. Cliff used several different printed marks, each of which incorporated a facsimile of her signature – and generally the name of the pattern.

Clews Pottery – (see also, Historical Staffordshire) was made by George Clews & Co., of Brownhill Pottery, Tunstall, England, from 1806-1861.

Clifton Pottery – William Long founded the

Clifton Pottery in Clifton, NJ, in 1905. Pottery was simply marked CLIFTON. Long worked until 1908, producing a line called Crystal Patina. The Chesapeake Pottery Company made majolica marked Clifton Ware, which oftentimes confuses collectors.

Coalport porcelain has been made by the Coalport Porcelain Works in England since 1795. The ware is still being produced at Stoke-on-Trent.

Coors Pottery – Coors ware was made in Golden, CO, by the Coors Beverage Co. from the turn of the century until the pottery was destroyed by fire in the 1930s.

Copeland-Spode – The firm was founded by Josiah Spode in 1770 in Staffordshire, England. From 1847 W.T. Copeland & Sons Ltd. succeeded Spode, using the designation "Late Spode" to its wares. The firm is still in operation.

Copper Luster – See Lusterwares.

Cordey – Boleslaw Cybis was one of the founders of the Cordey China Company, Trenton, NJ. Production began in 1942. In 1969, the company was purchased by the Lightron Corporation, and operated as the Schiller Cordey Company. Around 1950, Cybis began producing fine porcelain figurines.

Cowan Pottery – Guy Cowan produced art pottery in Rocky River, OH, from 1913 to 1931. He used a stylized mark with the word COWAN on most pieces. Also, Cowan mass-produced a line marked LAKEWARE.

Crown Ducal – English porcelain made by A.G. Richardson & Co. Ltd. since 1916.

Cup Plates were used where cups were handleless and saucers were deep. During the early 1800s, it was very fashionable to drink from a saucer. Thus, a variety of fancy small plates were produced for the cup to rest in. The lacy Sandwich examples are very collectible.

Davenport pottery and porcelain was made at the Davenport Factory in Longport, Staffordshire, England, from 1793 until 1887 when the pottery closed. Most of the wares produced there – porcelains, creamwares, ironstone, earthenwares and other products – were marked.

Dedham (Chelsea Art Works) – The firm was founded in 1872, at Chelsea, Massachusetts, by James Robertson & Sons, and closed in 1889. In 1891, the pottery was reopened under the name of The Chelsea Pottery, U.S. The first and most popular blue underglaze decoration for the desirable "Cracqule Ware" was the rabbit motif – designed by Joseph L. Smith. In 1893, construction was started on the new pottery in Dedham, Massachusetts, and production began in 1895. The name of the pottery was then changed to "Dedham Pottery," to eliminate the confusion with the English Chelsea Ware. The famed crackleware finish became synonymous with the name. Because of its popularity, more than fifty patterns of tableware were made.

Delft – Holland is famous for its fine examples of tin-glazed pottery dating from the 16th century. Although blue and white is the most popular color, other colors were also made. The majority of the ware found today is from the late Victorian period and when the name Holland appears with the Delft factory mark, this indicates that the item was made after 1891.

Dorchester Pottery was established by George Henderson in Dorchester, a part of Boston, Massachusetts, in 1895. Production included stonewares, industrial wares and, later, some decorated tablewares. The pottery is still in production.

Doulton – The pottery was established in Lambeth in 1815 by John Doulton and John Watts. When Watts retired in 1845, it became known as Doulton & Company. In 1901, King Edward VII conferred a double honor on the company by presentation of the Royal Warrant, authorizing their chairman to use the word "Royal" in describing products. A variety of wares were made over the years for the American market. The firm is still in production.

Dresden – The term identifies any china produced in the town of Dresden, Germany. The most famous factory in Dresden is the Meissen factory. During the 18th century, English and Americans used the name "Dresden china" for wares produced at Meissen which has led to much confusion. The city of Dresden which was the capital of Saxony, was better known in 18th century Europe than Meissen. Therefore, Dresden became a generic term for all porcelains produced and decorated in the city of Dresden and surrounding districts, including Meissen. By the mid-19th century, about thirty factories in the city of Dresden were producing and decorating porcelains in the style of Meissen. Therefore, do not make the mistake of thinking all pieces marked Dresden were made at the Meissen factory. Meissen pieces generally have crossed swords marks and are listed under Meissen.

Flowing Blue ironstone is a highly glazed dinnerware made at Staffordshire by a variety of potters. It became popular about 1825. Items were printed with Oriental patterns and the color flowed from the design over the white body, so that the finished product appeared smeared. Although purple and brown colors were also made, the deep cobalt blue shades were the most popular. Later wares were less blurred, having more white ground.

Frankoma – The Frank Pottery was founded in 1933, by John Frank, Sapulpa, OK. The company produced decorative wares from 1936-38. Early wares were made from a light cream-colored clay, but in 1956 changed to a red brick clay. This along with the glazes helps to determine the period of production.

Fulper – The Fulper mark was used by the American Pottery Company of Flemington, NJ. Fulper art pottery was produced from approximately 1910 to 1930.

Gallé – Emile Gallé was a designer who made glass, pottery, furniture and other Art Nouveau items. He founded his factory in France in 1874. Ceramic pieces were marked with the initials E.G. impressed, Em. Gallé Faiencerie de Nancy, or a version of his signature.

Gaudy Dutch is the most spectacular of the gaudy wares. Made for the Pennsylvania Dutch market from about 1785 until the 1820s, this soft paste tableware is lightweight and frail in appearance. Its rich cobalt blue decoration was applied to the biscuit, glazed and fired – then other colors were applied over the first glaze – and the object was fired again. No luster is included in its decoration.

Gaudy Ironstone was made in Staffordshire from the early 1850s until around 1865. This ware is heavier than Gaudy Welsh or Gaudy Dutch, as its texture is a mixture of pottery and porcelain clay.

Gaudy Welsh, produced in England from about 1830, resembles Gaudy Dutch in decoration, but the workmanship is not as fine and its texture is more comparable to that of spatterware. Luster is usually included with the decoration.

Gouda Pottery – Gouda and the surrounding areas of Holland have been one of the principal Dutch pottery centers since the 17th century. The Zenith pottery and the Zuid-Hooandsche pottery produced the brightly colored wares marked GOUDA from 1880 to about

1940. Many pieces of Gouda featured Art Nouveau or Art Deco designs.

Grueby – Grueby Faience Company, Boston, MA, was founded in 1897 by William H. Grueby. The company produced hand thrown art pottery in natural shapes, hand molded and hand tooled. A variety of colored glazes, singly or in combinations, were used, with green being the most prominent color. The company closed in 1908.

Haeger – The Haeger Potteries, Inc., Dundee, IL, began making art wares in 1914. Their early pieces were marked with HAEGER written over the letter "H." Around 1938, the mark changed to ROYAL HAEGER.

Hampshire – In 1871, James S. Taft founded the Hampshire Pottery Company in Keene, NH. The company produced redware, stoneware, and majolica decorated wares in 1879. In 1883, the company introduced a line of colored glazed wares, including a Royal Worcester type pink, blue, green, olive and reddish-brown. Pottery was marked with the printed mark or the impressed name HAMPSHIRE POTTERY or J.S.T. & CO., KEENE, N.H.

Harker – The Harker Pottery Company of East Liverpool, OH, was founded in 1840. The company made a variety of different types of pottery including yellowware from native clays. Whiteware and Rockingham type brown-glazed pottery were also produced in quantities.

Historical Staffordshire – The term refers to a particular blue-on-white, transfer-printed earthenware produced in quantity during the early 1800s by many potters in the Staffordshire district. The central decoration was usually an American city scene or landscape, frequently showing some mode of transportation in the foreground. Other designs included portraits and patriotic emblems. Each potter had a characteristic border, which is helpful to identify a particular ware, as many pieces are unmarked. Later transfer-printed wares were made in sepia, pink, green and black, but the early cobalt blue examples are the most desirable.

Hull – In 1905, Addis E. Hull purchased the Acme Pottery Company in Crooksville, OH. In 1917, Hull began producing art pottery, stoneware and novelties, including the Little Red Riding Hood line. Most pieces had a matte finish with shades of pink and blue or brown predominating. After a flood and fire in 1950, the factory was reopened in 1952 as the Hull Pottery Company. Pre-1950 vases are marked Hull USA or HULL ART USA. Post-1950 pieces are simply marked HULL in large script or block letters. Paper labels were also used.

Hummel – Hummel items are the original creations of Berta Hummel, born in 1909 in Germany. Hummel collectibles are made by W. Goebel Porzellanfabrik of Oeslau, Germany, now Rodenthal, West Germany. They were first made in 1934. All authentic Hummels bear both the signature, M.I. Hummel, and a Goebel trademark. However, various trademarks were used to identify the year of production.

Ironstone is a heavy, durable, utilitarian ware made from the slag of iron furnaces, ground and mixed with clay. Charles Mason of Lane Delft, Staffordshire, patented the formula in 1823. Much of the early ware was decorated in imitation of Imari, in addition to transfer-printed blue ware, flowing blues and browns. During the mid-19th century, the plain white enlivened only by embossed designs became fashionable. Literally hundreds of patterns were made for export.

Jackfield Pottery – is English in origin. It was first produced during the 17th century; however, most items available today date from the last century. It is a red-bodied pottery, often decorated with scrolls and flowers in relief, then covered with a black glaze.

Jasperware – is a very hard, unglazed porcelain with a colored ground, varying from blues and greens to lavender, red, yellow or black. White designs were generally applied in relief to these wares, and often reflect a classical motif. Jasperware was first produced by Wedgwood's Etruria Works in 1775. Many other English potters produced jasperware, including Copeland, Spode and Adams.

Jugtown Pottery – This North Carolina pottery has been made since the 18th century. In 1915 Jacques Busbee organized what was to become the Jugtown Pottery in 1921. Production was discontinued in 1958.

King's Rose is a decorated creamware produced in the Staffordshire district of England during the 1820-1840 period. The rose decorations are usually in red, green, yellow and pink. This ware is often referred to as "Queen's Rose".

Leeds Pottery was established by Charles Green in 1758 at Leeds, Yorkshire, England. Early wares are unmarked. From 1775, the impressed mark "Leeds Pottery" was used. After 1880, the name "Hartley, Greens & Co." was added, and the impressed or incised letters "LP" were also used to identify the ware.

Limoges – The name identifies fine porcelain wares produced by many factories at Limoges, France, since the mid-1800s. A variety of different marks identify wares made there including Haviland china.

Liverpool Pottery – The term applies to wares produced by many potters located in Liverpool, England, from the early 1700s, for American trade. Their print-decorated pitchers – referred to as "jugs" in England – have been especially popular. These featured patriotic emblems, prominent men, ships, etc., and can be easily identified, as nearly all are melon-shaped with a very pointed lip, strap handle and graceful curved body.

Lonhuda – In 1892, William Long, Alfred Day, and W.W. Hunter organized the Lonhuda Pottery Company of Steubenville, OH. The firm produced underglaze slip-decorated pottery until 1896, when production ceased. Although the company used a variety of marks, the earliest included the letters LPCP.

Lotus Ware – This thin, Belleek-like porcelain was made by the Knowles, Taylor & Knowles Company of Easter Liverpool, OH, from 1890 to 1900.

Lusterware – John Hancock of Hanley, England, invented this type of decoration on earthenwares during the early 1800s. The copper, bronze, ruby, gold, purple, yellow, pink and mottled pink luster finishes were made from gold painted on the glazed objects, then fired. The latter type is often referred to as "Sunderland Luster". Its pinkish tones vary in color and pattern. The silver lusters were made from platinum.

Maastricht Ware – Petrus Regout founded the De Sphinx pottery in 1835 at Maastricht, Holland. The company specialized in transfer printed earthenwares.

Majolica – The word "majolica" is a general term for any pottery glazed with an opaque tin enamel that conceals the color of the clay body. It has been produced by many countries for centuries. Majolica took its name from the Spanish island of Jamorca, where figuline (a potter's clay) is found. This ware frequently depicted elements in nature: birds, flowers, leaves and fish. English manufacturers marked their wares, and most can be identified through the English Registry mark and/or the potter-designer's mark, while most Continental pieces had an incised number. Although many American potteries produced majolica between 1850 and 1900, only a few chose to identify their wares. Among these were the firm of Griffen, Smith & Hill, George Morely, Edwin Bennett, Chesapeake Pottery Company, and the new Milford-Wannoppe Pottery Company.

Marblehead – This hand thrown pottery had its beginning in 1905 as a therapeutic program by Dr. J. Hall for the patients of a Marblehead, MA, sanitarium. Later, production was moved to another site and the factory continued under the management of A.E. Baggs until it closed in 1936. The most desirable pieces found today are decorated with conventionalized designs.

Matt-Morgan – By 1883, Matt Morgan, an English artist, was producing art pottery in Cincinnati, OH, that resembled Moorish wares. Incised designs and colors were applied to raised panels, and then shiny or matte glazes were applied. The firm lasted only a few years.

McCoy Pottery – The J.W. McCoy Pottery was established in 1899. Production of art pottery began after 1926, when the name was changed to Brush McCoy.

Meissen – The history of Meissen porcelain began in Germany in 1710 in the Albrechtsburg fortress of Meissen. The company was first directed by Johann Boettger, who developed the first truly white porcelain in Europe. The crossed swords mark of the Meissen factory was adopted in 1723.

Mettlach, Germany, located in the Zoar Basin, was the location of the famous Villeroy & Boch factories from 1836 until 1921, when the factory was destroyed by fire. Steins (dating from about 1842) and other stonewares with bas-relief decorations were their specialty.

Minton – Thomas Minton established his pottery in 1793 at Hanley, Stoke-on-Trent, England. During the early years, Minton concentrated on blue transfer painted earthenwares, plain bone china, and cream colored earthenware. During the first quarter of the 19th century, a large selection of figures and ornamental wares were produced in addition to their tableware lines. In 1968, Minton became a member of the Royal Doulton Tableware group, and retains its reputation for fine quality hand painted and gilded tablewares.

Mochaware – This banded creamware was first produced in England during the late 1700s. The early ware was lightweight and thin, having colorful bands of bright colors decorating a body that is cream colored to very light brown. After 1840, the ware became heavier in body and the color was often quite light – almost white. Mochaware can easily be identified by its colorful banded decorations – on and between the bands – including feathery ferns, lacy trees, seaweeds, squiggly designs and lowly earthworms.

Moorcroft – William Moorcroft established the Moorcroft Pottery, in Burslem, England, in 1913. The majority of the art pottery wares were hand thrown. The company initially used an impressed mark, MOORCROFT, BURSLEM, with a signature mark, W. MOORCROFT, following. Walker, William's son, continued the business after his father's death in 1945, producing the same style wares. Contemporary pieces are marked simply MOORCROFT with export pieces also marked MADE IN ENGLAND.

Newcomb – William and Ellsworth Woodward founded Newcomb Pottery at Sophie Newcomb College, New Orleans, LA, in 1896. Students decorated the high quality art pottery pieces with a variety of designs that have a decidedly southern flavor. Production continued through the 1940s. Marks include the letters "NC" and often have the incised initials of the artist as well. Most pieces have a matte glaze.

Niloak Pottery with its prominent swirled, marbelized designs, is a 20th century pottery first produced at Benton, Arkansas, in 1911, by the Niloak Pottery Company. Production ceased in 1946.

Nippon porcelain has been produced in quantity for the American market since the late 19th century. After 1891, when it became obligatory to include the country of origin on all imports, the Japanese trademark "Nippon" was used. Numerous other marks appear on this ware, identifying the manufacturer, artist or importer. The handpainted Nippon examples are extremely popular today and prices are on the rise.

Norse Pottery was founded in 1903 in Edgerton, WI. The company moved to Rockford, IL, in 1904, where they produced a black pottery which resembled early bronze items. The firm closed in 1913.

Ohr Pottery was produced by George E. Ohr in Biloxi, Mississippi, around 1883. Today Ohr is recognized as one of the leading potters in the American Art Pottery movement. Early work was often signed with an impressed stamp in block letters – G.E. OHR BILOXI. Later pieces were often marked G.E. Ohr in flowing script. Ohr closed the pottery in 1906, storing more than 6,000 pieces as a legacy to his family. These pieces remained in storage until 1972.

Old Ivory dinnerware was made in Silesia, Germany, during the late 1800s. It derives its name from the background color of the china. Marked pieces usually have a pattern number on the base, and the word "Silesia" with a crown.

Ott & Brewer – The company operated the Etruria Pottery in Trenton, NJ, from 1863 to 1893. A variety of marks were used which incorporated the initials O & B.

Owens – The Owens Pottery began production in Zanesville, OH, in 1891. The first art pottery was made after 1896, and pieces were usually marked OWENS. Production of art pottery was discontinued about 1907.

Paul Revere Pottery – This pottery was made at several locations in and around Boston, MA, between 1906 and 1942. The company was operated as a settlement house program for girls. Many pieces were signed S.E.G. for Saturday Evening Girls. The young artists concentrated on children's dishes and tiles.

Peters & Reed Pottery Company of Zanesville, Ohio, was founded by John D. Peters and Adam Reed about the turn of the century. Their wares, although seldom marked, can be identified by the characteristic red or yellow clay body touched with green. This pottery was best known for its matte glaze pieces – especially one type, called Moss Aztec, which combined a red earthenware body with a green glaze. The company changed hands in 1920 and was renamed the Zane Pottery Company. Examples marked "Zaneware" are often identical to earlier pieces.

Pewabic – Mary Chase Perry Stratton founded the Pewabic Pottery in 1903 in Detroit, MI. Many types of art pottery were produced here, including pieces with matte green glaze and an iridescent crystaline glaze. Operations ceased after the death of Mary Stratton in 1961, but the company was reactivated by Michigan State University in 1968.

Pisgah Forest Pottery – The pottery was founded near Mt. Pisgah in North Carolina in 1914, by Walter B. Stephen. The pottery remains in operation.

Quimper – Tin-glazed hand-painted pottery has been produced in Quimper, France, dating back to the 17th century. It is named for a French town where numerous potteries were located. The popular peasant design first appeared during the 1860s, and many variations exist. Florals and geometrics were equally popular. The HR and HR QUIMPER marks are found on Henriot pieces prior to 1922.

Redware is one of the most popular forms of country pottery. It has a soft, porous body and its color varies from reddish-brown tones to deep wine to light orange. It was produced in mostly utilitarian forms by potters in small factories, or by potters working on their farms, to fill their everyday needs. The most desirable examples are the slip-decorated pieces, or the rare and expensive "sgraffito" examples which have scratched or incised line decoration. Slip decoration was made by tracing the design on the redware shape with a clay having a creamy consistency in contrasting colors. When dried, the design was slightly raised above the surface.

Red Wing Art Pottery and Stoneware – The name includes several potteries located in Red Wing, MN. David Hallem established his pottery in 1868, producing stoneware items with a red wing stamped under the glaze as its mark. The Minnesota Stoneware Co. began production in 1883. The North Star Stoneware company began production in 1892, and used a raised star and the words Red Wing as it mark. The two latter firms merged in 1892, producing stoneware until 1920, when the company introduced a pottery line. In 1936, the name was changed to Red Wing Potteries. The plant closed in 1967.

Ridgway – Throughout the 19th century the Ridgway family, through partnerships, held positions of importance in Shelton and Hanley, Staffordshire, England. Their wares have been made since 1808, and their transfer design dinner sets are the most widely known product. Many pieces are unmarked, but later marks include the initials of the many partnerships.

Riviera – This dinnerware was made by the Homer Laughlin Company of Newell, WV, from 1938 to 1950.

Rockingham – See Bennington Pottery.

Rookwood Pottery – The Rookwood Pottery began production at Cincinnati, Ohio, in 1880 under the direction of Maria Longworth Nichols Storer, and operated until 1960. The name was derived from the family estate, "Rookwood," because of the "rooks" or "crows" which inhabited the wooded areas. All pieces of this art pottery are marked, usually bearing the famous flame.

Rorstrand Faience – The firm was founded in 1726 near Stockholm, Sweden. Items dating from the early 1900s and having an Art Nouveau influence are very expensive and much in demand.

Rose Medallion ware dates from the 18th century. It was decorated and exported from Canton, China, in quantity. The name generally applied to those pieces having medallions with figures of people, alternating with panels of flowers, birds and butterflies. When all the medallions are filled with flowers, the ware is identified as Rose Canton.

Rose Tapestry – See Royal Bayreuth.

Roseville Pottery – The Roseville Pottery was organized in 1890 in Roseville, Ohio. The firm produced utilitarian stoneware in the plant formerly owned by the Owens Pottery of Roseville, also producers of stoneware, and the Linden Avenue Plant at Zanesville, Ohio, originally built by the Clark Stoneware Company. In 1900, an art line of pottery was created to compete with Owens and Weller lines. The new ware was named "Rozanne," and it was produced at the Zanesville location. Following its success, other prestige lines were created. The Azurine line was introduced about 1902.

Royal Bayreuth manufactory began in Tettau in 1794 at the first porcelain factory in Bavaria. Wares made there were on a par with Meissen. Fire destroyed the original factory during the 1800s. Many of the wares available today were made at the new factory which began production in 1897. These include Rose Tapestry, Sunbonnet Baby novelties and the Devil and Card items. The Royal Bayreuth blue mark has the 1794 founding date incorporated with the mark.

Royal Bonn – The trade name identifies a variety of porcelain items made during the 19th century by the Bonn China Manufactory, established in 1755 by Elmer August. Most of the ware found today is from the Victorian period.

Royal Crown Derby – The company was established in 1875, in Derby, England, and has no connection with the earlier Derby factories which operated in the late 18th and early 19th centuries. Derby porcelain produced from 1878 to 1890 carries the standard crown printed mark. From 1891 forward, the mark carries the "Royal Crown Derby" wording, and during the 20th century, "Made in England" and "English Bone China" were added to the mark. Today the company is a part of Royal Doulton Tableware, Ltd.

Royal Doulton wares have been made from 1901, when King Edward VII conferred a double honor on the Doulton Pottery by the presentation of the Royal Warrant, authorizing their chairman to use the word "Royal" in describing products. A variety of wares has been produced for the American market. The firm is still in production.

Royal Dux was produced in Bohemia during the late 1800s. Large quantities of this decorative porcelain ware were exported to the United States. Royal Dux figurines are especially popular.

Royal Rudolstadt – This hard paste ware was first made in Rudolstadt, Thuringen, East Germany, by Ernst Bohne in 1882. The ware was never labeled "Royal Rudolstadt" originally, but the word "Royal" was added later as part of an import mark. This porcelain was imported by Lewis Straus and Sons of New York.

Royal Worcester – The Worcester factory was established in 1751 in England. This is a tastefully decorated porcelain noted for its creamy white lusterless surface. Serious collectors prefer items from the Dr. Wall (the activator of the concern) period of production which extended from the time the factory was established to 1785.

Roycroft Pottery was made by the Roycrofter community of East Aurora, New York, during the late 19th and early 20th centuries. The firm was founded by Elbert Hubbard. Products produced included pottery, furniture, metalware, jewelry and leatherwork.

R.S. Germany porcelain with a variety of marks was produced at the Tillowitz, Germany, factory of Reinhold Schlegelmilch from about 1869 to 1956.

R.S. Prussia porcelain was produced during the mid-1800s by Erdman Schlegelmilch in Suhl. His brother, Reinhold, founded a factory in 1869, in Tillowitz in lower Silesia. Both made fine quality porcelain, using both satin and high gloss finishes with comparable decoration. Additionally, both brothers used the same R.S. mark in the same colors, the initials in memory of their father, Rudolph Schlegelmilch. It has not been determined when production at the two factories ceased.

Ruskin is a British art pottery. The pottery, located at West Smethwick, Birmingham, England, was started by William H. Taylor. His name was used as the mark until around 1899. The firm discontinued producing new pieces of pottery in 1933, but continued to glaze and market their remaining wares until 1935. Ruskin pottery is noted for its exceptionally fine glazes.

Sarreguemines ware is the name of a porcelain factory in Sarreguemines, Lorraine, France, that made ceramics from about 1775. The factory was regarded as one of the most prominent manufacturers of French faience. Their transfer printed wares and majolica were made during the nineteenth century.

Satsuma is a Japanese pottery having a distinctive creamy crackled glaze decorated with bright enamels and often with Japanese figures. The majority of the ware available today includes the mass-produced wares dating from the 1850s. Their quality does not compare to the fine early examples.

Sewer Tile – Sewer tile figures were made by workers at sewer tile and pipe factories during the late nineteeth and early twentieth centuries. Vases and figurines with added decorations are now considered folk art by collectors.

Shawnee Pottery – The Shawnee Pottery Company was founded in 1937 in Zanesville, OH. The plant closed in 1961.

Shearwater Pottery – was founded by G.W. Anderson, along with his wife and their three sons. Local Ocean Springs, MS, clays were used to produce their wares during the 1930s, and the company is still in business.

Sleepy Eye – The Sleepy Eye Milling Company, Sleepy Eye, MN, used the image of the 19th century Indian chief for advertising purposes from 1883 to 1921. The company offered a variety of premiums.

Spatterware is soft paste tableware, laboriously decorated with hand-drawn flowers, birds, buildings, trees, etc., with "spatter" decoration chiefly as a background. It was produced in considerable quantity from the early 1800s to around 1850.

To achieve this type of decoration, small bits of sponge were cut into different shapes – leaves, hearts, rosettes, vines, geometrical patterns, etc. – and mounted on the end of a short stick for convenience in dipping into the pigment.

Spongeware, as it is known, is a decorative white earthenware. Color – usually blue, blue/green, brown/tan/blue, or blue/brown – was applied to the white clay base. Because the color was often applied with a color-soaked sponge, the term "spongeware" became common for this ware. A variety of utilitarian items were produced – pitchers, cookie jars, bean pots, water coolers, etc. Marked examples are rare.

Staffordshire is a district in England where a variety of pottery and porcelain wares has been produced by many factories in the area.

Stickspatter – The term identifies a type of decoration that combines hand-painting and transfer-painted decoration. "Spattering" was done with either a sponge or brush containing a moderate supply of pigment. Stickspatter was developed from the traditional Staffordshire spatterware, as the earlier ware was time consuming and expensive to produce. Although most of this ware was made in England from the 1850s to the late 1800s, it was also produced in Holland, France and elsewhere.

Tea Leaf is a lightweight stone china decorated with copper or gold "tea leaf" sprigs. It was first made by Anthony Shaw of Longport, England, during the 1850s. By the late 1800s, other potters in Staffordshire were producing the popular ware for export to the United States. As a result, there is a noticeable diversity in decoration.

Teco Pottery is an art pottery line made by the Terra Cotta Tile works of Terra Cotta, Illinois. The firm was organized in 1881, by William D. Gates. The Teco line was first made in 1885, but not sold commercially until 1902, and was discontinued during the 1920s.

UHL Pottery – This pottery was made in Evansville, IN, in 1854. In 1908, the pottery was moved to Huntingburg, IN, where their stoneware and glazed pottery was made until the mid-1940s.

Union Porcelain Works – The company first marked their wares with an eagle's head holding the letter "S" in its beak around 1876; the letters "U.P.W." were sometimes added.

Van Briggle Pottery was established at Colorado Springs, Colorado, in 1900, by Artus Van Briggle and his wife, Anna. Most of the ware was marked. The first mark included two joined "A's," representing their first two initials. The firm is still in operation.

Villeroy & Boch – The pottery was founded in 1841, at Mettlach, Germany. The firm produced many types of pottery including the famous Mettlach steins. Although most of their wares were made in the city of Mettlach, they also had factories in other locations. Fortunately for collectors, there is a dating code impressed on the bottom of most pieces that makes it possible to determine the age of the piece.

Watt Pottery – In 1935 the company began producing dinnerware with freehand decorations that has become very popular with collectors. Their most popular pattern is Apple which was produced in 1952. Early pieces in this pattern can be dated from the number of leaves. Originally, the apples had three leaves, but in 1958 only two leaves were used. Other popular patterns in this ware include Rooster (1955), Starflower and Tulip variations. New patterns were introduced annually until October, 1965, when the factory was destroyed by fire; it was never rebuilt.

Walrath – Frederich Walrath worked in Rochester, NY, New York City, and at the Newcomb Pottery in New Orleans, LA. He signed his pottery items "Walrath Pottery". He died in 1920.

Warwick china was made in Sheeling, WV, in a pottery from 1887 to 1951. The most familiar Warwick pieces have a shaded brown background. Many pieces were made with hand painted or decal decorations. The word ILGA is sometimes included with the Warwick mark.

Wedgwood Pottery was established by Josiah Wedgwood in 1759, in England. A tremendous variety of fine wares has been produced through the years including basalt, lusterwares, creamware, jasperware, bisque, agate, Queen's Ware and others. The system of marks used by the firm clearly indicates when each piece was made.

Weller Pottery – Samuel A. Weller established the Weller pottery in 1872, in Fultonham, Ohio. In 1888, the pottery was moved to Piece Street in Putnam, Ohio – now a part of Zanesville, Ohio. The production of art pottery began in 1893, and by late 1897 several prestige lines were being produced, including Samantha and Dickensware. Other later types included Weller's Louwelsa, Aurora, Turada and the rare Sicardo which is the most sought after and most expensive today. The firm closed in 1948.

Wheatley – Thomas J. Wheatley established the Wheatley Pottery in 1880. The Wheatley mark included joined letters WP with a dash below within a circle.

40-48

49-52

53-57

A-NH Nov. 2003 **Northeast Auctions**
Historical Staffordshire

40 **Tureen Stand** by Enoch Wood & Sons, Lafayette At Washington's Tomb, unmarked lg. 7⅝in. **$2,000**

No. 41-57, Landing of General Lafayette at Castle Garden, New York, 16 August, 1824 scene.

41 **Two Plates** by James & Ralph Clews, w/imp. factory mark, dia. 7 & 9in. **$300**

42 **Pitcher** by Clews, unmarked, ht. 7½in. **$800**

43 **Two Pitchers** by Clews, unmarked, hts. 7¾ & 10in. **$1,900**

44 **Soup Plate** by Clews w/impressed factory mark, dia. 9¾in. **$300**

45 **Bowl & Soup Plate** by Clews, each w/factory mark, dia. 7⅝ & 8⅝in. **$500**

46 **Sugar Box & Cream Pitcher** by Clews, latter unmarked. **$800**

47 **Waste Bowl** by Clews, unmarked, dia. 6¼in. **$600**

48 **Sugar Box & Cream Pitcher** by Clews, unmarked. **$550**

49 **Set of Four Plates,** each w/imp. factory mark, dia. 10¼in. **$1,000**

50 **Teapot** by Clews, unmarked, ht. 7¾in. **$1,000**

51 **Tea Service** by Clews, 5 pcs., comprising a teapot, coffee pot, sugar box w/cover, cream pitcher & waste bowl, unmarked, ht.of coffee pot 9¾in. **$2,750**

52 **Five Tea Bowls & Saucers** by Clews, each saucer w/imp. factory mark. **$1,900**

53 **Platters,** three by Clews, each w/imp. factory mark, lengths 10½, 12¼, & 15¼in. **$2,400**

54 **Well-And-Tree Platter** by Clews, unmarked, lg. 18¼in. **$1,700**

55 **Bowl** by Clews w/imp. factory mark, dia. 12½in. **$1,600**

56 **Four Graduated Vegetable Dishes** by Clews w/imp. factory mark. **$2,500**

57 **Soup Tureen & Cover** by Clews w/imp. factory mark, lg. over handles 14½in. **$4,800**

89-90

91-93

94-97

A-NH Nov. 2003 **Northeast Auctions**
Staffordshire
89 **Soup Tureen & Cover,** scene of Dix Cove On The Gold Coast, Africa. The printed title in underglaze-blue, lg. over handles 13¼in. **$600**
90 **Tureen & Cover,** Stand by James & Ralph Clews, Don Quixote & The Princess Series & Teresa Pansa & The Messenger, each printed title in underglaze blue, lg. of tureen over handles 15½in, stand 14in. **$1,200**
91 **Waste Bowl, Sugar Box & Cover,** each w/printed title Mount Vernon, The Seal of The Late Gen'l. Washington, ht. of sugar box 6¾ & dia. of waste bowl 7½in. **$600**
92 **Vegetable Dish & Cover,** Beauties of America Series, Mount Vernon Near Washington, by John & William Ridgway, lg. 11⅛in. **$600**
93 **Three Piece Tea Service,** Mount Vernon, comprising a teapot, sugar box w/cover & cream pitcher, both w/printer title, ht. of teapot 7in. **$3,500**
94 **Two Sugar Bowls & Covers** by Enoch Wood & Sons, unmkd., w/printed title Washington Standing At His Tomb, Scroll In Hand, ht. 4¾in. **$800**
95 **Tea Service,** 4 pcs. w/impressed Wood mark & title Washington Standing At His Tomb, ht. of teapot 7½in. **$750**
96 **Tea Bowl, Saucer, Cream Pitcher & Saucer** w/impressed Wood, & the scene on each, Washington Standing At His Tomb, Scroll In Hand. **$750**
97 **Egg Cup** by Wood, unmarked, Washington Series, ht. 2⅜in. **$4,000**

A-PA May 2004 Pook & Pook, Inc.
Chinese Export, 19th C.
518 **Large Canton Platter,** 19th C., lg. 20½, wd. 18in. **$920**
519 **Canton Serving Dishes,** two, shell form, together w/a reticulated tray. **$863**
520 **Two Large Canton Platters. $518**
521 **Canton Platter,** lg. 20¼, wd. 16in. **$1,035**

A-SC Dec. 2003 Charlton Hall Galleries, Inc.
146 **Chinese Export Covered Tureen,** 19th C. w/repr. to finial & handle. **$2,700**

A-PA June 2004
Conestoga Auction Co., Inc.
Gaudy Dutch
294 **Plate,** Oyster patt, dia. 10in. **$2,255**
295 **Plate,** Butterfly patt., dia. 10in. **$2090**
296 **Handleless Cup & Saucer,** Butterfly patt. **$1,375**
297 **Handleless Cup & Saucer,** Dahlia patt., **$3,300**
298 **Waste Bowl,** Butterfly patt. w/reprs., ht. 3in. **$577**
299 **Helmet Form Cream Pitcher,** War Bonnet patt., reprs. **$412**
302 **Waste Bowl,** Single Rose patt., ht. 3in., dia. 5½in. **$1,430**
303 **Cream Pitcher,** Sunflower patt., w/repr. handle. **$375**
304 **Plate,** War Bonnet patt., dia. 9¾in. **$1,375**
305 **Soup Plate,** Single Rose patt. w/line repr. **$357**
306 **Handleless Cup & Saucer,** latter w/repr., Sunflower patt. **$302**
307 **Handleless Cup & Saucer,** Urn patt. **$907**

A-PA June 2004 Conestoga Auction Co., Inc.
Spatterware Unless Noted
498 **Spatter Plate** w/rose & rosebud dec, dia. 10in. **$2,300**
499 **Stick Spatter Charger** dec. w/rabbits playing cricket, dia. 12½in., together w/a small similar plate w/rabbit border, not illus. **$978**
500 **Rainbow Spatter Waste Bowl,** dia. 6½in. **$690**
501 **Historical Blue Plate** depicting the Landing of Lafayette, dia. 10in., together w/another plate Peace & Plenty, dia. 10¼in. **$431**
502 **Five Stick Spatter Rabbit Plates,** 19th C., dia. 9¼in., and a similar large charger, dia. 13in. **$2,530**

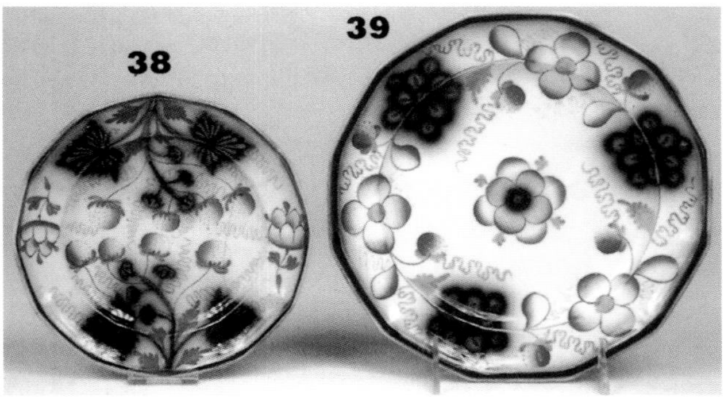

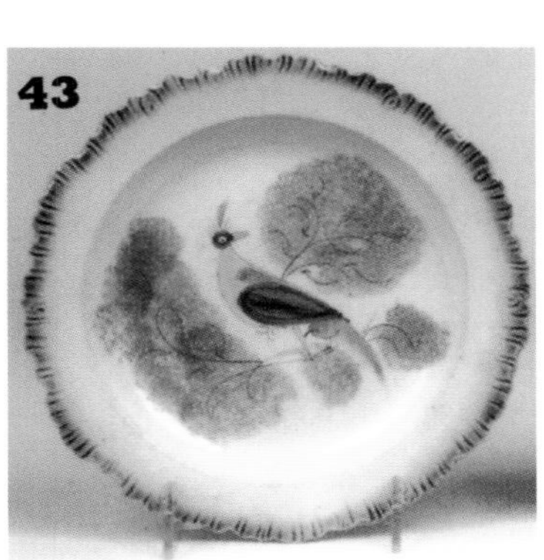

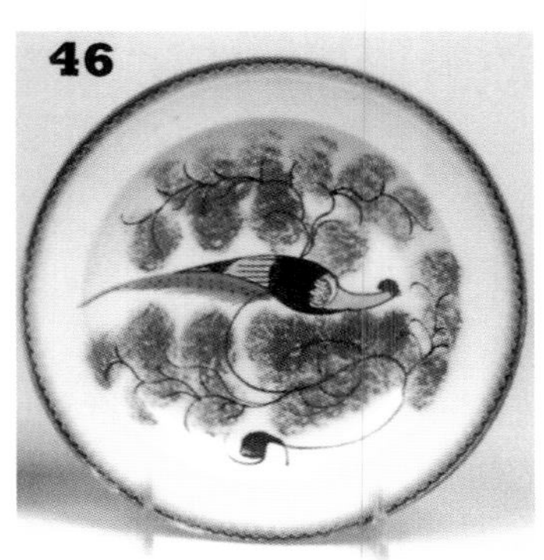

A-PA June 2004 Conestoga Auction Co., Inc.
38 **Gaudy Ironstone Plate,** Strawberry patt, dia. 6⅝in. **$176**
39 **Gaudy Ironstone Dinner Plate,** Strawberry patt., dia 8½in. **$137**

A-PA June 2004
Conestoga Auction Co., Inc.
43 **Leeds Plate,** dec. w/green feather edge & peafowl center, dia. 8⅜in. **$495**

A-PA June 2004
Conestoga Auction Co., Inc.
46 **Leeds Plate,** dec. w/brown feather edge & peafowl center, dia. 8⅛in. **$330**

A-PA June 2004 Conestoga Auction Co., Inc.
Gaudy Dutch
300 **Plate,** Urn patt., dia. 7½in. **$104**
301 **Plate,** Single Rose patt., dia. 8¼in. **$1,072**

A-PA Nov. 2003 Conestoga Auction Co., Inc.
Stick Spatter
708 **Set of Six Plates,** Virginia Patt., dia. 9¼in. **$440**
709 **Set of Four Plates,** Virginia Patt., dia. 8½in. **$220**
710 **Set of Ten Plates,** Virginia Patt., dia. 7½in. **$467**

A-NC Jan. 2004
Brunk Auction Service, Inc.
0380 **Canton Shallow Bowl** w/minor glaze chips, dia. 15in. **$480**
0382 **Canton Shallow Bowl** w/cloud & rain interior border, dia. 10½in. **$425**
0381 **Canton Cut-Corner Bowl** w/harbor scenes, pagodas & border w/clouds & rain, & minor firing flaws, dp. 5, lg. 9¾in. **$700**

Top: 19-23, Middle: 24-29, Bottom: 30-35

A-PA Dec. 2003 Pook & Pook, Inc.
Spatterware
First Row
19 **Rainbow Spatter Striped Plate,** dia. 9½in. **$4,830**
20 **Creamer** w/yellow, blue spatter & a red rooster, ht. 4½in. **$920**
21 **Red Spatter Plate** w/peafowl dec., dia. 9½in. **$920**
22 **Cup & Saucer** w/yellow & blue rainbow dec. in Star patt. **$5,750**
23 **Rainbow Spatter Bullseye Plate,** dia. 9½in. **$1,495**

Second Row
24 **Rainbow Spatter Bullseye Plate,** dia. 7½in. **$1,150**
25 **Rainbow Spatter Plaid Cup & Saucer. $1,495**
26 **Red Spatter Plate** w/star center, dia. 9½in. **$805**
27 **Miniature Mug,** w/rainbow spatter, ht. 1¾in., together w/a rainbow mini. cup. **$805**
28 **Blue Spatter Cup & Saucer** w/red schoolhouse & yellow roof. **$2,990**
29 **Sugar Bowl** w/spatter dec. & red thistle, ht. 6in. **$6,325**

Third Row
30 **Plate** w/red & blue rainbow crisscross panel dec., dia. 7½in. **$403**
31 **Yellow Spatter Sugar** w/peafowl dec.,ht. 6in. **$4,140**
32 **Miniature Tea Service** on tray, together w/purple sugar not shown. n/s
33 **Rainbow Spatter Bowl** w/bullseye, ht. 4½, dia. 9½in. **$920**
34 **Red Spatter Cup & Saucer** in Cherry patt. **$3,680**
35 **Blue Spatter Paneled Plate** w/tulip, dia. 8½in. **$345**

A-NH Nov. 2003 Northeast Auctions
Historical Staffordshire
Decorated w/Scenes of Landing of General Lafayette At Castle Garden, New York, 16 August, 1824
77 **Pitcher** by James & Ralph Clews, unmkd., ht. 6¼in. **$500**
78 **Pitcher** by Clews, unmkd., ht. 7½in. **$450**
79 **Two Graduated Pitchers** by Clews, unmkd., ht. 4½ & 8in. **$1,000**
80 **Pitcher** by Clews, unmkd., ht. 7¾in. **$1,700**
81 **Pitcher** dec. w/the Entrance Of The Erie Canal Into The Hudson At Albany & view of The Aqueduct Bridge At Little Falls, by Enoch Wood & Sons. **$550**

A-NH Nov. 2003 Northeast Auctions

275 **Nanking Circular Dish** w/flaring rim, dia. 16 ¼in. **$300**

276 **Canton Cider Pitcher** w/downturned spout, ht. 9¼in. **$1,300**

277 **Canton Salad Bowl** w/lobed edge, ht. 4, lg. 11in. **$450**

278 **Soup Tureen** w/boar's head handles & undertray, Canton, lg. 15in. **$1,800**

279 **Octagonal Canton Platter** w/Mazarin, lg. 18in. **$750**

280 **Two Canton Oval Covered Vegetable Dishes** w/pod finials, lg. 11in. **$500**

Top: 508-511 Bottom: 512-515

A-PA May 2004 Pook & Pook, Inc.

19th C. Canton Unless Noted

First Row

508 **Reticulated Bowl & Undertray,** bowl ht. 4, tray lg. 11¼in. **$1,725**

509 **Three Covered Dishes,** one w/undertray, together w/2 covered jars w/strap handles. **$920**

510 **Teapots** w/foo dog finials & strap handles, one illus., ht 8½in. **$1,495**

511 **Serving Plate,** dia. 9⅝in. **$374**

Second Row

512 **Hot Water Platter & Cover,** ht. 7¼, lg. 14¾in. **$1,035**

513 **Nanking Coffeepot** together w/2 small teapots, not illus. **$1,265**

514 **Water Bottle** w/tobacco leaf dec., together w/a water pitcher not illus., ht. 10in. **$1,610**

515 **Nanking Tureen & Cover,** ht. 8¾, wd. 13½in. **$1,035**

A-NH Aug. 2004 **Northeast Auctions**
Canton, Chinese Export Porcelain
244 **Large Square Tea Caddy,** ht. 17½in. **$900**
245 **Octagonal Platter w/Strainer,** dia. 17 x 14in. **$500**
246 **Rectangular Pin Tray,** lg. 10in. **$600**
247 **Tablewares** incl. a cylindrical vase, ht. 8in., a trencher salt, egg cup, salt shaker & butter pat. **$1,000**
248 **Octagonal Platter,** dia. 16½ x 13¼in. **$250**
249 **Rectangular Hot Water Serving Dish,** together w/a rectangular covered dish, & platter, wd. 13in. **$350**
250 **Circular Serving Dishes,** two, dia. 11 & 8in. **$200**
251 **Three-Piece Covered Rice Bowl** w/metal ring handles, ht. 5in. **$700**
252 **Octagonal Tea Caddy** w/lid, ht. 6½in. **$2,500**
253 **Round Tile,** dia. 6in. **$400**
254 **Milk Pitcher,** ht. 6¼in. **$800**
255 **Boar's Head Covered Soup Tureen,** ht. 8in. **$800**
256 **Circular Covered Rice Bowl,** dia. 9¼in. **$300**
257 **Three-Part Butter Dish,** ht. 4in. **$700**
258 **Tablewares,** 3 pcs. incl. an oval platter, 14½in., hot water plate, & a scalloped edge bowl, dia. 11in. **$400**
259 **Strap-Handled Covered Cider Jug,** ht. 9½in. **$3,100**
260 **Two Similar Shrimp Dishes,** wd. 9½in. **$300**
261 **Square Tile,** dia. 6¼in. **$300**
262 **Large Square Tea Caddy,** ht. 13¼in. **$2,100**
263 **Two Large Covered Ginger Jars,** ht. 7½in. **$400**
264 **Matching Candlesticks,** ht. 7½in. **$1,200**

719

A-Aug. 2004 **Northeast Auctions**
Pennsylvania Redware
719 **Three Glazed Plates** incl. two dec. w/cream slip wavy lines & coggled rim. The third plate w/modified zigzag dec., dia. 8in. **$1,500**
720 **Shallow Bowls,** one illus., pair w/three rows of cream slip double lines, dia. 7⅞in. **$600**

Top: 477-480, Bottom: 481-484

A-PA Dec. 2003 **Pook & Pook, Inc.**

Redware

First Row

477 **PA Two-Handled Crock,** 19th C., w/black manganese splash dec., ht. 5¼in. **$403**

478 **PA Pitcher,** 19th C. w/manganese sponge dec. & strap handle, ht. 8½in. **$633**

479 **New England Fish Shaped Food Mold,** 19th C., lg. 10¾in. **$115**

480 **PA Canister** w/mottled green & manganese sponge dec., ht.8in. **$575**

Second Row

481 **North Carolina Deep Dish,** 19th C., w/dark brown manganese squiggle & green slip circles, dia. 12in. **$2,070**

482 **PA Canister** w/brown manganese dec., ht. 5⅛in. **$345**

483 **Redware Pitcher** w/manganese splash dec & incised bands, ht. 10in. **$345**

484 **New England Bowl** w/swirling yellow slip dec., ht. 3½, dia. 11½in. **$575**

737-743

A-OH Nov. 2003 **Garth's Arts & Antiques**

Redware

First Row

737 **Apple Butter Cup** w/incised lines on shoulder & handle & dec. w/dark brown manganese daubs, ht. 5½in. **$460**

738 **Canning Jar** w/incised rings & pronounced rim w/dark green glaze w/spots of orange, ht. 8½in. **$201**

739 Pie Plates, one of three illus., two w/yellow slip dec., wear & damage, & the other w/matt brown glaze, dia. 7¼in. **$460**

Second Row

740 **Pie Plates,** one the size of a charger w/worn yellow slip, & edge chips, dia. 12in., The smaller plate has lines & dots in yellow slip w/edge drips, dia. 6¾in. **$690**

741 **Covered Jar** in mottled red & orangish-green glaze w/dark brown daubs. Minor wear w/flakes on base & lid edge, ht. 9in. **$2,185**

742 **Lady's Cuspidor** w/three-tier tooled rim, sage green & light orange glaze w/ brown daubs, ht. 2in. **$1,840**

743 **Stoneware Covered Jar** w/applied ribbed handles, fitted lid & dec. w/beaded edges & coggle wheel scallops. **$69**

A-NH Aug. 2004 **Northeast Auctions**

New England Redware

1126 **Slipware Loaf Pan,** CT, w/fishbone type lines. **$2,860**

1127 **Glazed Slipware Loaf Pan** w/notched edge & five line slip w/green splashes, a type historically found on Cape Cod, lg. 16, wd. 11in. **$14,000**

1128 **Wheel-Turned Slipware Plate** w/brownish-red glaze & double wavy slip dec., dia. 11¼in. **$1,000**

1129 **Wheel-Turned Slipware Plate,** Southwestern MA or CT, w/light orange-brown glaze & double line dec. w/green around rim, dia. 9¾in. **$1,700**

A-NH Aug. 2004 **Northeast Auctions**

1144 **Covered Redware Jar,** Hartford, CT., w/white slip splashes & abstract design of two fish, ht. 8in. **$1,300**

1145 **Marriage Jar,** Southeastern MA., w/orange glaze dec.w/squiggles & floret tips w/bright green splashes & drips, dated 1812 under one handle & initials AP, ht. 11½in. **$1,600**

1146 **Redware Jug,** probably MA, w/mustard brown glaze & concentric drip lines, ht. 8½in. **$650**

A-PA June 5, 2004
496 **Charger Bowl** w/yellow, green & black banding, dated 1791, minor chips, ht. 3, dia. 13½in. **$15,950**
497 **Large Plate** w/slip dec., coggle wheel edge & five line yellow slip. Minor chips & crazing to glaze, dia. 11¾in. **$7,700**
498 **Sgraffito Plate** w/yellow, orange,tulip & double bird design. Incised banding on rim, which has chips & repr., dia. 12in. **$4,128**
499 **Plate,** slip decorated w/orange & brown base color & four lines of yellow slip. Chips to coggle wheel rim. dia. 13¼in. **$2,750**
355 **Porringer** w/applied handle, orange glaze & brown brushed dec., w/minor chips, ht. 3¼in. **$1,100**
356 **Turned Mixing Bowl** w/applied handles & incised bands, chips to rim, ht. 6, dia. 13½in. **$1,100**
521 **Large Plate** w/coggle wheel rim, orange ground w/yellow slip spiral banding dec., minor wear, ht. 2⅞, dia. 12½in. **$770**
522 **Bowl** w/applied strap handles, incised & banded rim, orange ground w/black sunflower design. Exterior unglazed, ht. 5, dia. 12½in. **$1,210**
772 **Redware Crock** w/wide flaring mouth & lug handles, red-orange lead glaze brushed w/brown splotches & vertical crack, ht. 9½in. **$384**
359 **Cake Mold** w/raised center post, scalloped rim, yellow, orange & black mottled glaze. Crazing & chips to glaze, ht. 4½, dia. 11¾in. **$825**
519 **Cake Mold** w/spiral relief design & center post, orange ground w/dripped black highlights. Stamped on side John W. Bell, Waynesboro, ht. 5, dia. 8½in. **$2,200**

142

145

148

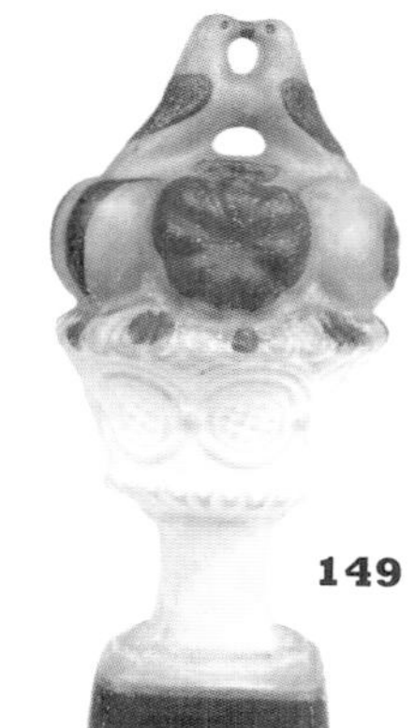

149

A-PA April 2004
Conestoga Auction Co., Inc.
Chalkware
142 **Large Seated Cat,** black ground w/red, yellow & deeper black dec., w/hollow base & body, ht. 15½, wd. 8in. **$20,900**
145 **Parrot On Ball** w/hollow base & body, ht. 8½in. **$2,310**
148 **Seated Rabbit,** w/hollow base & body, ht. 5, lg. 4in. **$11,550**
149 **Chalkware Compote of Fruit** w/birds, hollow form w/painted dec. ht. 11¾in. **$6,050**

A-IA Oct. 2003
Jackson's International Auctioneers
Hand Painted Nippon Unless Noted

60 **Scenic Vase** w/cottage lake scene in four panels & green M in wreath mark, ht. 9in. **$1,035**

61 **Urns,** matched pair w/gilt scrolling on cobalt blue ground & mkd. w/green M in wreath, ht. **$2,185**

62 **Portrait Vase** depicting a young lady in floral garden, mkd. w/blue maple leaf., ht. 8in. **$2,300**

63 **Bolted Urn** w/cobalt blue handles & pedestal base, lid missing, mkd. Nippon, ht. 12in. **$230**

64 **Noritake Footed Vase** w/floral dec. & Noritake Wheelmark, ht. 4in. **$416**

65 **Scenic Vase** w/scene of a lake & fisherman, w/green M wreath mark, ht. 6in. **$316**

66 **Scenic Vase** w/cartoon style dec. in four panels w/blue M wreath mark, ht. 5¼in. **$230**

67 **Footed Vase** w/handles, purple flowers & gilt scrolls. Paulowina flower mark, ht. 5in. **$201**

68 **Scenic Vase** w/six panels, gilt, grapevines & green M in wreath mark, ht. 7in. **$402**

A-OH Apr. 2004 **Garth's Arts & Antiques**

158 **Armorial Rose Medallion Plates,** hand painted w/center dec. of a belt surrounding a sword & laurel wreath with Fides Praestantior Auto. Slight wear, one has a short hairline, the other a small filled in rim chip, dia. 9⅝in. **$575**

159 **Rose Mandarin Shrimp Dish** w/gilt border, hair accents, bright butterflies, flowers, fruit & orange peel glaze. One shallow rim flake, dia. 10⅛in. **$805**

A-OH Apr. 2004 **Garth's Arts & Antiques**

214 **Mandarin Platter** w/gilt accents including the hair, twenty figures & a faint orange peel glaze, minor wear, 14 x 17in. **$1,955**

215 **Mandarin Plates,** each w/brilliant blue fretwork & detailed center scenes, minor wear, dia. 9¾in. **$460**

A-SC Dec. 2003 Charlton Hall Galleries, Inc.
130 **Chinese Export Armorial Tureen & Cover** w/artichoke finial & dec.w/continuous scenes, woven strap handles & motto Stand Fast & Craig Elachie. Portions of interior lid rim rest., ht 9, wd. 13½in. **$3,600**

188

A-SC Dec. 2003 Charlton Hall Galleries, Inc.
188 **Pair of Chinese Armorial Pot de Cremes,** ca. 1800. Each dome cover has a pomegranate finial, double strap handles & painted w/ floral bands, ht. of each 3½in. **$550**

134

A-SC Dec. 2003 Charlton Hall Galleries, Inc.
134 **Chinese Export Famille Rose Urn,** 3rd qtr. of 19th C., w/applied figures of foo dogs & one rim chip, ht. 24½in. **$800**

A-SC Dec. 2003 Charlton Hall Galleries, Inc.
129 **Chinese Export Famille Rose Urn,** late 19th C., w/applied figures of foo dogs & dec. w/court scenes. Chip to underside of base, ht. 24½in. **$800**

A-OH Apr. 2004 Garth's Arts & Antiques
199 **Mandarin Platter** w/court scene depicting 16 figures in brilliant colors & orange peel glaze, 14½ x 16½in. **$2,075**
200 **Celadon Plate** w/Rose Canton motif & underglaze blue square signature, wear & some inpainting, dia. 10¼in. **$207**

A-SC Dec. 2003 Charlton Hall Galleries, Inc.
190 **Covered Vegetable Tureens,** Chinese Export, ca. 1800 w/famille rose dec., w/gated garden on interior & wear to gilding, lg. 10, wd. 9in. **$4,000**

190

0382B

0382A

A-NC Jan. 2004 Brunk Auction Service, Inc.
0382B **Imari Bowl** w/minor loss to gilding & chips on foot ring, dia. 11¾in. **$250**
0382A **Imari Jardinière** w/flattened rim, loss to gilt & crack in bottom, ht. 11½, dia. 8½in. **$350**

142 143 144

A-SC Dec. 2003 Charlton Hall Galleries, Inc.

142 **Imari Vase,** Japanese, ca. 1870-1880 w/floral dec., one impr., ht. 14in. **$55C**

143 **Chinese Export Teapot,** ca. 1840, w/rest. ht. 9in. **$600**

144 **Imari Vase,** Japanese, ca. 1870, flaw & wear, ht. 14¾in. **$500**

145

A-SC Dec. 2003

Charlton Hall Galleries, Inc.

145 **Famille Rose Bowl,** Chinese Export, ca. 1860, dec. w/figures, flowers, birds & butterflies. Small crack from rim to base, dia. 11¼in. **$975**

A-NC Jan. 2004

Brunk Auction Service, Inc.

0649 **Imari Bottle-Form Vase** w/loss to highlights, ht. 18½in. **$1,100**

0649

0650

A-NC Jan. 2004

Brunk Auction Service, Inc.

0650 **Imari Charger** w/-scalloped rim & minor surface wear to rim, dia. 18in. **$700**

189

A-SC Dec. 2003

Charlton Hall Galleries, Inc.

189 **Chinese Export Armorial Plate,** ca. 1725 w/arms of Godfrey & motto Corde Fixam. Hairline to underside, dia. 8¾in. **$950**

176

A-NC Dec. 2003 Charlton Hall Galleries, Inc.

176 **Famille Rose Plates,** Chinese Export, ca. 1740, dia. 8½in. **$750**

304 305 306 307 308 309 310

A-IA Oct. 2003 Jackson's International Auctioneers

Royal Doulton Porcelain

304 **Pair of Handled Vases,** early 20th C., Babes in Woods series w/woman in a winter scene strolling a path. Printed green marks, ht. 13in. **$2,070**

305 **Vase,** Babes in Woods series w/green mark, ht. 6in. **$431**

306 **Large Vase,** early 20th C., Babes in Woods series, ht. 17in. **$1,380**

307 **Handled Vase,** Babes in Woods series w/gilt handles, scene of a woman w/ basket, ht. 6¼in. **$690**

308 **Vase,** early 20th C., dec. w/Babes in Woods, scene of a young girl w/basket, w/green mark, ht. 8¼in. **$431**

309 **Vase,** Babes in Woods series w/scene of woman strolling w/basket, ht. 6in. **$632**

310 **Vase,** Babes in Woods series w/scene of a woman w/basket & child, ht. 7in. **$747**

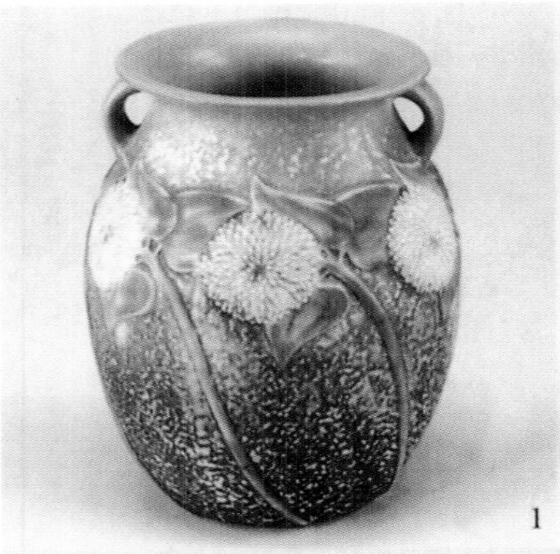

A-NJ Mar. 2004 **David Rago Auctions**

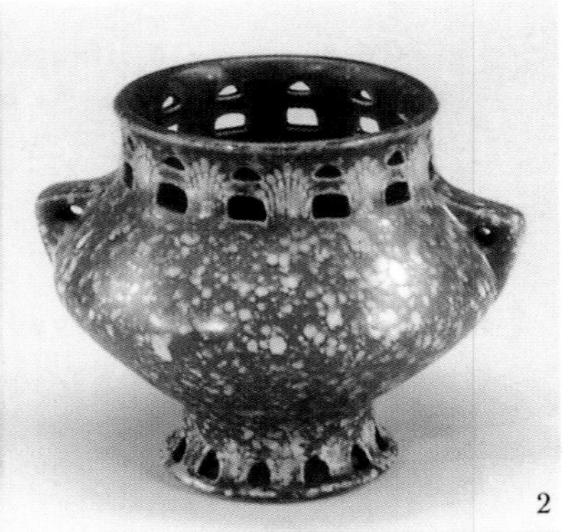

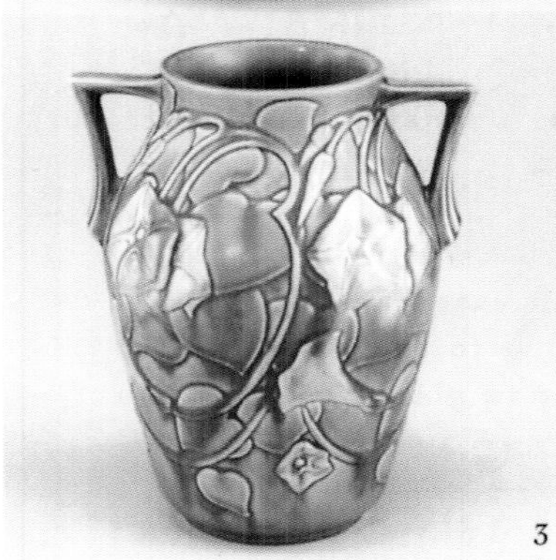

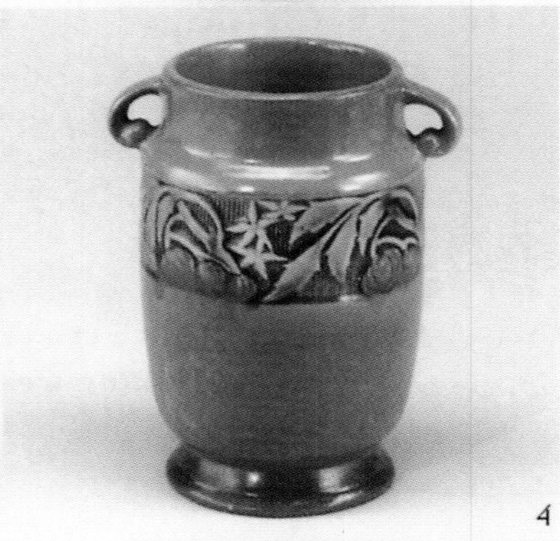

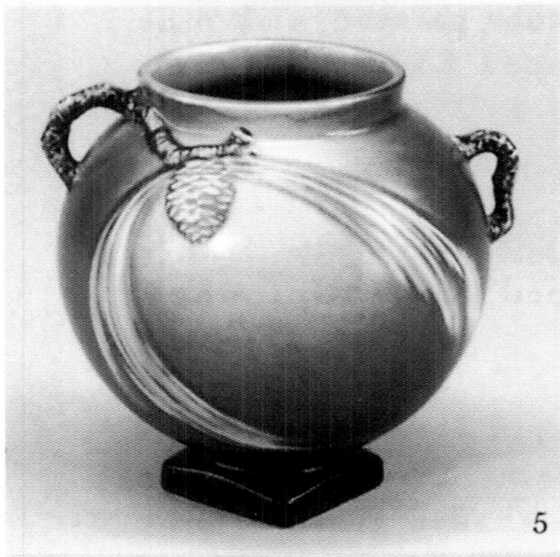

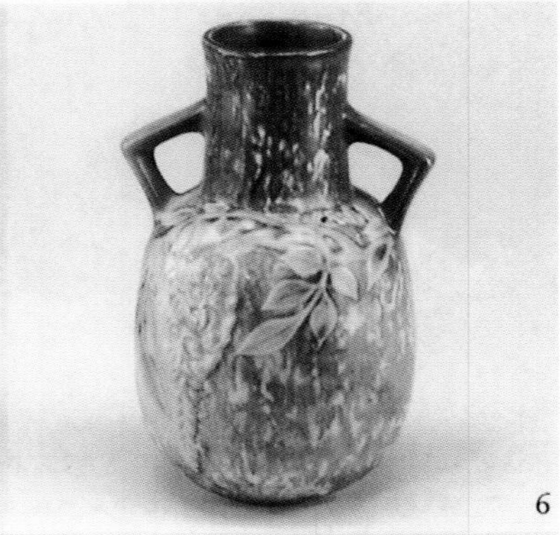

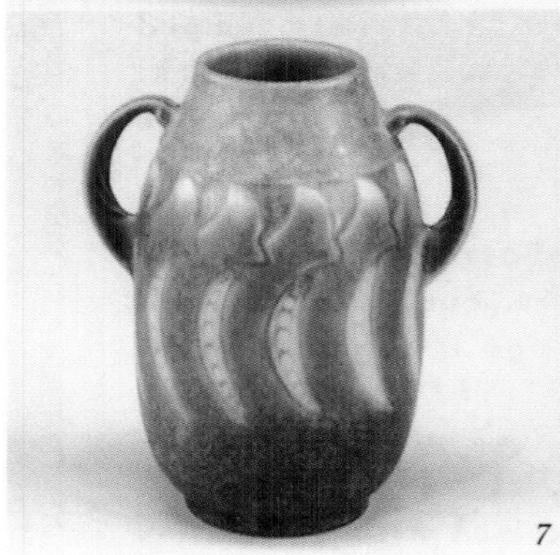

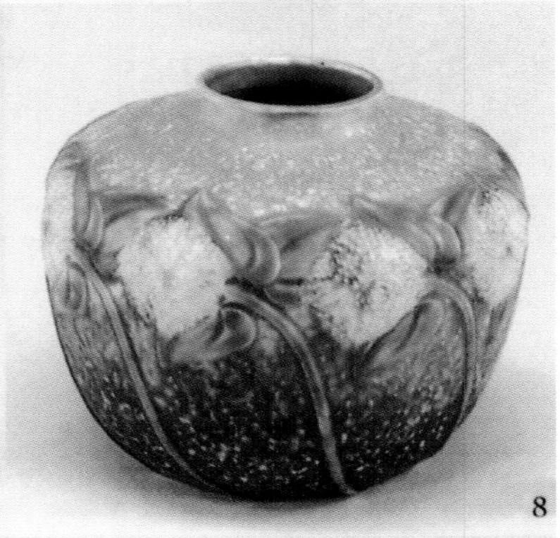

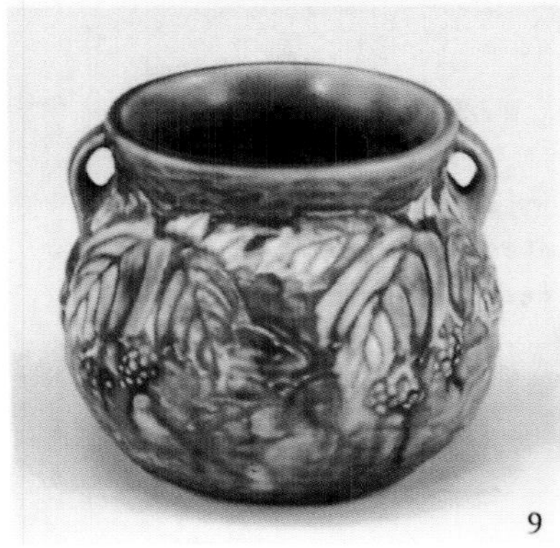

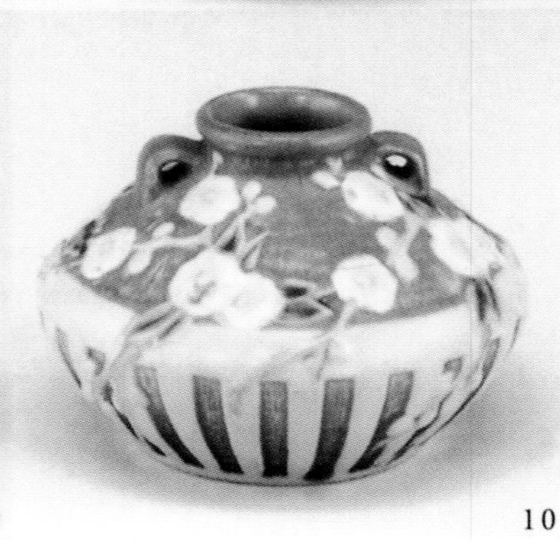

Oyster Plates

421 French Majolica, ca. 1890, dia. 8¼in. **$175**

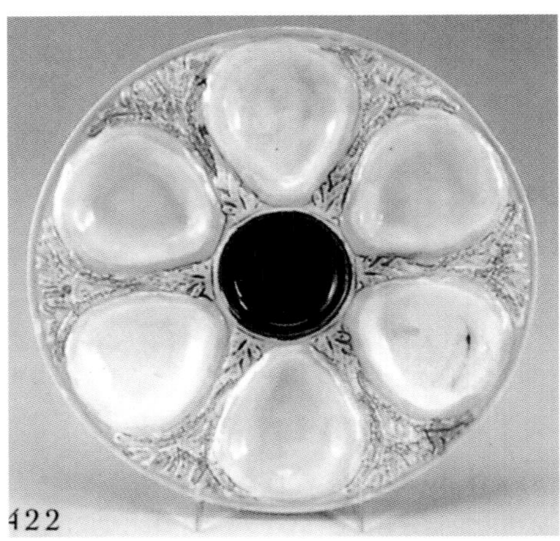

A-NJ Mar. 2004 **David Rago Auctions**

422 English Majolica, ca. 1880, dia. 10in. **$175**

A-NJ Mar. 2004 **David Rago Auctions**

Roseville Pottery

01 Two-Handled Vase w/sunflower dec., unmkd., ht. 8¼in. **$2,900**
02 Ferrella Squat Vase, red w/minor rest.to foot, unmkd. ht. 6¼in. **$850**
03 Two-Handled Vase w/morning glory dec., minute nicks to base, unmkd. ht. 8½in. **$800**
04 Pink Baneda Vase, unmkd., ht. 7in. **$450**
05 Pine Cone Spherical Vase w/foil label, ht. 7½in. **$650**
06 Wisteria Bottle-Shaped Vase, unmkd., ht. 9½in. **$1,000**
07 Blue Falline Vase, unmkd., ht. 6in. **$950**
08 Sunflower Vase w/flat shoulder, unmkd., ht. 6½in. **$950**
09 Blackberry Two-Handled Vase, unmkd., ht. 4in. **$275**
10 Squat Vessel w/cherry blossom dec., w/foil label, ht. 3½in. **$250**

426

A-NJ Mar. 2004 **David Rago Auctions**
426 **English Majolica,** ca. 1880 w/hairline to underside of rim, dia. 9in. **$375**

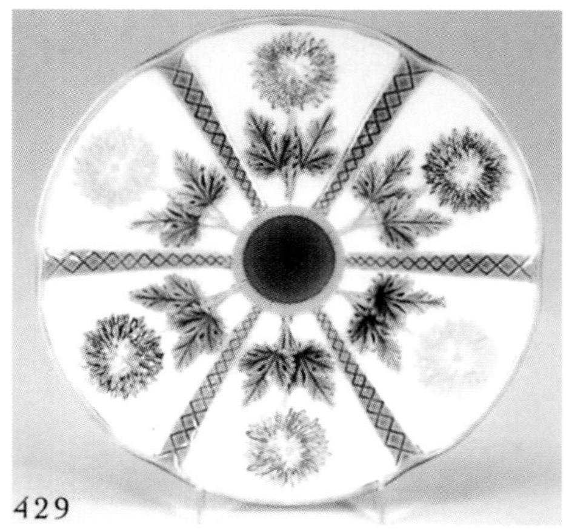
429

A-NJ Mar. 2004 **David Rago Auctions**
429 **Wedgwood Argenta Ware Plate** w/imp. marks & date code for 1884, dia. 9in. **$150**

A-NJ Mar. 2004 **David Rago Auctions**
452 **English Majolica Butter Dish,** ca. 1875 w/bird knop & Water Lily patt., base has hairlines & repr. crack, ht. 4½in. **$225**
453 **English Majolica Mugs** by Shorter & Co., ca. 1920 w/Fish patt., one w/rim flake, ht. 4½in. **$300**
454 **Cheese Stand,** George Jones majolica, Apple Blossom patt., ca. 1875, ht. 12½in. **$2,400**
455 **English Majolica Sardine Dish,** attributed to J. Holdcraft, ca. 1875, **$650**
456 **Wedgwood Majolica Game Dish,** ca. 1872, base rest., w/imp. marks & date, lg. 8½in. **$175**
457 **Majolica Jardinière,** ca. 1875, J. Holdcroft, w/ Minerva head handles, ht. 8¼in. **$650**
458 **English Majolica Teapot,** ca. 1875, rest. to spout, ht. 7¼in. **$325**
459 **Wedgwood Bread & Butter Plate** in Grapevine patt., ca. 1874, w/impressed mark, dia. 5½in. **$225**
468 **Etruscan Majolica Cake Stand,** ca. 1880 in Maple Leaf patt., w/imp. monogram, dia. 9½in. **$300**
469 **Etruscan Majolica Coffee Pot,** ca. 1880, Bamboo patt., w/minor loss to spout, ht. 6½in. **$225**

452 453 454 455 456 457

458 459

469

21

21A

28

29

13

23

24

25

26

27

A-NJ Dec. 2003 David Rago Auctions
Roseville Pottery
21 **Carnelian II urn** covered in mottled patt. w/sm. chip on bottom of one handle unmkd., ht. 15in. **$1,000**
21A **Fudji Bottle-Shaped Vase** w/Rozane Ware seal, ht. 8½in. **$2,100**
13 **Pink Baneda Vase** w/foil label, ht. 7¼in. **$650**
23 **Vista Jardinière & pedestal** w/tight line from rim of jardinière. Flake on base of pedestal, unmkd., ht. 28in. **$1,600**
24 **Blue Fuchsia Jardinière & pedestal** w/minor touch-up to base, ht. 30in. **$2,000**
25 **Jardinière & pedestal** dec. w/jonquils, ht. 29in. **$1,800**
26 **Chloron Pitcher** w/swirled design & ring handle, ht. 7½in. **$325**
27 **Hexagon Vase** covered w/ glossy blue glaze, RV ink mark, ht. 5½in. **$200**
28 **Vase** dec. w/jonquils, fleck to one handle, unmkd., ht. 10¼in. **$500**
29 **Dahlose Bulbous Vase,** unmkd., ht. 10in. **$1,400**

219

220

221

222

223

224

A-NJ Dec. 2003 David Rago Auctions
219 **Roseville Rozane Jug** dec. w/orange pansies, 2 flakes to rim, unmkd. ht. 4½in. **$325**
220 **Roseville Rozane Ewer** dec. w/berries & leaves, imper. & some lifting of glaze, stamped Rozane, ht. 10¾in. **$150**
221 **Owens Utopian corseted vase** dec. w/gooseberries & leaves, mkd., ht. 10¾in. **$225**
222 **Weller Pottery Ewer,** Louwelsa patt. w/impressed mark & dec. w/nasturtiums, ht. 7in. **$175**
223 **Weller Jug,** Louwelsa w/stamped mark, & dec. w/berries & leaves, ht. 6½in. **$375**
224 **Weller Louwelsa Squat Vessel** painted w/orange blossoms & mkd. ht. 3¼in. **$150**

269

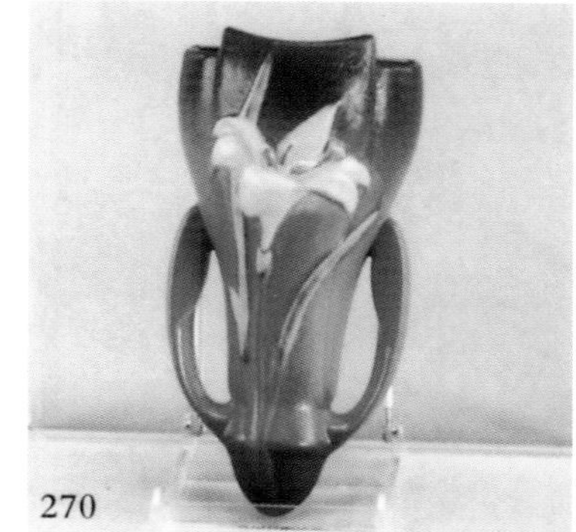
270

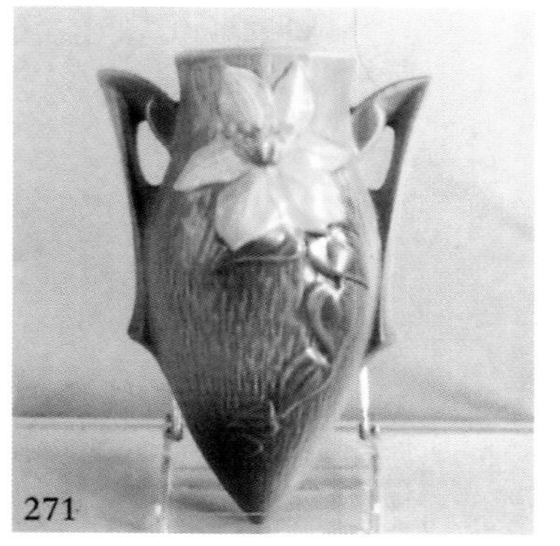
271

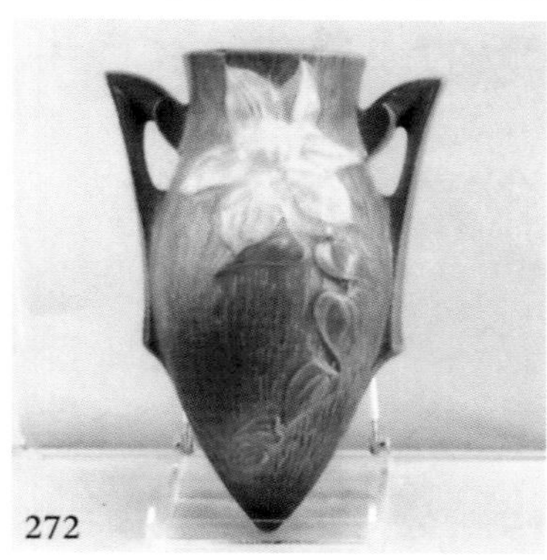
272

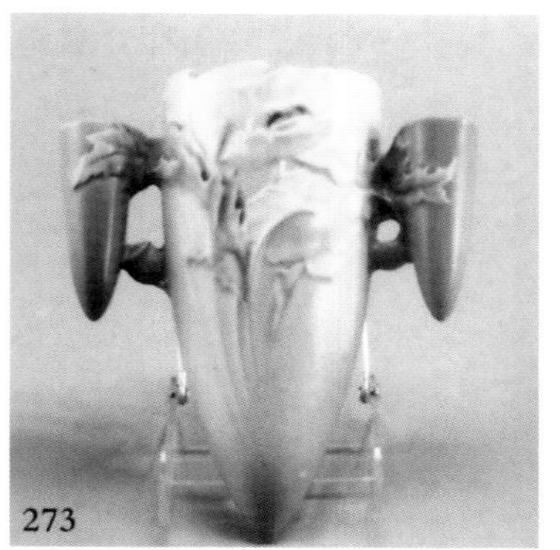
273

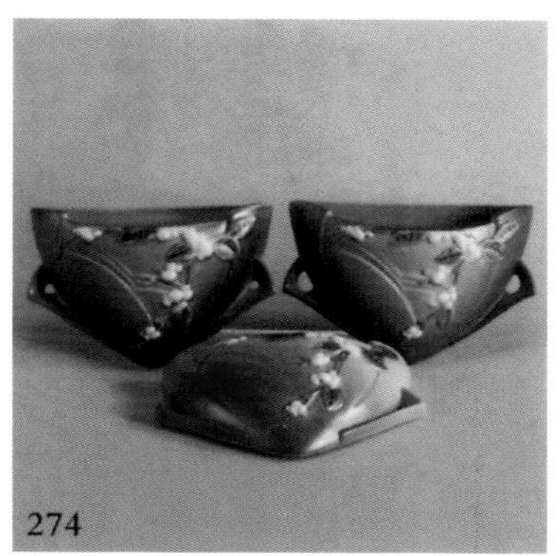
274

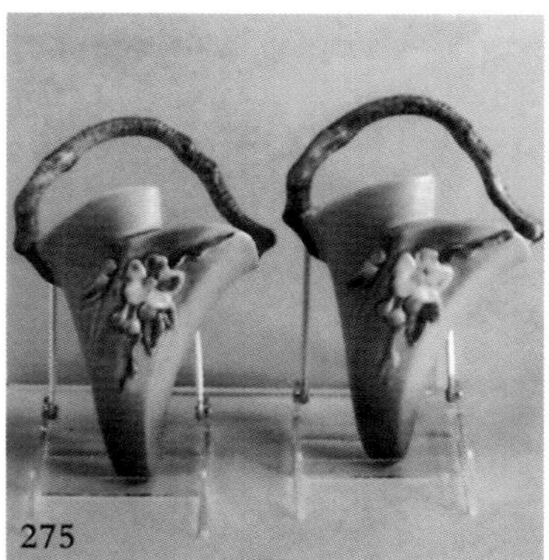
275

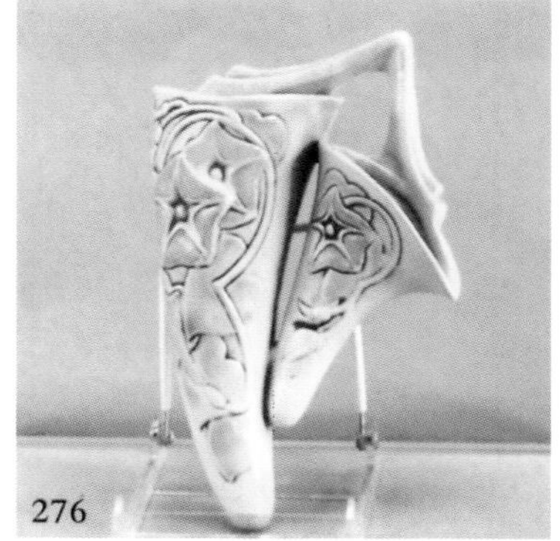
276

277

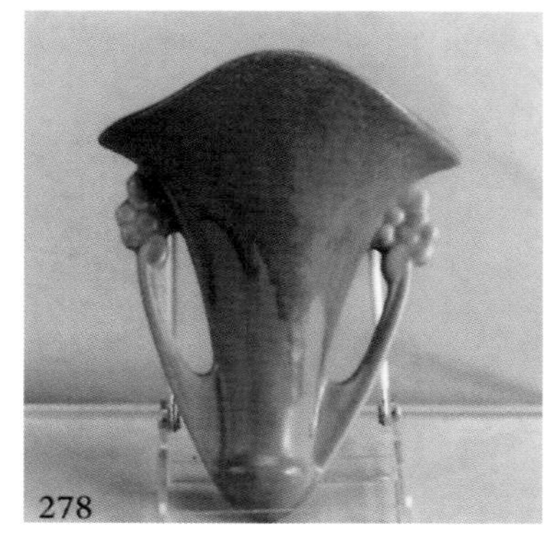
278

A-NH Aug. 2004 **Northeast Auctions**

71 **Bowl,** English Creamware w/black transfer of maritime interest w/English ship & six border vignettes of nautical emblems, dia. 10in. **$350**

72 **Liverpool Creamware Jug** w/black transfer dec. of Come Box The Compass w/reverse scene of an American ship, ht. 7¾in. **$700**

73 **Liverpool Creamware Jug** w/black transfer-printed Signals At Portland Observatory w/reverse of Am. ship Washington, ht. 8¾in. **$750**

74 **Liverpool Jug** w/black transfer dec. w/scenes of Am. ship & hospital, ht. 8¾in. **$500**

75 **Liverpool Jug** w/poly. & gilt painted eagle dec. for Am. market. The reverse w/crossed flags & medallion inscribed America, ht. 9in. **$350**

A-NJ Dec. 2003 **David Rago Auctions**

Roseville Pottery Unless Noted

269 **Freesia Wall Pocket** w/bruise on one handle & raised mark, ht. 8in. **$125**

270 **Zephyr Lily Vase** wall pocket, w/raised mark, ht. 8in. **$175**

271 **Wall Pocket** dec. w/ large Clematis, rest., ht. 8in. **$100**

272 **Green Clematis Wall Pocket** w/raised mark, ht. 8in. **$200**

273 **Poppy Triple Wall Pocket** w/impressed mark, ht. 8½in. **$600**

274 **Three Snowberry Wall Pockets,** all marked. **$650**

275 **Apple Blossom Wall Pockets,** pair, ht. 8in., crack to one, ht. 8in. **$250**

276 **Morning Glory Double Wall Pocket,** rest. to rim, unmarked, ht. 9in. **$600**

277 **Weller Quadruple Wall Pocket,** the Sydonia blank covered in blue-green glaze. Small chip to rear of hanging hook, ht. 9in. **$300**

278 **Carnelian I Wall Pocket** w/nicks to hanging hole, unmkd., ht. 7½in. **$200**

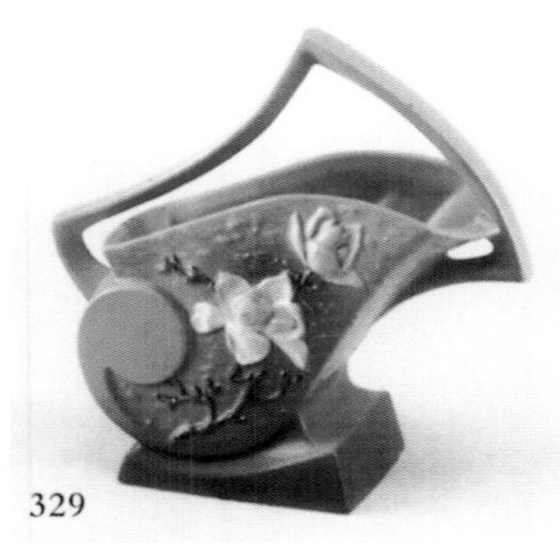
329

330

335

336

331

332

337

338

333

334

A-NJ Dec. 2003 **David Rago Auctions**
Roseville Pottery
329 **Magnolia Cornucopia-Shaped Vase** w/rest., ht. 12in. **$150**
330 **Snowberry Dish** w/raised mark, diam. 6in. **$50**
331 **Snowberry Vases,** both marked, ht. 6 & 7in. **$175**
332 **Zephyr Lily Pieces,** both marked, ht. 10 & 8in. **$275**
333 **Zephyr Lily Console Bowl** w/raised mark, lg. 14in. **$175**
334 **Zephyr Lily Vases,** both marked, ht. 7 & 8in. **$250**
335 **Three Clematis pieces,** all marked, ht. 6½, 7 & 10in. **$275**
336 **Apple Blossom pieces,** incl. a window box & pair of vases. **$275**
337 **Apple Blossom Ewer & Vase** w/raised marks. **$650**
338 **White Rose 3 pc. Console Set,** marked. **$175**

588

590

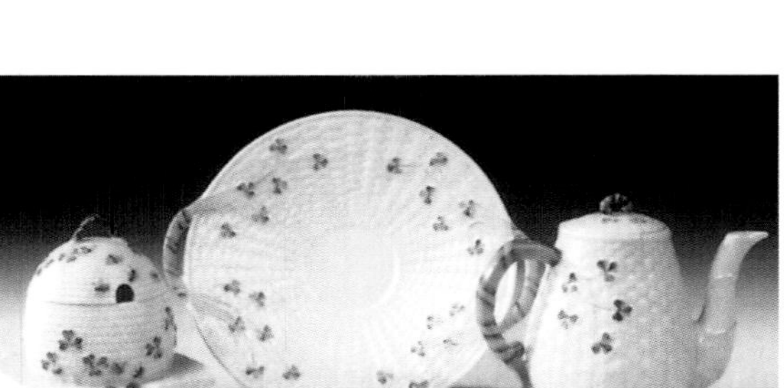
589

591

A-IA Oct. 2003
Jackson's International Auctioneers
Irish Belleek
588 **Dessert Set,** early 20th C., in Shamrock patt., incl. a handled cake plate, 8 dessert plates, 8 cups & saucers, tea pot, cream & sugar. All pieces mkd. w/black back stamp. **$546**
589 **Handled Cake Plate,** coffee pot, both w/green marks, & a honey jar w/black Belleek mark, all Shamrock patt. **$287**
590 **Belleek Bowl & three vases,** Shamrock patt., ht. of vases 2, 7 & 8in. **$145**
591 **Plates,** 24 pcs. in Tridacna patt., incl. 9 & 6½in. plates. **$201**

Lot 292

Lot 294

Lot 295

A-IA Mar. 2004 **Jackson's International Auctioneers**
Tealeaf Ironstone
292 **Collection of 18 pcs.** incl. gravy boats, coffee pot, cups, covered soup dish, butter pats, relish trays & two saucers. Some pcs. mkd. Meakin. **$287**
294 **Group of 9 pcs.** incl. platters, an open & covered vegetable, gravy boat, sugar & creamer. **$161**
295 **Collection of 68 pcs.** incl. 61 plates in various sizes & platters. **$207**

A-OH Nov. 2003 **Garth's Arts & Antiques**
Mocha Unless Noted
19 **Pepper Pot** w/dark brown stripes & an ochre band w/brown & white earthworm design. Blue starflower on top & repr. to foot, ht. 4½in. **$747**
20 **Pepper Pot** w/dark blue speckles on light blue ground & black & white tooled bands, some damage, ht. 4½in. **$172**
21 **Pepper Pot** w/dark brown stripes & an ochre band w/dark brown seaweed design & a blue strip. Small flakes, ht. 6in. **$517**
22 **Pitcher,** light blue & black stripes on pale grey band w/light blue, black & white earthworm & cat's-eye designs, flake & hairlines, ht. 6in. **$460**
23 **Two Pepper Pots,** one w/ tan bands & black strips, repairs, ht. 4¼in. Together w/a soft paste pot w/blue stripes & feathering & damage. **$115**
24 **Mustard,** blue w/feather edge & molded leaf ends. Minor stains & flakes,dia. 3⅜in. **$258**
25 **Two Mugs,** one w/blue & black stripes & a brown band w/seaweed design, wear, ht. 5in. Together w/blue stripes, mkd. Staffordshire England. Later examples. **$86**
26 **Mocha Pitcher** w/black stripes, a tooled green band & ochre, white & black cat's eyes on grey band. Prof. rest., ht. 6½in. **$1,035**
27 **Soft Paste Cache Pot** w/blue stripes & a white, black & brown pebbled band, mkd. FV, flakes & hairlines. n/s
28 **Yellowware Pitcher** w/dark brown strips, white bands & seaweed designs, one blue & one brown, ht. 6⅜in. **$920**
29 **Two White Clay Pieces** w/light blue glaze. Creamer w/tooled checkerboard design, ht. 2¾in. Mug has white slip designs, both have damage. **$115**

303 304 305 306 307 308 309 310

A-Feb. 2004 **Skinner, Inc.**
English Mochaware Unless Noted
294 **Pearlware Covered Mug,** early 19th C., w/minor glaze loss, ht. 7in. **$470**
295 **Flowerpot & Undertray,** ca. 1800, w/glaze flakes on interior & hairlines, ht. 6¾in. **$940**
296 **Quart Mug,** ca. 1790, w/stress cracks from rim, ht. 6in. **$881**
297 **Jug,** ca. 1820, barrel-form w/green glazed double diamond rouletting w/black, white & brown earthworms. n/s
298 **Slip-Splashed Quart Mug,** ca. 1790 w/extruded handle, rest. **$2,115**
299 **MacIntyre Pottery Slip-Marble Platter,** Staffordshire, 1860-67 w/imp. mark, dia. 10⅝in. **$400**
300 **Checker Banded Jug,** ca. 1790, rare red earthenware baluster-form, banded w/black & white slip, in fine checkerboard patt., spout repr., ht. 5½in. **$705**
301 **Chamber Pot,** ca. 1830, dec. w/tricolor black, brown & blue slip-trailed twigs, w/cat's eyes & looped earthwork dec. Rim chip & spider in base, ht. 5¾in. **$1,410**
302 **Bowl,** ca. 1860, w/seaweed dec.on salmon field. Hairline & foot ring chip, ht. 3¼, dia. 6in. **$353**
303 **Mug,** ca. 1800, half-pint w/minor lines in base, ht. 3¾in. **$470**
304 **Creamware bowl,** ca. 1800, banded in rust, butterscotch & dark brown slip w/black mocha trees, ht. 3½, dia. 7⅜in. **$470**
305 **Jar & Cover,** early 19th C., w/reddish brown band & black seaweed dec. The conforming cover has cracks, ht. 3¼in. **$1,116**
306 **Tea Caddy,** late 18th/early 19th C., pearlware w/green bands & slip-marbled ground in white, brown & ochre. Repair on rim, ht. 4½in. **$1,645**
307 **Jug,** possibly Copeland & Garrett, ca. 1833-47, w/strainer, banded in raw sienna-colored slip, imper. ht. 4¼in. **$176**
308 **Prattware Pottery Spirit Barrel** w/stylized initials LG, & dated 1822. **$999**
309 **Porter Mug,** ca. 1830, pearlware banded in brown w/tricolored slip trailings, one hairline to side, ht. 3⅛in. **$999**
310 **Small Creamware Bowl & Pitcher,** early 19th C., dec. w/floral dec., repr. to handle & hairlines. ht. 4⅜in. **$353**

A-OH Nov. 2003
Garth's Arts & Antiques
Staffordshire Figures Unless Noted
First Row
36 **Toby Pitcher** w/lid, rest. to hat & touch ups, ht. 10¼in. **$488**
38 **Two Sheep** w/black features, one w/repr. & a poodle w/puppies on a cobalt base w/gilding, ht. 5in. **$373**
Second Row
37 **Toby Pitcher** w/minor flaking, ht. 8¾in. **$230**
39 **Cats** w/black spots & pink luster accents. One w/hairline in front leg, ht. 7in. **$517**
40 **Red Whippet Dog,** curled up on grass, lg. 4½in. **$287**
41 **Bisque Crested Bird** w/minor flakes & a seated chalk dog w/-minor wear & base chip, ht. 6in. **$86**

A-OH Apr. 2004 Garth's Arts & Antiques
Staffordshire & Bisque Figures
First Row
83 **Chimney Piece,** multi-storied house w/coleslaw trim, topped w/vines, wear & few hairlines, ht. 9⅛in. **$316**
84 **Pair of Seated Spaniels** w/yellow collars,hairlines & minor flaking, ht. 7⅝in. **$316**
85 **Sportsman Figure** mounted on a horse, hairlines, ht. 7in. **$345**
86 **Scottish Couple,** she holds a basket, he has a horn, ht. 9¼in. **$115**
87 **Two White Poodles & Seated Spaniels,** minor flaking, ht. 5½ & 6½in. **$287**
88 **Two Bisque Figures** dressed in Indian attire & riding elephants, one w/a leopard, the other shooting an attacking tiger, some flaking, ht. 7½ & 7¾in. **$230**

A-OH Nov. 2003 Cowan's Historic Americana Auctions
833 **Toby Pitchers,** first a single face version w/raised dec. painted in poly. overglaze enamel on pearlware body. The second almost a perfect match, both w/prof. rest. **$705**

831

832

834

835

839

836

A-OH Nov. 2003 Cowan's Historic Americana Auctions
English Toby Pitchers
831 **Spatterware Pitcher,** ca. 1820-40 w/rainbow spatter overglaze dec., w/ cherubim handle & prof. repr. to spout, ht. 10¼in. **$230**
832 **Spatterware Pitcher** w/rainbow spatter dec., & cherubim handle. Minor wear & hairline in base. **$288**
834 **Lidded Pitcher,** ca. 1840-60, dec. w/poly. overglaze enamel on whiteware body w/a C scroll handle, ht. 9in. **$294**
835 **Standing Toby Pitcher,** ca. 1870 w/scarf forming the handle, ht. 11in. **$173**
839 **Lidded Toby, ca.** 1850-70 w/poly. overglaze enamel painted on a white-ware body & C scroll handle, ht. 10¼in. **$411**
836 **Sponged Decorated Toby,** ca. 1820 w/poly. overglaze enamel paint & a green sponged dec. coat w/floral C scroll handle, ht. 11in. **$374**

747

747A

748

749

750

751

752

753

A-OH Nov. 2003
Cowan's Historic American Auctions
Wedgwood
747 **Covered Cake Plate** w/relief dec. taken from An Offering To Peace by Lady Templetown, w/imp. mark, late Victorian. **$646**
747A **Wedgwood & Adams Jasperware,** 4 pcs. incl. a teapot w/relief dec., mkd. Wedgwood England, ca. 1900-39, ht. 5in.; a cylinder spill vase, mkd., a bud vase w/relief figures, & a flower bowl, ht. 4in. **$460**
748 **Wedgwood Jasper Vases** dec.w/classical musicians, floral swags, acanthus leaves & goat mask handles. Both mkd. Wedgwood England, ht. 6in. **$823**
749 **Wedgwood Lavender Dip Jasper,** incl. a pitcher w/silver plated hinged lid & Satyr mask spout dec. w/classical scenes, ht. 7in., & a tazza w/swags of vining grapes, both mkd., ht. 6in. **$470**
750 **Wedgwood Portland Vases** mkd. Wedgwood, England, ht. 6in. **$705**
751 **White Stoneware Creamer,** w/ lavender bellflowers & green acanthus leaves, ht. 4in., together w/a footed spill vase in cane-ware w/classical scenes, ht. 3¾in. **$646**
752 **Wedgwood Basalt Creamer** w/mixed floral dec., ca. 1810-30, together w/a bulbous creamer dec. w/scrolled floral symbols of the British Isles, ht. 4in. **$499**
753 **Wedgwood Tankard** w/rope handles & seal of Elkington & Co., in a medallion ht. 4¾in., together w/a three handled loving cup w/classical scenes & imp. mark, ca. 1880, ht. 4in. **$403**

33 34 36 37 38 39

A-IA Oct. 2003
Jackson's International Auctioneers
Hand Painted Nippon
33 **Scenic Vase** w/windmill scene & enameled handles, ht. 8in. **$172**
34 **Scenic Bowl** dec. w/a mountainous island scene & green wreath mark, dia. 9in. **$80**
35 **Cup & Saucer** w/moriage dec. & green maple leaf mark. **$230**
36 **Hand Painted Vase** w/enameled dec., & green M in wreath mark, ht. 9in. **$402**
37 **Hand Painted Vase** w/gilt, enameled jeweled swags on floral ground & mkd. w/green M in wreath, ht. 9in. **$1,092**
38 **Footed Bowl,** hand painted & mkd. w/green M in wreath, dia. 9in. **$69**
39 **Vase** w/pink roses & mkd. w/green M in wreath, ht. 9in. **$69**

A-IA Oct. 2004
Jackson's International Auctioneers
Silesia Old Ivory
253 **Chocolate Set,** ca. 1900, patt. 16, dec. w/roses, consisting of a pot & 6 cups & saucers. **$862**
254 **Biscuit Jar,** patt. 16, lg. 9in. **$517**
255 **Chocolate Set,** ca. 1900, patt. 84, incl. a pot, six cups & saucers, ht. of pot, 10in. **$517**

A-IA Oct. 2004
Jackson's International Auctioneers
927 **French Veilleuse** (the name derives from the French veiller, to keep a night vigil). Hand painted w/hairline in base, ca. 1900, teapot & warmer ht. 10in. **$115**
928 **French Ice Tub,** early 19th C., w/hand painted florals & swags, ht. 6¾in. **$258**
929 **French Veilleuse,** 19th C., teapot & warmer w/hand painted florals, overall ht. 9½in. **$86**
930 **Covered Sauces,** pair, French, 19th C., w/hand painted florals, unmkd. Sèvres, lg. 7in. **$201**

A-IA Oct. 2004
Jackson's International Auctioneers
R.S. Germany Porcelain
345 **Chocolate Set,** early 20th C., 13 pcs. w/floral transfer dec. on satin ground w/green mark, ht. of pot 9in. **$316**
346 **Chocolate Set** in the Art Deco style w/transfer dec., & gilt bands, ht. of pot 10in. **$373**
347 **Chocolate Set** w/transfer dec. of floral bouquet & wreath mark, ht. 9¼in. **$373**
348 **Porcelain 13 pc. Chocolate Set** w/floral transfer dec. & gilt accents, mkd., ht. 10in. **$316**
349 **Chocolate Set,** 20th C., w/floral transfer dec. on satin ground & blue mark, ht. 9¼in. **$373**

A-IA Oct. 2004

Jackson's International Auctioneers

Royal Worcester Porcelain

243 **Ewer,** late 19th C., hand painted w/embossed scrolled handle & printed purple mark, ht. 6in. **$345**

244 **Ewer** w/hand painted dec., & branch form handle w/printed purple mark, ht. 7¼in. **$287**

245 **Bamboo Form Vases** w/bronze & gilt dec. & printed purple mark, ht. 5in. **$92**

246 **Jug,** ca. 1900 w/floral dec., gilt handle & green crown mark, ht. 7in. **$258**

247 **Ewer,** late 19th C. w/floral dec. on ivory ground mkd. Royal Worcester, ht.10in. **$460**

248 **Ewer,** late 19th C., w/floral dec. on ivory ground & printed green mark, ht. 7¼in. **$201**

249 **Handled Vase** w/flaring waist on pedestal foot w/floral dec. on ivory ground & mkd. Royal Worcester, ht. 11in. **$603**

250 **Basket** w/embossed woven mold & hand painted highlights, purple mark, ht. 7in. **$258**

251 **Set of 3 Jugs** w/floral dec. & purple back stamp. **$402**

252 **Jug** w/hand painted dec. & purple back stamp, ht. **5in. $50**

A-IA Oct. 2003

Jackson's International Auctioneers

Staffordshire

462 **Covered Hen On Nest,** mid to late 19th C., w/poly. features on custard glazed base, lg. 11in. **$747**

463 **Hen On Nest,** bisque w/poly. features on amber base, lg. 9in. **$747**

464 **White Hen On Nest** w/black poly. highlights, hand painted, lg. 9in. **$747**

465 **Colorful Hen On Nest** w/poly. hand painted dec., lg. 9in. **$977**

Lot 1468

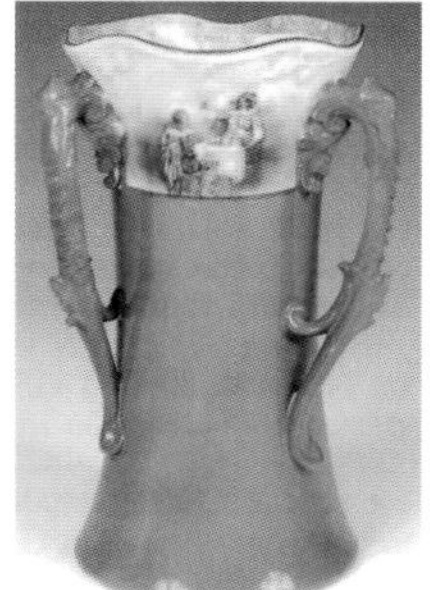
Lot 1469

Lot 1470

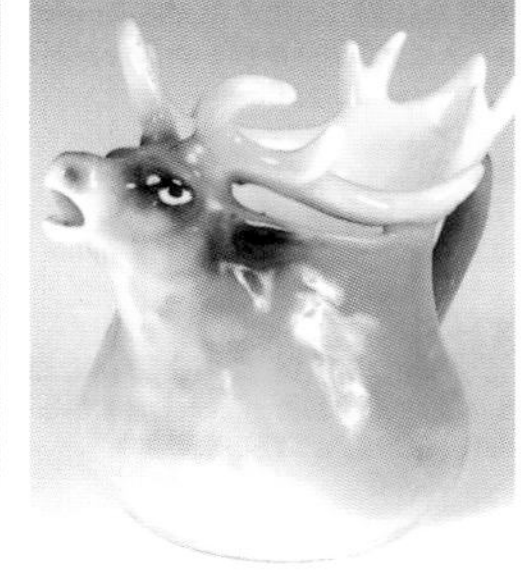
Lot 1471

Lot 1472

Lot 1473

Lot 1474

Lot 1475

A-IA Mar. 2004 Jackson's International Auctioneers

Royal Bayreuth

1468 **Apple Water Pitcher,** ht. 6in. **$287**

1469 **Ye Old Belle Vase** w/three handles & blue backstamp, ht. 7in. **$184**

1470 **Elk Water Pitcher** w/blue backstamp, ht. 7in. **$259**

1471 **Elk Creamer** w/blue backstamp, ht. 5in. **$138**

1472 **Vase** w/Skiff With Sail dec., & blue mark, ht. 7in. **$92**

1473 **Portrait Plate** w/Arab On Horse, & mkd. w/green backstamp, dia. 9in. **$46**

1474 **Vase** w/Cows Watering, landscape w/blue backstamp, ht. 4¼in. **$92**

1475 **Jug** w/Cows Watering, landscape w/blue backstamp, ht. 5in. **$103**

A-IA Oct. 2004 Jackson's International Auctioneers

394 **French Limoges Tankard,** early 20th C., artist dec. & mkd. J&P.L.France, ht. 14¼in. **$431**

395 **German Tankard,** artist sgn. & dec., mkd. RC Bavaria, ht. 15in. **$287**

396 **French Tankard,** early 20th C., dec. w/scene of a friar at tavern table, artist sgn. & marked Limoges, ht. 14in. **$517**

397 **Tankard,** hand painted w/grapes & embossed vine base & handle, mkd. T&V Limoges, ht. 15in. **$258**

398 **German Tankard,** artist dec. & sgn. Hohenzollen Germany, ht. 12in. **$258**

A-IA Oct. 2004 Jackson's International Auctioneers

399 **Beverage Set,** 6 pcs. early 20th C., mkd. T&V Limoges, ht. 11in. **$488**

400 **French Vase,** artist dec. & sgn Jorgenson, ht. 10in. **$287**

401 **Two-Handled Vase,** early 20th C., w/minor repr. to rim, ht. 7in. **$138**

402 **French Porcelain Tankard,** early 20th C., Am. studio dec. blank, artist sgn. Seidel, & mkd. Pickard, ht. 13in. **$1,495**

403 **Cider Pitcher,** early 20th C., artist sgn. Challinor & mkd. Pickard w/J&C for Limoges, ht. 9in. **$575**

404 **KPM Cake Plate** w/etched gold & hand painted flowers, Silesia, dia. 10in. **$69**

405 **Tankard,** artist dec. blank mkd. T & V France, ht. 11in. **$258**

Top: 646 - 650 Bottom: 651 - 655

A-PA May 2004 Pook & Pook, Inc.
Presidential Porcelain, First Row
646 **Benjamin Harrison Breakfast Plate** w/gold corn, goldenrod & 44 stars, dia. 9⅝in. **$2,645**
647 **Rutherford B. Hayes Oyster Plate,** Haviland, Pat. date 1880, the orig. set incl. more than 1000 pcs., dia. 8¾in. **$1,380**
648 **Benjamin Harrison Tea Cup & Saucer. $403**
649 **Rutherford B. Hayes Oyster Plate. $1,380**
650 **Benjamin Harrison Butter Plate. $1,380**
Second Row
651 **Benjamin Harrison Plate** w/wide blue border. **$230**
652 **Abraham Lincoln Cup & Saucer** made for sale in the 1870s. **$1,265**
653 **James Polk Bowl & Plate** w/US shield & gilt rim, dia. 9⅝in. **$8,913**
654 **Benjamin Harrison Plate** w/wide blue border, dia. 6⅛in. **$748**
655 **Benjamin Harrison Breakfast Plate,** dia. 8⅝in. **$575**

A-NH Mar. 2004 Northeast Auctions
124 **Creamware Molds,** English, a rose, berry sprig, iris & rose. **$500**
125 **Three Creamware Molds,** English, a conch shell mkd. Wedgwood, a fruit w/scalloped interior, and a vase of flowers, ht. of last 4½in. **$ $350**

Opposite
A-IA Oct. 2003
Jackson's International Auctioneers
502 **Royal Bayreuth Bowl,** mkd., ca. 1900 w/vine molded rim, dia. 10in. **$316**
503 **Tankard,** early 20th C., mkd. Vienna Austria, ht. 13in. **$258**
504 **R.S. Prussia Bowl,** ca. 1900, w/scalloped rim & floral dec., mkd. dia. 10in. **$402**
505 **R.S. Prussia Bowl** w/molded iris rim, mkd. w/hairline in glaze, dia. 10in. **$103**
506 **Royal Doulton Coronation Cup** for 1937 Coronation of George VI & Elizabeth, numbered 621 of 2000, mkd. Royal Doulton, ht. 10in. **$920**
507 **Hat Pin Holder,** mkd.Regina Ware Hand Painted Germany w/assortment of 15 various period hat pins. **$201**
508 **R.S. Prussia Bowl,** mkd. w/green lustre dec., dia. 10½in. **$161**
509 **Meissen Figure,** Woman w/Lamb, mid 19th C. w/crossed blue sword mark, repr. & losses, ht. 9¾in. **$368**
510 **R.S. Prussia Bowl,** ca. 1900 w/pink rose transfer dec., mkd. dia. 10in. **$172**
511 **Nippon Handled Urn,** ca. 1900 w/hand painted florals & gilt, unmkd. ht. 8in. **$92**
512 **Nippon Wine Jug,** unmkd., w/hand painted florals, ht. 6½in. **$57**
513 **R.S. Prussia Celery** w/embossed iris, mkd., lg. 12in. **$161**
514 **Royal Worcester Cream Jug,** ca. 1900 w/embossed basketweave dec., mkd. & No. 1881, ht. 3in. **$57**
515 **R.S. Prussia Sugar & Creamer** w/embossed floral dec., mkd. **$126**
516 **R.S. Prussia Celery** w/pierced handles & mkd. lg. 9½in. **$103**
517 **Royal Worcester Jug,** ca. 1900 w/gilt branch handle & floral dec., mkd., ht. 5in. **$69**
518 **Jasperware Hat Pin Holder,** German, w/raised classical designs, ht. 5in. **$103**
519 **R.S. Prussia Plate** w/embossed arch rim. **$184**
520 **Bisque Half Doll,** early 20th C., mkd. Made In Germany, loss to finger, ht. 4in. **$23**
521 **Meissen Hand Painted Vase,** mkd. w/blue crossed swords, ht. 5½in. **$28**
522 **R.S.Prussia Handled Cake Plate** w/water lily dec., mkd. dia. 11in. **$218**
523 **R.S.Prussia Handled Cake Plate** w/floral dec., mkd. dia. 10¼in. **$172**
524 **Rosenthal Console Group,** 3 pcs., in Chippendale patt., mkd. **$218**
525 **Royal Copenhagen Vase,** mid-20th C., w/apple blossom dec., ht. 8in. **$34**
526 **German Nappy,** leaf form, mkd Pirkenhammer, lg. 11in. **$46**
527 **Royal Bayreuth Biscuit Jar,** ca. 1900, hand dec. w/bronze lid, mkd. ht. 8in. **$69**
528 **Limoges Cologne Bottle** w/hand painted dec., & hairlines. Hairlines in glaze w/blue JP mark, ht. 5¼in. **$46**
529 **Belleek Handled Vase,** Shamrock patt. w/brown backstamp, ht. 6½in. **$52**
530 **Koch Dessert Set,** 5 pc., ca. 1900, each pc. mkd. Louise Bavaria. **$80**
531 **Nippon Dresser Tray** mkd. Royal Kinwan Nippon, lg. 12in. **$103**
532 **Limoges Nappy,** together w/two hand painted shakers, one w/repr. **$17**
533 **Sitzendorf Figure** of young boy w/grape vine, reprs. ht. 7½in. **$69**
534 **Dresser Set,** 5 pcs. w/hand painted dec., lg. 10in. **$138**
535 **German Invalid Feeder** in Onion patt., lg. 6in. **$34**
536 **Rose O'Neill Kewpie Plate** depicting 5 kewpies at play, sgn. dia. 7in. **$115**

502
503
504
505
506
509
511
507
508
515
510
512
517
513
514
516
518
519
521 
520
522
523
524
52
527
529
526
528
530
531
532
533
534
535
536

Opposite left
A-OH June 2004 Garth's Arts & Antiques
Steins

576 **Pouring Stein** w/impressed castle mark for 1885-1930 w/form No. 1578. Pewter top w/incised tavern scene w/relief banding & rosettes, minor bruise on rim beneath top, ht. 20in. **$862**
577 **German Stein** w/impressed letters HR on base & Germany. Dec. w/incised scene w/castle, king & queen w/swan boat, ht. 10in. **$258**
578 **Mettlach Stein** w/1885-1930 castle mark w/incised designs w/a knight pouring water on a man's head, fireman finial & titled Sangt Florian. Rest. to handle, ht. 8½in. **$546**
579 **French Steins,** pair, mkd. Déposé w/a building within a building on base. Both dec. w/outdoor scene of many playing bagpipes & people dancing, ht. 6½in. **$201**
580 **Mettlach Stein** w/impressed castle mark & domed fish scale lid in pewter. With impressed scene of man in armor pouring water on flames in a city below. Dragon handle has rest. to head, ht. 8¼in. **$115**
581 **Mettlach Stein** w/castle mark & tavern scene of three men & kegs, ht. 10½in. **$115**
582 **Mettlach Stein** w/relief scenes of a band playing & couples dancing, ht. 10½in. **$402**
583 **Mettlach Stein** w/impressed castle mark & shield medallion & portrait of a gentleman, foliage & banners. ht. 9in. **$373**
584 **Villeroy & Boch Mettlach Stein** w/green mark, artist sgn., w/colored transfer scene of a man playing a harp w/a cat & monkey drinking from a horn, hairlines, ht. 6¼in. **$143**
585 **Villeroy & Boch Mettlach Stein** w/black mark, brown glaze, a white six-point star & motto, ht. 6¼in. **$86**
586 **Mettlach Stein** w/impressed castle mark & a card playing scene. The pottery lid has a glued hairline,ht. 6¼in. **$383**
587 **Villeroy & Boch Mettlach Stein** w/green mark & scene of a hunter, staining, ht. 6½in. **$258**
588 **Mettlach Stein** w/impressed castle mark & relief panel of a man drinking while a dog looks on, ht. 5¾in. **$143**
589 **Villeroy & Boch Mettlach Stein** w/green mark & transfer scene of a brew meister & barrel, ht. 8in. **$143**
590 **Two English Syrupers,** a Wedgwood majolica stein w/raised bands & a motto, together w/a Doulton Lambeth stein w/floral dec. & silver plated top, ht. 6¼in. **$316**
591 **Two Steins,** one w/relief scenes of soldiers, German, ht. 8½in., & a French stein w/image of a monk. Bottom mkd. O'Hara Dial Co., Waltham, Mass., ht. 5½in. **$431**

Opposite right
A-PA May 2004 Pook & Pook, Inc.
Occupational Shaving Mugs & Display

148 **Oak Shaving Mug Display Hanging Rack,** ca. 1890 w/cubby holes, ht. 38,wd. 41¼in. **$575**

Inscriptions Included When Legible

149 **Mug depicting an engine & coal car,** mkd. R.D., ht. 3½in. **$230**
150 **Mug depicting a horse head inside a horseshoe,** together w/a mug dec. w/flowers, illus. **$115**
151 **Blacksmith's Mug,** depicting a man shoeing a horse & inscribed D.F. Knittle, ht. 3¾in. **$316**
152 **Mug depicting a touring car** & the name A.F. Gray, purportedly the first Ford dealer west of the MS, together w/mug depicting another car. **$1,380**
153 **Druggist's Mug** depicting a mortar & pestle, together w/mug dec. w/Star of David. **$460**
154 **Mug depicting the Pennsylvania State Seal** & inscribed George D. Thorn, deputy secretary of the Commonwealth in 1923. **$201**
155 **Mug depicting a steam engine,** together w/a similar mug, both w/inscriptions. **$690**
156 **Amish Horse & Buggy,** together w/mug decorated w/flowers & butterfly. **$288**
157 **Leatherworker's Mug** w/splitting knife, together w/transfer dec. mug of an elk's head. **$345**
158 **Mug depicting a caboose,** inscribed Reid, together w/another railroad mug. **$173**
159 **Barber Shop Mug** w/barbers & customers, together w/an artist's mug w/palette, brushes & inscriptions. **$518**
160 **Machinist Mugs,** one w/a steam engine, and one w/a shield, dividers, square & hammer. **$374**
161 **Mug depicting a passenger train** in a landscape, w/ inscription. **$575**
162 **Mug w/the Pennsylvania State Seal** & the name Mr. Rute, a sergeant-at-arms in the PA Senate in 1909. **$115**
163 **Knights of Columbus & Redmen Mug,** together w/ Knights of the Macabe mug. **$144**
164 **Son of Veterans Mug,** together w/ an Odd Fellows & Masonic mug. **$173**
165 **Mugs depicting a Baker & a Carpenter** w/inscriptions. **$748**
166 **Shaving Mug** w/a steer & butchering tools, artist sgn. **$259**
167 **A Bartender's Mug,** together w/a miner's mug w/printed names. **$460**
168 **Knights of Honor Shaving Mug,** together w/Knights of Pythias mug. **$345**
169 **Four Shaving Mugs,** one inscribed Kleeblatt, Sioux City, IA, w/a four leaf clover & another inscribed Arts Place. **$86**
170 **Patriotic Order of Sons of America Mug,** together w/a mug dec. w/shield & a railroad mug. **$86**

A-NH March 04 Northeast Auctions
English Pearlware

94 **Recumbent Lion** dec. in sponged orange, blue & black, lg. 4in. **$600**
95 **Prattware Pearlware Seated Lion,** dec. in manganese, brown, green & yellow, lg.4in. **$700**
96 **Caricature Figure of a Lion** in orange, green, yellow & brown, lg. 4½in. **$1,100**
97 **A Recumbent Lion,** dec. in brown, orange & green, lg. 4¼in. **$600**
98 **A Caricature Figure of a Lion** dec. in brown & green, lg. 4in. **$650**

681.

682.

691.

645.

648.

695.

696.

697.

666.

675.

651.

658.

660.

662.

A-PA Mar 2004 Glass Works Auctions
Occupational Shaving Mugs, ca. 1885-1925

681 **Mug depicting a man driving a horse drawn buggy,** inscribed A.F. Jenkins, & mkd. O&EQ Royal Austria on base, ht. 3⅞in. **$90**

682 **Shoe Cobbler's Mug**, inscribed Morris Friedman w/sm. chip, ht. 3¾in. **$210**

691 **Brick Mason's Mug,** inscribed A. Strempel, ht. 3½in. **$400**

645 **Fireman's Mug** w/detailed horse drawn steam fire engine, inscribed Wick C. Osborn. Barber Supply Co., St. Louis, stamped on base, ht. 3¾in. **$1,100**

648 **Mug depicting a man at soda fountain,** inscribed Fred Stern, ht. 3⅜in. **$2,500**

695 **Mug depicting a bar room scene** & inscribed Michael Crossin, mkd. T.V. France, **$130**

696 **Mug dec. w/a horse drawn delivery wagon** inscribed Pure Milk & H. Danehower, ht. 3⅞in. **$400**

697 **Mug depicting a man working at a sewing machine,** inscribed M. Jeanson, & Austria on base, ht. 3½in. **$650**

666 **A Tinsmith's Mug,** depicting a man making a pan & inscribed B.T. Clemett, ht. 6¼in. **$600**

675 **Automobile Mug** inscribed Ray T. Burson & stamped Germany, ht. 3¾in. **$425**

651 **Fireman's Mug depicting a fire engine** & inscribed F. Horn Rescue SGEHC No. 4, ht. 3¾in. **$950**

658 **Combination Train Car Mug** inscribed P.J. Kelley & stamped T&V France, ht. 3⅝in. **$425**

660 **A Tailor's Mug** depicting a man measuring a customer for a suit & inscribed J. Kilchenstein, mkd. D&Co., ht. 3½in. **$600**

662 **An Upholsterer's Mug,** depicting a man working on a parlor chair & inscribed Wm. Claus, ht. 3½in. **$2,000**

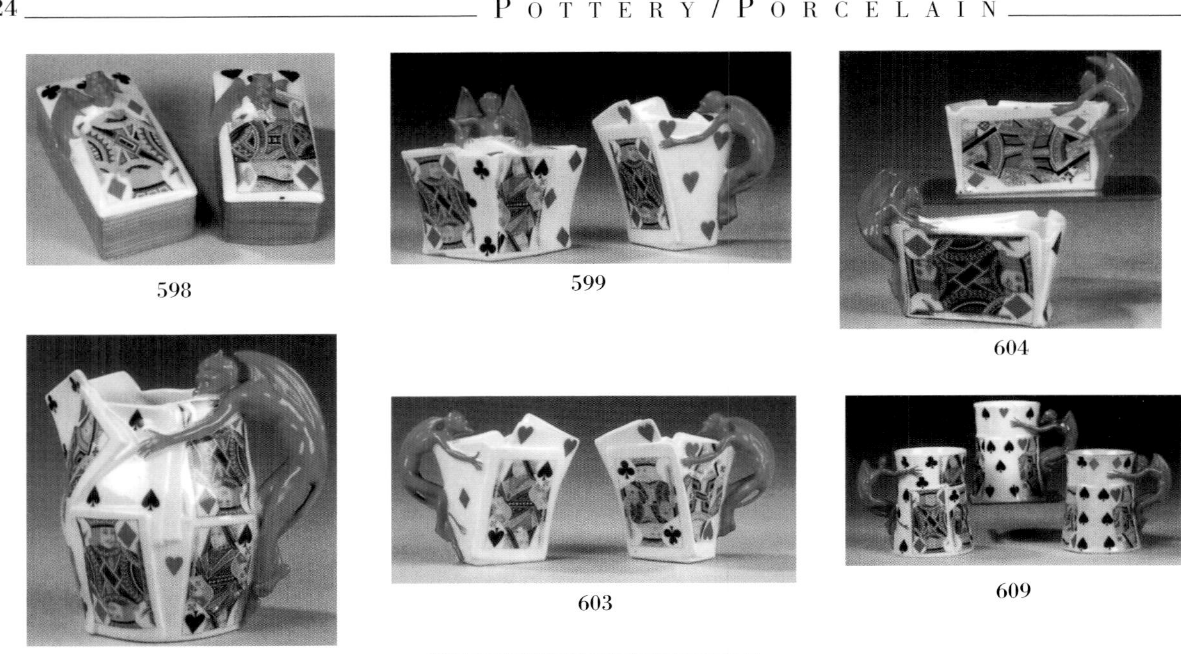

598

599

604

601

602

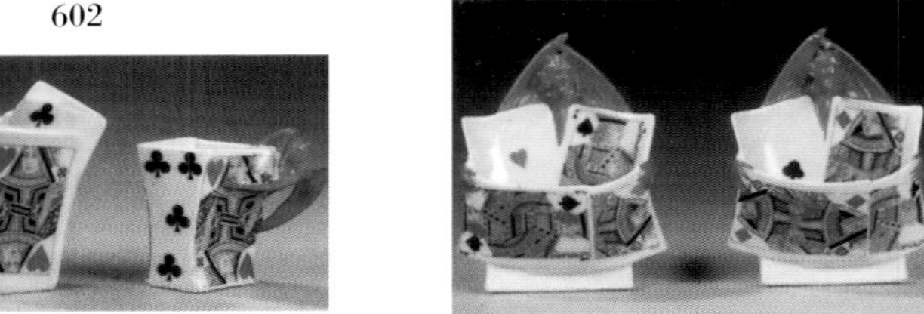

603

609

596

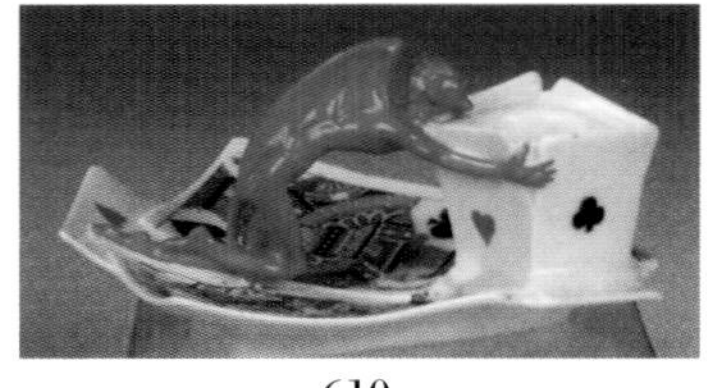

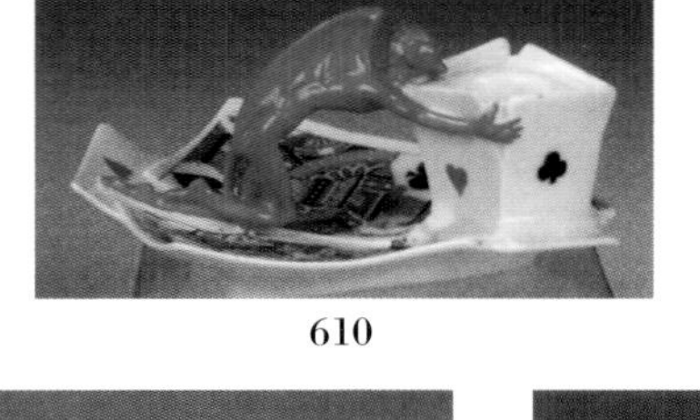

611

595

610

613

614

615

612

A-OH Nov. 2003

Historic Americana Auctions

Royal Bayreuth Devil & Cards

595 **Wall Pocket Match Holders,** pair, w/striking plate below, mkd. **$460**

596 **Cards Tray,** w/canted corners & devil in one corner, blue mark, rec. 7¼ x 10in. **$863**

597 **Milk Pitchers,** pair, w/devil handles & green mark, rest. to one handle. **$920**

598 **Stamp Boxes,** one unmkd. and one w/blue type mark. **$920**

599 **Creamer & Sugar,** matched pair, sugar has tiny flake under lip, both w/green mark. **$460**

601 **Tobacco Humidor,** square form w/blue mark, prof. rest. **$920**

602 **Large Water Pitcher** w/green mark, ht. 7¾in. **$518**

603 **Creamers,** lot of two, one w/blue mark & one w/green. **$219**

604 **Handled Master Salts,** two, each w/blue mark, one w/prof. rest. to wing tip. **$460**

609 **Beer Tankards,** lot of 3, marked, ht. 5in. **$805**

610 **Chamber Stick** w/blue mark, lg. 6in. **$575**

612 **Covered Card Box** w/reclining devil atop lid, blue mark. Chips on inner lip of lid. **$633**

613 **Ashtray** w/Match Holder w/blue type mark, one wing prof. rest. **$633**

614 **Cards Nappy** w/one prof. repr. to rim chip, blue mark. **$403**

615 **Cards Nappies,** lot of 2, both nearly matching, one w/green type mark, the other blue. **$633**

Opposite

A-IA Sept. 2004

Jackson's International Auctioneers

Cookie Jars

1759 **Raggedy Ann** by Brush Pottery, ht. 11in. **$747**

1760 **Donkey With Cart** by Brush Pottery, ht. 10in. **$126**

1761 **Dalmatians In Rocking Chair** by McCoy Pottery, ht. 10in. **$345**

1762 **Smiley Pig With Green Bandana,** some paint loss, ht. 11¼in. **$126**

1763 **Squirrel With Top Hat** by Brush Pottery, ht. 11in. **$218**

1764 **Little Red Riding Hood** by Hull Pottery, ht. 13in. **$126**

1765 **Bisque Spaceship,** ht. 12⅛in. **$126**

1766 **Winnie Pig** by Shawnee Pottery, ht. 11in. **$126**

1767 **Clown** by Brush Pottery, ht. 12in. **$184**

1768 **Happy Bunny** by Brush Pottery w/chip on rim, ht. 13in. **$184**

1769 **Cinderella's Pumpkin Coach** by Brush Pottery w/chip on rim, ht. 9in. **$115**

1770 **Farmer Pig** by Brush Pottery w/minor chip on face, ht. 11in. **$69**

1771 **Hobby Horse** by McCoy Pottery, w/chip & some paint loss, ht. 10in. **$69**

1772 **Humpty Dumpty** by Brush Pottery, ht. 10½in. **$115**

1773 **Bisque Tug Boat** w/minor crack on collar, ht. 9in. **$34**

1774 **Metlox Koala Bear,** ht. 12in. **$149**

1759 1760 1761 1762

1763 1764 1765 1766

1767 1768 1769 1770

1771 1772 1773 1774

277

278

279

280

281

282

283

284

285

286

287

288

Opposite and above
A-IA Nov. 2003
Jackson's International Auctioneers

277 **Pair of French Chantilly Porcelain Figures** w/hand painted features, ht. 20in. **$977**

278 **German Heubach Bisque Figures,** early 20th C., ht. 15in. **$947**

279 **Pair of Bohemian Royal Dux Porcelain Figures,** early 20th C., w/applied pink triangle mark, ht. 20in. **$1,725**

280 **Bohemian Royal Dux Figures,** mid-20th C., w/hand painted features & applied pink triangle marks, ht. 17in. **$1,955**

281 **German Heubach Bisque Figures,** ca. 1900, hand painted, ht. 13in. **$977**

282 **Pair of German Porcelain Figures,** ca. 1900 w/poly. dec., unmkd. ht. 14in. **$201**

283 **Victorian Bisque Figure** w/blue diamond R mark, ht. 20in. **$103**

284 **Pair of Heubach Bisque Figures,** ca. 1900 w/poly. dec., ht. 20in. **$201**

285 **Heubach Bisque Figures,** ca. 1900 w/hand painted features, unmkd. ht. 17in. **$143**

286 **German Heubach Bisque Figures,** ca. 1900, w/hand painted features, unmkd., ht. 16in. **$316**

287 **German Bisque Figures,** ca. 1900, hand painted w/gilt accents, unmkd., ht. 16in. **$172**

288 **Pair of German Bisque Figures,** late 19th C., w/hand painted features, unmkd. ht. 16in. **$287**

A-IA Sept. 2004
Jackson's International Auctioneers

*875 **Austrian Majolica Figural Compote,** 19th C., w/an art nouveau figure & lily forms, ht. 17in. **$1,035**

A-NH May 2004 Northeast Auctions
Bennington

13 **Book Flask** w/dark flint-enamel glaze & imp. Bennington Companion on spine, ht. 10¾in. **$1,200**

14 **Book Flask** w/dark flint-enamel glaze & imp. Buntlines Companion on spine, 2 qt., ht. 7¾in. **$800**

15 **Flint-Enamel** flask w/imp. Bennington Bank on spine, ht. 5¾in. **$800**

A-NH May 2004 Northeast Auctions
Bennington

16 **Flint-Enamel Candlesticks,** each w/cylindrical stem surrounded by molded rings, ht. 9½in. **$2,400**

17 **Flint-Enamel Chamberstick** w/nozzle of ribbed baluster form & applied scroll handle, ht. 3¼in. **$2,700**

18 **Pair of Flint-Enamel Candlesticks** w/mottled olive-green & brown glaze on domed base, ht. 8½in. **$700**

A-NH May 2004 Northeast Auctions

69 **Pie Dish** w/flint-enamel glaze & bowl, each w/imp. 1849 mark, dia.10¾ & 7in. **$750**

70 **Tobacco Jar & Cover** w/Bennington Rockingham-glaze, alternate rib patt., w/ imp. 1849 mark, ht. 8in. **$800**

71 **Candlesticks,** matched pair w/Rockingham-glaze, ht. 8¾ & 9in. **$600**

72 **Toilet Box & Cover** w/flint-enamel glaze & imp. 1849 mark, together w/a soap dish w/imp. 1849 mark. **$450**

73 **Rockingham-glazed Goblet & Beaker,** hts. 4 & 3in. **$700**

74 **Ogee-Molded Picture Frame** w/flint enamel glaze w/a daguerreotype depicting a mother & two children, together w/a flint-enamel name plate. **$650**

75 **Two Rockingham-glazed Boots,** ca. 1849-58, ht. 2⅞ & 1¾in. **$350**

76 **Circular Fluted Cake Mold** w/flint-enamel glaze, dia. 3¾in. **$350**

A-NH May 2004 Northeast Auctions
Bennington

53 **Rockingham-Glazed 3 qt. Pitcher** w/hound handle. Body molded w/two stag & hound scenes in wooded setting, neck & spout w/grapes & vines, ht. 9½in. **$600**

54 **Pitcher,** 6 qt., w/Rockingham glaze & hound handle. Molded scene same as No. 53., ht. 11in. **$400**

55 **Pitcher** w/hound handle & hunt scene, 2 qt. w/Rockingham glaze,ht 8¾in. **$350**

56 **Rockingham-glazed 2 qt. Pitcher** w/hound handle, body molded w/hunt scenes, ht. 9in. **$400**

A-NH May 2004 Northeast Auctions
Bennington

29 **Flint-Enamel Coffeepot & Cover** w/imp. 1849 mark, ht. 12½in. **$800**

30 **Flint-Enamel Sugar Bowl & Cover** w/imp. 1849 mark, ht. 9in. **$2,000**

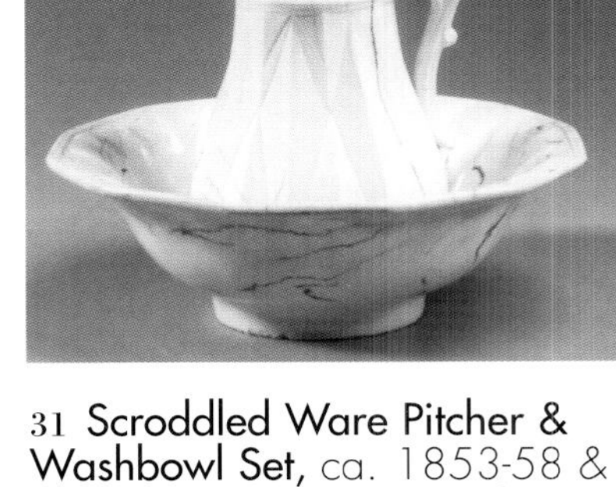

31 **Scroddled Ware Pitcher & Washbowl Set,** ca. 1853-58 & mkd. U.S.P. oval mark H for the United States Pottery Company, ht. 11in. & wd. of bowl 13in. **$2,250**

37 **Book Flask,** flint enamel w/imp. Bennington Battle on the spine, pt., ht. 5½in. **$600**

38 **Two-Quart Book Flask,** flint-enamel w/imp. Bennington Suffering on spine, ht. 7¾in. **$600**

39 **Book Flask,** flint-enamel, 4 qt. w/imp. Bennington Companion on spine, ht. 10¾in. **$3,250**

A-NH May 2004 Northeast Auctions
Bennington

36 **Mottled Flint Enamel Standing Lion** w/coleslaw mane & lowered tongue, ht. 8in. **$4,000**

40 **Coachman Bottle,** flint-enamel, molded w/a mustache, wearing tassels & holding a bottle, w/imp. 1849 mark A, ht. 10⅝in. **$850**

41 **Coachman Barrel Bottle** dated 1848, ht. 10⅞in. **$300**

42 **Toby Snuff Jar & Cover,** mottled olive green flint-enamel w/imp. 1849 mark, ht. 4¼in. **$1,200**

43 **Rockingham glazed sitting Toby Pitcher** w/c-scroll handle, ht. 6½in. **$600**

44 **Toby Snuff Jar** w/cover, flint-enamel, w/imp. 1849 mark, ht. 4¼in. **$400**

264 265 266 267

268 269 270 271

272 273 274 275

276 277 278 279

A-IA Oct. 2003

Jackson's International Auctioneers

264 Spongeware Wash Bowl & Pitcher w/minor hairline & glaze flake, ht. 12in. $632

265 Sleepy Eye Pottery Pitcher w/prof. repr. to lip, ht. 8in. $115

266 Calla Lily Wash Pitcher w/chip on base, ht. 10in. $138

267 Spongeware Pitcher w/large mottle dec., ht. 9in. $402

268 Spongeware Pitcher w/small mottle dec., ht. 9in. $287

269 Pitcher dec. w/small Dutch children & chip on lip,ht. 7in. $57

270 Dutch Children Pitcher w/small glaze flaw, ht. 7in. $115

271 Stoneware Pitchers in cherry band & cattail pattern, ht. 7 & 8in. $184

272 Pair of Pitchers, one w/cherry band and one dec. w/a windmill. $149

273 Stoneware Pitchers w/floral dec., possibly Whites, Utica, NY, ht. 8 & 9in. $259

274 Spongeware Butter Jar & Pitcher. The latter has chip on base. $218

275 Stoneware Covered Jar w/embossed surface design, bail handle missing & chip on base, ht. 7in. $92

276 Butter Crocks w/embossed designs, minor losses, ht. 4¼in. $103

277 Advertising Spongeware Bowl & a butter crock. $259

278 Spongeware Salt Crock w/firing flaw, together w/ an embossed pitcher. $316

279 Stoneware Pitcher w/chips & an advertising beater jar. $92

The Shaker movement in America began in 1774 when Mother Ann Lee, an untutored English textile worker, arrived in this country with a small group of ardent followers. By the time of the Civil War membership had increased to around 8,000 brothers and sisters living in eighteen communities from Maine to Ohio. Shakers believed in celibacy and lived in communities that were largely self supporting. They were very traditional, believing in simplicity and conservatism which were heightened by religious strictures against any type of unnecessary decoration. Deliberately withdrawing from the world around them, members of this religious communal sect have left us a heritage of simplicity and beauty in their furniture, as well as every other Shaker craft. Their lifestyle is wholly without parallel in American history.

Shaker furniture is a major creative force in our decorative arts heritage because it is the only truly original American style of furniture. Harmony and quiet simplicity came naturally to the Shaker craftsman. His ambition was to produce works of the highest quality with the best materials to be found. Most Shaker pieces have simple, geometric lines and ingenious features such as complex drawer arrangements. Oftentimes, surfaces were left unpainted or covered with a thin coat of stain.

Since the "discovery" of Shaker designs during the 1920s, a number of American museums and collectors have amassed distinguished collections of the sect's furniture and artifacts. The word "Shaker," as in every other Shaker craft, is now being very appreciated at its true value and has become a magic term to collectors these days. Recent auctions have attracted serious collectors, as well as museum representatives, and their frenzied bidding has literally driven prices upward until many new heights have been realized in recent years.

A-MA Oct. 2003 **Skinner, Inc.**

191 **Walnut Tool Box,** sgn. Gilbert Avery 1881, Enfield, CT, w/hinged lid opens to an interior fitted w/lift-out tray, stains, ht. 12, wd. 26¾in. **$1,763**

192 **Basket,** finely woven splint, 19th C., w/double lashed rim, carved handles & raised dome at center, ht. 7¼, dia. 14⅜in. **$2,468**

193 **Wood Box,** Enfield, CT., pine w/dovetail const. w/hinged lids & orig. dark red finish, ht. 15¼, wd. 49in. **$1,058**

195 **Black Walnut Bowl,** Enfield, CT w/carved handholds, age crack, ht. 6, wd. 15⅝, lg. 28¼in. **$441**

A-MA Oct. 2003 **Skinner, Inc.**

180 **Pantry Box,** covered, ash & pine painted blue, 19th C. w/lapped ash sides fastened w/iron tacks & orig. surface, ht. 6¼, dia. 12in. **$558**

A-MA Oct. 2003 **Skinner, Inc.**

139 **Drop-leaf Table,** cherry & birch, ca. 1830, MA or ME w/hinged leaves which flank legs w/three ring turnings above swelled & tapered legs, minor imper., ht. 27¼in. **$2,233**

A-MA Oct. 2003 **Skinner, Inc.**
Shaker Chairs & Stool, Mount Lebanon, NY

130 Meeting House Chair No. 3, 3rd qtr. 19th C., repl. tape seat, imper. $382

131 Child's Chair w/rockers, No. l, w/old black paint, imper. ht. 29in. $470

132 Meeting House Chair No. 3 w/orig. br. stain, seat missing, ht. 34in. $382

133 Armless Production Chair w/rockers, No. 7, repl. rush seat, imper. $382

134 Rocking Chair No. 4, late 19th C. w/orig. taped seat, imper. $323

135 Rocking Chair w/arms, Production Chair, No. 7, repl. seat, imper. $823

136 Child's No. O Production Chair w/rockers, ca. 1880-1920, imper. $558

137 Production Footstool, early 20th C., w/Shaker's Trademark decal. $264

138 Child's Production Armchair w/dark maple stained surface & mushroom caps above tape seat. $646

A-MA Oct. 2003 Skinner, Inc.
166 **Step-back Cupboard,** NY, ca. 1860, poplar, stained dark red w/old surface & orig. hardware, minor imper., ht. 78, wd. 25, dp. 19in. **$9,988**

A-MA Oct. 2003 Skinner Inc.
161 **Built-in-Cupboard,** MA, ca. 1845 w/panel door opening to four pine shelves, mostly orig. finish, left side & molding are additions, ht. 68, wd. 21, dp. 7¾in. **$5,875**
162 **Wooden Spit Box,** 19th C. w/yellow painted surface & lapped sides secured w/iron tacks, ht. 4, dia. 11in. **$470**
163 **Oval Box** w/brown paint, pine & maple w/four fingers secured w/copper tacks, minor wear, ht. 3½, dia. 9⅛in. **$1,410**
164 **Butter Churn** painted blue, ME, 19th C. w/iron hoop & pine stave const. Pine dasher w/maple handle. Minor wear to painted surface, total ht. 46in. **$353**

A-MA Oct. 2003 Skinner, Inc.
104 **Shaker Pine Box Forms,** two, Hancock, MA, 20th C. used for molding poplarware boxes w/applied molding fastened w/copper tacks, ht. 2¼in. **$176**
105 **Doll Bonnet, Box & Two Maple Thread Spools, $382**
106 **Leather Covered Sewing Case,** late 19th C., lined in lavender satin w/ velvet pincushion, thimble holder w/silver thimble & scissors holder, clasp loose, 2½ x 4in. **$176**
107 **Darners,** 19th C., mushroom form w/handle & egg form of alternating light & dark woods, attrib. to Thomas Fisher, normal wear, lg. 5, 6¼in. **$206**
108 **Shaker Baskets,** three covered together w/small unfinished basket, dia. of largest 5in. **$529**

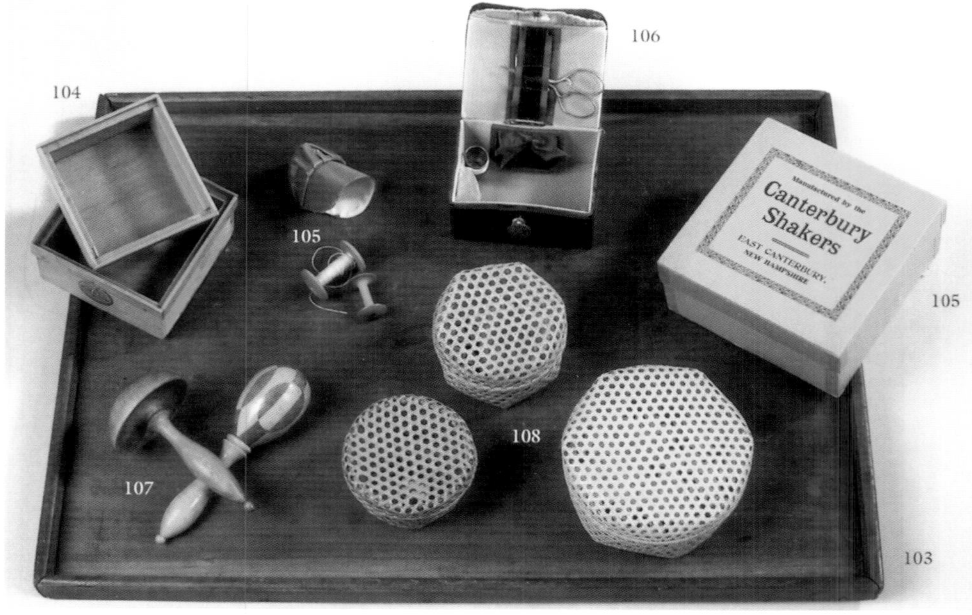

A-MA Oct. 2003 Skinner, Inc.
165 **Adjustable Wooden Candlestand & Two Hogscraper Candlesticks** not illus., early 19th C., possibly a shoemaker's candlestand, painted red, burlwood base w/orig. surface, minor age cracks, ht. 20⅝in., candlesticks 8⅛in. **$8,813**

A-MA Oct. 2003 Skinner, Inc.
116 **Shaker Set of Steps,** pine stained brown, Enfield, CT, ca. 1830-50, ht. 30¼, wd. 18, dp. 22¼in. **$3,819**

A-MA Oct. 2003 Skinner, Inc.
18 **Shaving Mirror On Stand,** Enfield, CT, written in script in ink T. Fisher 1869 on mirror frame, ht. 10⅛in. **$1,175**
19 **Cherry Grain Scoop,** Enfield, CT, 19th C. w/handle, lg. 10in. **$823**
20 **Pin Cushion Stand,** 19th C. w/gold velvet cushion on turned stand w/metal spool holders affixed to base, ht. 4½in. **$176**
21 **Woven Splint Basket,** round w/single lashing over square base, carved handle w/dark brown stain, few breaks & losses, ht. 5⅞in. **$588**
22 **Miniature Woven Splint Basket,** 19th C. w/round shallow form, domed center & small compartment, probably Taghkanic, NY, ht. 1½, dia. 5½in. **$2,115**
23 **Miniature Splint Basket** w/sq. base, ht. 5⅛in. n/s
24 **Cherry Tray & Shaker Hair Restorer Bottle** not illus., tray cracked. **$353**
25 **Shaker Bottles** w/labels, Sabbathday Lake, ME, ht. 7⅜, 6¼in. **$441**
26 **Nerve Bitter's Bottle** w/assorted Shaker items not illus, but consisting of assorted Shaker labels, herb products, etc. from various Shaker communities. **$3,173**
27 **Wooden Cream Skimmer,** Sabbathday Lake, ME, lg. 6¼in. **$264**
28 **Shaker Tools,** 19th C., incl. butter paddle, clothes brush, screw starter, tool & thin paddle. **$343**
29 **Wooden Mattress Smoother,** 19th C. w/tapered ends, lg. 22⅛in. **$118**

84
85
85
83
86
87
87
88
88
87
89
90
SHAKER'S CHOICE VEGETABLE SEEDS
SHAKER SEED CO.
91
92
93
93
93
93
93
95
97
94
96
96
96

A-MA Oct. 2003 Skinner, Inc.
201 **Cherry Trestle Table,** MA, ca. 1830, a communal dining table w/rectangular two-board top, arched feet & pointed toes. Rest., ht. 28½, lg. 72, wd. 30½in. **$4,406**

A-MA Oct. 2003 Skinner, Inc.
41 **Built-in Cupboard & Case of Drawers,** Enfield, CT, 1825-50, pine & butternut w/yellow ochre stain, orig. surface, top & bottom moldings are additions, ht. 87¾, wd. 37, dp. 19⅛in. **$31,725**

A-MA Oct. 2003 Skinner, Inc.
5 **Splint Utility Basket,** 19th C. w/domed base, minor breaks, ht. 15⅝in. **$118**
6 **Wooden Splint Basket,** 19th C., ht. 8¼, dia. 25in. **$705**
7 **Rectangular Splint Basket,** 19th C., w/canted sides & carved handle, wear, ht. 12¼, lg. 21½in. **$705**
8 **Pie Safe** w/yellow paint, Mount Lebanon, NY, 1845-60 w/5 shelves, orig. hdw. & surface, repl. punched screen panels, imper. ht. 76¾in. **$3,819**

Opposite
A-MA Oct. 2003 Skinner, Inc.
83 **Shaker Utilitarian Shelving Unit,** MA or NY, mid-19th C., dovetailed shelves; w/orig. darkened surface, minor imper., ht. 75¾, wd. 52in. **$588**
84 **Sap Bucket,** painted red, NH, late 19th C., base mkd. NF Shakers over Enfield NH, minor stains, ht. 9⅛, dia. 11⅞in. **$441**
85 **Sap Buckets,** two, late 19th C., tongue & groove pine staves w/iron hoops & single iron tape hangers,one painted yellow, the other red, mkd. as No. 94, wear, ht. 9¼in. **$588**
86 **Berry Basket,** 19th C. w/pierced wood panels, applied tin rim & base band, minor crack, ht. 4⅝in. **$206**
87 **Wooden Pails,** striped, attrib. to Thomas Fisher (1823-1903), Enfield, CT, w/iron hoops, imper. ht. to rim 5⅞in., three. **$764**
88 **Wooden Buckets,** two, both w/turned handles, wire bails & sheet iron hoops. Larger bucket painted green w/white int., smaller one painted salmon w/white int., imper. ht. to rim 5¾ & 4⅜in. **$1,058**
89 **Wooden Bowl** painted blue, 19th C. w/wear & minor age cracks, ht. 4, dia. 14½in. **$499**
90 **Covered Box,** Shaker green, 19th C. w/minor paint wear, ht. 4⅝in. **$323**
91 **Wooden Apple Butter Scoop** painted Shaker yellow, 19th C. w/pierced handle carved from one piece of wood, wear & edge losses, lg. 11⅝in. **$206**
92 **Wooden Seed Display Box** w/Paper Label, Mount Lebanon, NY, ca. 1885, six sections w/labels depicting flowers & vegetables, wear & lacking cover, ht. 4½ x 9¼in. **$470**
93 **Six Shaker Tin Items,** 19th to early 20th C. incl. pail, milk pan, colander, sm. crimped tart pan, coffeepot & sm. round pan. **$206**
94 **Round Wooden Covered Pantry Box,** red w/vertical seams fastened w/iron tacks, imper. ht. 10, dia. 13¾in. **$705**
95 **Sap Bucket** w/yellow paint, pine staves & iron three-hoop const. & imp. on base NF Shakers over Enfield NH, ht. 11¼in. **$235**
96 **Shaker Ash Measures,** three, Sabbathday Lake, ME, late 19th C. w/lapped sides secured w/iron tacks, mkd. Shaker Society, Sabbathday Lake, ME, ht. 6, 8 & 6¾in. **$705**
97 Wire Sieve w/lapped ash bands fastened w/iron tacks, wire screen w/ crossed wire strands. **$125**

Stoneware is another type of country pottery that has swung into prominence. Its production in America got underway around the mid-1700s and, because of its popularity, it was mass produced until the late 1800s.

Stoneware is a weighty, durable, dense pottery made from clay mixed with flint or sand, or made from very siliceous clay that vitrifies when heated to form a nonporous base. The common household vessels were glazed inside and/or outside to prevent porosity and resist chemical action. Most of the ware produced is salt-glazed. To produce this type of glaze, common table salt was heated and then thrown into the ware-filled kiln when firing was at the maximum temperature. The intense heat caused the salt to vaporize instantly, covering the objects with a clear, thin glaze; hence the term "salt-glaze". Frequently, the salt particles hit the vessels before being transformed into vapor, creating a pitted or pebbly surface on the stoneware.

When not salt-glazed, stoneware was coated with a slipglaze, often referred to as brown "Albany" slip, which consisted of a mixture of clay mixed with water. When applied as a finish, the mixture would fuse into a natural smooth glaze at certain firing temperatures.

The earliest stoneware was plain and unadorned but, by the turn of the 19th century, potters were using splashes of cobalt blue to decorate the gray and tan jugs and crocks. Gradually, their first squiggles evolved into the highly sophisticated freehand figures of the mid-1850s and '60s, then to the usage of stenciled patterns as interest declined.

Interest in stoneware today is not in its beautiful forms or colors, but in its decoration, the maker's name, location, and in rare instances a date, painted or incised into the clay. But, as a general rule, the more fanciful cobalt blue decorated vessels continue to increase in value, forcing the serious collector to be more discriminating.

A-MD July 2004 Crocker Farm Auction
10 **Stoneware Chicken Waterer,** attrib. to Western PA pottery companies, ca. 1875, ht. 12in. **$5,225**

A-MD July 2004 Crocker Farm Auction
69 **Stoneware Pitcher** w/incised dec., attrib. to Henry Remmey, Sr., Baltimore, ca. 1820, ht. 9in. **$35,000**

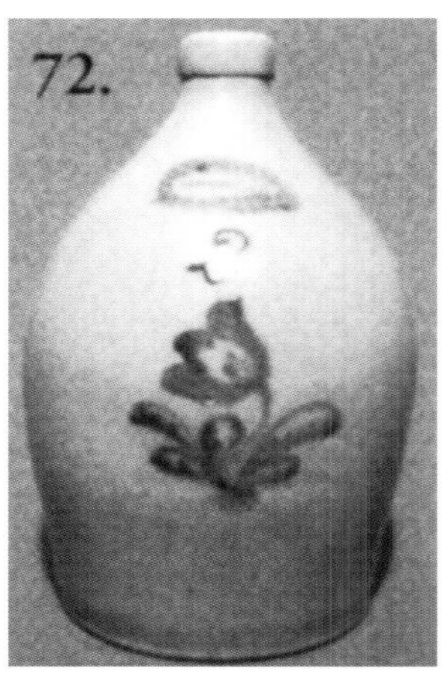

A-MD July 2004 Crocker Farm Auction
72 **Jug,** mkd. Burger & Lang/Rochester, NY, ca. 1869-1877, 2gal. w/line near handle, ht. 14in. **$990**

A-MD July 2004 Crocker Farm Auction
Decorated Stoneware
15 **Jar,** mkd. H. Glasier/Huntingdon, PA, ca. 1831-1854 w/crack & lines on underside, ht. 10in. **$2,200**

16 **Rundelet,** attrib. to NJ or NY potter, early 19th C., mkd. F&B on each side of spigot, prof. rest., ht. 7¾in. **$1,000**
17 Jar, Baltimore, ca. 1825, approx. 1qt., ht. 6in. **$3,520**
18 **Pitcher,** Baltimore, ca. 1840 w/repair to spout, ht. 10in. **$1,320**

A-MA Aug. 2004 **Skinner, Inc.**

Stoneware

608 **Crock** w/cobalt tulip dec., mkd. Wm. Farrar & Co., NY, 4gal. **$646**

609 **Crock** w/cobalt floral dec., mkd. Frye & Burrill, MA, 4gal. **$118**

610 **Crock** w/floral dec., 3gal. **$147**

623 **Jug** w/cobalt floral dec., mkd. J.& F. Norton, Bennington,VT. **$529**

624 **Crock** w/cobalt floral dec., mkd. O.L. & A.K. Ballard, Bennington, VT. **$118**

625 **Crock,** w/lid & cobalt blue dec.of flowerpot, 2gal. **$323**

635 **Pitcher,** w/cobalt floral dec. & strap handle, 1gal. **$147**

651 **Bardwell's Root Beer** w/cobalt blue floral dec. & a stag, molded stoneware. **$558**

652 **Three Stoneware Butter Crocks,** w/cobalt leaf dec., 2 w/bail handles & two w/covers. **$441**

661 **Prosit** dec. molded stoneware pitcher & mug set, 7 pcs. **$206**

740 **Molded barrel-form Water Cooler,** glazed & dec., & labelled PORTER. **$176**

846 **Three Cobalt Setter & Horse dec. stoneware humidors** & a matchstrike holder. **$235**

847 **Ovoid Redware Jug** w/slip glaze. **$411**

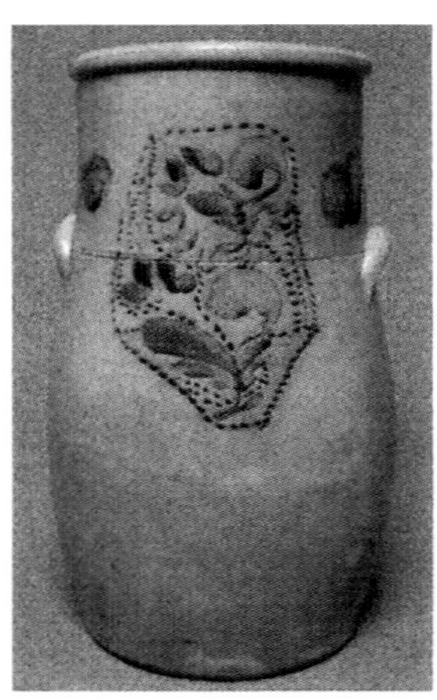

A-MD July 2004 Crocker Farm Auction

30 **Pitcher** ½gal., attrib. to H.H. Zigler, ca. 1852-1865, w/chips & roughness to rim, ht. 8in. **$1,760**

31 **Churn,** 3gal., Ohio, ca. 1860 w/handles, ht. 15in. **$605**

32 **Pitcher,** 2gal., Baltimore, ca. 1860 w/minor chip to int. of rim & nick to collar, ht. 12in. **$1,540**

33 **Pedestal Water Cooler,** attrib. to NY potter, ca. 1850 w/ext. rest., ht. 12in. **$990**

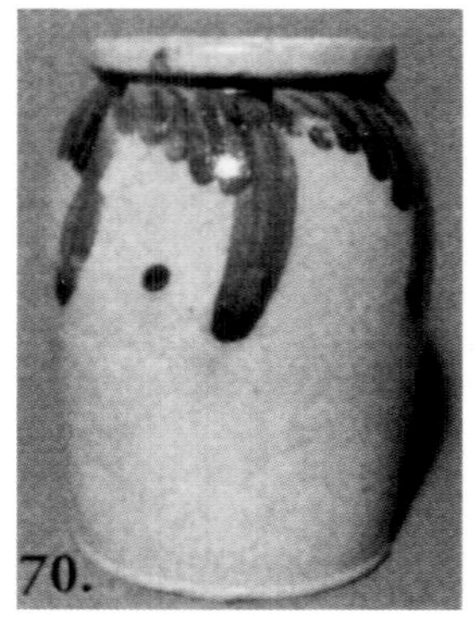

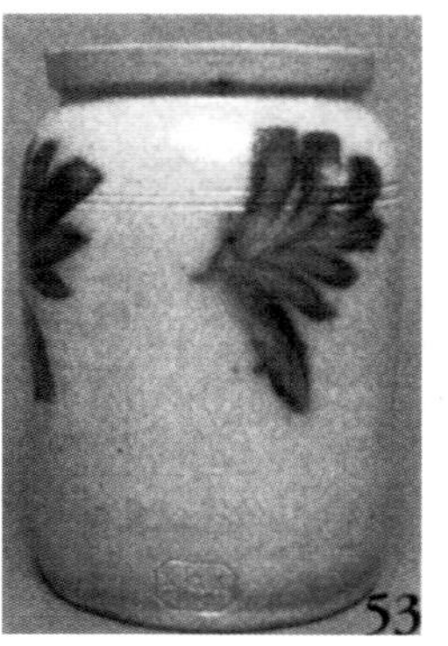

A-MD July 2004 Crocker Farm Auction

70 **Jar,** mkd. H. Myers, Baltimore, ca. 1825 w/one nick & base chip, ht. 9in. **$660**

71 **Pitcher,** 1gal., attrib. to Remmey Pottery, ca. 1860 w/spout chips, ht. 10in. **$1,320**

A-MD July 2004
Crocker Farm Auction

49 **Jug,** mkd. F. Stesenmeyer, Rochester, NY, ca. 1855-1857, 2gal. w/chip on base, ht. 14in. **$1,430**

A-MD July 2004 Crocker Farm Auction

53 **Crock,** 1gal., mkd. made at pottery of Richard Clinton Remmey, Philadelphia, w/rim chips & lines near base, ht. 10in. **$385**

54 **Jar,** attrib. to Remmey Pottery, mint, ht. 7in. **$440**

A-MD July 2004 Crocker Farm Auction

134 **Cake Crock** w/lid, 5gal, Philadelphia, ca. 1865, w/lines & rim chips, ht. 10in. **$1,815**

A-OH July 2004 Garth's Arts & Antiques

73 **Harvest Jug,** mkd. G. Hormell, Newport, OH, 1872 w/base lines & chip on smaller spout, ht. 13¾in. **$7,017**

198 **Cooler,** sgn. by J. Lambright, Newport, OH, 1873, no lid, ht. 1in. **$7,245**

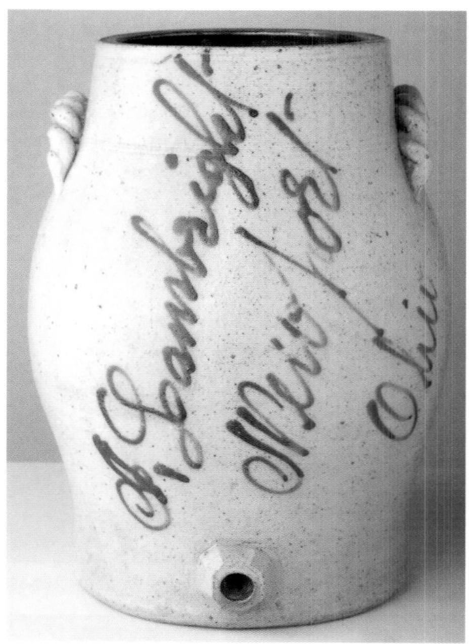

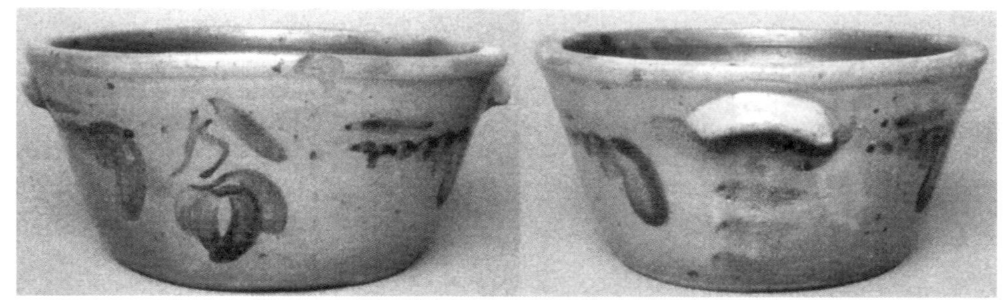

A-MD July 2004 Crocker Farm Auction
91 **Bowl,** 1½gal., mkd. Solomon Bell, Strasburg, VA, ca. 1850-1880, w/one rim chip, ht. 5in. **$2,200**

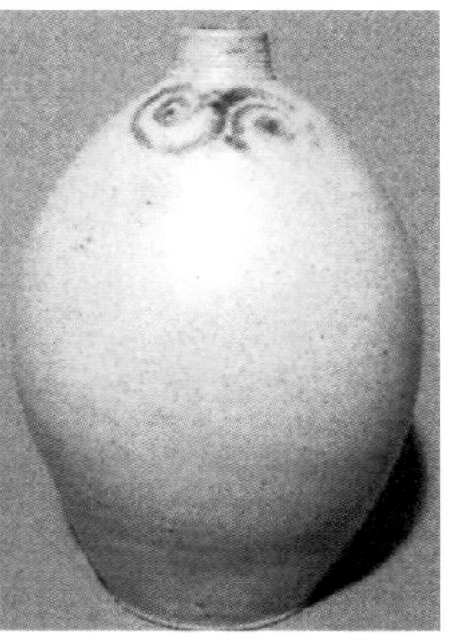

A-MD July 2004 Crocker Farm Auction
112 **Crock,** 3gal. mkd. D.Weston, Ellenville, NY, ca. 1849-1875 w/repr., ht. 10in. **$1,100**
113 **Crock,** 3gal. mkd. F.T. Wright & Son, Taunton, MA, ca. 1870 w/glaze loss & rim chips, ht. 10in. **$82**
114 **Jug,** w/Clock Spring dec., Northeastern U.S., 1st qtr. 19th C., w/incised lines at spout, ht. 16in. **$1,045**

A-MD July 2004 Crocker Farm Auction
119 **Crock,** attrib. to Fulper Pottery, NJ, late 19th C., w/Albany slip int. & two chips on rim,ht. 7in. **$577**

A-MD July 2004 Crocker Farm Auction
116 **Pitcher,** ½gal., att. to Remmey Pottery, w/minor rim chip, ht. 9in. **$1,100**
117 **Jar,** 3gal., mkd. Whites Utica, NY, ca. 1865, ht. 12in. **$247**
118 **Water Cooler,** att. to NY or New England potter, ca. 1880 w/line near spigot, ht. 12in. **$192**

A-MD July 2004 Crocker Farm Auction
176 **Stoneware** Lid mkd. John Bell, Waynesboro, ca. 1850-1880, w/repairs, wd. 9½in. **$275**

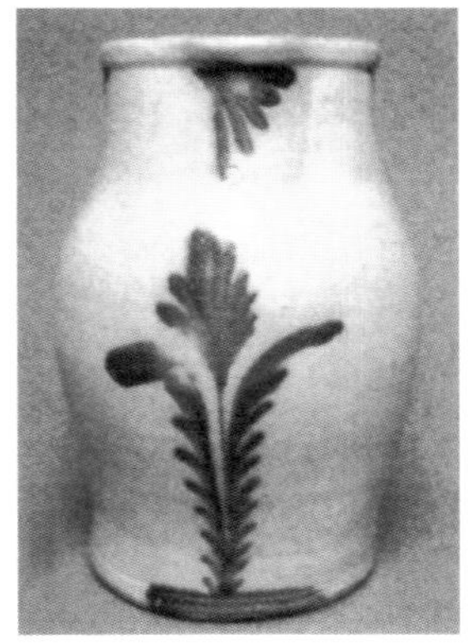

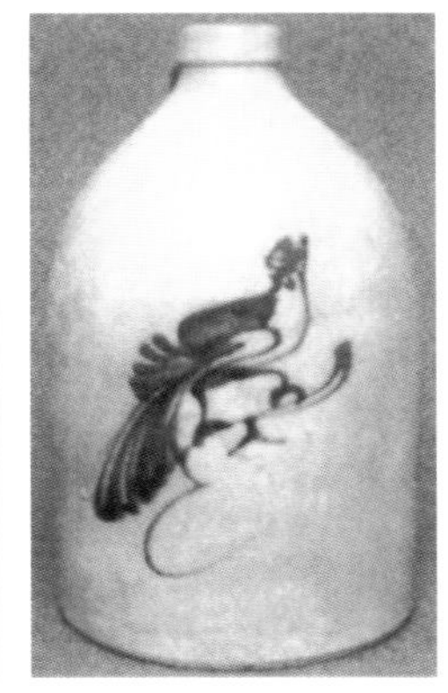

A-MD July 2004 Crocker Farm Auction
87 **Pitcher,** attrib. to Remmey Pottery, 3gal., ht. 10in. **$1,210**
88 **Jug,** att. to Brady & Ryan, Ellenville, NY, w/craze lines, ht. 14in. **$357**

A-MD July 2004 Crocker Farm Auction
170 **Jar,** 6gal., Eastern PA, ca. 1860 w/crazing to base & chip on handle, ht. 17¾in. **$1,320**

A-MD July 2004
Crocker Farm Auction
175 **Churn,** 6gal., mkd. Williams & Reppert, New Geneva, PA, ca. 1885 w/chip to handle terminal & age lines, ht. 19in. **$770**

A-MD July 2004 Crocker Farm Auction
96 **Bowl,** mkd. Sipe, Nichols & Co., Williamsport,PA, ca. 1875 w/chip on rim, wd. 10in. **$137**
97 **Butter Crock,** att. to Remmey Pottery, w/rim chips & line from rim, ht. 5, wd. 8in. **$247**
98 **Milkpan,** Baltimore, ca. 1870 w/handles & tiny rim chips, ht. 6¾, wd. 12in. **$770**

A-MD July 2004
Crocker Farm Auction
171 **Jar,** 4gal., mkd. J. Weaver, Beaver Co., PA, ca. 1860 w/small chips on handles, ht. 13in. **$770**

19.

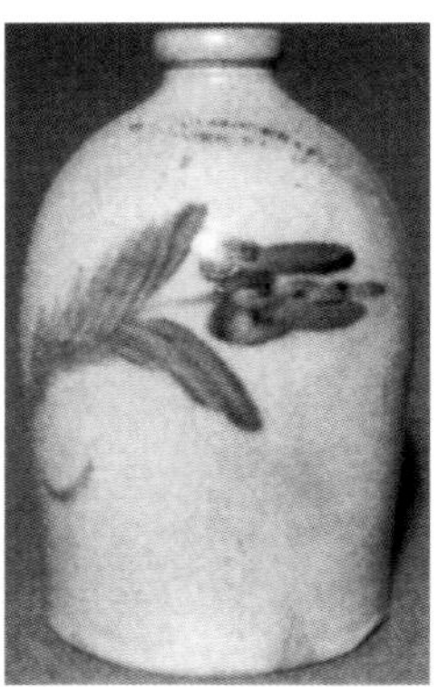

21.

19 **Crock,** 4gal., possibly Perine Pottery, Baltimore, MD, ca. 1870, w/large rim chip & base chips, ht. 15in. **$330**
21 **Jug,** 5gal., PA or NJ potter, ca. 1880 w/chips to spout, ht. 18in. **$385**

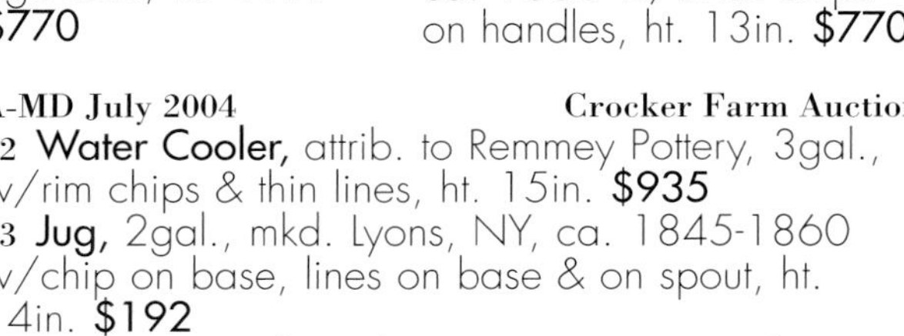

A-MD July 2004 Crocker Farm Auction
92 **Water Cooler,** attrib. to Remmey Pottery, 3gal., w/rim chips & thin lines, ht. 15in. **$935**
93 **Jug,** 2gal., mkd. Lyons, NY, ca. 1845-1860 w/chip on base, lines on base & on spout, ht. 14in. **$192**
94 **Pitcher,** 1½gal., Baltimore, ca. 1879 w/Line in rim & spout chip, ht. 11in. **$990**

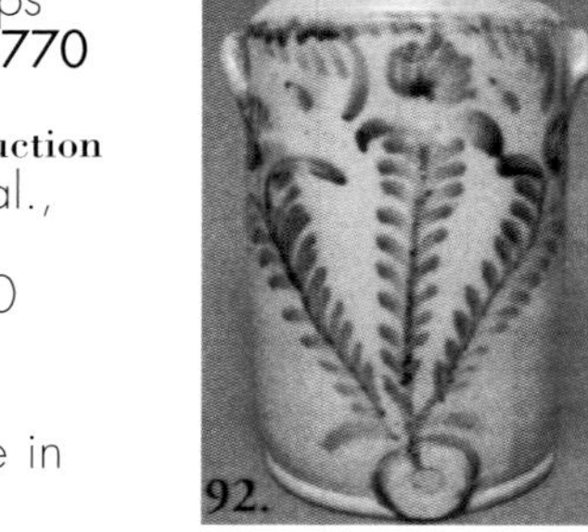

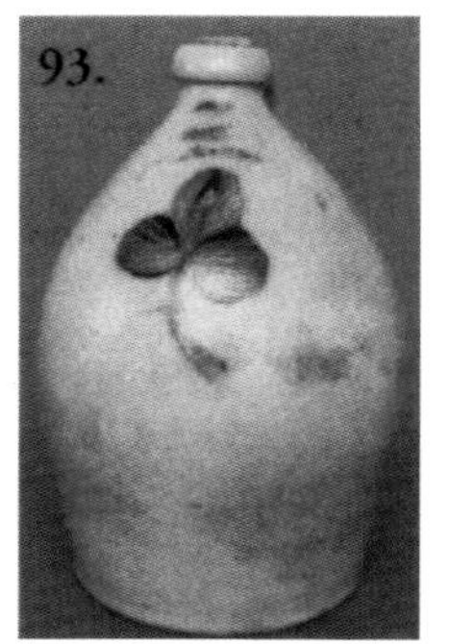

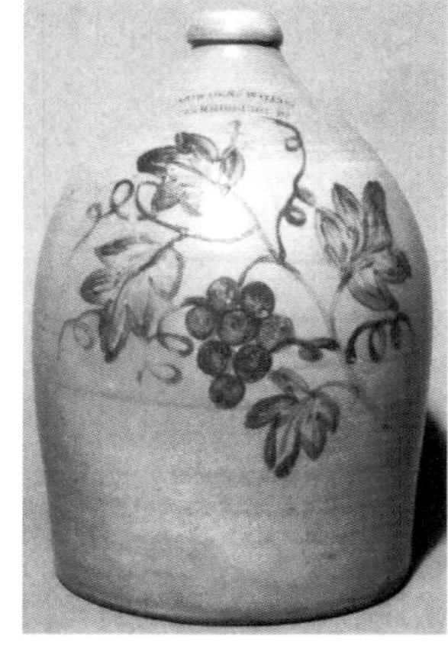

A-MD July 2004
Crocker Farm Auction
284 **Jug,** mkd. Cowden & Wilcox, Harrisburg, PA, ca. 1865, w/prof. rest. to handle, ht. 17in. **$4,675**

290 **Pedestal Water Cooler,** w/incised double birds, mkd. L.&.B.G. Chance, Somerset Mass., ca. 1845-1882, w/pewter spigot. Lines and chip to base, ht. 16in. **$4,290**

A-OH July 2004
Garth's Arts & Antiques
134 **Stoneware Cooler** w/relief molded dec. & imp. P.J. Spencer, w/minor chips on base & under rim, ht. 17in. **$18,975**

227 **Stoneware Crock** w/applied double handles, possibly Akron, OH, or Red Wing potter, ht. 17in. **$3,737**

A-MA Aug. 2004 **Skinner, Inc.**
Stoneware

401 **Three Salt-Glazed Stoneware Items,** Am., 19th C., incl. two ovoid jugs w/strap handles, one w/incised flower & the other mkd. Goodwin & Webster, Hartford, CT, ca. 1810-1840, together w/a slope shouldered cylindrical churn w/Albany slip int., all w/miner imp., ht. 15,16 & 13in. **$1,087**

402 **Two Jars** w/cobalt blue dec. NY & NJ, mid-19th C., both 2gal. jars w/wide mouth, one w/stylized blue flower design & maker's mark A.E.Smith & Sons, Manufacturers, N.Y.; the other w/applied lug handles & stylized blue tulip, mkd. Union Pottery Newark N.J., hairlines & rim chips, ht. 11 & 12in. **$176**

403 **Jug,** 3gal., Boston, 19th C. w/applied strap handle & mkd. Boston, w/wide brown glazed bands, repair to rim & handle, ht. 14in. **$353**

404 **Two Jugs & Small Crock,** Am., 19th C., ovoid jugs w/strap handles, one mkd. T. Mabbett & Co Po'keepsie, NY, the other mkd. L. Norton & Son, together w/wide mouth jar w/applied loop handles & cobalt blue dec., w/imper., ht. 11, 11, & 7in. **$264**

405 **Butter Churn** w/dec. & mkd. Frank B. Norton, Worcester Mass, 3rd qtr. 19th C., 4gal. w/Albany slip int. & minor rim chips. ht. 17in. **$764**

The early settlers brought to these shores the best handworked patterns and techniques of their native lands. Women were accomplished with the needle and their creations were a matter of pride, as well as necessity. They literally threaded themselves into the patchwork of a new American life-style as they settled into their new environment. Every handcrafted, surviving example is an expression of their talent, and textiles are among the more diverse of American collectibles.

It has become increasingly difficult to find an early colorful quilt or woven coverlet these days. Coverlets remain among one of the more expensive of American textiles. The quilt collector focuses on the quality and vintage of the needlework, the diverse forms and condition. Within the past thirty years, prices for fine quilts and coverlets have escalated dramatically... yet good buys remain for the resourceful collector.

Many collectors have turned to other forms of bed covers such as the embroidered blanket, bedspreads of the white variety, stenciled spreads and all forms of embroidery including show towels made by the Pennsylvania Germans.

Colorful hooked and braided rugs command much attention these days, and fetch very substantial prices ... especially those with original designs.

Samplers and needlework pictures became popular during the 18th and 19th centuries. More of these works of art have survived than any other type of fancy American needlework. The most intricately stitched American samplers and needlework, including elaborate mourning pictures, are extremely pricey. Many less elaborate pieces are still available ... and, like other fine American textiles, very good investments.

A-OH Nov. 2003 Historic American Auctions
1033 **Jacquard Coverlet** w/corner blocks by L. Post Benton, N.Y. 1833,slight wear to margins, 78in. sq. **$235**
1034 **Coverlet,** one piece, linen w/minor edge wear, 68 x 80in. **$230**

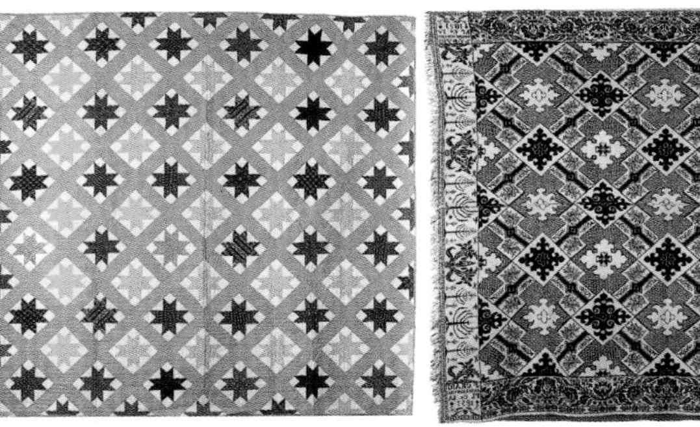

A-OH Nov. 2003 Historic American Auctions
1024 **American Star of LeMoyne Quilt,** mid-19th C., hand quilted calico in unused condition, 78 x 80in. **$259**
1036 **Jacquard Coverlet,** two-piece by Js. Craig/Andersonvill/Fl.Co., IA/1851, browned w/some staining, 78 x 90in. **$863**

A-OH Nov. 2003 Historic American Auctions
1031 **Jacquard Coverlet,** two-piece w/corner blocks by A.H. Church, Illinois, 1840, linen & wool w/U.S. eagle & tree border, reversible, 78 x 85in. **$1,645**
1032 **Jacquard Coverlet,** New York, mkd. in corner blocks L. Post Benton, NY, 1833 w/U.S. shield-breasted eagle, roses & tree border, 75 x 87in. **$764**

A-OH Nov. 2003 Historic American Auctions
1027 **American Multiple Star Quilt,** pieced, hand-quilted calico, ca. 1870s, minor wear, 79in. sq. **$259**
1023 **Morning Star Pieced Quilt,** ca. 1870s, hand-quilted calico, 70 x 9in. **$403**

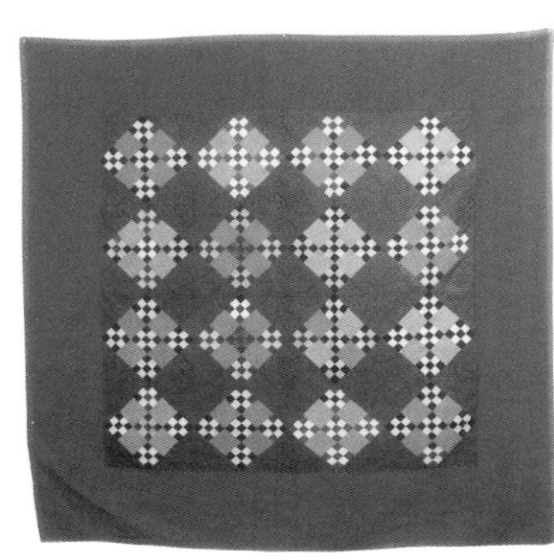

A-OH Jan. 2004 Garth's Arts & Antiques
431 **Amish Quilt,** Lancaster Co., PA, pieced & hand stitched w/flower & feather quilting, print backing, small holes, 82in. sq. **$977**
432 **Amish Quilt,** Lancaster Co., PA, hand stitched, print backing, 82in. sq. **$345**

A-MA Oct. 2003 Skinner, Inc.
151 **Hooked Rug,** wool, possibly Shaker, 19th C., w/bands of multicolored diamond shaped segments & applied wool braided edge, wear, dia. 79in. **$5,875**

A-MA Jun. 2004 Skinner, Inc.
20 Needlework Pocketbook, Am., 1740-90 w/crewel embroidery w/interior lining of blue glazed wool w/two compartments, imper. 4⅝ x 7⅝in. **$10,575**

A-PA June 2004 Conestoga Auction Co., Inc.
304 **Colorful Hooked Rug** w/black horses, M.H. in script & dated 1897, w/printed cloth backing an later addition, 40 x 28in. **$275**

A-PA May 2004 Pook & Pook, Inc.
387 **Pictorial Hooked Rug** ca. 1900 w/birds & potted flowers, 37 x 26½in. **$489**
388 **Pictorial Hooked Rug** ca. 1900 depicting a dog, 44 x 28in. **$920**

A-PA June 2004 Conestoga Auction Co., Inc.
367 Hooked Rug depicting farm scene w/people & animals, 38 x 53in. $302

A-PA June 2004 Conestoga Auction Co., Inc.
368 Hooked Rug depicting a conestoga wagon & animals, 31 x 4 in. $715

A-PA June 2004 Conestoga Auction Co., Inc.
302 Hooked Rug depicting cat in center w/border & cloth backing, 27 x 11½in. $220

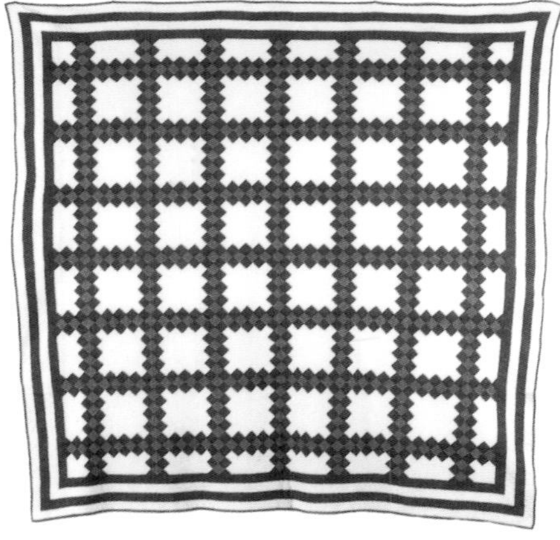

A-PA Dec. 2003
Pook & Pook, Inc.
126 American Patchwork Cotton Quilt, ca. 1900, sawtooth & block patt. $1,380

A-MA Nov. 2003 Skinner, Inc.
102 Civil War Memorial Quilt, pieced & appliquéd, made by Mary Bell Shawvan, ca. 1863, composed of solid color & calico printed cotton w/dark green scalloped border w/off-white muslin backing, minor imper., 81 x 84½in. $149,000

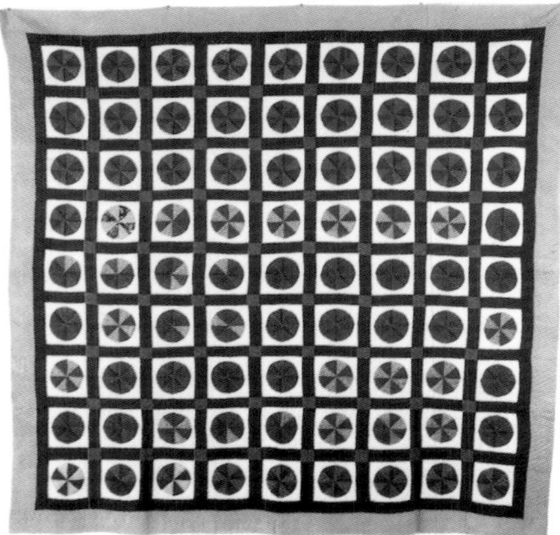

A-PA Dec. 2003
Pook & Pook, Inc.
154 Pieced & Appliquéd Quilt, 19th C., w/81 circles within grid. $633

A-NC Jan. 2004

Brunk Auction Services, Inc.

0553 **Pieced Quilt,** 30 blocks w/radiating red & beige sashing, 19th C., w/small stains, 82 x 67in. **$450**

0121 **Appliqué Quilt** w/eagle central medallion, early 20th C., 95 x 80in. **$1,900**

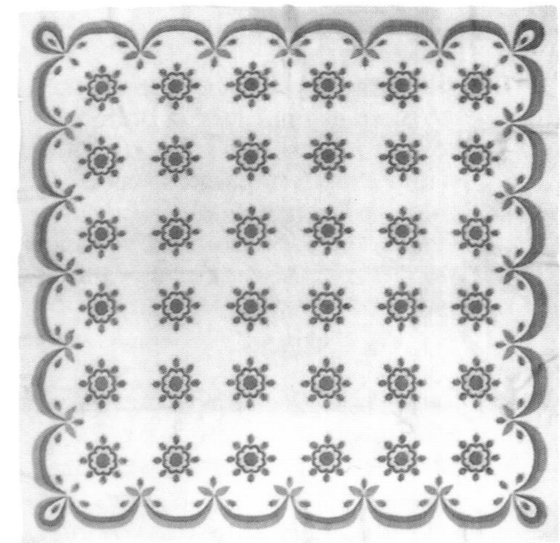

0122 **Pieced Quilt** w/detailed quilting, mid-19th C., KY, stains, 112 x 115in. **$375**

0123 **Pieced Quilt,** Caesar's Crown or Grecian Star variant, late 19th C., KY provenance, light stains, fading, 61x77in. **$400**

A-MA Feb. 2004

Skinner, Inc.

109 **Baltimore Album Quilt,** ca. 1840s, pieced & appliquéd, sgn. w/printed calico border, 106½in. x 108in. **$11,750**

0124 **Pieced & Appliquéd Quilt,** variant of Whig's Defeat, detailed quilting w/some flowers stuffed, stains, 74 x 96in. **$850**

A-OH June 2004 Garth's Arts & Antiques

Jacquard Coverlets

605 Agriculture & Manufactures are the Foundations of our independence. A two-piece double weave in navy & natural, flanked by Masonic columns, monkeys & small human figures. Attrib. to Duchess County, NY, by an unidentified weaver, w/bound edges, 80 x 85in. **$1,035**

606 Two-piece double weave coverlet w/unusual border of leopards & monkeys by unidentified weaver, possibly New York or Ohio, ca. 1830-40 w/ fringe loss,the two halves are separate, 70 x 72in. **$719**

607 Double Weave, two-piece w/corner blocks by Jacob Impson 1832-45. Some staining, minor wear & bound edges, 78 x 90in. **$805**

608 Two-piece Biederwand w/floral & geometric medallions. Corner block Made by Jacob Long, Knox County, Ohio 1843. Minor stains, 76 x 84in. **$1,201**

A-OH June 2004 Garth's Arts & Antiques

Jacquard Coverlets

701 Two-piece Biederwand w/circular medallions, a bird, foliage & swag border. Corner blocks w/W. in Mt. Vernon, Knox County, Ohio by Jacob & Michael Ardner 1853. Minor wear & fringe loss, 76 x 86in. **$1,495**

702 Two-piece Biederwand w/eagle corner blocks & Knox County, Ohio, 1845, 72 x 84in. **$920**

703 Two-piece Biederwand w/corner blocks Winesburg, Holmes County, Ohio 1844, Christian Nusser. Fringe loss & some edge damage, 74 x 82in. **$977**

704 One-piece Biederwand w/a Christian & Heathern border, wear & some damage, 74 x 84in. **$201**

A-OH June 2004 Garth's Arts & Antiques

Jacquard Coverlets

666 Two-piece Biederwand w/W. in Mt. Vernon, Knox County, Ohio by Jacob & Michael Ardner 1854. Minor fringe loss, 71 x 84in. **$2,242**

667 Two-piece double weave w/four-part corner block w/American eagles & Liberty. Damage w/some stitched repair, 73 x 76in. **$230**

668 Two-piece Biederwand w/nesting birds & corner blocks by Sebastian Hipp 1853, working in Mifflin Township, Richland County Ohio w/minor fringe loss, 74 x 84in. **$1,265**

669 Two-piece Biederwand w/unusual corner block of bars, leaves, stars & wide bird border, 72 x 78in. **$575**

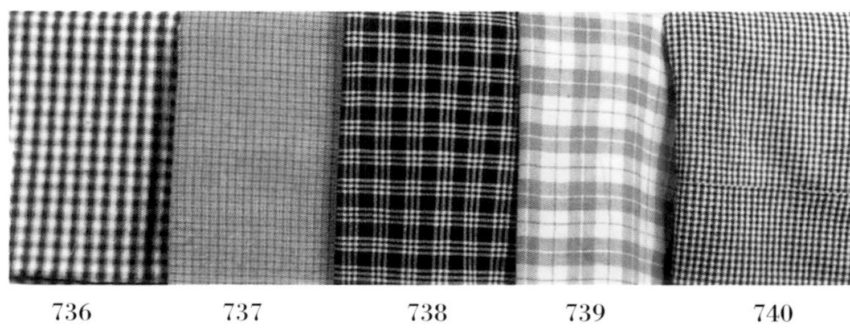

736 737 738 739 740

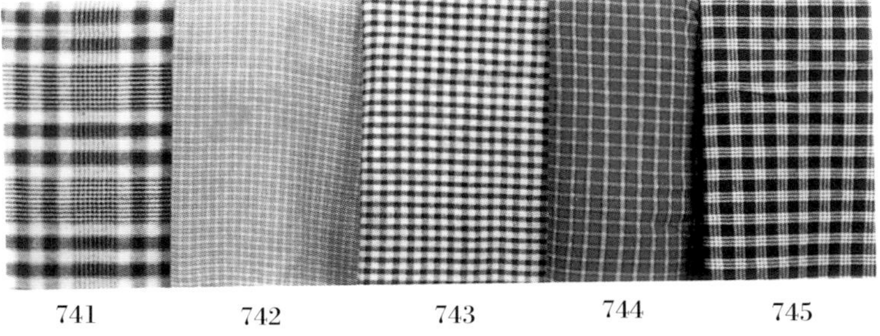

741 742 743 744 745

335 336 337 338

A-PA Nov. 2003 **Conestoga Auction Co., Inc.**
Homespun Textiles

736 **Plaid Linen** w/seam running full length w/minor discolorations, 74 x 44in. **$137**

737 **Plaid Mattress Cover,** linen w/seam running full length, minor discolorations, 70 x 44in. **$1,100**

738 **Cotton Mattress Cover** w/seams, minor staining, 67 x 62in. **$165**

739 **Large Plaid Linen** w/holes & minor staining, 72 x 68in. **$660**

740 **Checked Mattress Cover,** linen w/full seam and string ties with initials S.Y.6 in red thread, staining, 86 x 58in. **$357**

741 **Two large pieces of homespun** applied together, 69 x 40in. **$330**

742 **Checked Linen** w/minor discoloration, 53 x 35in. **$330**

743 **Mattress Cover** w/two applied pieces, old repairs, initialed, 72 x 59in. **$385**

744 **Checked Homespun Linen** w/discoloration, 42 x 39in. **$385**

745 **Plaid Mattress Cover,** cotton w/seam in middle & discoloration, 69 x 58in. **$137**

335 **Tablecloth** w/dyed homespun wool & seam running length, repairs & holes to seams, 98 x 36in. **$165**

336 **Plaid Coverlet** w/homespun dyed wool, bound & fringed, 104 x 81in. **$770**

337 **Plaid Coverlet** w/homespun dyed wool, bound & fringed, sm. holes, 90 x 80in. **$192**

338 **Plaid Coverlet** w/homespun dyed wool, seam & fringed edges & minor discoloration, 106 x 90in. **$385**

A-PA June 2004 **Conestoga Auction Co., Inc.**
397 **Ohio Sampler** by Charity Trimble, born in 1789, done in 1807 w/silk thread in good color featuring bands of dec. that include a verse, flowers, women w/parasols, Noah's ark, birds & brick building. Ht. 16, wd. 14⅜in. **$14,950**

A-OH June 2004 **Garth's Arts & Antiques**
398 **Ohio Sampler** by Ann Alletta Schenck, Franklin, Ohio, CVB Schencks School 1818. Silk thread on linen w/rows of alphabets, floral border, bowls of fruit, buildings & trees. Unframed w/minor stains, 15½in. sq. **$18,400**

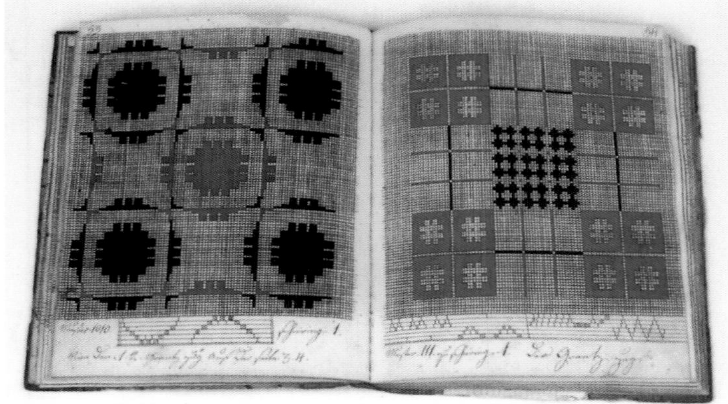

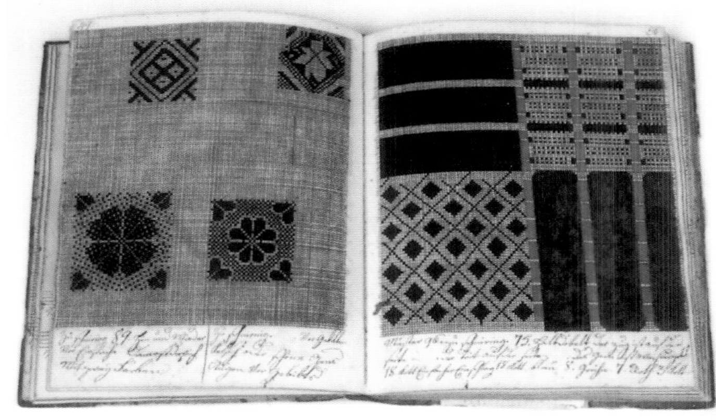

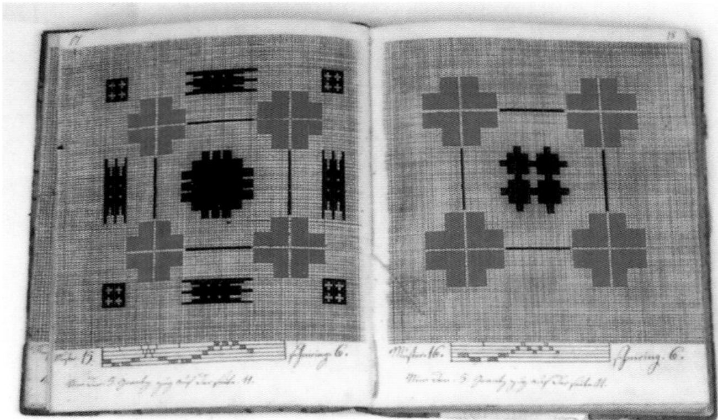

A-PA Jan. 2004

Conestoga Auction Co., Inc.

168 **Weaver's Loom Coverlet Pattern Book** made in Schaefferstown, Lebanon Co. in the State of Pennsylvania by Johannes Schmidt 1818. The first page shows loom, wool wheel & clock reel. Other pages show 28 full page patterns drawn in red & black ink, written in German & leather bound w/wallpaper cover, w/minor ink damage to paper, 10⅝ x8½in. **$30,800**

A-PA Jan. 2004 Conestoga Auction Co., Inc.

174 **Appliquéd Quilt** w/colorful calico wreaths on white ground w/multiple signatures in centers with 1850 date. Foliated needle work on border, minor staining, 86 x 88in. **$1,980**

A-PA Jan. 2004 Conestoga Auction Co., Inc.

169 **Coverlet** by G.Renner & P. Leidig & dated on two corners 1837, cotton weave w/white base, 98 x 86in. **$2,420**

170 **Coverlet** by John Smith & S. Leman & dated on two corners 1837,cotton weave w/white base, staining, 80 x 106 in. **$550**

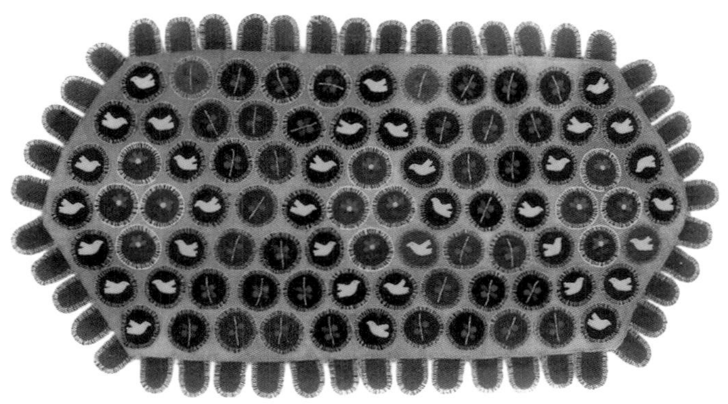

A-PA Jan 2004 Conestoga Auction Co., Inc.

306 **Penny-rug Table Cover,** six sides w/ appliquéd felt pennies of yellow birds, red berries on stems, green leaves & orange daisies w/yellow centers on light background. Scalloped border, 57 x 32in. **$2,090**

Early, interesting old toys – especially the hand-carved examples – are truly vivid expressions of the American craftsman's art of imagination. They are continuously in demand, and prices increase sharply each year. Those worthy of consideration as a "folk art" are very pricey, even though some are crudely whittled; others show fine craftsmanship and detailing. Among the most interesting of the early toys are the carved wooden dolls, squeak toys, wood and metal jumping figures, wood and chalk animals, whistles, miniatures, and the ever-popular "Sunday" toys when boisterous play was banned. The carved "Noah's Arks" were especially designed for this purpose. They oftentimes contained as many as fifty minutely carved and decorated animals, in addition to human figures.

The American toy industry was brought into being during the first decades of the nineteenth century. William S. Tower of South Hingham, MA, a carpenter by profession, has often been called the founder of the toy industry in America. In spite of the availability and wide usage of wood during this period, an increasing number of tin and iron toys were made. Many of the mass-produced toys were made during the 1870s, including the popular cast iron mechanical banks.

Because of the scarcity of earlier toys, today there is a rapidly growing band of enthusiasts buying up toys, almost regardless of the era – sometimes the items haven't been around as long as those doing the prospecting! But, whether it is indicative of a universal yearning for the good old days, or simply a case of monkey-see, monkey-do, the rush goes on.

A-MA Aug. 2004 **Skinner, Inc.**
296 **Wooden Child's Velocipede Coach,** made by E.W. Bushnell, Philadelphia, mid-19th C. Levers at the side propel the cart forward, orig. paint, iron wheels & partial manufacturer's paper label affixed to underside, minor paint wear, ht. 30¾, wd. 22, dp. 39in. **$14,100**

A-PA Dec. 2003 **Pook & Pook, Inc.**
354 **Rocking Horse,** carved & painted, ca. 1900, retaining black & white smoke dec. & mounted on wheels, ht. 24, lg..38in. **$690**
359 **Stuffed horse** pull toy/rocker, early 20th C., w/carved mouth & hooves. The base retains its orig. red painted surface w/yellow pinstriping, ht. 33, lg. 49in. **$690**
356 **Carriage,** Victorian, carved & painted w/3 wheels, retains orig. black painted surface w/gold & red pin-striping, ht. 35½in. **$690**
357 **Bears,** Steiff jointed blond teddy bear, early 20th C., w/tan embroidered nose, mouth & claws, and cream colored felt pads, lg. 19in.; together w/ another jointed yellow bear, lg. 27in. **$2,990**

A-NH Nov. 2003 Northeast Auctions
171 **Child's Amish Two-Wheel Carriage,** painted & dec. w/crest of spreadwing eagle, lg. 56in.; together w/a Greiner doll, lg. 26in. **$2,250**
172 **Carved & Painted Mansard Roof Doll House** w/furnishings. The lower level w/ parlor, drapes, stamped brass w/appliqués, scroll arm sofa, five side chairs & table. The upstairs w/bed & two bureaus, ht. approx.27½, base 20 x 21in. **$1,000**
173 **Noah's Ark,** carved & painted w/dove on roof & numerous pairs of figures, animals & birds. One side sliding open to interior, lg. 19½in. **$2,600**
174 **Seated Dog,** Gallé Faience, painted overall w/blue & white spots on pale yellow ground, sgn. E. Gallé/Nancy on top of rear paw, ht. 11½in. **$650**

A-NH Nov. 2003 Northeast Auctions
177 **Wooden Soldiers Mechanical Bank.** The opposing figures in uniforms & black hats fitted to hold coin, each facing a trapezoidal tower w/slot, mounted on a rectangular case w/shaped apron & bracket feet. Prototype for cast iron mechanical bank, 10 x 10in. **$800**

A-NH Nov. 2003 Northeast Auctions
175 **Daisy Pull Toy** w/bell, cast iron, painted, lg. 8½in. **$1,300**
176 **Landing of Columbus Pull Toy** w/bell, cast iron, by J.& E. Stevens Co., Made for the Columbian Exposition, Chicago, 1892. Together w/ the copper printing block w/Stevens brand, lg. 7½in. **$1,400**

A-ME June 2004 James D. Julia, Inc.
2367 **Horse Drawn Penny Toy,** tin litho. toy w/one split on tin, lg. 3½in. **$120**

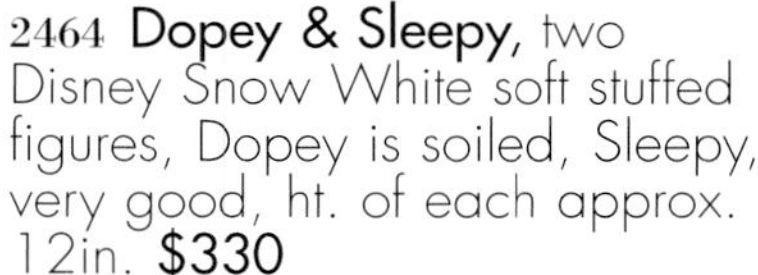

2464 **Dopey & Sleepy,** two Disney Snow White soft stuffed figures, Dopey is soiled, Sleepy, very good, ht. of each approx. 12in. **$330**

A-ME June 2004 James D. Julia, Inc.
2397 Tin Figural Charlie Chaplin Spring Rider, litho. image, working, lg. 8in. $201

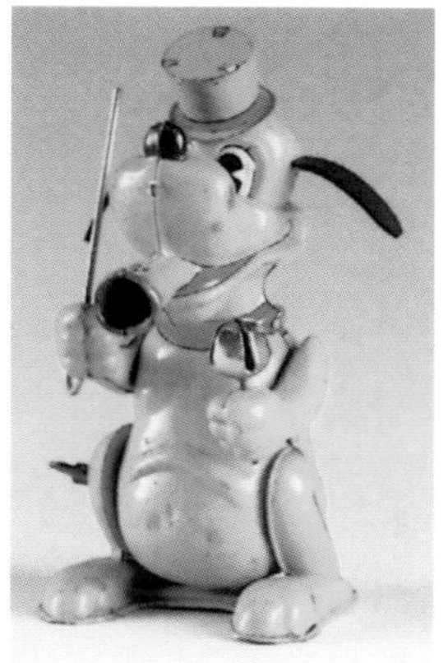

A-ME June 2004 James D. Julia, Inc.
2370 Linemar Pluto The Band Leader, Disney Prod., Japan, all tin wind-up, replaced ears, working. Ht. 6in. $180

A-ME June 2004 James D. Julia, Inc.
2464E Glass Tray featuring Mickey & Minnie w/metal frame & carrying handles, w/paint loss, lg. 16, wd. 11in. $275

A-ME June 2004 James D. Julia, Inc.
1074 Mickey Mouse Handcar, Lionel, restored, ex. cond. & working, lg. 8in. $2,070

A-ME June 2004 James D. Julia, Inc.
1073 Mickey Mouse Souvenir Bank, cast metal, marked Delaware Water Gap, figure mkd. Walt E. Disney & Germany. Bank retains orig. brass padlock, w/few losses on the in-flaps at seams, ht. 15in. $1,552

A-ME June 2004 James D. Julia, Inc.
1072 Mickey Mouse Celluloid Nodder, pre-war Japan w/orig.paper label, mkd. & dated 1928, ht. 7in. $2,185

A-ME June 2004 James D. Julia, Inc.
1071 Mickey Mouse Mechanical Jazz Drummer, 1930s, w/plunger action mechanism, mkd., some light abrasions, working, ht. 7in. $402

A-ME June 2004 James D. Julia, Inc.
2361 Porky The Pig Wind-up Toy, by Marx, 1939, tin, working, ht. 8in. $172

A-ME Jan. 2004 James D. Julia, Inc.
2431 **Arcade Fire Engine,** cast iron, Am., 2 pc, firemen & ladders, not orig. to toy. lg. 16in. **$570**

A-ME Jan. 2004 James D. Julia, Inc.
2432 **Kenton Fire Truck,** shows orig. paint & nickel plated areas & rubber hoses. Spool retains original string cord fire hose. lg. 14½in. **$1,020**

A-ME Nov. 2003 James D. Julia, Inc.
Teddy Bears
1186 **Brown Mohair Bear** w/jointed limbs, glass eyes & flat back, w/fur loss to back, one eye re-attached & repair to leg, ht. 25in. **$115**
1187 **German Mohair Bear** w/jointed limbs, glass eyes, velvet pads & mild hump. Some fur loss to back side & pads show wear, ht. 15in. **$488**
1188 **Steiff Bear,** blond mohair w/glass eyes, jointed limbs & retains button in ear. Foot pads replaced. **$316**
1189 **Mohair Bear** w/long jointed limbs, button eyes, pointed snout & oilcloth nose. Repair to neck. **$420**

A-ME Nov. 2003 James D. Julia, Inc.
1190 **Brown Mohair Bear** w/button eyes, jointed limbs, large hump & woven cloth paws. Left ear reattached & area where growler was has been resewn. **$780**
1191 **White Mohair Bear** w/black button eyes, jointed limbs & woven cloth paws. Some fur loss to back of legs & around face. **$720**
1192 **Light Brown Mohair Bear** w/jointed limbs,brown button eyes & stubby ears. Some fur loss & repair to legs. **$488**

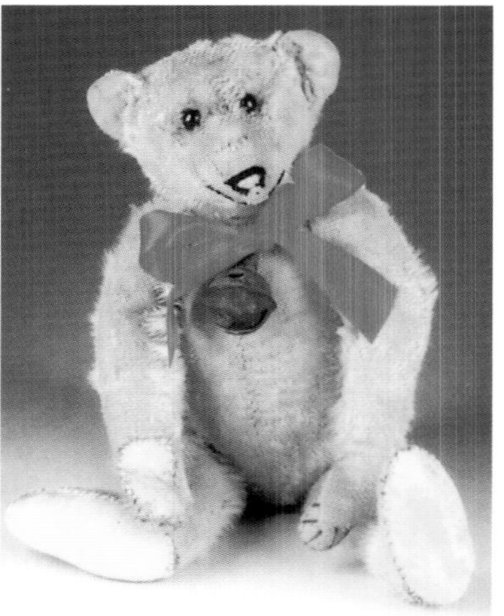

A-ME June 2004 James D. Julia, Inc.
2107 **Steiff Bear,** mohair fur loss w/shoe-button eyes, felt pads repl., lacks button on ear. **$488**

A-ME June 2004 James D. Julia, Inc.
2332 **Steiff Animal Collection,** Germany, lot averages good to near excellent, all mohair toys & many retain ear buttons. The lot includes a standing polar bear, dinosaur, rabbit, ferret, penguin, seal, monkey & large lion. **$862**

A-ME June 2004
James D. Julia, Inc.
2331 Steiff Teddy Bears, German, partial lot, all with ear tags. Lot includes Dicky, a fully jointed 13in. replica of a 1930 issue, a Teddy w/growler, little bear, off white; a golden bear, black bear; a Teddy child's purse w/glass eyes; a panda & a white bear w/outfit. As new cond. $600

A-ME June 2004 James D. Julia, Inc.
2105 Lot of 3 Bears, the first a Steiff teddy w/chest tag, ear button & yellow tag, ht. 6in. The other two bears are of unknown manufacture, & show fur loss. $2100

A-ME June 2004
James D. Julia, Inc.
2104 White Steiff Bear w/glass eyes, Steiff button in ear w/remnants of orange tag under button. Fur loss throughout. $1,782

A-ME June 2004
James D. Julia, Inc.
1192 Lionel No. 44 U.S. Army Missile Launching Locomotive. $57

A-ME June 2004 James D. Julia, Inc.
1424A Yellow Mohair Steiff Bear, ca. 1940/50s, honey colored w/glass eyes. Partial cloth tag remains on bear's right arm stating Made in US Zone. Germany. Minimal fur loss, ht. 26in. $4,312
1423B Mohair Bear w/long jointed limbs, black button eyes & oilcloth nose, ht. 21in. $390

A-PA Nov. 2003
Conestoga Auction Co., Inc.
169 Trotting Horse, tin pull toy, ht. 8¾, lg. 11in. $467

170 Tin & Metal Steam Engine, key wind, ht. 8¾, lg. 11¼in. $4,620

A-ME June 2004 James D. Julia, Inc.
Santa Candy Containers
2456 **Santa Riding Nodding Donkey,** Santa w/papier mâché face & rabbit beard. Fading & loss to nap of clothing & donkey. Ht. 8in. **$2,012**

A-ME June 2004 James D. Julia, Inc.
2457 **Later Santa** w/rabbit beard. Candy container is housed within his body and accessed by removing his legs. Light soiling/fading to clothing. **$1000**

A-ME June 2004
James D. Julia, Inc.
2455 **Papier mâché Santa** stands atop a mica covered wood base w/paper store label affixed to underside of base. **$1200**

A-ME June 2004
James D. Julia, Inc.
2450 **Santa Trudger w/Sled,** dragging his wooden sled/candy container which is mounted on wood base w/mica covering. Yoke to pull sled is repl. **$2,300**

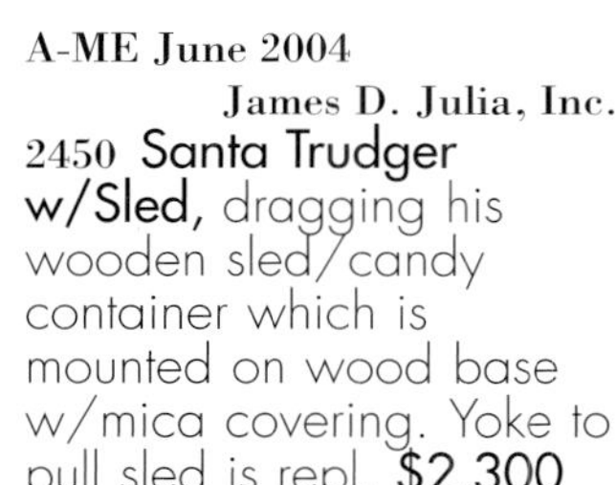

A-ME June 2004
James D. Julia, Inc.
2449 **German Papier Mâché Santa** in virtually untouched cond. standing on top of wood base w/mica covering. Uniform w/light soiling & minor nap loss. Ht. 18in. **$3,680**

A-ME June 2004
James D. Julia, Inc.
2453 **Reindeer Candy Container** w/papier mâché Santa. Removing reindeer's head/neck reveals the candy container. Some paint loss to metal antlers, ht. 6in. **$1,725**

A-IA Mar. 2004
Jackson's International Auctioneers
466 **Carved Wooden Horse Pull Toy** by Converse, w/orig. bridle & saddle, mounted on oak platform w/cast iron wheels, lg. 16, ht. 20in. **$747**

A-IA Mar. 2004
Jackson's International Auctioneers
467 **Cast Iron Child Size Stove,** Bucks Junior, missing one door & 3 surface lids. **$184**

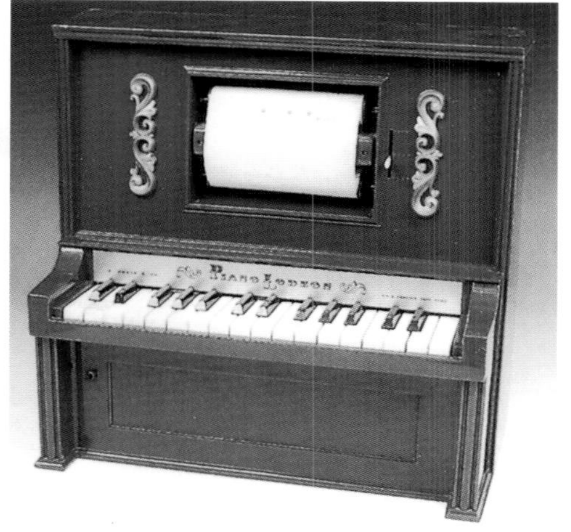

A-IA Mar. 2004
Jackson's International Auctioneers
468 **Pianolodeon Player Piano** by J. Chein & Co., ca. 1949, plastic. **$69**

A-ME June 2004 James D. Julia, Inc.
2349 **Mechanical horse** on platform, all tin, hand painted, working. ht. 5in. **$450**

A-ME June 2004 James D. Julia, Inc.
2355 **Lehmann Wind-Up Coach,** lithographed & hand-painted tinplate in working condition, lg. 5¼in. **$360**

A-ME June 2004 James D. Julia, Inc.
2365 **Taxi Touring Car Penny Toy** by J.D., Germany, ca. 1925. Meter reads For Hire, lg. 3in. **$460**

A-ME June 2004
James D. Julia, Inc.
2359 **Shoenhut Mr. Peanut Wooden Figure,** fully jointed & all original advertising character for Planters Peanuts, ht. 8½in. **$126**
2360 **Marx Joe Penner & His Ducks,** tin wind-up, Am., working, ht. 8in. **$287**

A-ME June 2004 James D. Julia, Inc.
2348 **George Brown Yankee Notions Wagon,** ca. 1880s, tin, w/some paint touch up. One horse has had rest., lg. 11in. **$920**

2368 **Li'1 Abner Wind-Up Dogpatch Band** by Unique Art, Am., ca. 1945, lithographed tin. Box is incomplete, toy in excellent working cond. **$546**

2371 **Three wind-up vehicles,** tin, Marx Dipsy, G.I. Joe & Marx Milton Berle Dipsy, all working. **$300**

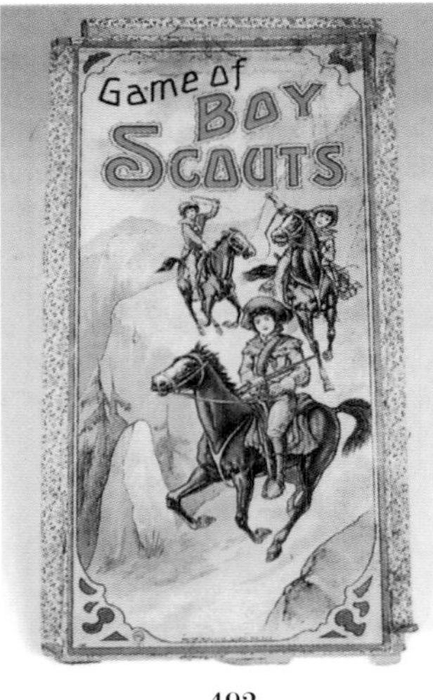

492

493

494

495

496

497

498

499

A-IA Oct. 2003
Jackson's International Auctioneers

492 **Game of Boy Scouts** w/orig. box & playing board by Milton Bradley, some losses & staining. **$46**

493 **Toy Village** by Milton Bradley, w/orig. box in played with condition. **$46**

494 **The Gypsy Fortune Teller Game,** w/orig. box by Bradley. **$126**

495 **Collection of Paper Dolls,** ca. 1920s, Dolly Dingle Fairy Tales. **$5**

496 **Comic Book,** Charlie Chaplin's Funny Stunts by J. Keeley, 1917. **$51**

497 **Tintograph Stencil Outfit of Soldiers & Sailors** by Baumgarten & Co., Pat. 1915, in orig. box w/16 stencils. **$109**

498 **Boy Scouts Marching Group** by McLoughlin Brothers w/42 figures. **$103**

499 **Pair of Games** by Milton Bradley, incl. Uncle Sam's Postman & Fish Pond. **$69**

A-ME June 2004 James D. Julia, Inc.

2351 **Schuco Wind-Up Toys,** lot of 6, German, incl. 2 violin monkeys, a drumming monkey, drumming boy figure, a dressed figure raising mug & a boy lifting celluloid child. All working toys, tallest 6in. **$287**

Opposite
A-IA Oct. 2003
Jackson's International Auctioneers

102 **Pedal Tractor,** M Farmall w/chain drive, sgn. J.L. Ertl, lg. 39in. **$115**

103 **Pedal Car,** Super Sport, incomplete w/rest., lg. 37in. **$103**

104 **Pedal Car** w/Murray hubcaps, 1960s Ford, missing windshield, lg. 41in. **$69**

105 **Pedal Car,** Western Flyer, Fire Battalion No. 1, by Murray, w/paint loss & replaced ladders. Red light added to hood, lg. 40in. **$92**

106 **Pedal Tractor,** Murray TRAC w/chain drive, all orig., lg. 39in. **$144**

107 **Riding Horse,** Mobo Metal w/orig. paint & saddle, English, lg. 39in. **$172**

108 **Cast Iron Car**, lg. 5in. & bus 4in. **$126**

109 **Contractor's Dump Wagon** w/horse, repainted & bottom missing, lg. 12in. **$80**

110 **Tin Car** mkd. Made in Germany, dents & spring wind broken. lg. 7in. **$374**

111 **Thrashing Machine,** McCormick Deering, repro., lg. 11in. **$29**

112 **Shoenhut Circus Toys,** 9 pcs. including 2 elephants, 2 barrels, donkey, clown, elephant drum, chair & ladder. **$113**

113 **Schuco Wind-up Fiddler** in orig. box, toy horse missing platform. **$115**

114 **Collection of 4 toys,** late 1930s, including woman w/laundry, black comp. wind-up doll & comp. sailor doll. **$161**

115 **Renwal Metal Doll House** w/approx. 60 pcs. furniture, in played with cond. **$604**

116 **Marx Metal Ranch House Dollhouse** w/approx. 100 pcs. of furniture. **$138**

102 103 104

105 106 107

108 109 110

111 112 113

114 115 116

A-ME June 2004 James D. Julia, Inc.

1037 Locomotive & Tender, original Lionel AC Gilbert Erector Hudson. $1,782

1030 Lionel 400 E Locomotive w/12-wheel oil tender & some paint loss to frame. $2,300

1034 American Flyer Standard Gauge Passenger Set w/mirror chips. $2,587

1022 **Lionel Standard Gauge Stephen Girard passenger set** w/minor paint loss to frames. **$3,450**

1010 **Lionel Standard Gauge 329 E Locomotive & Tender,** boiler front clasp is missing. **$2,300**

1009 **Lionel No. 7 Locomotive & Tender** w/minor chips on tender frame. **$3,450**

1018 **American Flyer Standard Gauge Hamiltonian Passenger Set** w/minor scratches overall. **$1,320**

A-OH Oct. 2004 Garth's Arts & Antiques
420 **Game Board,** maple w/old mustard paint & a walnut inlaid checkerboard on each side, 29x19in. **$345**
421 **Wooden Rocking Horse,** carved Appaloosa in grey & white w/high relief mane, saddle blanket & harness, mid-20th C., ht. 36, lg. 48in. **$575**

A-OH Oct. 2004 Garth's Arts & Antiques
First Row
423 **Two Carved Wooden Chickens** w/crosshatched combs w/minor edge flakes & glued repairs on each, ht. 3⅛ & 2¾in. **$2,300**
424 **Folk Art Rooster,** hand carved w/dark patina & minor edge damage, ht. 5in. **$431**
425 **Pipsqueak Toy,** fancy fowl w/orig. poly. paint, leather bellows silent & wear, ht. 5in. **$373**
Second Row
Butterprints
426 **Deer & Sunburst** w/scrubbed finish & inset handle missing, dia. 4in. **$575**
427 **Acorn,** well carved w/one-piece handle, dia. 4in. **$402**
428 **Compass Star & Hearts,** one-piece handle & scrubbed surface, dia. 4in. **$488**
429 **Flying Am. Eagle** w/shield, old ref. & one piece handle, dia. 2in. **$230**
430 **Stylized Am. Eagle** w/shield on breast, stained w/minor edge flakes, dia. 4⅝in. **$316**

A-OH July 2004 Garth's Arts & Antiques
211 **Cannon Ball Rope Bed,** tiger maple w/old ref., extended rails & elaborate headboard, lg. 76in. **$1,035**
212 **Stoneware Jar,** 5 gal. w/Greentown 1891 in blue & cracks, ht. 16in. **$718**
213 **Stoneware Jug** w/blue floral dec. & imp. mark of J.Stadden, Summit Co., OH, ht. 15¾in. **$690**
214 **Churn** w/cobalt dec., 4 gal., stains & chips, ht. 17in. **$373**

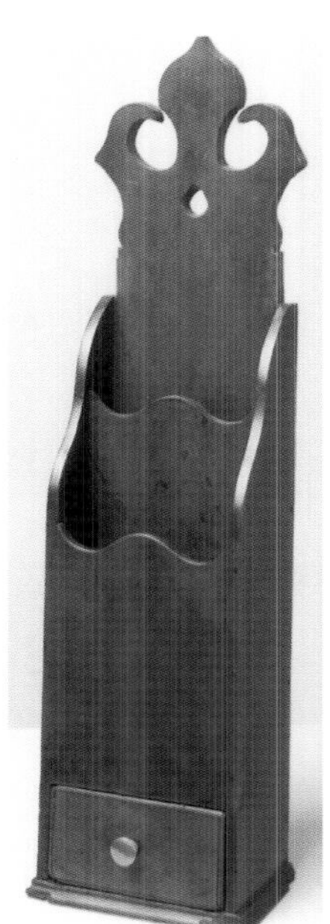

A-OH Oct. 2004 Garth's Arts & Antiques
13 **Pipebox,** cherry w/orig. dark red surface, pine secondary wood, CT, w/few minor chips on base, ht. 23¼, wd. 6⅛in. **$5,462**

A-OK July 2004 Garth's Arts & Antiques
441 **Bookplate,** watercolor on laid paper & dated 1796, w/stains & fold lines, old frame w/dark graining & gilt liner, ht. 7⅞, wd.6⅝in. **$977**
442 **Redware Turk's Head Food Mold** w/mottled spots, wear & hairline, dia. 9¾, ht. 2¾in. **$374**
443 **Brass Candlestick** w/seamed stem, repairs, ht. 7in. **$316**
444 **Bellows** w/mustard ground, stenciled red & green fruit, releathered & repaired edge damage, lg. 16½in. **$690**
445 **Baleen Oval Box** w/three fingers & copper tacks, & lid, ht. 2½in. **$632**

A-OH July 2004 Garth's Arts & Antiques
446 Queen Anne Lowboy, cherry w/old mellow finish, two-board top, drops & returns missing & feet have rest. ht. 29¾in. $6,612
447 Embroidery Frame w/dec., 20th C., adjustable. $1,495
448 Brass Candlestick, frying pan form w/pierced heart handle, ht. 3½in. $402
449 Redware Storage Jar, pumpkin colored glaze w/brown floral dec., flaking & rim rest., ht. 9⅝in. $1,495

A-NH Aug. 2004 Northeast Auctions
760 Queen Anne Cherry Candlestand, ca. 1790-1800, ht. 27, dia. 16½in. $1,600
761 Black Bellied Plover Decoy mkd. R.J.de la Grange, lg. 9⅛in. $200
762 Sheet Metal Stag Weather Vane in old green paint, late 19th C. Fitted on stand, lg. 37in. $2,900
763 Pull-Toy & Cart in green paint, hideskin covered horse on platform w/ spoked wheels, ht. 9in., overall lg. 30in. $300

A-NH Mar. 2004 Northeast Auctions
450 Hanging Candlebox, poplar w/old blue green paint, sq. nail construction & rest., ht. 8, lg. 11¾in. $287
451 Ladderback Arm Chair, woven splint seat w/damage, legs have been ended out, ht. 46in. $517
452 Butter Churn w/stave construction, original worn red paint, overlapping staves & a hewn top. The dasher appears to be later, ht. 27in. $1,466
453 Wooden Barrel & Lid, pine & hickory w/old brown patina, ht. 18in. $373
454 Two Woven Splint Baskets, one finely woven shown, ht. 8in., together w/an oblong gathering basket w/arched handle, lg. 12in. $230

A-NH Aug. 2004 Northeast Auctions
605 Circular Box, brown w/circular black & yellow dec., ht. 8½in. $1,500
606 Treen Kitchenware, four pcs., incl.two small jars, a bowl & blue butter mold w/starflower motif. $230
607 New Hampshire Queen Anne Tea Table w/old red painted base, scrubbed top & button feet, ca. 1770, ht. 26, top 32x28in. $6,750
608 Two Woven Splint Baskets in red & green paint, rectangular w/twin swing handles, lg. of green 14½, red one 13½in. $1,400
609 Pigeon Decoys, set of three, cast & gray painted, ht. 7, lg. 10in. $2,000

A-PA May 2004 Pook & Pook, Inc.
400 Pewter Deep Dish w/Edward Danforth touchmark, 1788-1794, dia. 13¼in. $633
401 Pewter Flagon w/lion touchmark, impressed Boardman, ht. 11¾in. $345
402 Q.A. Dining Chair, ca. 1745, walnut w/oxbow crest rail above a vasiform splat & slip seat. $3,450
403 Drop Leaf Table, Q.A., maple, ca. 1760 & retaining old mellow surface, ht. 27, wd. open 35¾in. $3,105
404 Boston Q.A. Dining Chair, cherry, ca. 1745 w/oxbow crest above a vasiform splat & slip seat. $2,530

A-NH Mar. 2004 Northeast Auctions
467 **Federal Banjo Clock,** MA w/eglomisé panels by E. Howard & Co., ht. 32in. **$2,300**
468 **Sheraton Blind Door Secretary,** mah. w/inlay, ht. 52, wd. 40in. **$2,200**
469 **Sheraton Stand,** cherry w/one drawer, ht. 28½, wd. 17½in. **$1,600**
470 **Sheraton Work Table,** mah. w/two drawers, square top & fluted legs, ht. 29½, sq. top 20in. **$1,900**
471 **Hepplewhite Corner Washstand,** mah. w/inlay, ht. 42, wd. 23in. **$1,600**

A-NH Mar. 2004 Northeast Auctions
232 **Cherry Corner Cupboard,** in two parts on molded base, ht. 76, wd. 44in. **$2,100**
233 **Staffordshire Pearlware Tablewares** by various makers incl. a large platter, pitcher, two cups & saucers, two toddy plates & cup plate. Together w/a Staffordshire blue/white teapot & coffee pot cover. **$1,400**
234 **Sheraton Chairs** w/painted decoration, set of six, two illustrated. n/s
235 **N. Eng. Hooked Rug,** ca. 1900, Cat On The Roof, mounted on a stretcher. 26x48in. **$400**
236 **Pillar & Scroll Shelf Clock,** labeled Seth Thomas, mah., ht. 30in. **$1,600**
237 **Hepplewhite Chest of Drawers,** tiger maple w/panel ends, ht. 42, wd. 42in. **$2,000**
238 **Amber Glass Chestnut Bottles,** five, ht. of tallest 8¼in. **$1,750**
239 **Sheraton Stand,** tiger maple w/sandwich glass opal. knob, ht. 29, top 18x25in. **$1,400**

A-MA Feb. 2004 Skinner, Inc.
112 **Veneer Dressing Bureau,** Classical, mah., ca. 1825 w/repl. brasses, ht. 66, wd. 36in. **$1,175**
113 **Carved Mirror,** Classical, gilt gesso, ca. 1825, ht. 36, wd. 16in. **$353**
114 **Classical Carved Mirror** w/molded egg & dart cornice, regilded, ht. 39, wd. 23in. **$940**
115 **Work Table,** mah. & mah. veneer, ca. 1825 w/repl. pulls, old finish, bag drawer, imper., ht. 31, wd. 20½in. **$1,293**
116 **Classical Lady's Work Table,** ca. 1825 w/hinged top opening to a fitted interior & two drawers below, repl. pulls, imper. ht. 30, wd. 24in. **$2,820**
117 **Classical Carved Ottoman,** mah., Boston, old finish w/minor imper. **$1,116**
118 **Chamber Stand,** classical, mah., ca. 1820-25 w/drawer, ref. & minor rest., ht. 38, wd. 19½in. **$1,880**
119 **Kazak Rug,** Southwest Caucasus, early 20th C. w/moth damage. n/s

A-MA Aug. 2004 **Skinner, Inc.**
79 **Hooked Wool Rug** w/floral design, late 19th/early 20th C., mounted on a wooden frame, 26x37in. **$264**
80 **Painted Cake Board,** Am. 19th C. w/polychrome dec., dated 1831 & age cracks; wd. 31½in. **$1,293**
81 **Four Braced Windsor Side Chairs** w/orig. worn paint, N. Eng., late 18th C., & minor imper. **$4,113**
82 **Wrought Iron Candleholder,** adjustable tabletop, 18th/early 19th C., w/ penny feet, ht. 19, wd. 11in. **$1,998**
83 **Burl Bowl** w/scrubbed interior & remains of orig. exterior paint, dia. 15, ht. 4½in. **$5,581**
84 **Tavern Table** w/old red finish, rectangular top pinned to base, dov. drawers, ht. 29½in. **$1,410**

A-PA Oct. 2004 **Pook & Pook, Inc.**
824 **English Woolwork Ship Portrait,** dated April 1880 w/a 3-masted frigate flying 31 flags of various countries, 14x23in. **$4,140**
825 **Woolwork Ship Portrait,** late 19th C. of a frigate flying a British flag, orig. bird's-eye maple frame, 17x26in. **$1,380**
826 **PA Federal Tiger Maple Sideboard,** ca. 1815 w/bowed cupboard doors, flanked by bottle drawers, ht. 40¼, wd. 53in. **$6,325**
827 **English Woolwork Coastal Scene,** late 19th C. w/British frigate & buildings, 10x15in. **$1,610**

A-NH Mar. 2004 **Northeast Auctions**
207 **English Oak Windsor Armchairs,** similar w/bowbacks & splayed legs. **$450**
208 **English Sheraton Four-Tier Etagère,** mah. w/turned supports & drawer, ht. 52, wd. 18in. **$2,000**
209 **Beau Brummel Dressing Table,** mah. w/fitted interior, ht. 23, wd. 17in. **$1,000**
210 **Dome-Top Box on Frame,** mah. w/inlay, ht. 24in. **$900**

A-NH Mar. 2004 **Northeast Auctions**
175 **Chippendale Mahogany Mirror** w/double line inlay, ht. 39, wd. 21in. **$400**
176 **Fan-Back Windsor Chairs,** pine, set of four w/plank seats, **$2,200**
177 **Hutch Table,** pine w/circular top pivoting above a box base w/hinged lid, ht. 30½, dia. 47in. **$800**
178 **Brass Jelly Buckets,** three w/applied steel curved handles, ht. of largest 16, dia. 16½in. **$400**
179 **Folk Art Coffer,** painted & dec. w/hinged top, 45 recessed panels, each w/a yellow daisy, & iron handles, ht. 10, lg. 21in. **$1,500**
180 **Chippendale Blanket Chest,** maple w/hinged top above a case w/two simulated over three actual long drawers, ht. 48, wd. 36in. **$1,200**
181 **Candlestand,** adjustable w/tripod base, ht. 44in. **$500**

A-MA June 2004 Skinner, Inc.

235 **Blue Painted Box** w/dome top, NY, early 19th C., w/hinged top, iron latch & dec., wear cracks, ht. 11, wd. 27in. **$1,880**

236 **Folk Art Carved Wooden Bald Eagle,** OH, probably early 20th C., painted w/glass eyes, stippled surface & mounted on carved pine base, age cracks, ht. 11in. **$4,994**

237 **Child's Chair,** painted brown w/floral dec. on crest & splat w/gilt accents; minor wear & cracks, ht. 20⅛in. **$264**

238 **Grain Painted Chest of Drawers** w/carving, ME or NH, late 18th C. w/rest. ht. 49in. **$4,406**

239 **Lift Top Chest,** N. Eng., early 19th C. The hinged top opens to a storage cavity above two drawers, w/burnt umber & ochre, dec., old brasses; & minor imper., ht. 39, wd. 39in. **$2,350**

240 **Two Small Child's Chairs,** late 19th C., painted w/minor wear. **$206**

241 **Miniature Stool,** pine w/painted stenciled dec., repairs, ht 5½in. **$558**

242 **Grain Painted Six-Board Chest,** N. Eng., ca. 1830, old surface w/imper. ht. 24, wd. 37in. **$3,000**

A-PA Oct. 2004 Pook & Pook, Inc.

304 **Pair of Celestial & Terrestrial Table Top Globes,** early 19th C., each supported by 4 columns w/ball feet,ht. 6¾in. **$3,680**

A-PA May 2004 Pook & Pook, Inc.

First Row

111 **Candlebox,** PA, ca. 1800 w/floral painted tombstone panel over ochre grained dov. case, ht. 5, wd. 15½in. **$1,035**

112 **Folk Art Folding Seat,** ca. 1840, one side carved w/figure of a man, the other a lady, possibly a love token to be used at public events, lg. 34in. **$3,335**

113 **Cookie Cutter,** tin, in the form of Uncle Sam, ht. 12¼in. **$460**

114 **Miniature Butter Churn,** pine staved, 19th C., ht. 14in. **$115**

Second Row

115 **Pair of Stirrup Cups,** Stevenson & Hancock, Staffordshire, ca. 1900 & inscribed Tally Ho, lg. 5¼in. **$4,370**

116 **Tole document Box,** N. Eng., yellow,gilt floral dec. w/inscription & dated 1835, ht. 9½in. **$748**

117 **Miniature Chest of Drawers,** Am. Chippendale, ca. 1800, ht. 8½in. **$1,610**

Third Row

118 **Stoneware Jug,** Charlestown, MA, ca. 1800 w/brown glazing, mkd., ht. 9½in. **$574**

119 **Redware Bank** in form of a monkey, 19th C. ht. 8in., together w/ an earthenware recumbent spaniel, 19th C. ht. 3½in. **$1,495**

120 **Watch Safe,** cherry, Lancaster Co., PA, ca. 1830, w/scalloped top & glazed door, ht. 10¾, wd. 6in., together w/a Seth Thomas gold pocket watch. **$1,380**

121 **Stoneware Jug,** New Jersey, early 19th C. w/ incised cobalt bird & tree dec, ht. 12½in. **$1,380**

A-PA Nov. 2004 Conestoga Auction Co. Inc.

379 **Hooked Rug** depicting farm landscape, mounted on frame, ht. 21, lg. 48in. **$715**

A-NH Aug. 2004 Northeast Auctions
772 **Tinware Pitcher,** large size, possibly an advertising sign, w/flaring strap handle & scroll thumb-piece, ht. 37, wd. 23in. **$800**
773 **Sheet-Metal Running Horse Weather Vane,** ca. 1900, w/remnants of red & black paint, ht. 19½, lg. 43in. **$700**
774 **Rooster Weather Vane,** sheet metal, Maine, late 19th C., ht. excluding stand 31¼in. **$800**

A-NH Aug. 2004 Northeast Auctions
759 **Hooked Rug** in Log Cabin patt., 36 blocks w/black border. Mounted on stretcher, 40x78in. **$1,700**

A-MA Nov. 2003 Skinner Inc.
Items in Cupboard
299 **Set of Flow Blue Ironstone Tableware,** England, 19th C., many pieces in the Manilla patt. by Podmore, Walker & Co., Tunstall, Staffordshire, including 19 dinner plates, 23 salad plates, 12 dessert plate, 18 tea bowls, 23 saucers, 6 small plates, 6 serving bowls & some w/covers. **$4,113**
300 **Federal Cherry Corner Cupboard,** early 19th C., ref. & imper. ht. 74, wd. 38, dp. 20in. **$2,820**
301 **Oil Painting,** dated 1887, unsgn., imper., sight size 17x27in. **$1,293**
302 **Federal Chest of Drawers,** walnut, 19th C. w/repl. brasses, ref. & imper., ht. 26½, wd. 23in. **$2,468**
303 **Cast-Iron Jenny Lind Dressing Mirror,** 19th C, w/wear, ht. 23, wd. 13½in. **$411**
304 **Yarn Swift** w/painted floral dec. & repl. ribbons, ht. 22½in. **$235**
305 **Portrait** w/inscriptions & dated 1805, oil on panel, framed, sight size 9½ x 7½in. **$823**
306 **Cherry Carved One-Drawer Stand,** ca. 1825, old ref. & imper. ht. 28in. **$529**
307 **Fereghan-Sarouk Rug,** West Persia, late 19th C. w/wear & end fraying, 6 x 4 ft. **$1,880**

A-OH July 2004 — Garth's Arts & Antiques

531 **Small Chippendale Mirror,** mah. veneer, old glass & reprs., ht. 15in. **$172**
532 **Skewer Rack & Five Skewers,** wrought iron rack w/ram's horn finials, ht. 4½, skewers 9¾ to 15½in. **$632**
533 **Windsor Cheese Carrier,** hickory w/natural dry finish. The basket has a round top & is attached to mortised crosspieces on base, ht.9¼, lg. 29½in. **$460**
534 **Early Windsor Low-Back Chair,** attributed to Rhode Island w/old black paint over earlier red, repr. to rolled backrest, ht. 27¾in. **$3,220**
535 **Bamboo Windsor Cradle,** poplar & hickory w/natural finish, sq. nail const., & rest., ht. 20, lg. 39in. **$402**
536 **Firkin** w/stave const., pine w/hickory bands w/mix of rose & square head nails w/raised tabs on either side have pierced handles, ht. 11¼, dia. 15in. **$345**

A-NH Aug. 2004 — Northeast Auctions

523 **Twig Armchair on Rockers** w/heart motif, mid-19th C. **$5,500**
524 **Candlestand,** early 19th C., red painted birch w/square top & tapering legs, ht. 29, top 17½ x 18in. **$1,750**
525 **Dome-Top Box,** miniature w/blue paint & dec. w/stylized tulip buds, 19th C., the lid is pinned, ht. 2¾, lg. 4in. **$550**

Cupboard 406, Pewter - Shelf 1: 407 - 410, 407
Shelf 2: 408, 411, 407, 411, 408, 412, 409
Shelf 3: 410, 411, 411, 408, 413, 409, 411

A-PA May 2004 — Pook & Pook, Inc.

406 **N. Eng. Pewter Cupboard,** walnut, one-piece w/scrolled sides, ht. 70, wd. 38in. **$3,220**

Shelf One

407 **Continental Lidded Tankard,** together w/a pewter cider mug, & a flagon inscribed 1746. **$1,725**
408 **Whale Oil Lamps,** two Am., together w/two small fluid lamps. **$288**
409 **Pewter Porringers,** four, N. Eng. or NY pewter, ca. 1800 w/crown handles, one mkd. WW. **$394**
410 **Pewter Candlesticks,** Q.A. form, together w/pair of scalloped base Q.A. candlesticks. **$575**

Shelf Two includes

411 **Love Pewter Plate,** dia. 8in., together w/five English plates, 18th & 19th C. **$2,875**
412 **Pewter Plate** w/2 eagle touchmark & impressed Samuel Danforth, dia. 7¾in., together w/a pewter plate by Yates. **$374**

Shelf Three includes the following:410, 411, 408, 413, 409 & 411.

A-NH April 2004 Garth's Arts & Antiques
649 Chippendale Mirror w/phoenix crest, ref. mah., ht. 23in. $258
650 Country Q.A. Work Table, walnut w/old finish, dov. drawers, orig. brass pulls & three board top is missing pins for the aprons, ht. 29, wd. 48in. $1,150
651 Pewter Charger w/Samuel Ellis, London touchmarks, wear & knife scratches, dia. 16⅜in. $345
652 Pewter Measures, assembled set of seven w/minor wear. $230
653 Van Briggle Figural Vase in form of a Native Am. Indian, mkd., ht. 8in. $460
654 Decorated Box, dov., basswood w/old brown over tan vinegar dec., iron lock w/hasp & keyhole, square cut nail const., ht. 16, wd. 30in. $316

A-NH Nov. 2003 Northeast Auctions
254 Maple Double Ladderback Settee, N. Eng. w/mushroom cap finials & box stretchers, ht. 33, lg. 36in. $1,500
255 Federal Tiger Maple Stand w/one drawer, ht. 28, top 18x20in. $2,250
256 Q.A. Maple Desk on Frame, N. Eng. w/dov. top & scalloped skirt supported by cabriole legs ending in pad feet, ht. 38, wd. 28in. $3,000
257 Tavern Table w/oval top, turned legs joined by stretcher base, ht. 24¼, top 19x30in. $3,000
258 Federal Stand, N. Eng. tiger maple on square tapering legs w/an X stretcher, ht. 26, top 18x19in. $1,750

A-PA Mar. 2004 Pook & Pook, Inc.
Stoneware, ca. 1820-1850
101 Mug, attributed to Wingender w/pewter lid, ht. 8in. $230
102 Pitcher, Wingender w/pewter lid & floral design, ht. 9in. $288
103 Mug, Wingender w/pewter & brass lid, ht. 11in. $305
104 Pitcher, Wingender w/pewter lid & inscribed Thos. Hogan, ht. 13in. $403
105 Mug, Wingender w/pewter lid, ht. 15in. $431
106 Large Pitcher, attributed to Wingender w/elaborate designs, ht. 19in. $805

A-PA Oct. 2004 Pook & Pook, Inc.
883 Watch Safe, Federal, PA, mah., ca. 1815 w/painted dec., one drawer & ball feet, ht. 14⅝in. $1,850

A-PA Oct. 2004 Pook & Pook, Inc.
889 Spread Winged Eagle Plaque, carved & painted by G. Stapf, PA, 1862-1958, w/applied stars flanked by Am. flags & eagle holding a laurel brand & bundle of arrows in his talons, ht. 14, wd. 29½in. $17,250

Huntboard 183, Chalk 184, Bowl 187, Basket 188
Tole 189, 191, Box 190, Stool 192

A-PA Dec. 2003 Pook & Pook, Inc.
183 **Hunt Board,** Federal, Southern, ca. 1810, yellow pine, ht. 40, wd. 47in. **$3,450**
184 **Chalkware Stag** w/polychrome dec., 19th C., ht. 15¼, wd. 15in. **$1,093**
187 **Burlwood Footed Bowl,** N. Eng., ca. 1800, w/incised rim & base, ht. 4, dia. 10½in. **$3,220**
188 **Double Handled Basket,** Maine, late 19th C., w/handles & dec., ht. 7in., wd. 15¾in. **$1,840**
189 **Toleware Tray,** 19th C., w/classical landscape & figures on red ground, wd. 19½, lg. 15in. **$805**
190 **Wallpaper Hatbox,** late 19th C., w/vibrant multi floral dec., ht. 6¼, wd. 14¼in. **$863**
191 **Fireman's Toleware Parade Fire Horn,** late 19th C. **$6,900**
192 **Basswood Stool,** N. Eng. w/painted dec., ca. 1860, ht. 6¼in. **$518**

A-NH Nov. 2003 Northeast Auctions
329 **Pillowback Writing Armchair** w/drawer, Hitchcock w/painted & stencil black & russet dec. overall. **$700**
330 **Cherry Tripod Candlestand,** CT Chippendale, one drawer w/Rockingham knob, cabriole legs & slipper feet. **$3,000**
331 **Child's Sled** on iron runners, painted red w/green & yellow dec., lg. 31in. **$700**

A-OH Jan. 2004
Garth's Arts & Antiques
182 **Child's Sled** w/orig. dec. & scrolled steel runners, splits, lg.44in. **$2,415**

A-PA Dec. 2003 Pook & Pook, Inc.
370 **Sheraton Dropleaf Work Table,** tiger maple, ca. 1820, ht. 28¾in. **$2,760**
371 **Child's Cradle,** tiger maple, ca. 1800 w/heart cut-outs on scalloped head & footboard, dov. frame & cheese cutter rockers, ht. 19, lg. 36in. **$2,070**
372 **Chippendale Pembroke Table,** tiger maple, ca. 1795, NY, w/square beaded legs. **$1,150**

A-PA May 2004 Pook & Pook, Inc.
322 **Leather Fire Helmet,** Montgomery, dated 1847, ht. 8½in. **$920**
323 **Fireman's Parade Hat,** 19th C., painted w/spread winged eagle over a banner, & inscribed Montgomery Hose Company, & monogrammed on blue ground. **$9,775**
324 **Work Table,** PA, Sheraton, ca. 1820 w/two drop leaves & Sandwich glass pulls, table retains an old red stained surface, ht. 30, wd. 20¾in. **$4,370**
325 **Toleware Fire Horn,** PA, 19th C., lg. 26in. **$3,450**
326 **Presentation Fire Trumpet,** brass & silver, inscribed & dated 1865, ht. 19in. **$1,610**

A-PA Oct. 2004 Pook & Pook, Inc.
331 **Red Covered Bridge** painting by William J. Forsyth, Am. 1854-1935, egg tempera on artist board, sgn., sight 29x36in. **$1,840**
332 **N. Eng.Blanket Chest,** ca. 1810 w/orig. vibrant ochre sponge dec. ht. 40, wd. 40¾in. **$748**
334 **N. Eng. Tall Case Clock,** ca. 1820 w/overall red & black grain dec., the face is inscribed R. Whiting, Winchester, ht. 84in. **$3,220**

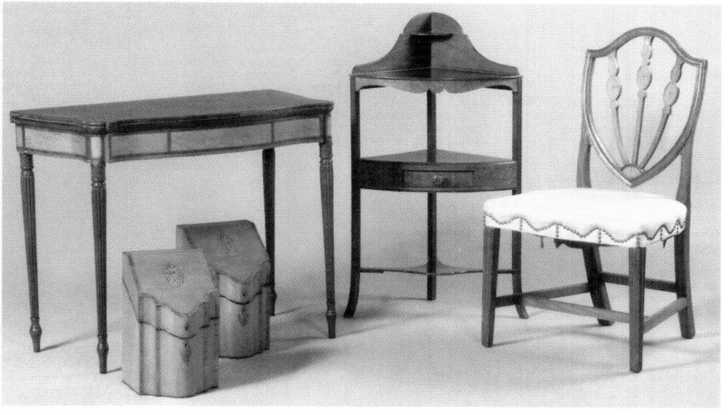

A-NH Nov. 2003 Northeast Auctions
1837 **N. Eng. Card Table,** mah. & flame birch w/serpentine hinged top, ht. 29½, wd. 36in. **$5,500**
1838 **Hepplewhite & Bird's-Eye Maple Wash Stand,** ht. 39in. **$1,100**
1839 **Salem Shield-Back Side Chair,** inlaid mah. w/fan inlay. **$1,200**
1840 **English Knife Boxes,** inlaid satinwood, serpentine front & lid w/inlaid shell, interior fitted. **$16,000**

A-NH Mar. 2004 Northeast Auctions
759 **Windsor Bow-back Side Chairs,** NY, faux bamboo spindles w/gilt highlights & retaining fragment labels of DeWitt & Gallatian. **$1,000**
760 **Q.A. Drop-Leaf Dining Table,** mah., & pad feet w/disks, ht. 28¾, lg. 40¾ & opens to 49in. **$1,500**
761 **Chopping Bowl,** hand turned w/blue-green painted exterior, dia.18in. **$1,700**
762 **Sack-back Windsor Armchair** in brown paint w/ring turned legs. **$950**
763 **Herb Splint Woven Basket** w/X-form handle, ht. 8, dia. 12in. **$1,600**
764 **Splint Melon Basket** w/hickory handle, ht. 9, lg. 12½in. **$250**

A-NH Mar. 2004 Northeast Auctions
639 **Chippendale Blanket Chest,** Southern walnut, dov. const. w/till, ht. 27, wd. 48in. **$1,500**
640 **Copper Buckets,** Eng., one w/brass base, rim & handle, ht. 11in.; the second of incurved form w/cast-iron handle, ht. 8¼in. **$900**
641 **Copper circular pan & a candy bowl,** dia. 15½ & 13¼in. **$900**
642 **Cast-iron Kettles,** each w/raised straight feet, ht. 12 & 14in. **$300**
643 **Five Ladderback Side Chairs,** two illus., Delaware River Valley w/splint woven seats, mixed woods. **$250**
644 **Country Federal Tavern Table,** walnut w/oval top & slightly raked square legs, ht. 27½, top 36x25in. **$2,800**
645 **Copper Ale Jug & Flagon,** hts. 10 & 12¼in. **$2,600**

A-OH July 2004 Garth's Arts & Antiques
621 **Tin Candlestand,** old green paint over other colors w/weighted cone base, top is adjustable w/two candle sockets, ht. 36½in. **$1,380**
622 **Blanket Chest,** pine w/worn orig. smoke graining, molded one board top, wear & edge chips, ht. 23, wd. 43¼in. **$1,035**
623 **Embroidery Hoop on Stand** w/rectangular base & hoop swivels on top of uprights, ht. 15in. **$891**
624 **Two Tin Coffee Pots,** both w/raised bands & rest. **$178**

A-OH July 2004 Garth's Arts & Antiques
59 **High Back Dry Sink,** two-piece, pine & walnut w/old red & yellow paint, ht. 52, wd. 56in. **$2,185**
60 **Stoneware Crock** w/tulip dec., mkd. T. Reed, OH, chips & flakes,ht. 14in. **$862**
61 **Ohio Stoneware Crock** mkd. Harmell & Smyth, Tuscarawas Co., OH, imper., ht. 14¼in. **$ 1,495**
62 **Graphic Hooked Rug,** light wear & stains, 21x39in. **$115**

A-OH July 2004 Garth's Arts & Antiques
831 **Tin Candle Sconces,** three w/crimped round crests & pans, one w/slightly rusted surface & splits, ht. 14in. **$747**
832 **Kraut Cutter,** thick ash panel w/two blades, box frame is missing, ht. 49in. **$201**
833 **Blanket Chest** in orig. red paint, six-board, pine w/rose head nail const., hinges repl. & section of till lid is missing. **$632**
834 **Windsor Candlestand,** pine & birch w/green paint over earlier, single board round top & repl. legs. ht. 24in. **$230**
835 **Redware,** three pieces incl. a canning jar, crock & jug w/strap handle. **$373**

A-PA Dec. 2003 Pook & Pook, Inc.
342 **Theorem** by David Y. Ellinger, oil on velvet w/basket of fruit, orig. dec. frame & sgn. 23x28in. **$4,600**
343 **Glazed Face Jug** by Burlon B. Craig, NC, w/broken china teeth, ht. 9½in. **$1,150**
344 **Dome Top Storage Box,** N. Eng., pine, ca. 1820 w/floral design on an ochre grained surface w/red highlights, ht. 9½, lg. 18½in. **$288**
345 **Rocking Horse,** carved & painted, ca. 1870 w/leather bridle & saddle, orig. dec., ht. 37, lg. 59in. **$2,415**
346 **Secretary Desk,** two-part, w/fliptop writing surface w/overall ochre grain dec., ht. 56½, wd. 35¼in. **$2,185**
347 **Glazed Face Jug** w/applied ears & handles, ht. 10½in. **$575**
348 **Lead & Manganese-glazed redware pitcher**, mkd. Bell, ht. 9in. **$2,760**

A-MA Aug. 2004 Skinner, Inc.

71 **Corner Cupboard** w/red stain, CT, last half 18th C, w/three serpentine shape shelves & paneled door opening to a single shelf, rest., ht. 92, wd.49, dp. 15¼in. **$2,115**

72 **Combware Loaf Dish**, probably Eng., early 19th C., red earthenware w/coggled rim, linear combed slip design in brown on creamy white ground, wear & hairlines, ht. 2½, dia. 12¼in. **$999**

73 **Redware Jug**, Am., late 18th/early 19th C. w/brown streaked speckled glaze on ochre ground & base chips, ht. 7¼in. **$353**

74 **Redware Jar** w/lug handles, brown slip-glaze floral dec. & inscribed 1841 w/ squiggle line dec. on reverse, minor rim chips & flaking, ht. 10in. **$5,875**

76 **Redware Pottery Jar**, possibly Rensselaer Co., NY, early 19th C. w/mustard glaze & brown speckles, wear & base chips, ht. 10¾in. **$529**

75 **Small Redware Plate** w/yellow slip dec. n/s

A-PA May 2004 Pook & Pook, Inc.

328 **PA Federal Corner Cupboard**, tiger maple, ca. 1815 w/glazed upper section above base w/two doors & bracket feet, ht. 87in. **$18,600**

329 **Chinese Export Plates**, nine, 19th C. in Thousand Butterfly patt, dia. 9½in. **$633**

330 **Chinese Export Plates**, twelve, 19th C. in above patt., dia. 9in. **$690**

331 **Chinese Export Covered Vegetable Dish**, in the Thousand Butterfly patt., together w/a covered tureen & undertray, 20th C. **$460**

A-OH Nov. 2003 Garth's Arts & Antiques

189 **Wall Cupboard**, two-piece, poplar w/old red paint, dov. drawers & interior painted w/thin cream colored wash. The high pie shelf has a plate rail, ht. 83, wd. 49in. **$10,062**

190 **Pewter Coffee Pot** by Boardman & Hart, NY w/tooled lines around body, handle & wafer repainted, ht. 11¾in. **$747**

191 **Nantucket Basket** w/worn green paint, turned wooden base & swing handle. Several broken splints at rim, ht. 14½in. **$917**

192 **Pewter Flagon** w/raised rings, scrolled handle & domed lid, ht. 12in. **$805**

193 **Bellows** w/old painted dec. of fruit & foliage on yellow ground, smoke dec. on back & brass spout. Re-leathered, lg. 17¼in. **$143**

A-MA Feb. 2004 Skinner, Inc.

180 **Chippendale Cherry Side Chair**, late 18th C., slip seat, ref. & minor imper., ht. 38in. **$2,115**

181 **Federal Pembroke Table**, cherry, ca. 1790 w/pierced scrolled stretchers, ref. & minor imper. , ht. 28, wd. 36in. **$5,581**

182 **Rose Medallion Porcelain Punch Bowl**, China, 19th C., ht. 6, dia. 16in. **$1,538**

A-PA Dec. 2003 Pook & Pook, Inc.

59 **Walnut Dutch Cupboard,** PA, early 19th C., 2 piece w/rattail hinges, bobbin turned columns over two candle drawers & turned feet, ht. 86, wd. 54in. **$12,650**

60 **Stoneware Crock,** 4 gal., w/stencil dec. & mkd. Hamilton & Jones, Greensboro PA, ht. 14½in. **$575**

61 **Stoneware Crock,** 3 gal., sgn. Harght & Co., Shinnston W. VA, ht. 13in. **$460**

62 **Stoneware Crock,** 3 gal., 19th C. & mkd. Made for Emerick & Hopkins, ht. 14in. **$403**

63 **Redware Plate,** PA, 19th C., w/yellow slip dec., dia. 12½in. **$978**

64 **Redware Jug,** PA, early 20th C., w/inscription & retains green & orange slip ht. 7¼in. **$230**

65 **Toleware Teapot,** PA, 19th C., w/floral dec. on black ground, ht. 10½in. **$920**

A-PA May 2004 Pook & Pook, Inc.

670 **Am. Powder Horn,** 18th C., inscribed Abner Robinson's Horn Dated Crown Point Octr__1759, w/scenes of towns, an elaborate mermaid, dragon, bird, & flowers, etc. **$7,475**

A-PA Mar. 2004 Pook & Pook, Inc.

29 **Victorian Carved & Painted Bird House,** late 19th C., wood & wire frame w/painted turrets, brick accents & elaborate entrance, ht. 82, wd. 69in. **$5,750**

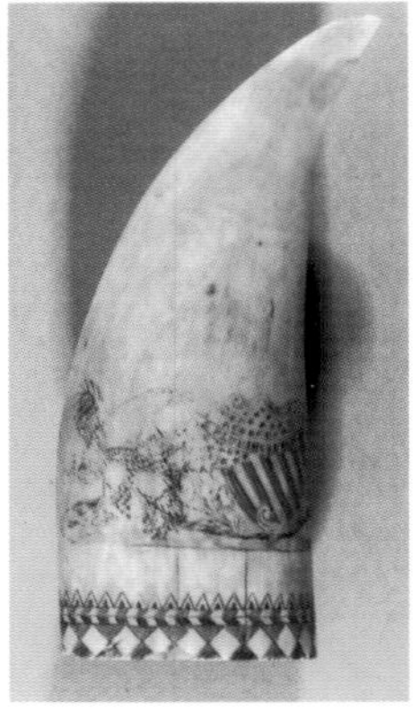

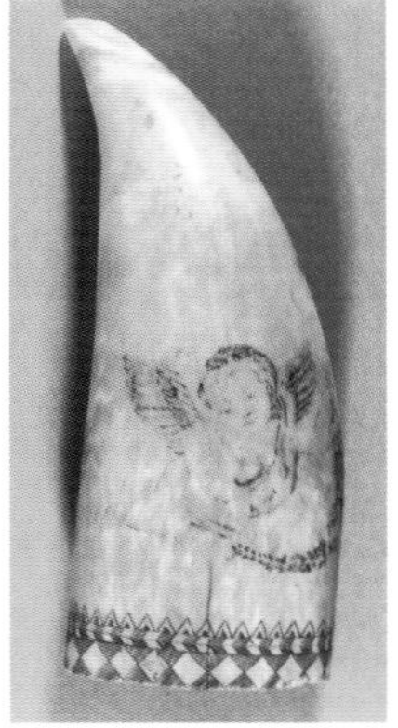

A-PA May 2004 Pook & Pook, Inc.

673 **Scrimshaw Whale's Tooth,** 19th C., dec. w/a spread winged eagle flanked by an Am. flag and banner inscribed E Pluribus Unum, the reverse side w/a winged cherub holding a floral garland above a checkerboard sawtooth base, lg. 5¾in. **$1,610**

671 **Powder Horn dated** 1777 & inscribed David Egleston's Horn Made Decr. 17 AD 1777 In the Army, w/scenes of cities incl. Philadelphia & New York, as well as ships, a mermaid, fish, rivers, etc., lg. 10in. **$8,625**

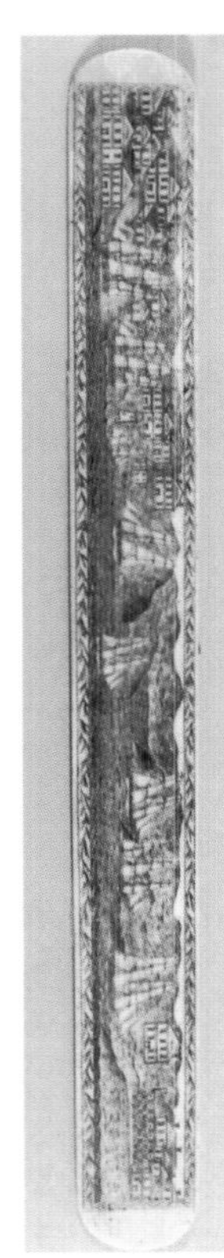

A-PA May 2004 Pook & Pook, Inc.

674 **Scrimshaw Baleen Busk,** 19th C, w/dec. of a ship, Am. flag, fort, hearts & a cottage within a sawtooth border w/inscribed initials, lg. 13¾in. **$1,610**

677 **Scrimshaw Whale Bone Busk,** 19th C. w/detailed scene of New Bedford, 8 sailing ships, lighthouse & houses, lg. 14½in. **$3,910**

676 **Scrimshaw Whale's Tooth,** 19th C. w/dec. of a spread winged eagle atop an Am. flag & cannon & inscribed Peace Independence & Plenty, ht. 5½in. **$5,175**

A-OH Oct. 2004 Garth s Arts & Antiques

325 **Hepplewhite One-Drawer Stand,** walnut w/orig. dark surface, line inlay around the two board top, dov. drawer & repl. brass, ht. 28¼in. **$3,220**

326 **Country Chippendale Chest,** tiger maple w/old finish, top old replacement, ht. 44, wd. 36in. **$8,628**

Bentwood Shaker Boxes

327 **Natural Finish** w/two-finger lapped const. & copper tacks, lg. 3¾in. **$632**

328 **Natural Finish** w/two-finger lapped const. & copper tacks,lg. 6in. **$460**

329 **Box** w/old finish & coat of varnish, three-finger const., lg. 9in. **$402**

330 **Box** w/golden brown surface w/slight loss to lower edge on side of lid, lg. 11in. **$690**

331 **Large Oval Box** w/natural finish & four-finger const., lg. 13½in. **$1,092**

A-MA Feb. 2004 Skinner, Inc.

216 **Still Life With Fruit,** unsgn., oil on canvas, 19th C., 14x16in. **$1,116**

217 **Farmstead In Winter,** unsgn., oil on canvas w/paint loss & punctures, 15x20in. **$499**

218 **Wood & Iron Chandelier,** Am., late 18th C. w/eight tin candle sockets supported by iron wire arms, imper., ht. 15, dia. 29in. **$2,820**

219 **Still Life With Fruit,** unsgn.,oil on artist board, w/paint losses & imper., 10x12in. **$411**

220 **Carved Ash Bowl,** northeastern Iroquois tribe, 18th or early 19th C. w/carve hand holds, age cracks, ht. 8, wd. 10, lg. 29¼in. **$2,055**

221 **Roundabout Chair,** N. Eng., 18th C. w/early salmon-red surface over earlier paint, ht. 28½in. **$1,293**

222 **Maple Tavern Table,** N. Eng., ca. 1730-50 w/box stretcher, old ref. & rest., ht. 26½, wd. 27, dp. 44½in. **$1,763**

223 **Q.A. Side Chair,** Hudson River Valley or CT, late 18th C., w/old brown paint & gilt striping. Minor imper., ht. 40½in. **$2,350**

224 **Hooked Rug,** Am., 19th C. w/wear to edges. n/s

A-NE Aug. 2004 Northeast Auctions

143 **Ship's Wheel,** eight-spoke wood & brass bound w/secondary brass handle, dia. 59in. **$1,300**

144 **Pond Model of the Sloop May 2nd,** wood const. w/cloth sails, on stand w/plaque stating boat was built in 1931, ht. 70, lg. 36in. **$900**

145 **Model of the Powerboat Dolphin** w/inboard steam engine by Boucher Mfg. Co., New York, on stand including orig. blueprints, lg. 43in. **$2,500**

146 **Seascape** w/lighthouse, oil on canvas by W.F. Halsall, Am., 1844-1919, 12x36in. **$750**

147 **Chest of Drawers,** British mah. brass-bound campaign chest, ht. 44, lg. 42in. **$1,500**

148 **Navigational Boxed Ebony & Ivory Inlaid Octant** w/brass arm in green keystone case w/maker's label, lg.of case 12in. **$1,300**

149 **Painted Wood Ship Weather Vane** w/copper sail, N. Eng., two sided & fitted on stand, ht. 28, lg. 34in. **$1,200**

150 **Three Masted Schooner Weather Vane,** sheet-brass w/applied lead wave & brass post w/scrolled supports, ht. overall 33, lg. 33in. **$1,600**

A-Nov. 2003 Northeast Auctions
1463 **Sheraton Chairs,** pair w/faux tiger maple paint & shell dec. **$1,300**
1464 **Dressing Table,** N. Eng., yellow painted & dec., ht. 56, wd. 32in. **$3,900**
1465 **Arrow-Back Side Chair,** painted & decorated. **$500**
1466 **Painted Model,** the Riverton Congregational Church, ht. 14in. **$350**

A-OH Nov. 2003 Garth's Arts & Antiques
436 **Chippendale Three-Drawer Blanket Chest,** attributed to NC, walnut, rest., ht. 28¾, wd. 48½in. **$805**
437 **Game Board,** pine w/old red paint, checker squares on one side & backgammon on opposite side, hinged & folds into a box, 15x14in. **$718**
438 **Pease Covered Jars,** two w/old mellow finish, imper. **$230**
439 **Wooden Bowl,** poplar w/ring turnings, in old blue paint, dia. 18in. **$575**
440 **One-Door Cabinet** w/orig. smoke dec. in black on yellow w/red door & side panels. Shaped interior shelf, ht. 15in. **$488**

A-NH Aug. 2004 Northeast Auctions
803 **PA Red Painted Pine Hutch Table** w/curved rails, ca. 1820 & C-curved side stretchers, ht. 27¾, top 29 x 44in. **$1,900**
804 **Pottery Seated Spaniel** w/blue glaze, Ohio, mid-19th C., ht. 11½in. **$2,750**
805 **Two Woven Splint Buttock-Type Baskets** w/center handles, one a large shallow flower gathering basket, the other w/wide handle. **$550**
806 **Corn Decoys,** early 20th C., used to attract crows, ducks & geese. **$200**
807 **Redware Tree Trunk-Form Umbrella Stand,** relief molded, attributed to J. Eberly & Co., Strasburg, PA, 1892-1903, ht. 21¾in. **$400**

A-MA Feb. 2004 Skinner, Inc.
82 **Wrought Iron Wall Sconces,** pr., Am. or Eng., early 19th C, w/iron candle sockets fitted into iron wall mounts, ht. 15, wd. 15⅛in. **$2,115**
83 **QA. Mirror,** Am. or Eng., 18th C., ht. 17, wd. 14½in. **$940**
84 **Carved Wooden Spoon Rack** w/chip carving & fan dec., initials IVP & 1766, ht. 24, wd. 7⅜in. **$14,100**
85 **CT Side Chair** w/three slats, hand grips on vase & ring-turned supports continuing to legs joined by stretchers, old red surface, ht. 42in. **$3,055**
86 **Wool Floral Hooked Rug,** 19th C. w/woven cotton backing, dia. 42in. **$1,293**
87 **Lift Top Blanket Chest** w/drawer & orig. painted brown surface, pine & maple, ca. 1725-35, ht. 36, wd.38in. **$31,725**

A-OH Sep. 2004 Garth's Arts & Antiques
353 **Bennington Frame,** oval w/Rockingham glaze, opening 3½ x 4¼in. **$488**
354 **Bennington Frame,** oval w/dark Rockingham glaze, opening same as above. **$604**
355 **Burl Compote & Wax Fruit,** dated 1764 on bottom w/age split & some charring on base, ht. 3½, dia. 8½in. **$862**
356 **Oversize Staffordshire Mug** w/hand painted enamel tavern scene, ht. 4¾in. **$143**
357 **Staffordshire Teapot** w/molded scroll & acanthus designs w/hand painted flowers, stains & crazing, ht. 6½in. **$201**

A-OH July 2004 Garth's Arts & Antiques
786 **Tin Cookie Cutters,** a Shaker lady & horse, some wear & rust. **$517**
786A **Three Tin Cookie Cutters,** a large heart, ht. 8¼in., a horse, lg. 7in. & a rooster not illus. **$402**
787 **Fanback Windsor Side Chair** w/blue green paint & evidence of an earlier black, rest. & a restored split on crest, ht. 36in. **$345**
788 **Empire Chest** w/painted dec., cherry, old glass pulls & paneled ends, ht. 47, wd. 40in. **$1,035**
789 **Pair of Skates** w/steel plates, attachment spikes & wooden toe supports, minor wear, lg. 14¼in. **$258**
790 **Copper Fish Poacher** w/brass handles, tin lined, lg. 13in. **$172**

A-MA Nov. 2003 Skinner, Inc.
7 **Portrait,** unsgn. but attributed to Robert Street, Am., 1796-1865 w/sitter labels affixed to the reverse. Oil on canvas, sight size 32x26in. **$2,350**
8 **View of Mount Washington,** ca. 1875, unsgn., oil on canvas, sight size 11x19½in. **$1,998**
9 **Chippendale Slant-lid Desk,** carved mah., ca. 1780, replaced brasses & old finish, imper. ht. 40, wd. 39in. **$2,938**
10 **Chippendale Chest of Drawers,** N. Eng., late 18th C. w/old finish, repl. brasses & minor rest., ht. 43, wd. 35in. **$2,703**
11 **Q.A. Maple Tea Table,** MA, last half 18th C., base retains orig. red paint, top has been ref., imper., ht. 26, dia. 30in. **$7,050**
12 **Chippendale Carved Side Chair,** walnut, ca. 1780, ref. & imper. **$1,116**

A-SC Dec. 2003
Charlton Hall Galleries, Inc.
535 **Knife Urns,** Adam style, opening to fitted interiors for cutlery, painted w/scrolling leaf, bow & garland designs, ht. 25¾in. **$2,000**

A-OH Oct. 2004 Garth's Arts & Antiques
Bentwood Pantry Boxes With Handle

160 **Old Green** surface w/overlapping seam, copper tack const., dia. 9¼in. **$661**

161 **Old Red** dry paint w/overlapping seams & steel tacks, dia. 10in. **$1,063**

162 **Box** w/old green paint & steel tack const., minor edge chip, dia. 11¼in. **$805**

163 **Old Red** paint w/earlier paint on lid, steel tack const., rim chip on lid & repl. bottom. **$345**

164 **Box attrib. to the Shakers** w/lapped const. & copper tacks. Wear & chip on baseboard, dia. 13¼in. **$891**

165 **Comb-back Windsor Armchair** w/old black painted alligatored surface, ht. 36in. **$7,762**

A-OH July 2004 Garth's Arts & Antiques

486 **Treenware,** maple compote w/scrubbed surface, ht. 5, dia. 8in., together w/a birch rolling pin w/minor chip to handle, not illus. **$460**

487 **Windsor Stool** w/old red repaint, round dish shaped seat & split on one foot, ht. 18¼in. **$460**

488 **Ironware,** two pcs., a cast teakettle w/gooseneck spout, ht. 7½in., together w/a wrought iron trammel, adjusts from 29 to 41in. lg. **$345**

489 **Comb-back Windsor Armchair** w/black painted surface, feet ended out & one arm rail rest., ht. 41in. **$2,760**

490 **Early Wooden Tape Loom,** pine w/orig. dark brown surface & one split at end has been lightened for lacing, lg. 21¼in. **$1,092**

A-MA Nov. 2003 Skinner, Inc.

20 **Chippendale Mirror,** mah. gilt gesso, 18th C., probably Eng. w/imper., & a phoenix above frame, ht. 46½in. **$7,050**

21 **Brass Wall Sconces,** Eng., pair, mid-18th C. w/swollen candlecup & drip pan supported on scrolled arm, ht. 6, dep. 10in. **$3,290**

22 **Chippendale Carved Slant-lid Desk,** late 18th C. w/old finish, repl. brasses & minor imper., ht. 43in. **$3,525**

23 **Chippendale Carved Side Chair,** mah., ca. 1780 w/minor imper. **$1,175**

A-PA Mar. 2004 Pook & Pook, Inc.

203 **PA Bench Table,** pine, early 19th C. w/rectangular top tilting over a case w/two lift lids, ht. 28, wd. 48, lg. 96in. **$3,680**

204 **Stoneware Jug,** 4 gal. w/handles & stencil dec., inscribed Hamilton & Jones, ht. 17½in. **$690**

205 **Stoneware Crock,** 3 gal., by Remmey & mkd. R.C.R. Phila. w/2 sided cobalt dec., ht. 13¼in. **$575**

206 **Stoneware Jug,** 2 gal., 19th C. & mkd. J & E Norton Bennington VT, w/cobalt dec., ht. 14in. **$748**

207 **Stoneware Crock,** 10 gal., Greensboro, 19th C., w/free hand stenciled cobalt dec. of Williams & Reppert, above an eagle's head, ht. 21in. **$978**

208 **PA Pieced Quilt,** 19th C., in log cabin patt., approx. 76x78in. **$518**

209 **Appliqué Star Quilt,** PA., ca. 1900, together w/a similar example, 80x82in. **$518**

210 **Pieced Log Cabin Quilt,** early 20th C. w/red & green border. **$518**

211 **Carved English Oak Candlestand,** mid-18th C. w/adjustable ratchet mechanism & wrought iron, ht. 31in. **$748**

212 **Child's Armchair,** PA, early 19th C. w/orig. dec. on yellow ground, ht. 18in. **$1,610**

A-PA May 2004 Pook & Pook, Inc.
710 **N. Eng. Banjo Clock,** mah., ca. 1815 w/painted face & eglomisé panel depicting a naval battle of the War of 1812, ht. 34in. **$518**
711 **Chippendale Looking Glass,** mah., ca. 1780 w/gilt phoenix, ht. 41in. **$1,495**
712 **Federal Banjo Clock** inscribed S. Willard's Patent, ht. 40½in. **$1,725**
713 **Candlesticks,** pair, cobalt blue, 19th C., ht. 6⅜in. **$748**
714 **Sandwich Glass Lamp,** clambroth & milk glass w/double font fluid ca. 1830, ht. 12in. **$489**
715 **Double Font Fluid Lamp** mkd. D.C. Ripley & Co., w/blue opalescent glass, electrified, ht. 16in. **$1,150**
716 **Vaseline Glass Fluid Lamp** w/paneled reservoir, together w/a clear glass hurricane globe. **$633**
717 **Two Blown Glass Bottles,** 19th C. by Granite Glass Co., Stoddard, NH, together w/a Success to the Railroad bottle. **$920**
718 **Canary Glass Candlesticks,** three, together w/a clear glass example. **$575**
719 **Blue Cut to Opaque to Clear Glass Lamp,** 19th C., w/green shaft & marble base, ht. 17¾in. **$575**
720 **Vaseline Glass Candlesticks,** 19th C., ht. 9in. **$748**
721 **Sandwich Glass Cobalt Overlay Fluid Lamp,** ca. 1830, together w/a Sandwich glass green & milk glass overlay fluid lamp w/marble base, and two fluid lamps **$1,150**
722 **N. Eng. Hepplewhite Dining Table,** cherry, two part, ca. 1810 w/line inlays, ht. 29½, lg. 91in. **$1,036**
723 **Shaving Mirror,** George II, mah., mid-18th C. w/line inlays, ht. 24in. **$402**
724 **Brass Fluid Lamp,** Cornelius type, ca. 1830 w/etched shade & prisms. **$623**
725 **Sandwich Glass Fluid Lamp,** ca. 1830 w/clear glass reservoir & green & milk glass shaft, together w/a green cut to clear fluid lamp. **$518**

Cupboard 135 Pewter: 136 - 141

A-PA May 2004 Pook & Pook, Inc.

135 **Pewter Cupboard,** walnut, ca. 1810 w/recessed paneled doors & scalloped skirt, ht. 73½, wd. 48in. **$2,990**

136 **Pewter Pitcher,** Sellew & Co. w/a pewter beaker by James Dixon & Sons, & a salt. **$230**

137 **Pewter Teapot,** mkd. Porter, together w/a pewter pitcher by Dunham. **$748**

138 **Pewter Measures,** seven in graduated sizes mkd. J.R. **$374**

139 **Pewter Coffee Pot** w/etched dec. by Israel Trask, mkd. I. Trask, ht. 11in. **$374**

140 **Pewter Oil Lamps,** matched pair mkd. R. Gleason, ht. 9in. **$403**

141 **Pewter Coffee Pot** mkd. Griswold w/an eagle touch, ht. 11in. **$230**

A-PA May 2004 Pook & Pook, Inc.

177 **Stick Spatter,** seven, plates 7¾ & 9in. dia., bowls 7in. **$546**

178 **Floral Stick Spatter Shallow Bowls,** one w/sawtooth border, dia. 14in. **$316**

179 **Stick Spatter Bowls,** five blue & white w/dahlia centers, dia. 9½ & 11¼in. **$489**

180 **PA Dutch Cupboard,** cherry, ca. 1820 w/rattail hinges, reeded stiles & bracket feet, w/rest., ht. 90, wd. 54in. **$2,530**

A-OH July 2004 Garth's Arts & Antiques

727 **Hutch Table** w/extra top, pine w/alligatored red paint over earlier red, orig. top, age splits,nailed drawer & legs ended out, ht. 28, dia. 52in. The additional round top includes six boards, dia. 70in. **$3,565**

728 **Pieced Quilt,** blue & white calico w/light stains, hand stitched, 73x72in. **$431**

729 **Large Rye Straw Basket** w/a few splint breaks, ht. 10½, dia. 22in. **$230**

A-OH June 2004 Garth's Arts & Antiques

16 **Pictorial Hooked Rug,** winter scene w/minor rest., 30x47in. **$230**

17 **Settle Bench,** PA w/old dec., deep plank seat, wear & one arm rest., lg. 71½in. **$1,200**

18 **Oval Penny Rug,** hand stitched wool w/minor moth damage, 42x34in. **$172**

A-OH Oct. 2004 Garth's Arts & Antiques

264 **Two-Drawer Mule Chest,** pine w/orig. brown over yellow sponging, orig pulls & slight loss of height, ht. 37¾, wd. 37in. **$11,500**

265 **Wooden Butter Churn** in old blue grey paint w/overlapping bands, rosebud nails, orig. lid & dasher. Damage to lower bands, ht. 45½in. **$345**

266 **Adams Rose Platter** w/large red roses, green & blue foliage, stains, lg. 16¼in. **$1,035**

267 **Stick Spatter Bowls,** two w/floral dec. **$345**

A-OH Sep. 2004 Garth's Arts & Antiques
187 **Virginia Pie Safe,** cherry w/dov. drawers & four punched tin panels in each door, and two in each side, all w/pinwheel medallions & floral spandrels, ht. 49, wd. 53in. **$10,350**

A-NH Aug. 2004 Northeast Auctions
779 **Georgian Style Armchair,** mah. w/foliate carved knees & ball & claw feet. **$1,400**
780 **Chippendale Dumbwaiter,** mah., three-tier w/cabriole legs & pad feet,ht. 40½in. **$1,400**

A-NH Aug. 2004 Northeast Auctions
678 **Sack-back Windsor Armchair** w/carved knuckles & fitted for a potty chair, 19th C. w/green painted surface. **$1,500**
679 **Child's Staffordshire Pearlware Mug** w/transfer dec. inscribed Love/Liberty School, ht. 2¾in. **$600**
680 **Federal Birch Candlestand,** NH, ca. 1800-1820, ht. 27, dia. 14in. **$4,250**

A-OH April 2004 Garth's Arts & Antiques
64 **Currier & Ives Lithograph,** handcolored, Scenery of the Upper Mississippi, An Indian Village, imper. 10x14in. **$287**
65 **Pewter Coffee Pot** w/touchmark of I.C. Lewis, Meriden, CT, 1834-1852, ht. 11in. **$258**
66 **Miniature Blanket Chest** w/dov. case, poplar w/old red wash, rest. to hinge rail, ht. 7¾, wd. 15in. **$460**
67 **Burl Mortar w/Pestle** which appears to be lignum vitae, age splits, ht. 7in. **$373**
68 **Sugar Bucket** in old mustard paint, stave const. w/copper tacks, ht. 13in. **$460**
63 **Sugar Chest,** Sheraton style, cherry w/two dov. drawers. Interior divided into four compartments, a handmade reproduction, ht. 34¾in. **$862**

A-MA Feb. 2004 Skinner, Inc.

163 **Theorem,** assortment of fruit in basket, unsgn., watercolor on paper in molded giltwood frame, imper., 13x17in. $1,880

164 **Theorem,** basket. of fruit w/parrot & butterfly, unsgn., watercolor on velvet, framed size 12x16in. $3,760

165 **Theorem,** a bouquet of flowers in footed bowl, unsgn., watercolor on velvet, sight size 17x13in. $999

166 **Blanket Box,** poplar w/orig. orange & amber grain paint & imper. $1,175

167 **Dower Chest,** PA., ca. 1825-30 w/original amber & green vinegar putty painted dec. & minor imper., ht. 29½, wd. 46in. $4,406

168 **Writing-Arm Windsor,** ca. 1825-30 w/orig. freehand & stencil dec. of fruit w/minor imper. ht. 46in. $4,800

169 **Youth's Highchair,** maple & ash w/ chrome yellow paint, N. Eng., early 19th C., orig. surface, ht. 33½in. $4,994

170 **Grain Painted Pine Box** with drawers, 19th C., in shades of mustard & brown w/imper., ht. 12, wd. 15in. $940

A-MA Feb. 2004 Skinner, Inc.

150 **Hanging Cupboard** w/grain paint, pine, early 19th C. w/orig.red-brown paint resembling mahogany, imper. ht. 23½, wd. 19¼in. $1,500

151 **Pine Checkerboard,** probably 19th C., w/minor paint wear, 16⅝ in sq. $588

152 **Copper Rooster Weather Vane,** late 19th/early 20th C., flattened full-body w/embossed sheet copper tail, painted w/minor dents, ht. 25, lg. 21in. $3,055

153 **Wooden Pipe Box,** white painted, 19th C. w/single drawer, wear, ht. 17¼in. $705

154 **Large Copper Arrow Weather Vane,** 19th C., mounted on spire-topped shaft, corrugated sheet copper tail, verdigris surface, dents & bullet holes, ht. 28, lg. 48in. $1,645

155 **Copper Weather Vane,** 19th C., small copper sphere terminals on an arrow rod w/minor joinery separation on tail, lg. 24½in. $353

156 **Dressing Table,** N. Eng., ca. 1825-35 w/orig. yellow paint, ochre putty vinegar & gilt stencil dec., orig. glass pulls & minor imper. $823

157 **Gilt Copper Crowing Rooster Weather Vane,** molded full body figure standing on small sphere, bullet holes & gilt loss, black metal stand incl. $1,880

158 **Grain Painted Chest-over-Drawers,** 19th C., w/attached strap hinges above cavity & two cockbeaded drawers on molded base, repl. pulls & imper., ht. 42, wd. 36in. $5,875

159 **Side Chairs,** pair, grain painted & stenciled, ca. 1825 w/neoclassical gold leaf images, orig. surface w/abrasions & repl. caned seats. $1,645

160 **Six-Board Chest,** grain painted poplar w/lidded till & old smoke-grained green & black surfaces,minor imper., ht 26¼, wd. 42in. $1,175

161 **Federal Dressing Table** w/paint dec., N. Eng., Ca. 1825, old brass pulls & imper., ht. 33½, wd. 35in. $823

162 **Wooden Game Board,** 19th C, minor wear, 15½ x 18in. $1,645

A-OH Nov. 2003 Garth's Arts & Antiques
731 **Oil Painting** sgn. Hesky, on canvas w/small hole & gilt frame, 29x37in. **$172**
732 **Twin Beds,** tiger maple, pair w/old ref., rails match, no bolts, one illus. ht. 59, wd. 49, lg. 77in. **$1,380**
733 **Stoneware Jar,** 4 gal., w/blue dec., Burger Bro's & Co., ht. 15½in. **$316**
734 **Stoneware Jug,** 4 gal., mkd. Higgins & Co., Cleveland, Ohio w/hairlines, ht. 16½in. **$373**

A-PA Mar. 2004 Pook & Pook, Inc.
497 **Crosshatch Carving of a Spaniel,** 19th C., Am., w/old brown painted surface, ht. 13½, lg. 23½in. **$3,335**

A-ME June 2004 James D. Julia, Inc.
2557 **General Store Nuts & Bolts Revolving Cabinet,** eight sided w/88 drawers, ht. 38in. **$1,035**

A-OH Apr. 2004 Garth's Arts & Antiques
46 **Jelly Cupboard,** PA, poplar w/old salmon paint, three interior shelves, wear & chips, ht. 54in. **$1,380**
47 **Tin Candle Lanterns** w/removable bases, glass panels & ring carriers, ht. 12in. **$373**
48 **Ironstone Meat Platter** mkd. Mason's Patent Ironstone China w/gaudy dec., 18x14in. **$235**

A-OH June 2004 Garth's Arts & Antiques
192 **Centennial Exhibition Handkerchief,** silk, w/printed designs including Fairmont Park, Philadelphia 1776-1876. Stitched to a cloth covered back board & framed, staining, 29x33in. **$431**
193 **Two-Part Mirror** w/orig. reverse painting of the White House, flaking, ht. 22, wd. 13¼in. **$258**
194 **Country Sheraton Day Bed,** pine w/old brown finish & contemporary cushions, ht. 36, lg. 70½in. **$891**
195 **Jacquard Coverlet,** Agriculture & Manufacturers are the Foundations of our Independence, two piece double weave in navy & natural by an unidentified weaver, stains & edge damage, 78x82in. **$862**

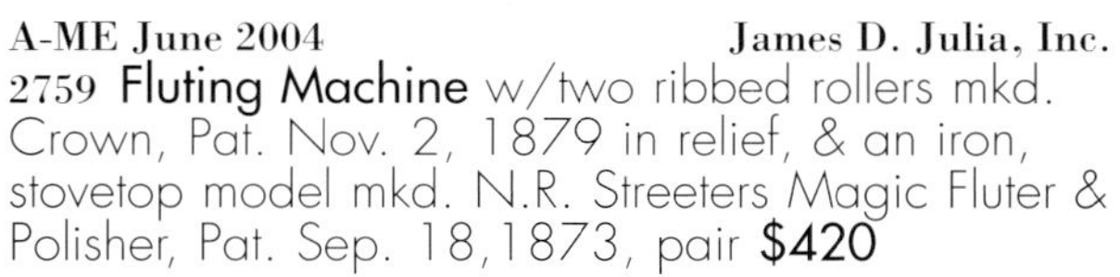

A-ME June 2004 James D. Julia, Inc.
2759 **Fluting Machine** w/two ribbed rollers mkd. Crown, Pat. Nov. 2, 1879 in relief, & an iron, stovetop model mkd. N.R. Streeters Magic Fluter & Polisher, Pat. Sep. 18,1873, pair **$420**

A-OH June 2004 Garth's Arts & Antiques
31 **Decorated Game Board,** old painted dec. w/a parcheesi game on one side & a checkerboard on the other, small plated feet at corners of each side, & age split, 18½in. sq. **$4,485**

A-June 2004 Garth's Arts & Antiques
159 **Decorated Game Board** w/old painted dec. reminiscent of Soap Hollow furniture & dated 1878. Applied decals of hunters in each corner w/minor splits & a corner chip, 18½ x 18¼in. **$2,415**

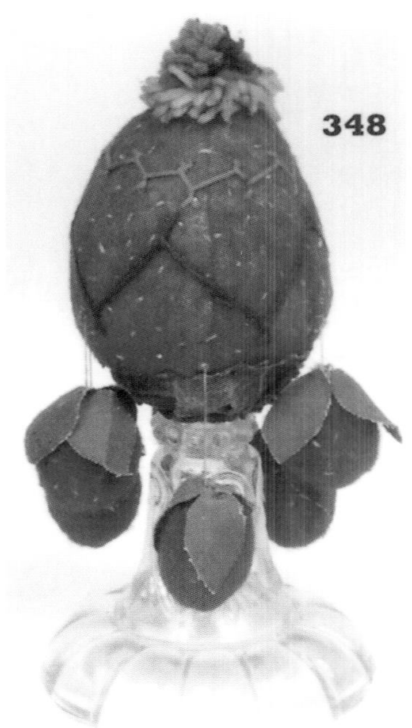

A-PA Apr. 2004
Conestoga Auction Co. Inc.
248 **Amish Strawberry Make Do Pin Cushion,** felt & yarn mounted on an old pattern glass pedestal, ht. 9½in. **$3,080**

A-OH July 2004 Garth's Arts & Antiques
839 **Stone Fruit in Wire Basket,** ten large pieces including peaches, pear, fig, oranges, cherries, lemon & plum w/minor damage. **$517**
840 **Stone Fruit,** thirteen pieces in realistic colors & some wear. **$575**
841 **Pillar Mold Compote,** clear w/plain stem & round base, ht. 7½in. **$546**
842 **Stone Fruit,** twelve pieces incl. cherries, pears, grapes, plums, peaches & a lime. **$575**
843 **Redware bowl** w/brown daubed stripes & flared rim, wear & hairlines. **$460**

A-OH Jan. 2004
Garth's Arts & Antiques
134 **Hooked Rug,** N. Eng. winter landscape w/minor wear, 17x34in. **$258**
135 **Copper Eagle Weather Vane** perched on a ball w/wings spread & old rest., by Washburne, ht. 55in. **$920**
136 **Wallace Nutting Comb-back Windsor Armchair,** branded, w/brown finish,ht. 44in **$1,955**

A-OH Nov. 2003
Cowan's Historic Americana
310 **Civil War Era Drum,** hand-painted band, drumheads held w/rope, leather tighteners & brass tacks. An interior label reads Ernest Vogt, Manufac. of Drums, Philadelphia, December 29,1864, ht. 16, dia. 16in. **$7,475**
311 **Wooden Confederate Canteen,** identified, stave const. of cedar, cypress or spruce, double iron bands w/scratched initials GAH & dated 1862 when mustered into D Co. North Carolina 55th Infantry, dia. 7, wd. 2¼in. **$2,415**

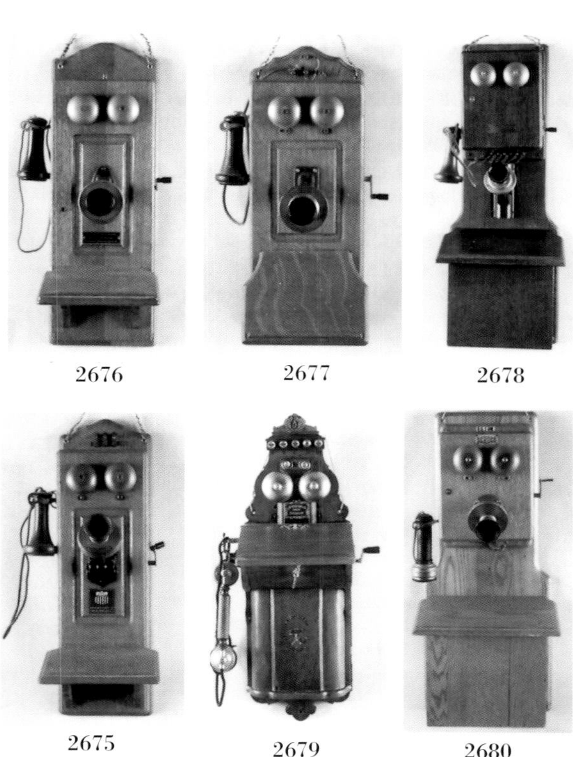
2676 2677 2678

2675 2679 2680

A-ME June 2004 James D. Julia, Inc.
2675 **Oak Wall Telephone** mkd. American Electric Telephone Co., Mfg. Co., Chicago, adjustable mouthpiece & double bell front, ht. 25½in. **$230**
2676 **Oak Wall Telephone** by American Electric w/tarnish to mouthpiece. **$230**
2677 **Oak Wall Telephone** w/foldaway bottom oak shelf, no key, ht. 26in. **$230**
2678 **Large Oak Telephone** by V. North Electric Co., Cleveland, OH, w/small writing shelf & orig. finish, ht. 33in. **$287**
2679 **Early Walnut Telephone** by L.M. Ericsson & Co., Pat. Stockholm, w/small writing surface, ht. 29in. **$402**
2680 **Oak Wall Telephone** by Seroco w/brass bells, mouthpiece & earphone w/orig. finish, ht. 29in. **$201**

A-ME June 2004 James D. Julia, Inc.
2622 **Clark's O.N.T. Spool Cabinet,** tabletop oak display, ht. 23, wd. 20in. **$805**

2624 **Merrick's Spool Cabinet,** round oak tabletop display on revolving base, Pat. July 20, 1897, ht. 20, dia. 18in. **$3,162**

A-MA Aug. 2004 Northeast Auctions
588 **Splint Woven Buttocks Basket** w/22 Velvet Pincushions, ht. of basket 5in. **$400**

0674

A-NC Jan 2004
Brunk Auction Services, Inc.
0674 **Brass Sewing Bird,** feather & flower designs in relief, spring auction & pincushion top ,4¼ x 3¾in. **$325**

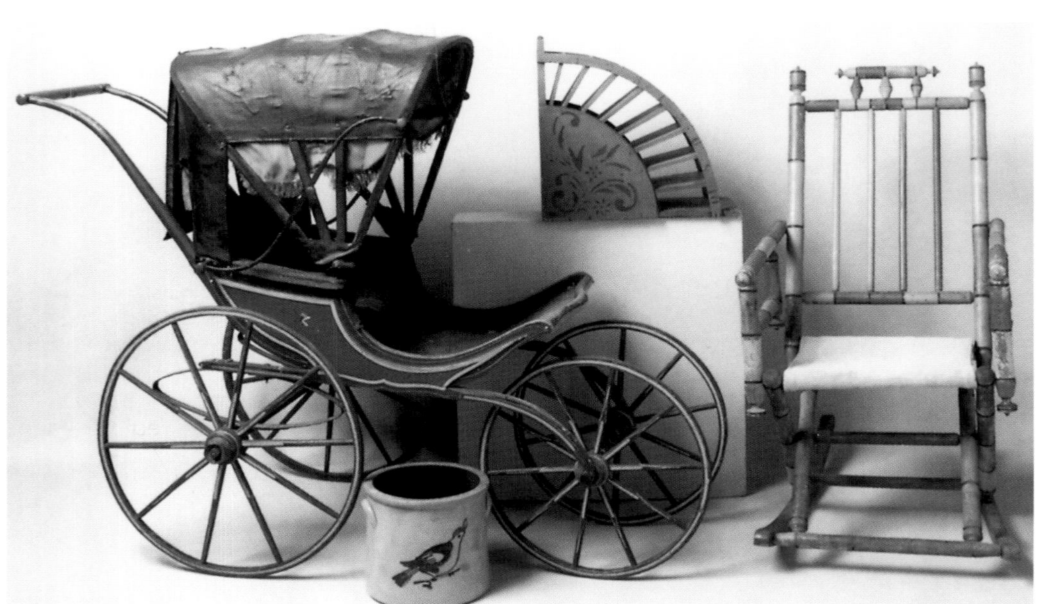

A-OH June 2004
Garth's Arts & Antiques
175 **Child's Carriage** w/painted dec., & mkd. A.C. Double Wheel, Pat. April 24, 1866 w/orig. black oilcloth covers, ht. 29in. **$517**
176 **Country Store Sack Holder** w/orig. painted dec., w/size numbers painted on side, ht. 15in. **$805**
177 **Stoneware Crock** w/cobalt bird dec., 6 gal. **$747**
178 **Rocking Chair** w/painted bamboo & spool turnings & old cloth seat. **$115**

G